Real Estate & the New Economy

The impact of information and communications technology

Real Estate & the New Economy

The impact of information and communications technology

Timothy Dixon

Director of Research, The College of Estate Management,
Reading

Bob Thompson

Consultant, RETRI

Patrick McAllister

Lecturer in Valuation and Property Management,
University of Reading

Andrew Marston

Research Analyst, ATIS REAL Weatheralls

Jon Snow

Chairman, iX Consulting Ltd

Blackwell
Publishing

Editorial offices:
Blackwell Publishing Ltd, 9600 Garsington Road, Oxford OX4 2DQ, UK
   Tel: +44 (0)1865 776868
Blackwell Publishing Inc., 350 Main Street, Malden, MA 02148-5020, USA
   Tel: +1 781 388 8250
Blackwell Publishing Asia Pty Ltd, 550 Swanston Street, Carlton, Victoria 3053, Australia
   Tel: +61 (0)3 8359 1011

First published 2005 by Blackwell Publishing Ltd

Library of Congress Cataloging-in-Publication Data

Real estate & the new economy : the impact of information and communications technology / Timothy Dixon . . . [et al.].– 1st ed.
      p. cm.
Includes bibliographical references and index.
   ISBN 1-4051-1778-8 (pbk. : alk. paper)
1. Real estate business–Data processing. I. Dixon, Timothy J., 1958-

HD1380.R43 2004
333.33′0285–dc22   2004013965

ISBN 1-4051-1778-8

A catalogue record for this title is available from the British Library

Set in 10/13pt Trump Mediaeval
by Kolam Information Services Pvt. Ltd, Pondicherry, India
Printed and bound in India
by Replika Press Pvt. Ltd

For further information on Blackwell Publishing, visit our website:
www.thatconstructionsite.com

RICS **FOUNDATION**

The **RICS Foundation** was established by the Royal Institution of Chartered Surveyors to promote and highlight the importance of the built and natural environment. The RICS Foundation supports and develops programmes of research to explore the key issues relevant to the way in which we manage, finance, plan and construct our built and natural environment, to make best and most effective use of the resources available to us.

Real Estate Issues

Series Managing Editors

Stephen Brown   RICS Foundation
John Henneberry   Department of Town & Regional Planning, University of Sheffield
David Ho   School of Design & Environment, National University of Singapore
Elaine Worzala   Real Estate Institute, University of San Diego

Real Estate Issues is an international book series presenting the latest thinking into how real estate markets operate. The books have a strong theoretical basis – providing the underpinning for the development of new ideas.

The books are inclusive in nature, drawing both upon established techniques for real estate market analysis and on those from other academic disciplines as appropriate. The series embraces a comparative approach, allowing theory and practice to be put forward and tested for their applicability and relevance to the understanding of new situations. It does not seek to impose solutions, but rather provides a more effective means by which solutions can be found. It will not make any presumptions as to the importance of real estate markets but will uncover and present, through the clarity of the thinking, the real significance of the operation of real estate markets.

Books in the series

Guy & Henneberry *Development & Developers*
Adams & Watkins *Greenfields, Brownfields & Housing Development*
O'Sullivan & Gibb *Housing Economics & Public Policy*
Couch, Fraser & Percy *Urban Regeneration in Europe*
Allen, Barlow, Léal, Maloutas & Padovani *Housing & Welfare in Southern Europe*
Leece *Economics of the Mortgage Market*
Evans *Economics & Land Use Planning*
Evans *Economics, Real Estate & the Supply of Land*
Byrne & Matysiak *Real Estate Investment*
Seabrooke, Kent & How *International Real Estate*
Ball *Markets and Institutions in Real Estate & Construction*
Dixon, Thompson, McAllister, Marston & Snow *Real Estate & the New Economy*
Adams, Watkins & White *Planning, Public Policy & Property Markets*
McGough & Tsolacos *Real Estate Market Analysis & Forecasting*
Byrne & Matysiak *Real Estate Investment*
Jones & Murie *The Right to Buy*

Contents

The Authors   xi
Foreword by Paul McNamara, Prudential Property
Investment Managers   xiii
Preface   xv
Table of Responsibilities   xviii

1 Introduction   **1**
   Background   1
   Aim and objectives   2
   Definitions   3
   Technological change: alternative perspectives   5
   Summary – an overview   32
   An integrative socio-technical framework
   for ICT and real estate   33
   Examples of the socio-technical approach   35
   Key themes and layout of the book   37
   Notes   38

Part 1   Context and Framework   **41**

**2   The Social, Economic and Political Context
    of ICT Transformation**   **43**
   Introduction   43
   Understanding the role of technological change in society   44
   Towards an information society and the new economy?   50
   The role of knowledge and innovation in policy   56
   Information society policy development in the UK   58
   Measuring the information society   66
   Implications of the development of an information society   69
   Summary   80
   Notes   81

**3   Technological Change: Diffusion and Adoption of ICT
    by Consumers, Businesses and Government**   **84**
   Introduction   84
   Technology diffusion   84
   Implications of ICT diffusion for consumers,
   businesses and government   87
   Internet-driven business activities: eBusiness, eCommerce
   and eWork   107

Some implications of ICT adoption for real estate   121
Summary   125
Notes   125

4   Business Process and Organisational Change   128
Introduction   128
Understanding corporate change   128
ICT and the design of organisations   131
Generic business processes   135
Procurement   139
Operational management   142
Marketing   143
Customer relationship management   145
Accounting   146
Recruitment   146
Stock management   146
Financial management   147
Mapping processes to property   148
Summary   158
Notes   158

5   The New Economy and Real Estate   160
Introduction   160
What is the new economy?   161
The evidence for a new economy   165
The role of real estate in the new economy   178
Summary   194
Notes   195

Part 2   Real Estate Spaces and the Impact of ICT   197

6   Real Estate Spaces   199
Introduction   199
The paradox of location in the new economy   201
Physical form and virtual reality   204
Transactions in space   206
Personal space   209
Private space   213
Summary   224
Notes   225

7 **Real Estate Use and ICT**   **226**
   Introduction   226
   Sales   226
   Processing   235
   Manufacturing   250
   Distribution   257
   Leisure and living   265
   Summary   275
   Notes   275

8 **Real Estate Service Providers and ICT**   **279**
   Introduction   279
   The changing context of real estate investment   281
   The owner's manager   288
   The occupier's manager   301
   Appraisers   313
   Brokers   318
   Summary   327
   Notes   327

Part 3 The Future   **329**

9 **New Directions and Policy Implications: The Future
   of Real Estate in the New Economy**   **331**
   Introduction   331
   The socio-technical framework   332
   New types of real estate   342
   Implications of ICT transformation for existing real estate   349
   Policy issues   351
   Future visions   358
   Is there still a future for real estate in the new economy?   366
   Notes   368

References   372
Index   412

The Authors

Dr Tim Dixon is Director of Research at the College of Estate Management in Reading. With more than 20 years experience in real estate research and education, he is a chartered surveyor, a Member of the Institute of Learning and Teaching, and a member of the Editorial Boards of five leading, international academic real estate journals. He is also a member of the EPSRC Infrastructure and Environment Strategic Advisory Team and RICS Research Policy Committee. He has written widely on the subject of ICT in property/real estate, and he is currently working with his team on major funded research projects concerned with both technology and environmental issues in real estate. He also co-authors a regular, Technology Trends column with Bob Thompson for *Property Forecast* magazine. The College is a member of the PIREC (Partners in Real Estate Connectivity) consortium.

Bob Thompson is a freelance consultant with his own consultancy, RETRI. Formerly head of research at King Sturge and Co., he undertakes a wide range of consultancy for clients across the business spectrum, contributing regularly to leading press and academic publications, and speaking at strategic conferences. He is former President of the European Real Estate Society, and is currently senior research associate at the College of Estate Management and a senior research fellow at the University of Reading. He is also a member of the advisory board of Property Economics and Finance Research Network (PEFRN). RETRI is a member of the PIREC consortium.

Patrick McAllister is a lecturer in valuation and property management in the Department of Real Estate and Planning at the University of Reading. He has published widely on a range of topics related to property investment and valuation. In the past he has researched the valuation implications of the generation of 'new economy' income streams by property investors from broadband and eProcurement. His research includes a project which investigated the consequences of property owners developing new business opportunities (including broadband) from their tenant base.

Andrew Marston is Research Analyst at ATIS REAL Weatheralls. From 1999 he was research officer in the Research Department at the College of Estate Management, where he worked with Dr Tim Dixon on a series of research reports and academic papers examining the relationships between real estate markets and the use of eCommerce and eBusiness technologies by retail and office occupiers. In 2004 he moved to ATIS

REAL Weatheralls, a leading European real estate property consultancy. He is also a Committee member of the Society of Property Researchers.

Jon Snow is Chairman of iX Consulting Ltd. Jon Snow founded iX Consulting in March 2001 as a niche research house focusing on the emerging relationship between Internet technologies and real estate. iX Consulting supply subscription services to over 150 companies in 13 countries. Prior to founding iX Consulting, Jon was a researcher in the School of Real Estate Management at Oxford Brookes University, and eBusiness Associate at international property consultants Weatherall Green and Smith (now ATIS REAL Weatheralls) where he headed a team developing business in the technology sectors.

Foreword

It is said that, with technological change, most people overestimate the short term impacts but underestimate the long term impacts.

Certainly it did seem as though the real estate market of the late 1990s was somewhat thrown into panic by the perceived threats of both internet retailing to the continuing viability of established retailing centres and of business-to-business and business-to-customer on the continuing requirements for office space. That neither fear has yet turned into the reality that property investors and landowners worried they might, has encouraged a more sanguine, some might say complacent, view about the impact of developments in information and communication technology (ICT) on the real estate market.

With this in mind, there probably couldn't be a better time than the present for someone to conduct a thorough review of these crucially important issues. Over and above this, there is also a need to get away from the one-dimensional perspective on the impact of ICT that dominated thinking in the real estate markets of the late 1990s. We need to understand how the straightforward economics of the emerging technologies influence and are, in turn, influenced by social, economic and political forces. Only when seen in the round will we fully understand how ICT will ultimately influence real estate markets at local, regional, national and international levels.

On both counts, the authors of this book are to be applauded. They have sought, through their 'socio-technical' approach, to look at the complex interactions between technology, society and economics. Instinctively we know that new technologies might well allow us to work from home, but we might look on work as a social activity and not want to do so. We might not be able to work from home given the nature of our homes. Local planners may not be keen to accommodate such changes to individual residences and employers might vary in their willingness to see staff work away from home. Similarly, we might well be able to shop from home, but might still want to visit shops to see and feel the merchandise before we buy. We might see shopping trips as a leisure and social experience that forms a focus to daily or weekend life. In short, we might well turn our faces away from the 'atomisation' of social and economic interaction that ICT could now facilitate. As such, at a micro scale at least, there is no simple read-off of the effects of new technologies on individual activities or the real estate market.

Meanwhile, we also need to consider at a macro scale how ICT can relocate entire work functions across countries, continents and time zones, creating significant impacts for local labour markets and triggering heated political debate (viz. the debates in the UK and the USA with respect to the economic and social impact of 'off-shoring' work to the Indian sub-continent and elsewhere).

Certainly, writing as someone who earns his living by advising one of the UK's largest property investors on which properties to own and where, this book is very timely. Developments in ICT, mediated through economic, social and political processes, will clearly impact the absolute and relative utility of different types of locations and different types of properties to users, causing some to appreciate in value whilst others depreciate. Understanding the nuance of how this will unfold is, therefore, crucial to me. However, it is not just investors that will need to understand these processes – tenants, planners and communities at large, also need to understand them well.

In writing this comprehensive and very fully referenced text, the authors have done us all a great service.

Paul McNamara
Director: Head of Research
Prudential Property Investment Managers

Preface

If you had walked around Reading 20 years ago, the shape and form of the town centre and the urban fringe would have been very different from the pattern we see today. In 1984, business and office parks were starting to take off, driven by the inexorable rise in car transport and desire for peripheral locations; the town centre shopping was of a conservative and traditional high street form, without a major shopping centre; and despite its Thames Valley location, Reading was still not really in the upper echelons of UK towns and cities in terms of economic growth and wealth. Twenty years on, things are very different: office and business parks pervade; the Oracle has launched Reading into the top 12 shopping centres in the UK; and the area has one of the highest wealth indices outside London, founded on the growth of hi-tech business, the knowledge economy and financial services.

Reading's growth and prosperity have been founded on its location, skilled workforce and transport links, but technological change, and the growth of transport and allied infrastructure, as well as the telecommunications and information and communications technology (ICT) that we so often take for granted, have all played their role in this transformation.

But what is the evidence for this? Today's offices, shops and industrial property may not look that dramatically different on the outside, but there have been changes on the inside. For example, shops have become bigger: electronic point of sale technology has driven down the amount of storage space needed and freed up more sales space. Also, office technology has shifted space demand requirements, and changes in process have provided a re-emphasis, as 'call centres' and other types of new real estate space have developed. Reading's role in the growth of the new or knowledge economy in the region has also been driven by the trend towards a service economy, as successive governments have emphasised the importance of knowledge and enterprise as tools for economic growth. In turn, as service and other companies have sought to become more agile, flatter and more responsive to consumer choice, this has led to a move towards shorter leases and a desire to outsource property functions. Similarly, more business and commerce are being 'virtually' conducted on the web than before.

In short, as Kevin Kelly observed in 1998: 'People will inhabit places, but increasingly the economy inhabits a space' (see cartoon). But what will such continued transformation hold in store for Reading and other cities and towns in 20 years' time? In 2004, can we even imagine what Reading will look like in 2024? Will teleworking be the dominant form of working? Will Internet shopping have made major inroads into conventional shopping? Will manufacturing space be completely obsolete? What new types of real estate will emerge? What will be the balance and mix of real estate?

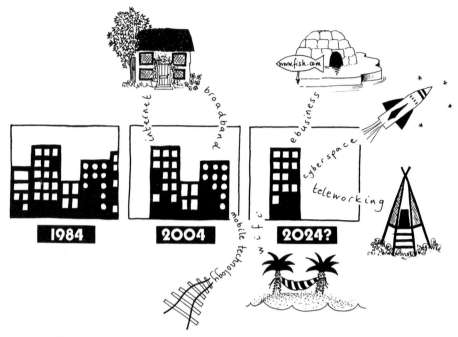

People will inhabit places, but increasingly the economy inhabits a space.

Our thesis in this book is that ICT is important, and does make a difference to the shape and form of real estate products and services that we see today, but what is also clear is that ICT does not act alone to transform real estate. Indeed, unravelling the effect of ICT from other forces for change in society is fraught with difficulty. As the Urban Task Force report, commissioned by the UK government in 1998, pointed out, the three main factors transforming our towns and cities are:

- Technical change, based on ICT and new networks connecting people at a global and local level.
- Ecological threat, including the role of sustainable development, on the future urban agenda.
- Social transformation, reflecting structural demographic and economic forces.

As we will argue, a full understanding can only be achieved by placing ICT in its social, economic and political context, or using a 'socio-technical' approach, and highlighting the importance of ICT within a conceptual framework that acknowledges the importance of this context. The book therefore seeks to steer a balanced path between the hype of the dot.com years, which, at its most extreme, suggested technology would lead to the 'death of real estate', and the more sceptical view that institutional and other barriers prevent ICT from influencing real estate demand and location to any large degree. In arriving at our conclusions we examine work from a range of disciplines including real estate studies; economics; spatial studies and geography; management literature and sociological studies. To that extent our approach is also multidisciplinary, and we also base our conclusions on continuing empirical research within our organisations.

Acknowledgements

The authors would like to thank colleagues, family and friends for their help and support during the course of writing this book. In particular, Tim Dixon would like to thank Rachel for just being there, with all her help and support including her cartoon artwork; and Bob Thompson would like to thank Jane for reminding him constantly why he bothers!

Table of Responsibilities

The writing of this book has been very much a joint effort between the authors. However, dividing the writing explicitly between us by chapter in terms of 'lead author' made sense from a project management point of view. We therefore outline below the responsibilities that were taken, and this may help readers who have particular queries over points raised in the individual chapters.

Chapter	Lead author(s)	Additional comments
1	Dixon	Thompson, Snow, McAllister, Marston
2	Dixon	Thompson, Snow, McAllister, Marston
3	Dixon	Thompson, Snow, McAllister, Marston
4	Thompson	Dixon, Snow, McAllister, Marston
5	Dixon	Thompson, Snow, McAllister, Marston
6	Thompson	Dixon, Snow, McAllister, Marston
7	Dixon, Thompson, Marston, Snow	McAllister
8	McAllister, Dixon, Thompson	Snow, Marston
9	Dixon, Thompson	Snow, Marston, McAllister

Book website
A website to accompany the book has been developed at www.cem.ac.uk/neweconomy. The website contains useful links, updates and other resources on real estate, the new economy and ICT.

Dr. Tim Dixon, College of Estate Management, Reading
(t.j.dixon@ cem.ac.uk) October 2004

1

Read all

Introduction

Background

The overall aim of this book is to show how new technology (i.e. Information and Communications Technology (ICT)) is impacting on the shape and form of real estate in our towns and cities, and how it is influencing and is being influenced by other forces within what many commentators call the 'new economy', as part of an 'information society'.

UK private sector commercial property (office, industrial and retail) is a large and important asset, representing some £400 bn or 34% of total business assets. Business property also represents 17% of UK fixed tangible assets (Capital Economics 2002). Yet social and economic forces for change, linked with new technology, are leading owners and occupiers to question the very nature of property and real estate, and the purpose it should serve. The key question therefore arises: what are the implications of ICT impact for the amount, location, configuration and type/nature of real estate assets? In this sense, if ICT is improving productivity (in space and output terms), will this reduce the demand for real estate in certain sectors (i.e. retail, offices and industrial), and the overall demand for real estate floor-space? Will new and existing property be reconfigured?

Typically, linear models of technological innovation have highlighted the transformational aspects of technology and the key social processes from which it emerges. However, such models adopt a deterministic view of technological change and imply that science, technology, markets and organisations are linked in a linear and causal chain. The reality is very different: invention, use and exchange of technology operate in a cyclical and reciprocal way. If this latter model is adopted as a starting point, then ICT is also a product and a manifestation of forces, which include social, economic and political factors, organisational change and business process change.

It is therefore dangerous to assert that technology operates in a vacuum, and the theoretical framework adopted in the book (which we term a 'socio-technical' model) views ICT as operating within the context of other factors, and as a product and manifestation of these forces. It acknowledges that these forces for change are shaping what may be called a 'new economy', and are also working together to influence real estate patterns and processes.

The book (and accompanying website, www.cem.ac.uk/neweconomy) is based on the authors' own research,[1] and a growing body of new, international research in the field. Drawing on the authors' extensive knowledge of research, and examples from the UK, USA and elsewhere, it addresses the following, related questions:

- How do new technology, organisational change and economic factors interact, and what is the impact of their interaction on working practices and demand for commercial and residential real estate?
- What are the resultant implications for real estate strategies (i.e. for landlords, tenants and other stakeholders) and for the provision of real estate services?
- What is the impact on the spatial form, geography, and specification of commercial and residential real estate?
- What are the changes in urban shape and form likely to be in the future?

This introductory chapter therefore sets the scene for what follows by:

- focusing on the key aims and objectives of the book;
- outlining the basis of the theoretical 'socio-technical' framework adopted (set in the context of a literature review of alternative frameworks); and
- highlighting the key themes which are explored in the book.

Aim and objectives

The key aim of the book is to examine how ICT, as one of a number of forces for change in property and real estate, is impacting on real estate markets and services.

The objectives are to:

- examine how new technologies, incorporating eCommerce and eBusiness, combined with organisational change and social, political and economic factors, are affecting the demand for space and working practices in office, retail and industrial real estate markets;
- analyse how real estate owners' and occupiers' real estate strategies are changing to reflect these trends. The effect on residential property through smart homes and teleworking is also considered as well as the effect on professional real estate services through disintermediation and reintermediation;
- assess how technology is impacting on the geography and space of commercial and residential real estate and the implications for infrastructure in our towns and cities;
- examine how urban shape and form are likely to change over the next decade and beyond, as a result of changes in demand for real estate and accompanying changes in the use, location, occupancy and type/nature of real estate.

It should be noted that the framework we adopt in the book highlights the interlinkage between ICT and other factors. As we shall see throughout the book, isolating and decoupling the impact of ICT from other factors are fraught with difficulties and, in fact, we adopt our framework because we argue that ICT cannot be understood in isolation from other related factors, which include globalisation, demographic change, flexible production and organisational change.

Definitions

It is important to examine how we define *technology*, *new economy*, *information society*, and *real estate* in this book. Historically, the Information Technology (IT) sector has been defined in a variety of ways. However, existing national and international statistical classifications and systems (see, for example, OECD 2000) have failed to keep up to date with a rapidly evolving IT sector. Computing and telecommunications technology has also converged and is now commonly referred to as 'the ICT sector'. In fact, in 1998 OECD member countries agreed to define the ICT sector as 'a combination of manufacturing and service industries that capture, transmit and display data and information electronically', and we adopt this definition in the book to include those technologies which underpin the sector. Therefore we use 'ICT' and 'technology' interchangeably, but our definition of technology is more restrictive than other definitions (see, for example, Green & Vandell, 2001 and Scarbrough & Martin Corbett 1992), which frequently include components beyond ICT.

As far as the most recent 'new economy' is concerned, Castells (2000) points out that this emerged in the last quarter of the twentieth century and is informational, global and networked. However, there have always been new economies (Rowlatt *et al.* 2002) and the concept is not tied to time or technology. Over the centuries there have been periods when changes in technology or social organisation brought about:

- radical changes to market boundaries, expanding the scope to exploit intellectual capital;
- access to new products and services for major sections of society;
- significant changes in the interactions and operating processes of enterprises; and
- a redefinition of customer–supplier relations.

Examples (also see Perez 2002; Gordon 2000) include printing; steam power; canals and railroads; mass media and more recently ICT. Each changes the structure of economies and relationships in society but none is purely economic in nature. Most proceed and succeed from an initial step providing limited intellectual capital to a small sector, to a point at which access is potentially available to all. Today the notion of a new economy is closely tied to the effects of technical progress on economic growth, and in the present debate the role played by information and communications technologies (ICT) on economic performance is vitally important.

However, in this book we adopt the following definition (Progressive Policy Institute, 1998: 8): 'a knowledge and idea-based economy where the key to job creation and higher standards of living are innovative ideas and technology embedded in services and manufactured products'.[2]

It is also important to note that the new economy is the driving force behind the emergence of the 'information society', which is explored in more detail alongside the 'new economy' in Chapter 2 of this book. A precise definition of the information society is difficult to pin down. For instance, a DTI/Spectrum report (1996: 1) suggested that the term could not be precisely defined, because it was still evolving and carried different meanings across Europe and elsewhere, but it conveyed a society that: '...uses information intensively and in a way that is not constrained by time or space, a society where transactions of all sorts can be processed electronically, a society whose working and living practices have been modified fundamentally by technology'.

Put simply, the term 'information society' stresses the societal, inclusive transformations of technology, whereas the term 'new economy' emphasises more restricted, economic aspects. The term 'information society' also stresses inclusivity: an information society is supposed to be enjoyed by all, and not just a particular group(s). In this book we argue that the information society is closely associated with the new economy, which is providing the engine for economic growth.

Finally, 'real estate' is used interchangeably with the term 'property' in this book and follows the *Dictionary of Real Estate Terms* definition (Friedman *et al.* 1993: 278) to 'encompass in law, land and everything more or less attached to it and, in business, the activities concerned with ownership and use transfers of the physical property'. In the book we use the term 'real estate' to encompass the main sectors of retail, industrial, offices and residential. However, we also suggest that the hard and fast distinctions between sectors are becoming more blurred as ICT impacts on real estate. Also, the term 'real estate' is inclusive of new types of property and use being created by ICT transformation (for example, smart homes, co-location centres or server farms). Within our definition of real estate, we also investigate both the real estate and corporate property sectors and include a detailed examination of the impact of ICT on the real estate services sector. Finally, we are concerned with addressing ICT impacts within the key stages of the real estate production process: namely, construction, development and investment.

Technological change: alternative perspectives

Technology's impact (in its widest sense) on society has been viewed in a variety of different ways and through different strengths of lens. In order to understand the rationale for the framework adopted in this book it is important to review the development of these views at four different levels within both non-spatial and spatial perspectives.

Within a 'non-spatial' perspective, two sets of frameworks have been developed (Table 1.1). First, frameworks of technological change which examine the impact on the economy as a whole and, second, frameworks of how the management, structure and form of organisations have been affected. Generally, this latter group does not consider the spatial aspects of technology explicitly (which would normally include the locational and space demand/supply dynamics at a meso/micro level).

Table 1.1 Perspectives on technology.

Perspective	Framework	Examples
Non-spatial	Economy-level	Schumpeter (1939)
		Beniger (1986)
		Gordon (2000)
		Perez (2002)
	Firm-level	Winner (1996)
		Scarbrough and Martin Corbett (1992)
Spatial	Urban and regional-level	Berry (1973)
		Storper (1997)
		Castells (2000)
		Graham and Marvin (2001)
	Real estate-level	Borsuk (1999)
		Green and Vandell (2001)
		Gibson and Lizieri (2001)
		Dixon and Marston (2002a)

In contrast, 'spatial' views and perspectives have also been developed to assess the impact of technological change on the shape and form of our towns and cities, and on the real estate occupied or owned by organisations.

It is also true that a number of frameworks view 'technology' in the widest sense of the word, and in a way that includes Information and Communications Technology. An example is that adopted by Green & Vandell (2001), which is discussed in more detail later in this chapter. Our definition of 'technology' is more restricted (see above) referring simply to ICT, but nonetheless we draw on some of the key themes and principles from previous theory in developing our 'socio-technical' framework, which we discuss in further detail later in this chapter. Although there is a degree of implicit overlap between some of the frameworks, models and paradigms, the typology now discussed serves to identify themes, and to place our framework in the context of work by others. The intention is to provide an overview, and the discussion is by no means exhaustive. There have been a whole range of models conceptualising the impact of technological change on society from a variety of disciplines, and so space prevents a detailed discussion of all of these. The key perspectives from the fields of economics, geography, planning, sociology and real estate are therefore now presented.

Non-spatial perspective

Economy-level framework

Over the last hundred or so years, there have been several approaches to the study of technology and technological change at an 'economy-level' (Bruun & Hukkinen 2003). Perhaps the most popular of these was developed in the field of evolutionary economics, which draws on the work of Joseph Schumpeter and sees knowledge as a connecting link between technological change and economic dynamics. In this sense, knowledge gives competitive advantage, but as technology diffuses throughout the economy prices fall, which means other firms start to innovate. Evolutionary economics increased in popularity because neo-classical economics had failed to explain technological change, which was seen as based solely on core assumptions regarding market equilibrium (sustained through the forces of demand and supply). Instead, evolutionary economics focused much more on an institutional framework of decision making, and based itself on a new theory of economic agency. The discipline was further developed in the 1980s to include 'innovation systems' which identified institutions and economic structures as important constraints and drivers for technological change. But technological change was also seen by many as systemic in nature, and so concepts in the field were developed further (Freeman & Louca 2001).

Although technological change was also important to proponents of evolutionary economics, previous theories, including those by Schumpeter (1939), had failed to recognise the vital role of institutions in shaping the outcome of technological transformation. Much existing theory was seen as being guilty of technological determinism, or the tendency to see technology and economic growth as directly linked. Instead, it was argued that economic growth can only be understood in the context of a sequence of eras corresponding to clusters of new technologies. Carlota Perez's work in 1983 on structural change and the assimilation of new technologies (see Freeman's Preface to Perez 2002) was therefore influential, because it demonstrated that big technology changes (for example, iron, coal, steel, oil or microprocessors) led not only to the rapid growth of new industries, but also spawned the rejuvenation of older industries over a longer period. These older industries found new ways of using the new technology and made changes in their organisation and management, brought about by technology. This comprised, in her view, a new way of thinking about the systems of production, including the organisation, techniques and interdependencies within what she termed a 'techno-economic paradigm'. The concept of a paradigm change at each technological revolution is fundamental to this view.[3]

Perez's work also emphasised the importance of 'meta-paradigm' changes which affect the whole economy and entailed the very widespread use of new inputs. These created economies of scale, leading to price falls, which made technologies more attractive for economic and technical reasons.

Her work also illustrated the fallacy of technological determinism, and she argued that transformation can only happen through an interactive and accompanying process of social, political and managerial change. She also showed that there is a great deal of interdependency between technology, management and organisation within the context of regulation and other societal forces. Paradigm change therefore has an impact at the firm level, but is also affected by the entire system of social and political regulation, and this is true of education and training, intellectual property rights and other legal frameworks in what many refer to as the 'information society' today.

Building on this work, Perez (2002) extended these ideas and those of Schumpeter still further in an attempt to develop a highly abstracted, interdisciplinary paradigm that linked long waves of technological growth to financial capital cycles. Schumpeter (1939) had referred to the 'creative destruction' of innovations, leading to progress but also recurring recessions. However, Perez argued that long waves of economic change could only be understood in the context of complex, society-wide processes. Such periods have frequently been the source of chaotic and contradictory social effects which meant internal re-composition, a redesign of institutions, markets and economic activity which could then lead to a new 'golden age'. She cites the example of the Victorian boom from the mid-nineteenth century which materialised some 20 years after George Stephenson's *Rocket* had run on the Liverpool–Manchester railway (Perez 2002: 24). This had followed the installation of a network of railways and occurred prior to (and during) a time of chaos and panic in the financial markets. The resultant boom was therefore founded on a new set of markets and institutions that led to more regulation, which, in turn, led to further expansion of the railway network and urban growth.

Perez (2002: 6) suggested that there were, in fact, three main features in the functioning of the capitalist system which interacted and determined the recurrent surges she identified:

- Technological change tends to occur in clusters of radical innovations leading to successive and separate eras that modernise the whole production system.
- Financial and production capital are interrelated but functionally separate, each following paths with different criteria and behaviours.
- Inertia and resistance to change are higher in the socio-institutional framework than in the techno-economic sphere, which is driven by competition.

She uses the term 'technological revolution' (Perez 2002: 8) to represent '...a powerful and highly visible cluster of new and dynamic technologies, products and industries, capable of bringing about an upheaval in the whole fabric of the economy and of propelling a long-term upsurge of development'. Inevitably, this includes a strongly linked 'constellation'[4] of technical innovations, which comprises an important all-pervasive low-cost input such as an energy industry, but sometimes a raw material, and new products and processes within a new infrastructure. The impact of these revolutions spreads far beyond the original industries and sectors in which they occurred and each provides interrelated generic technologies and organisational principles that enable upsurges in potential productivity. This in turn leads to regeneration and modernisation of the whole system with a recurrence of the cycle about every 50 years.

Perez (2002) sees the process of diffusion of the revolution and its paradigm throughout the economy as a great surge of development. This builds on the work of Dosi (1982), who related technological change to various trajectories of growth. Each surge in the trajectory is seen as having two distinct periods, over a period of 50 years (Figure 1.1). The first 20–30 years

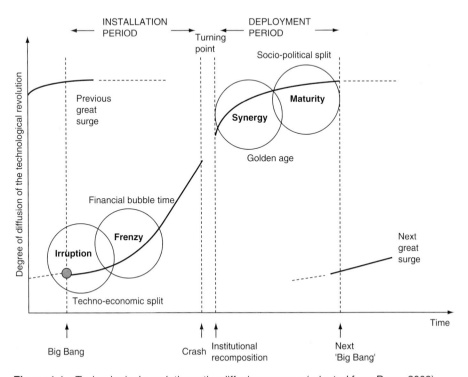

Figure 1.1 Technological revolutions: the diffusion process (adapted from Perez 2002).

are the period of 'installation', comprising a period of 'irruption' followed by 'frenzy', as a critical mass of industries and infrastructures develop, which seek to overturn the established paradigm, driven on by access to financial capital. After a mid-surge period there follows a 'turning point' when the tensions that have built up are surmounted and a period of deployment (also lasting 20–30 years) then follows. This phase is characterised by a spreading of the revolution throughout the economy, as 'synergy' and 'maturity' occur.

The framework developed by Perez links technological phases with new constellations of industries and infrastructures and paradigm changes to support and drive forward the change. This concept of technological revolution is also closely related to the ideas of Simon Kuznets (1971) who conceived the idea of 'epochal innovations' (over longer periods of several centuries), which were able to induce significant growth. Other authors such as Suarez-Villa (2003) have also used similar concepts to explain the evolution of technology, although Suarez-Villa employs the term 'techno-capitalism' to encapsulate the evolution of market capitalism rooted in rapid technological innovation and its supporting intangibles.

Perez suggests that since the end of the eighteenth century there have been five distinct phases of economic growth associated with particular revolutions (Table 1.2).[5] These have been characterised by clusters of growth occurring in particular countries or even regions: Lancashire as the cradle of the first industrial revolution and Silicon Valley as the centre of the microelectronics revolution. All require some form of low-cost 'attractor' or 'big bang' in order to spark further breakthrough in the revolution. Just as Richard Arkwright's Cromford Mill drove the irruption of the Industrial Revolution, so the microprocessor in 1971 started the 'information age'.

Similarly, each revolution is founded on the linkages and synergy between various industries and infrastructures. But many of the products and industries had already existed, and each revolution's role was in bringing them together. Coal and iron had been used for a long period prior to the Industrial Revolution, but it was the steam engine that transformed their power: the same can be said for oil and the internal combustion engine and mass car production. Electronics had also existed since the 1900s but broke through in the 1970s because of the potential of cheap microelectronics. So each 'constellation' also reveals technologies developing at different rhythms and with feedback loops: for example, the information revolution began with a upsurge and explosion in microprocessors and hardware which led to rapid growth in software and telecommunications, followed by the Internet boom with each benefiting from the previous

Table 1.2   The industries and infrastructures of each technological revolution (adapted from Perez 2002).

Technological revolution	New technologies and new or redefined industries	New or redefined infrastructures

FIRST:
From 1771
The Industrial Revolution, Britain
	Mechanised cotton industry
	  Wrought iron
	  Machinery
		Canals and waterways
		  Turnpike roads
		  Water power (highly improved water wheels)

SECOND:
From 1829
Age of Steam and Railways, in Britain and spreading to continent and USA
	Steam engines and machinery (made in iron; fuelled by coal)
	  Iron and coal mining (now playing a central role in growth)[*]
	  Railway construction
	  Rolling stock production
	  Steam power for many industries (including textiles)
		Railways (use of steam engine)
		  Universal postal service
		  Telegraph (mainly nationally along railway lines)
		  Great ports, great depots and worldwide sailing ships
		  City gas

THIRD:
From 1875
Age of Steel, Electricity and Heavy Engineering, USA and Germany overtaking Britain
	Cheap steel (especially Bessemer)
	  Full development of steam engine for steel ships
	  Heavy chemistry and civil engineering
	  Electrical equipment industry
	  Copper and cables
	  Canned and bottled food
	  Paper and packaging
		Worldwide shipping in rapid steel steamships (use of Suez Canal)
		  Worldwide railways (use of cheap steel rails and bolts in standard sizes)
		  Great bridges and tunnels
		  Worldwide telegraph
		  Telephone (mainly nationally)
		  Electrical networks (for illumination and industrial use)

FOURTH:
From 1908 Age of Oil, the Automobile and Mass Production, in USA and spreading to Europe
	Mass-produced automobiles
	  Cheap oil and oil fuels
	  Petrochemicals (synthetics)
	  Internal combustion engine for automobiles, transport, tractors, airplane, war tanks and electricity
	  Home electrical appliances
	  Refrigerated and frozen foods
		Networks of roads, highways, ports and airports
		  Networks of oil ducts
		  Universal electricity (industry and home)
		  Worldwide analogue telecommunications (telephone, telex and cablegram) wire and wireless

FIFTH:
From 1971
Age of Information and Telecommunications, in USA, spreading to Europe and Asia
	The information revolution:
	  Cheap microelectronics
	  Computers, software
	  Telecommunications
	  Control instruments
	  Computer-aided biotechnology and new materials
		World digital telecommunications (cable, fibre optics, radio and satellite)
		  Internet/electronic mail and other e-services
		  Multiple source, flexible use, electricity networks
		  High-speed physical transport links (by land, air and water)

Note: [*]These traditional industries acquire a new role and a new dynamism when serving as the material and the fuel of the world of railways and machinery.

market and potential. It may well be, in Perez's view, that biotechnology, bioelectronics and nanotechnology may form the next revolution.

The concept of 'revolution' means that old organisational models cannot cope or take full advantage of the new technology (Perez 2002). Techno-economic paradigms are therefore created. This comprises (Perez 2002: 15): '... a best practice model made up of all-pervasive generic technological and organisational principles, which represent the most effective way of applying a particular technological revolution and of using it for modernising and rejuvenating the whole of the economy'. When these are adopted they become the accepted way for organising activity and structuring institutions.

In essence a 'design, product and profit space' is opened up into which entrepreneurs, engineers and innovators pour to develop new practices. Perez suggests that paradigms are elusive and difficult to grasp but nonetheless argues strongly that they lead to a set of common principles which diffuses between actors in their decisions and decision making and that they promote 'isomorphism' in changes occurring across institutions, including firms. For example, the fifth revolution (the Age of Information and Telecommunications) within which, until the 1980s, the prevalent organisation was a centralised, hierarchical pyramid with functional divisions. Perez argues that this structure was applied to the economy by almost every institution from government through to firm level. However, with the advent of ICT, such structures are no longer tenable: decentralised, flexible networks are seen to be more efficient. These have a strategic core and rapid communications, which enable the linkage of global and local organisations (see also Castells 2000).

A useful contrast to this view is provided by Beniger (1986), who also uses a perspective which focuses on spans of technological change to illustrate how a 'control revolution' operates through bureaucratic change. In fact, he argues that bureaucracy remained the single most important technology of the control revolution in the era of ICT. In this respect, control is inseparable from information processing and communication, and ICT exerts control in much the same way that rail and telegraph systems did earlier through communication and feedback loops.

The work of Robert Gordon (2000) also provides an interesting and contrasting view to Perez. Like Perez, Gordon supports the view of transformational, technological eras or epochs in history, and uses the term 'clusters' in a similar sense to Perez[6] to represent a primary breakthrough invention, grouping together the 'Group of Five' as: electricity, the automobile, molecular re-arrangement, communications, and running water. These underpinned the Second Industrial Revolution of 1860–1900, and, he suggests, drove the golden age of productivity growth from 1913 to 1972. However, he poses the question: have the computer and the Internet brought about a Third Industrial Revolution? In this sense he is more sceptical than Perez and uses US empirical data to argue that ICT has not transformed productivity outside durable manufacturing. He suggests that ICT may be 'fun and informational' but cannot compare with the great inventions of the past in terms of economic impact. However, new evidence emerging from the OECD (2003) suggests that productivity impact is increasingly evident (see Chapter 5).

Perez (2002) does concede that there are barriers to be overcome with any new technology, however, and in fact one can argue that both views are not irreconcilable, given that Gordon's analysis was based on data from the 1990s. Perez (2002) therefore suggests that it is important to note that the techno-economic paradigm acts as a propeller of diffusion and as a delaying force. Although the model can be followed by all, the integration and configuration take time and new principles need to learned: there will also be resistance from the largest firms and organisations who have fixed asset structures based on existing technology. Effective solutions may also therefore take the form of mergers, migration and financial capital experiments, and the change of paradigm creates 'inclusion–exclusion' mechanisms which avoid departure from the norm, until the potential is exhausted. Finally, within the economy, the relationships between financial and production capital influence the rhythm and direction of growth. Production capital ensures the full deployment and spread of the revolution throughout the economy and new financial capital enables the succession of surges, which can help overcome conservative production 'lock in' at the end of the maturity period.

Although the evolutionary economics view of technological change within economies offers a compelling and persuasive perspective, it is not without criticism (Lemola 2000). As Bruun and Hukkinen (2003) point out, the whole field of evolutionary economics has been criticised for placing too much emphasis on individuals and radical innovations. Bruland (2001) also casts doubt on neo-Schumpeterian attempts to divide economic history into what she considers to be arbitrary chronologies, and she suggests that frequently such analysis fails to provide evidence on the economic impact of technologies. Others (see, for example, Lemola 2000) have also suggested that it is difficult to operationalise evolutionary economics mathematically or that it is guilty of positivism and has poorly defined concepts. Alternatives such as social construction of technology

(SCOT) and actor network theory (ANT) have therefore been formulated based on constructivism.

Philosophically, constructivism is a contrasting view to determinism, and in the constructivist view, free agency, individual will, conscious deliberation and choice amongst human agents are stressed (Ryder 2003). This is in stark contrast to determinism, which sees technology as a driving force with far reaching consequences regardless of social context (Smith & Marx 1994). Therefore social constructivists have sought to try and explain how and why particular technologies arise and are adopted at particular times. Technology is seen as a process in which differing interpretations emerge depending on social context (Boxes 1.1 and 1.2) Their proponents (see, for example, Pinch & Bijker 1997) suggest that they better explain why technical solutions become paradigmatic, claiming evolutionary economics is more appropriate for describing the outcomes of change. However, in many cases, such perspectives are often equally difficult to implement and conceptualise.

Firm-level frameworks

Turning to the firms and businesses, Brock (2000) suggests that there are various research streams which influence the impact of ICT at this level, ranging from computer science through behavioural science, decision science, organisation science, social science and management science to economics and political science. He suggests that the key research areas that have developed in this field over time include:

Box 1.1   Social construction of technology (SCOT)

The social construction of technology (SCOT) school was guided by three main principles flowing from the sociology of scientific knowledge: interpretative flexibility, relevant social groups and closure (Bijker *et al.* 1987). Interpretative flexibility means the way in which different social groups attach meaning to different technical artefacts. Contests between different social groupings based on power and influence are an important part of the process and so some may take actions to exclude the interests of others. Bijker (1995) introduced the concept of a 'technological frame' to develop an understanding of how such groups interacted. Closure and stabilisation of technology can occur because a particular technology appears to present fewer problems than others and so it comes to dominate (McGrath 2003). This also permits multiple or parallel forms of technology (for example, PCs and laptops), which become shaped not only in design but also in their use. SCOT essentially challenges the view that ICT is adopted because it works better; instead SCOT seeks to ask why is it thought that a new artefact works better?

Box 1.2   Actor network theory (ANT)

Another branch of the social constructivist school relates to actor network theory (ANT) (see the work of Latour (1993a,b)). ANT is an evolving body of theory, but put simply can be seen as a systematic approach to highlighting agency dynamics in the context of scientific and technological developments. ANT analysis attempts to describe the progressive development of networks in which human and non-human actors (or 'actants') assume identities according to the strategies of interaction which prevail. Actors' identities are therefore defined during the process of negotiation between the human and non-human actants. For example, as Hanseth and Monteiro (1998) state, when driving a car or writing a document using a word processor, there are many things that influence the action. When driving a car, a driver is influenced by traffic regulations, prior driving experience and the car's handling. The use of a word processor is influenced by earlier experience, the functionality of the word processor and work–leisure balance. ANT suggests that all these factors are important and the act and all of the independent factors should be considered together. An actor network, then, is the act linked together with all of its influencing factors (which again are linked), producing a network.[7] ANT differs from SCOT in two key respects (Bruun & Hukkinen 2003): ANT does not explain the action of actors by reference to their social context; and it argues that the technological openness of the situation does not end with enrolment or closure.

- adoption research;
- implementation research;
- strategic management research; and
- impact research.

Adoption research (see, for example, Fink 1998; Thong & Yap 1995) is interested in explaining the determinants of organisational adoption of ICT. One of the key questions is to address the factors influencing adoption and non-adoption of ICT.

Implementation research, on the other hand, is concerned with examining post-adoption processes, mainly the implementation process. Building on organisational innovation and diffusion theory (Zaltman *et al.*, 1973; Rogers 1995) other authors (Zmud & Apple 1992) see various phases comprising initiation, adoption, implementation, routinisation and infusion in this process.

The use of ICT as a strategic tool in an organisation is now well established, and during the 1990s the concept of a 'technology-strategy' connection was much vaunted. Michael Porter's models, for example, were adapted to develop business strategy frameworks and systems analysis frameworks. They were designed to highlight specific strategic opportunities and/or clarify business strategies to demonstrate options for using ICT in a strategic role. For example, Porter and Millar (1985), McFarlan (1984) and Cash and Konsynski (1985) built on Porter's 'Five Forces of Industry Competition'. Their work is summarised in Table 1.3. Barriers to entry can be used as a defensive strategic action, and in this sense ICT is seen as a powerful weapon, which can increase economies of scale, raise the cost of entry and tie up distribution channels. ICT can also be used as a source of innovation because it can be built into new products and add to product and service value.

Generally, however, such studies are not based on empirical work and ICT impact on strategic performance of firms still remains relatively ambiguous.

Impact research focuses on the effects of ICT on the operations of individuals, groups or whole organisations and so is an integral part of the previous research streams, although Brock (2000) considers it a separate stream because performance measurement is at the heart of impact analysis. Measuring the impact of ICT on firms is quite difficult because of the problems in measuring the overall value of ICT to organisations. This is the result not only of measuring productivity impact, where intangible goods are becoming important, but also because there is often a time lag between ICT investment and its impact (Brynjolfsson & Hitt 1998). Moreover there is a methodological problem here in that cross-sectional studies, the most popular form of research in this field, find it difficult to track change over time. Also, as ICT becomes more and more an integral part of business, it becomes difficult to isolate and separate its impact from other important influences (Dempsey *et al.* 1998).

Empirical research has also shown that organisational factors play an important role in determining the success or otherwise of ICT investment.

Table 1.3 Exploiting ICT in the competitive arena (adapted from Earl 1991).

Competitive force	Potential of IT	Mechanism
New entrants	Barriers to entry	Erect
		Demolish
Suppliers	Reduce power	Erode
		Share
Customers	Lock in	Switching costs
		Customer information
Substitute products and services	Innovation	New products
		Add value
Rivalry	Change the basis	Compete
		Collaborate

Brynjolfsson and Hitt (1998) found in an analysis of firm-level data in the USA that about 50% of ICT value is due to the unique characteristics of firms, while the remaining part is shared generally by all firms. The 'black box' processes inside a firm are therefore very important in determining the productivity of IT investments. Their research also showed that the organisational factors that unlock the value of ICT are costly and time consuming. This could therefore explain the finding from their research that ICT tends to be unusually productive in the long term: the benefits are not just from ICT but from a combination of technology and organisational changes.

This also has implications for restructuring of organisations. For example, the vast literature from business management (see, for example, Drucker 1977) suggests that diffusion of ICT into the workplace means organisations need to restructure. A typical example here is the issue of flatter, less hierarchical organisations, with workers operating in a decentralised environment (Drucker 1977). Alongside these changes, others (see, for example, Kanter 1989; Peters 1987) have highlighted additional trends such as business process redesign, emergence of high performance work systems, and shifts to flexible modern manufacturing. Some studies (Lichtenberg 1995) suggest that such practices do make a difference: organisations that have utilised decentralised decision making and have greater levels of workforce skill invest more in ICT. Indeed, Brynjolfsson and Hitt's (1998) research shows that firms that combine IT investments with decentralised work practices are about 5% more productive than firms that do neither. But firms can also become worse off if they invest in new ICT systems without new work systems. However, they also note that many organisations have not redesigned management infrastructure to match the changes in ICT.

The lesson from this is that it is not just ICT alone that drives productivity, but 'softer' organisational factors are also important. ICT does not automatically increase productivity (the book will cover this issue in more detail in Chapter 5). In other words, as with economy-level models, technological determinism does not give an accurate model of technological change. This point is also made by Scarbrough and Martin Corbett (1992) who suggest that although the typical linear model of technological innovation highlights the transformational aspects of technology and the key social processes from which it emerges, it clings to a deterministic view of technological change (Figure 1.2). It implies that technological necessity operates by welding science, technology, markets and organisations together into an objective and interlocking causal chain. Scarbrough and Martin Corbett argue for a rather different model, viewing invention,

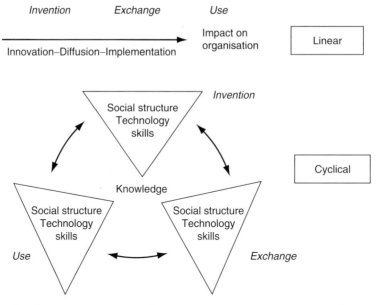

Figure 1.2 Two contrasting views of technological change (adapted from Scarbrough & Martin Corbett 1992).

use and exchange of technology in terms of subjective actions and loosely coupled forms of social organisation, giving rise to a cyclical and reciprocal process rather than a linear process.

Their analysis is a valuable one because it focuses on the relationships between technology and organisation. As they point out, the growing fluidity in organisational form presents theoretical challenges of understanding at the firm level. The linkage between technological and organisational form makes it difficult to 'know the dancer from the dance'. They see technology and organisation therefore as interlocking processes rather than as the finished articles of structures, systems and machines, and they therefore refute not only deterministic models of firm-level change, but also organisational choice models as well.

Put simply, deterministic, firm-level models (see Winner 1996) suggest that organisations have little choice but to adapt their skills and organisational practices in order to implement technology. In contrast, organisational choice models show that the process of change and technology is shaped by actors inside organisations. For example, a number of authors (such as Buchanan & Huczynski 1985; Pettigrew 1973; Buchanan & Boddy 1983) suggest that the relationship between technology and organisation is largely determined by managerial intentions and values, and organisational politics. Technology therefore embodies the intentions and interests of particular groups.

Clearly, the linear model shown above in Figure 1.2 proposes that technologies are generated and diffused by transfers of knowledge and artefacts between three different processes, comprising invention, where new ideas and forms of technological knowledge are generated; exchange process, where product-market and labour-market factors influence the design of the technology, and finally, a use or production process, where technologies are applied to particular tasks. This reflects a deterministic view of technological change and implies that organisations have little choice other than to apply the most advanced technologies. Technology is therefore viewed as a necessity, and cements science, technology, markets and organisations together in an interlocking chain. Scarbrough and Martin Corbett (1992) argue for a more cyclical process between invention, use and exchange. The individual organisation is therefore neither merely a passive receiver of technology nor an autonomous controller of technological change. Organisations, in their view, shape the technology, at the same time as it is shaped by them, and flows of knowledge are organised between different elements of the technology process. Social processes therefore also interact to create a cyclical and reciprocal process.

Spatial perspective

Urban and regional level frameworks

There have been a diverse range of models which have sought to explain the impact of ICT on urban form. In the view of Audirac and Fitzgerald (2003), for example, place, community and region form a 'triptych' in the current policy discourse in this field. Similarly, Audirac (2002a) suggests that urban IT analysts from a variety of perspectives highlight three issues (see, for example, Castells 2000; Graham & Marvin 1996; Storper 1997; Florida 2000) as being important:

- A shift to a new type of knowledge economy, in which intellectual capital is replacing other types of capital in wealth generation.
- Understanding where in the metropolitan region the new breed of knowledge/hi-tech workers want to live, work and take leisure.
- Designing liveable spaces that attract these key workers and protect local communities and promote economic growth.

They also suggest that various authors refer to a typology of cities which is synonymous with the impact of technology on urban shape and form. For example, 'megalopolises' (Gottman 1991); 'networked cities' (Clark & Kuijpers-Linde 1994); 'global cities' (Sassen 1991); 'informational cities' (Castells 2000); and 'post-industrial cities' (Hall 1997).

In contrast, other authors have used theoretical and descriptive perspectives to describe the flux at the edge of the city: the 'technoburbs' (Fishman 1990); 'edge-cities' (Garreau 1991); and 'postsuburbia' (Kling *et al.* 1995). The transformation of the city edge through new development has also engendered different perspectives such as 'post-Fordist' (Storper 1997); 'post-industrial' (Hall 1997) or 'informational' (Castells 2000).

Similarly, movements and manifestos have also evolved to offer responses to the trends being promoted by new technology and its impact on urban form. These include, particularly in the USA, Smart Growth; Congress of New Urbanism; New Economy Towns; Liveable Communities and New Regionalism, which also reflect the construction of new IT-embedded social networks and synergistic interaction between digital and physical space (Storper 1997; Castells 2000).

In the view of Audirac and Fitzgerald (2003) therefore the relevant literature in this field can be grouped around two major theoretical traditions:

- deconcentration; and,
- restructuring.

Building on the work of Frey (1993), they point out it has been frequently argued that spatial deconcentration perspectives related to IT and communications emphasise the travel substitution effects of technology, whereas restructuring perspectives emphasise technology's face-to-face generation effects. Deconcentration would lead to the disappearance of urban agglomeration, in contrast to the restructuring perspective that urban centres would continue to predominate.

However, these distinctions fail to recognise the similarities between the two traditions. In the view of Audirac and Fitzgerald, both 'traditions' recognise centripetal and centrifugal forces, but differ in the way that IT and telecommunications are theorised. However, it is also important to note that there is also some degree of overlap between the two traditions. In other words, the authors stress that the typology is a 'heuristic' device, which places the theoretical views as two poles of a continuum.

The deconcentration tradition focuses on technology as a way of extending and substituting human functions, and enhancing space and time spanning capabilities. Key agents here are individuals, households and firms exercising their locational preferences. On the other hand, the restructuring school places technology within a new technical and economic paradigm, which permeates social/institutional practices. In this perspective, key agents are corporate, state and institutional agents operating in local and global contexts.

The deconcentration school contains work in the human ecology tradition of urban sociology and microeconomic, neoclassical approaches in location decision theories. Since the 1970s geographers have been suggesting that IT is leading to a decentralised polycentric settlement pattern with high growth in the information services sector (see Berry 1973). In human ecology, technology is theorised as an integral part of culture, and technological change is a societal, adaptive response to changes in the environment. In this tradition, instant communications are seen as reducing travel costs and stimulating peripheral growth (Audirac 2002b), and this raises the need for controlling and co-ordinating dispersed operations (Hawley 1986). The ultimate fate of cities could therefore be 'unthinkable', because as new technologies substituted for face-to-face contact, core cities could evaporate, leaving a world without cities.

Others have taken a more sanguine view, and suggested that face-to-face contact will still mean that cities can play an important role. This view was promoted by Gottman (1991) who used the term 'megalopolis' to define an expanding network of cities. In this view, IT and telecommunications have expedited and intensified networking trends associated with past innovations (e.g. telegraph and telephone) rather than replacing face-to-face contact. More recent work has theorised a new 'economy of presence', which suggests planners can harness the power of the combination of socio-spatial forces into community design and planning (Mitchell 2000).

'Edge cities' (first alluded to by Berry (1973) and others in the deconcentration school) are also seen as being created by the result of interaction between economies of scale, mobility and transport costs. Land and buildings are immobile and so telecommunications and IT effects are 'captured' through a reduction in transport costs. Most research in this field sees urban form as the result of 'atomistic agents' (Medda *et al.* 1999) and travel trade-offs which are made possible by ICT. There is therefore a heavy focus on transportation studies, which frequently investigate the interaction between IT and travel, using spatial interaction models, scenario building, forecasting models, adoption/diffusion models or choice models. Telecommuting and homeworking have also been very popular areas for research in this school, although Audirac and Fitzgerald (2003) and Audirac (2002a) suggest that evidence from telecommuting adoption and travel substitution forecasts has been overstated and that at an aggregate level (citing Mokhtarian 1998) travel generation effects may be higher than the substitution effects.

In contrast to the deconcentration school, the restructuring school is anchored in Marxist political economy and regulation theories. The latter, frequently associated with post-Fordism, attempts to explain the technological and macroeconomic aspects of capital accumulation and spatial distribution. Within the overall tradition, there are a variety of views, but the main emphasis is on spatial and economic restructuring resulting from (Audirac & Fitzgerald 2003):

- technological change, which is the result of (and the transformational force affecting) the capitalist mode of production; and,
- the role of the state in shaping conditions for economic growth (capital accumulation).

The restructuring school sees both the local and global scales as operating together, and also sees technology as restructuring organisations and regions (i.e. contemporary socio-technical regimes enable the transformation of firms, labour–capital relations and global capital mobility, which all reflect international banking strategies and multinational corporation policies). Cities are also seen as the focus for local–global interplay and leading to new modes of capitalist development which have been termed 'informational' (Castells 2000), or 'reflexive' (Storper 1997).

In the same tradition, Sassen (1994) sees cities as concentrating producer services, leading to command-and-control centres in the capitalist world economy. Edge cities in this framework are centred on the needs of multinational and national corporations. This view is based on the assumption that urban growth and form result from complex strategic decisions by private/public corporate agents pursuing economic growth and sustained rates of profit within a regime of accumulation, in turn affecting the spatial dispersion/concentration ratio.

Therefore the perspective highlights the powerful combination of the ICT revolution and new labour market regulation (e.g. wage labour relations, pro-market regulation and local political devolution), which it sees as enabling new, highly networked socio-technical regimes. But the same regimes have also increased both spatial and social polarisation amongst workers, and have also led to both a spatial and temporal loosening of work. In turn, the latter has led to a higher demand for flexible working leading to congestion in networks of travel and communications. This has also led to dispersion and reconcentration of restructured firms in locations outside the city where incentives can include low taxes, broadband access and accessibility. In the USA and elsewhere this has created increased competition for new economy firms and elite workers. Audirac and Fitzgerald (2003) suggest this highlights a new urbanism theme of 'world-class connected communities', which provide the potential remedy for gridlock and social inclusion within mixed use neighbourhood development. Therefore metropolitan industrial cores provide brownfield recycling opportunities to cater for the needs of elite workers preferring job proximity and access to cultural facilities, and the built environment evolves through a process of restructuring. In summary, research in this school typically includes geographic and descriptive analyses of new occupations, employment and the distribution of firms in particular sectors, which are seen as representing new socio-technical transformations (for example, part-time workers, high technology workers, data processing).

As Audirac and Fitzgerald (2003) point out, much of the research embodied in ICT and urban change is 'speculative and futuristic'. They also emphasise the need to improve theorising and research, given the pace of technological change, the complexity of socio-economic and spatial relations, and the dearth of data. In their view, policy discourses on the new economy abound: many reports from the late 1990s concoct 'Disneyan' visions of a new era characterised by a growing number of entrepreneurial firms fast replacing major multinational corporations. In other words, a cleaner, new economy, spawning growth in new knowledge-based industries. These in turn attract workers who want to move to lifestyle choices based around flexible living and working. But they also suggest that such visions are prone to criticism, as they offer a clever combination of 'media-savvy' marketing and selective interpretation of research, and can be described as 'compelling but fanciful', based on the new economic reflexivity of information age market economies (i.e. institutional actors have greatly amplified the potential to shape conditions for their economic advantage).[8] Such reflexivity is only possible, however, if such organisations can adapt in rapid, strategic and innovative ways, and network collaboratively and reinterpret new realities upon which people can act (Storper 1997).

A particularly interesting model here is that of Castells (2000) which features elements of both the deconcentration and restructuring schools.

He suggests that in fact ICT can lead to both dispersal and concentration and this view has been taken forward by other authors such as Christie and Hepworth (2001) and Gillespie *et al.* (2001). They also developed key concepts first formulated by Alfred Marshall (1890) who drew attention to the battle between centrifugal forces and centripetal forces in the spatial organisation of the new economy: 'Every cheapening of the means of communication alters the action of forces that tend to localise industries'. Castells (2000) also builds on this fundamental concept and refers to an 'informational economy', in which information generation, processing and transmission become the fundamental sources of productivity and power. A 'space of places' has been joined by a 'space of flows'. The latter refers to the technological and organisational possibility of orchestrating social and work practices simultaneously without physical proximity (Box 1.3).

Box 1.3   Manuell Castells

Castells' work is considered by many to be seminal. Using extensive historical and empirical work from around the world he attempts to prove the claim that in the late twentieth century a new social structure and morphology emerged as part of the new network society. For Castells this is best understood as a new layer or dimension which emerged within and between societies. It was this layer that he termed the 'space of flows', but it is not a term that should engender geographic context; instead Castells argued that it was a new kind of layer based around the time-space organisation of social practices (Mol & Spaargaren 2003). Castells defines the term (2000) as 'the material organisation of time-sharing social practices that work through flows', where flows include all possible ones except for people: that is, capital, information, technology, organisational interactions, sounds, images and so on (Kellerman 2002). Essentially therefore the term refers to new social dynamics and to new concepts of time, space and power. The space of flows consists of three layers:

- a circuit of electronic exchanges within networked cities;
- a layer of nodes and hubs stretched over the global network of cities; and
- a layer of managerial elites who control the space of flows within the context of a range of other actors in the global flow of information.

In contrast, Castells uses the term 'space of places' to refer to a 'locale whose form, function and meaning are self contained within the boundaries of physical contiguity' (Castells 2000: 453). Although Kellerman (2002) argues that the precise relationship between space of flows and space of places is not clarified in Castells' work, it is evident that Castells envisages the two forms of space co-existing but creating tensions. As Castells notes, the dominant tendency is towards a space of flows imposing its logic over scattered, segmented places, or 'parallel universes'.

Building on this, Stephen Graham and Simon Marvin (1996) have tried to capture the impact of ICT on urban form. They use the term 'electronic space' to represent spaces constructed inside ICT networks whilst 'urban places' refers to the built environment or physical space. In this sense, ICT can lead to both centralisation and decentralisation of spatial developments. Gepts (2001) marries these concepts in a single model which suggest that four types of impact can occur:[9]

- **Synergy**. This means electronic spaces and urban places coincide as ICT infrastructure maps onto existing infrastructure: fibre-optic cables follow roads and railways.
- **Substitution**. ICT can also lead to a dispersal of economic activities, as teleworking and organisational functions can be separated (for example, innovations such as telebanking can also lead to space of flows replacing a space of places).
- **Generation**. ICT also generates physical flows of data giving rise to new forms of structure: co-location units, satellite ground stations and telecoms towers. Flows of traffic are also generated because virtual contact may widen networks and travel.
- **Enhancement**. ICT can optimise the efficiency of transport systems through traffic management or spatial planning.

In related work, Graham (1998) suggests a rather different taxonomy of 'spatial metaphors' to Audirac and Fitzgerald (2003). Indeed, in positing this, he suggests that concepts like 'information society' and 'information superhighway' have important roles in shaping the ways in which technologies are socially constructed, the uses to which they are put, and the effects and impacts of the power relations surrounding their development. He argues not only for a stronger embodiment to discourses on technological impact but also for a conscious decision to think through how new information technologies relate to and are embedded in space and place. Building on previous work (Graham & Marvin 1996) he identifies three broad perspectives stemming from a body of literature in urban theory, and dealing with the conceptual treatments of IT systems and space and place:

- **Substitution and transcendence**: the essentially deterministic view that human territoriality is directly replaced with new technologies.
- **Co-evolution**: the idea that both electronic space and territorial space are necessarily produced together as part of the restructuring of the capitalist political system.
- **Recombination**: this draws on actor network theory (ANT) to argue for a fully relational view of the links between technology, time, space and

social life. This perspective shows how new technologies become en-
veloped and integrated within a complex network of human actors and
technical artifacts to form actor networks, leading to the recombination
of new spaces and times.

Graham concludes that the most informative perspectives maintain a link
between the relational conceptions of ICT and space and place. He suggest
Latour's (1993b) 'skein of networks' (involving relational assemblies
linking technological networks, space and place and the space and place-
based users (and non-users) of networks) offers a valuable insight, because
this highlights how impossible it is to isolate or divorce technological
networks from space and place.

Following on from this, Graham and Marvin (2001) adopt what they call a
'socio-technical' perspective to explain the fragmentation of urban areas.
As their starting point they argue that infrastructure networks are the key
to physical and technological assets of modern cities. These networks both
influence and are influenced by the social relations which are encapsulated within cities and in turn social relations are entwined within these
networks. This view is defined in 'hybrid' terms (Graham & Marvin 2001:
429) as a sociological concept designed to overcome the modern dualism of
society/technology, and stresses the subtle blending of the social and the
technical in contemporary societies. They also suggest that previous
theory surrounding infrastructure networks has been guilty of determinism: frequently new infrastructural and technological innovations are seen
to impact linearly on city life (see, for example, Garrison 1990). This also
carries resonance with Aibar and Bijker's (1997) view that infrastructural
technology has often been regarded as unproblematic and autonomous in
shaping cities.

Real estate-level frameworks
Frameworks to examine and analyse the impact of ICT on real estate have
been much less common than those dealing with the impact at the urban
level. One model that adopts an all-embracing view of technology within
an economic framework is that of Green and Vandell (2001). They explore
the impact of technology (in its widest sense) on real estate, and examine
technology and its application to real estate through the impact on real
estate markets and the wider world.

They define technology more widely than the sense adopted in this book,
using the 1996 *Academic Press Dictionary of Science and Technology*
definition:

The application of scientific knowledge for practical purposes; the employment of tools, machines, materials and processes to do work, produce goods, perform services or carry out other useful activities.[10]

They therefore use an economic definition of technology to provide a formal frame of reference for their study. Essentially technology is viewed in an economic context as any intervention that changes the nature of the production function for economic goods, including real estate, so that new goods are developed or improved, or produced at lower costs. Therefore the production function links inputs (to the production of real estate stock and services) to output. All economic goods, including real estate, are assumed to be created from factors of production, which comprise labour (the efforts of developers, contractors, construction workers and others), land (the site, its location and other amenities) and capital (including both physical capital in the form of physical inputs and financial capital). They suggest that technology has three impacts or points of entry, through influence on (Green & Vandell 2001):

- the efficiency of production, or quality levels of inputs to the production process (for example, upstream inputs, such as improved insulation of glass curtain walls and the spread of secondary market and securitisation services);
- the production function for the real estate product through the construction and operation of the real estate structure itself (for example, a shift in production function which provides higher level of production at lower cost);
- the production functions associated with tenants of the real estate product and with unrelated firms (for example, downstream benefits by an increased demand for technological products, such as the surge of demand for office space by dot.coms in the late 1990s).

In their view, technology can operate at any of these points of entry at one of three levels: it can reduce costs through incremental improvement; it can lead to the production of an improved product; and it can lead to entirely new technologies. Their technology definition also embraces all aspects of technology in its widest sense, including innovations in capital markets, such as the introduction of real estate investment trusts (REITS) as financial engineering instruments. Their definition also includes political, legal and institutional engineering including the removal of trade barriers, which make the market more efficient, more competitive and more complete. Furthermore, they suggest six major events are the end result of recent transformations in technology:

- Introduction of new and improved consumer goods such as electronics, new drugs and health therapies and biotechnology products. These are creating downstream demand for users of real estate space to house production, distribution and marketing of goods.
- Enhanced transportation technology and development of cities will continue the trends of decentralisation of growth in urban areas. They are sceptical of the impact of telecommuting because of the continuing need for face-to-face contact and a desire for proximity to entertainment and socialising. Conurbations are the likely end scenario, as cities reach their physical limits.
- Improved construction technology has had an historic impact through three main innovations: the development of steel frame construction; the invention of the elevator by Elisha Graves Otis in the 1850s; and the introduction of mass manufacturing building methods. Smart buildings, which are based around high-technology control systems and are wired for broadband, are part of this process also.
- Financial engineering improvements through the provision of debt and equity capital. Both REITS on the equity side and commercial mortgage-backed securities (CMBS) on the debt side are examples of technology-driven impacts through service/product improvements which themselves are also being underpinned by the facilitation of growth through online service provision on the Internet.
- Improved manufacturing systems. These have impacted on industrial real estate through the improvement of supplier–producer relationships and just-in-time supply chains. This impacts on the necessity for localised storage facilities.
- Internet revolution. In Green and Vandell's view this is perhaps the most important technological innovation to impact on real estate since the invention of the automobile and the elevator. They suggest the Internet provides four degrees of influence in real estate markets through the provision of information, analysis, online transactions, and real-time auctions.

Their view on how technological innovation is driven is also an interesting one. Focusing on the demand side, they suggest that Gary Becker's (1996) work (building on the work of Veblen (1934) and conspicuous consumption thesis) on consumer demand helps in understanding the formation of consumer tastes, which lead to technological innovation and economic progress. In other words, technological innovation is most rapid when consumer tastes for improved quality of life exceed the existing capacity of the economic system to provide it in an affordable way.

An alternative perspective is provided by Guy and Shove (2000). Although not covering ICT as such, their work is also important for highlighting the importance of a sociological perspective in relation to energy technology in real estate *vis à vis* a wider definition of 'technology'. They challenge what they refer to as the 'techno-economic' model of change, which posits that technology diffusion occurs smoothly and in a linear fashion, if technical knowledge is rigorously tested and proven, and if market forces are undisturbed. Drawing on the work of Bijker (1995) and Latour (1987), their work suggests that to understand technology diffusion one must also understand 'need' and the creation of demand for technologies rather than simply understanding the obstacles and barriers in the way of a technology trajectory.

A more deterministic view of technology within the narrower remit of ICT is provided by Borsuk (1999). For example, in retail property Borsuk sees technology impact on real estate as a linear relationship in Figure 1.3. The first-order consequence is that consumers gravitate online for convenience, device and control and so the 'geocentric' shopping pattern, based on distance and location, becomes much less important. As a second-order consequence of this, retailers decide to lead or follow their customers online, which causes a migration of sales to the Internet, creating a downward shift in individual store performance. Retailers then alter their sales channel matrix and this impacts on leasing strategy. The third-order consequence is therefore an impact on rent and property values and lender and investor expectations. Landlords need to evaluate tenants in a different way through a tenant screen that incorporates questions on the retailer's ability to adopt and use the Internet effectively. Property owners might similarly need to consider the adoptive reuse potential of their premises.

However, this perspective ignores what may broadly be described as 'institutional barriers' to the impact of ICT in the workplace. For example, Lizieri (2003) argues that although much research assumes that property, as a derived demand, will simply be supplied in response to changed demand, in practice, the market's institutional structure can act as a

Figure 1.3   eCommerce and retail space demand (adapted from Borsuk 1999).

constraint on the provision of appropriate space. He also suggests that empirical research into new working practices and their impact on the property portfolio suggests that any change is 'muted and gradual'. Focusing largely on the office sector in relation to corporate real estate, he highlights the fact that changing occupier requirements will influence the level and stability of rental income. Moves towards shorter, more flexible leases, for example, increase development/investment risk, which will also affect space supply. Pointing to previous work, Lizieri suggests that three main sets of literature have emerged in real estate, which discuss and debate the optimal organisation of business and industrial activity:

- Building design, architecture and facilities management (FM) – which argues not only that the arrangement of space is an important part of re-engineering business, but that buildings can influence knowledge exchange and promote flexibility (see, for example, Becker 1990, 1998; Becker & Joroff 1995).
- Real estate decisions on the financial performance of the corporation (see, for example, Rodriguez & Sirmans 1994).
- Corporate real estate research, which attempts to combine varying perspectives from facilities management, business organisation and finance to provide a more informed strategic overview (see, for example, O'Mara 1999; Carn *et al.* 1999).

Focusing on the last group Lizieri addresses such questions as: How are firms altering their work practices? How does this affect the use of space? Does the property market facilitate change or does it lead to inertia? He suggests that corporate real estate literature draws on a variety of traditions and varied research methods, although he also concedes that his threefold division contains elements of overlap. The research in this field suggests that forces for change have increased in their intensity over the last 20–30 years. These forces comprise:

- globalisation;
- innovation/convergence in ICT;
- reorganisation of the workplace; and,
- drive for flexibility in goods and services production.

Trends such as these have intensified, and represent new ways of conducting business activity. These forces tend to change locational requirements and space requirements, as locational freedom is increased. They have also encouraged moves towards outsourcing, and a core/non-core designation of space. In the US and UK the impact of changing business practice on corporate real estate requirements has been the subject of much recent research (Manning & Roulac 2001; Gibson & Lizieri 1999, 2001). Much of the emphasis has also been on the office sector, and this research draws on a wide range of diverse social science literature (through such fields as 'new economic geography', post-Fordist production systems, post-modernism and business reorganisation) to suggest that business factors have changed the organisation of activity and requirements for business space.

Citing work by Gibler *et al.* (2002) and Gerald Eve (2001), for example, the empirical evidence for such change is meagre. However, according to Lizieri (2003), much depends on the views of senior executives in anecdote or case study work, and he argues that the evidence available does not suggest that businesses are likely to become digital in the near future. Moreover, in his view the major changes probably relate to the retail sector. This has led to business transformation through changes in management systems, working practices and technology-led change, which have led in turn to changes in the demand for real estate and the locational requirements of firms. This 'gradual' rather than 'revolutionary' change is, in Lizieri's view, partly due to the fact that managers do not have sufficient power or authority to influence corporate strategy; that property and other business infrastructure elements (such as IT provision) are rarely integrated; and that management resources are hindered by poor information systems.

In related work, Gibson and Lizieri (2001) also suggest that constraints in institutional and market structures outside the organisation can act as barriers: for example, although ICT can potentially reduce space requirements and affect the locational focus of real estate, in a market characterised by standard institutional leases, as in the UK, discarding surplus space may prove problematic for businesses. Their survey of 45 UK businesses focused not only on the demand side of the corporate real estate equation, through economic restructuring, the management response and the corporate real estate requirement, but also on the supply side which examined structures, the key player responses and the provision of business space.

However, they also suggest that change is occurring within the UK real estate market: the growth of the serviced office sector (for example, offering flexible space and lease terms) has been underpinned by property outsourcing schemes through real estate partnerships, which also offer flexible lease arrangements based on the UK Private Finance Initiative[11] model (see also Dixon *et al.* 2000). Nonetheless Gibson and Lizieri's work concludes that the impact of business reorganisation and new working practices on corporate real estate is less dramatic than often supposed.

However, more recent real estate research (see, for example, Dixon & Marston 2002b; Dixon *et al.* 2003), has found a growing impact of ICT in both the retail and office sectors. Indeed, part of the problem with much of the previous research in this field is that it is cross-sectional in nature, preferring to take snapshots in time rather than tracking trends longitudinally. Changes in organisational management and business process change are much harder to map. Moreover, the majority of studies do not compare current working practices with historic work practices: it is inherently more difficult to identify 'step changes' in process if you have only recently become part of the 'revolution' in technology, and part of the issue may be to do with who is surveyed in these studies, what their role is in the organisation, and how they see technological change as altering their business models. Focusing too narrowly on institutional barriers also fails to recognise the very important role that consumer demand is playing in shaping business processes (Coyle & Quah 2002).

Summary – an overview

So far in this chapter we have examined how technology can make an impact at four levels: the economy; the firm; urban and regional levels; and the real estate within those urban and regional areas. A number of lessons can be learned from the theoretical perspectives that have been examined. Non-spatial economy- and firm-level frameworks show that technological determinism is too simplistic a view. Technology can only be understood within the context of social, political and economic structures and institutions. At the firm level this is also reinforced by the view that 'softer', human factors are important to bear in mind in understanding technology impact, and that measuring ICT productivity impact is by no means straightforward. It is also true that ICT comes in a long line of technological innovations which have required particular circumstances at an economy and firm level to emerge successfully.

Similarly, spatial frameworks at the urban level teach us that ICT can lead to both clustering and dispersion. Both the deconcentration and restructuring schools can also provide valid frameworks for analysing the impact of ICT. A number of these models or frameworks also highlight the importance of the 'new economy' as a concept, and link policy agenda concepts such as 'new urbanism', 'knowledge workers' and 'sustainable communities'.

There is therefore a need for a new, 'socio-technical' framework, which looks at ICT within the context of other factors to examine its impact at a real estate level. Although institutional barriers are important, these are being overcome and new evidence is suggesting that ICT is affecting both location and space requirements in real estate markets.

An integrative socio-technical framework for ICT and real estate

The theoretical framework ('socio-technical' model) adopted in the book, and which includes the new economy, is shown in Figure 1.4 and is based on the research programme already undertaken by the authors. This underpins and forms the foundation for the empirical work in the book.

It can be argued that the socio-technical framework offers a number of advantages over those based either purely on a deterministic view of technology or on a purely supply-and-demand-led model. In particular, the framework is able to link economy-, firm- and urban/regional-level impacts more closely to the real estate level and sets technology in context. Institutional barriers and market barriers can still be examined but must be seen in the context of broader political, social and economic factors governing the transformation of technology. These ideas bear a degree of synergy with the work of Kling (2000) who was at the forefront of the development of the field of 'social informatics', which examines the design, uses and consequences of ICT in ways that take into account their interaction with institutional and cultural contexts. Arguing that ICT is socially shaped, Kling differentiated between standard (tool) models and socio-technical models (Table 1.4) to explain ICT impact.

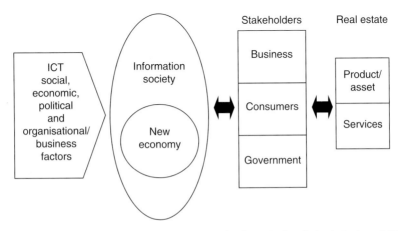

Figure 1.4 Key new economy drivers in property/real estate ('socio-technical model').

Table 1.4 Conceptions of ICT in organisations/society (adapted from Kling 2000).

Standard (tool) models	Socio-technical models
ICT is a tool	ICT is a socio-technical network
A business model is sufficient	An ecological view is also needed
One-shot ICT implementations are made	ICT implementations are an ongoing social process
Technology effects are direct and immediate	Technological effects are indirect and involve different timescales
Politics are bad or irrelevant	Politics are central and even enabling
Incentives to change are unproblematic	Incentives may require restructuring (and be in conflict)
Relationships are easily reformed	Relationships are complex, negotiated, multivalent (including trust)
Social effects of ICT are big but isolated and benign	Potentially enormous social repercussions of ICT
Contexts are simple	Contexts are complex
Knowledge and expertise are easily made explicit	Knowledge and expertise are inherently tacit/explicit
ICT infrastructures are fully supportive	Additional skill and work are needed to make ICT work

A socio-technical framework, which is based on similar concepts in a real estate setting, therefore enables us to take a critical view of technology's impact on real estate because it combines technical and social elements within an integrated framework.[12] Real estate literature in the field frequently seems to ignore social, political and economic context, and fails to make the link between economy-, firm-level, and property-level impacts. This book seeks to address these shortcomings and examines the barriers and drivers to ICT at these three levels. This is therefore intended to be the book's main focus and contribution to existing literature on the subject.

It is clear from our broad overview of literature that a deterministic view of technology (probably first promulgated by Veblen 1964) essentially holds that the world is a mechanism, and that by creating technology, future change will automatically occur. Such a view is monistic and mono-causal and involves a process of reductionism founded on a single independent variable, technology. From the economy level through to the real estate level therefore, alternative perspectives have been developed, which seek to place ICT in context. Graham and Marvin (2001) use the term 'socio-technical' to describe their preferred framework, which seeks to join society and technology in an overarching perspective which can explain alterations to urban shape and form. At a building or real estate level this approach has not been instituted to any large extent (but see Guy & Shove 2000).

We also adopt what we call a 'socio-technical framework' in this book, but distinguish it from other frameworks carrying the same terminology in three main ways:

- It is the first time, so far as we are aware, that such an approach has been used at a real estate level in seeking to explain the impact of ICT on real estate products and service.
- We do not use SCOT or ANT as the foundation for our framework, preferring to set ICT in the context of other drivers such as social and economic factors and organisational factors. In this sense we argue that ICT must be seen in context, and this follows the way in which our empirical work has been conducted.
- Sociological concepts and analysis play no part in our thesis, although in Part 2 of the book we contrast our framework with others, where these are relevant to the arguments we make, having already anchored these alternatives within the earlier literature review of the current chapter.

Examples of the socio-technical approach

The socio-technical approach is best illustrated by two examples. In retailing many have argued (see Borsuk 1999) that technology impacts on the demand for real estate. However, the development of eCommerce comes at a time when retailing is facing pressures on a number of fronts. In the UK these include the following:[13]

- **Changing work and leisure patterns**. Time pressures have increased during the 1990s giving rise to the expression 'money rich, time poor'[14] consumers. Despite this, there has been a trend towards increased spending on leisure (recreation and culture).
- **Demographic changes**. By 2020 the UK will have an aged population with perhaps as many as 25% of the population aged 65 or over. There will also be a decline in the proportion of younger people, whilst the middle-aged population takes off dramatically, and the number of single-person households increases. These changes will all have implications for spending patterns.
- **Decreasing number of shop units and increasing consolidation of sales**. The number of small, single independent retailers has fallen in the UK in parallel with their market share. In contrast, multiples have increased in number and have increased their share in turnover.
- **Evidence of falling real sales densities in the early 1990s, deflation and lower margins**. From 1990 to 2000 average sales densities in the UK rose

by 41%. But neighbourhood shops have improved by only 16%, with out-of-town up by 54% and in-town up by 39%. However, in inflation-adjusted terms, real sales densities have declined for all but out-of-town in the early 1990s, before rising again in the period to 2000. Recent official figures have also suggested the British economy is now in the most sustained period of low inflation since the Great Depression. Finally, price deflation in some sectors comes at a time when UK retailers' margins are also being squeezed.

- **Increasing globalisation**. The saturation of domestic markets and the desire for growth have fuelled increasing globalisation in retailing through self-start, merger and acquisition and franchising. The increasing merger activity in the retail sector has also been partly driven by global shortages of real estate available to retailers to build stores, particularly with strong growth restrictions in Western Europe.

Unravelling the impact of these pressures from the impact of eCommerce is difficult because they are, in many ways, interrelated. For example, there is clear evidence that the Internet is reinforcing price deflation through greater transparency. Nonetheless, any framework which seeks to understand the relationship between ICT and real estate must also understand these other factors.

Similarly, the impact of ICT on office markets should also consider ICT alongside other factors. Research by Dixon *et al.* (2003) suggests that there are factors in addition to ICT which are driving business change and the demand for real estate in offices (Table 1.5). These can be categorised according to whether they are 'centripetal' or 'centrifugal'. In practice, ICT may also partly act as a centripetal force if technology maps itself onto existing economic activity and continues to promote 'clustering'. If home working and other ICT-based activities grow then ICT will clearly promote 'dispersion'. Similarly there is also an argument for saying sustainable development would be promoted by encouraging living and working in cities.

Therefore our previous empirical work suggests that adopting a framework based around the factors in Figure 1.4[15] provides a sound basis for explain-

Table 1.5 Centripetal and centrifugal drivers in City of London offices (adapted from Dixon *et al.* 2003).

Centripetal (agglomeration)	Centrifugal (dispersion)
Face-to-face contact	ICT
Location	Transport
Clients	Sustainable development
Clustering	Human resources

ing and understanding the importance of technological change alongside other factors in transforming real estate markets and services.

Key themes and layout of the book

There are therefore three key themes to the book within the overall aim of examining how ICT is impacting and transforming real estate.[16] The first theme focuses on the fact that all markets operate in the context set for them by political, social, economic and technological factors. The framework in the book is therefore underpinned by Part 1, which examines the components of the framework in more detail and the relationships between them, and also explores the concept of a new economy. A number of the chapters in this part contain generic material which is designed to provide context for the real estate examples which are included. The relevant chapters and their role in this part are as follows:

Chapter 2	Examines the social, economic and political forces which help shape technological change in the information society and the new economy.
Chapter 3	Examines the nature and role of technological change in business process and organisational transformation in relation to the real estate sector, covering consumers, businesses and government.
Chapter 4	Analyses, through case studies, how business process change is driven by ICT and can transform real estate.
Chapter 5	Draws together the key themes emerging in previous chapters, and explores the new economy in detail to examine the changing role of real estate, including recent evidence for productivity increases created by ICT.

The second theme of the book is that ICT is impacting on real estate space and services in conjunction with other factors, which also include those discussed in the first part. Part 2 of the book therefore examines the relationship between physical and virtual space, redefining the typology and classification for describing real estate space in a digital world. The relevant chapters and their role in this section are as follows:

Chapter 6	Examines the changing concepts of space in the new economy and how these concepts can aid our understanding of real estate transformation.
Chapter 7	Examines the transformation of sales, processing, manufacturing, distribution and leisure/living space brought about by ICT, in alliance with other factors.
Chapter 8	Examines the transformation of real estate services and the changing role of real estate service providers, as a result of ICT and other drivers.

The third and final theme is that policymakers, planners and real estate specialists and other stakeholders must build technology impact into future decision making. The linkages between space, environment and technology are very real, and issues of sustainable development are raised as rapid urban growth continues. Part 3 therefore examines future scenarios, patterns and trends in real estate space, and also draws together other key themes and issues identified in the book. The relevant chapter and its role in this part is as follows:

Chapter 9   Draws together the main themes from the book, by critically reviewing the 'socio-technical' framework adopted, and examines the future for real estate in the new economy.

Notes

1   For example, the authors have been involved in a range of research projects, which are focusing on the impact of technology on real estate.

2   The concept of the new economy is dealt with in more detail in Chapters 2 and 5 of this book.

3   The concept of the microprocessor revolution as the most recent era of technological transformation also finds resonance in the comments of Alan Greenspan on the upsurge in economic growth in the late 1990s in the USA. Alan Greenspan, a renowned economist and chairman of the US Federal Reserve Board, is widely acknowledged as one of the first to identify the emergence of the 'new economy' in the USA, based on rapid technological growth and an upsurge in productivity.

4   In Perez's work (2002: 13) 'constellation' comprises the full combination of new industries, technical systems and infrastructure needed to underpin the transitional phase of a new technology.

5   At a macro level the importance of technological 'clusters' has long been recognised by authors who have studied technological change. Building on work by Schumpeter, Grubler (1998), for example, recognises four clusters: textiles, turnpikes and water mills (1750–1820); steam, canals and iron (1800–1870); coal, railways, steel and industrial electrification (1850–1940); and oil, roads, plastics and consumer electrification (1920–2000).

6   This should be distinguished from the use of the term 'clusters' in a spatial sense in regional economics (Porter 1998).

7   See also the very useful website on ANT at: http://carbon.cudenver.edu/~mryder/itc_data/ant_dff.html (checked 20 November 2003).

8   Reflexivity is an increasingly important issue in many areas of social science. The ability of institutional actors to affect and be influenced by the outcome of the future because of a critical mass of power and influence is a theme adopted

by Soros (1994), in a different context, in relation to equity markets. This was based on the premise that previous studies had separated events from observations relating to them and had ignored participants' thinking and behaviour. A prime example was classical economics. Instead, an understanding of markets needs to capture reflexivity, which is a two-way feedback mechanism in which the reality helps shape participants' thinking, and participants' thinking shapes reality.

9 These concepts are examined in more detail in Chapter 6.

10 This definition has some similarities with the one adopted by Castells (2000) building on the work of Brooks (1971:13), namely that technology is 'the use of scientific knowledge to specify ways of doing things in a reproducible manner'. Castells also included genetic engineering in his definition of information technologies.

11 The concept of outsourcing property in corporate real estate, which has gained in popularity over recent years, has been driven by a variety of factors including cost reduction and the promotion of shareholder value. ICT impact therefore is likely to strengthen the arguments for further outsourcing initiatives (see Chapter 5).

12 Linked to these changes is the concept of 'eProperty', which we define as 'property within which the Internet and related technologies are fully integrated and combined to enable owners and tenants to maximise value' (Dixon & Marston 2001). In evolutionary terms, eProperties or 'digital buildings' represent a 'fourth age' of development, where property and their population of tenants and employees have the ability to emerge as business portals, combining physical presence with virtual linkages, based on the developing complexity of IT linkages.

13 See also Chapter 3.

14 However, recent research by Mintel (2004) has shown that 'time freers' such as fast food, self-medication, and telephone and Internet services have provided people with more time, not less, for leisure and travel in the UK. In 1998 only 380 000 bank accounts were online. By 2003 there were 17.21 million.

15 The findings from this research are explored in more detail in Chapter 7.

16 It is important to note that this book is not about the precise detail of ICT, which is rapidly changing. Although reference is made to concepts such as the Internet, eCommerce, eBusiness, wireless and broadband, we prefer to avoid technical discussions not only to avoid out-datedness, but to promote a stronger thesis and storyline to the book. Readers who are interested in more technical details relating to ICT are therefore referred to other texts.

Part 1

CONTEXT AND FRAMEWORK

2

The Social, Economic and Political Context of ICT Transformation

Introduction

Chapter 1 introduced the socio-technical framework that runs throughout this book. In this chapter we explore the social, economic and political context of ICT transformation. The first part of the chapter explores the role of technological change in society, setting it in the context of other transformative factors, such as demographic, organisational and socio-economic factors, and their impact on real estate. Short examples are provided to add to the context.

We also explore the transformation of society through technology and analyse the emergence of the 'information society' in more detail, building on our introductory discussion in Chapter 1. The second part of the chapter then traces the emergence of this concept in theory and in policy.

Clearly, the political perspective is also important and there is a connection between the new economy and the political agenda and policies of many Western governments. Given that government policy has been designed to underpin the transformation of society through ICT, it is important to understand the emergence and rationale of these policies. For example, the new economy that has emerged over the last 15 or so years is seen by many of its advocates as being technology led. In turn, ICT has been 'borrowed' as both an instrument and concept to bolster arguments and rationales for economic growth and development in the 'knowledge economy' or 'new economy'. This view of the world is also incorporated in many of the political arguments put forward by advocates of the 'Third Way', which have influenced left of centre governments in the West (see, for example, Giddens 2000). Giddens (2000) argues that, in conjunction with the broader aspects of globalisation, the knowledge economy (or new economy) marks a 'major transformation' in the nature of economic activity. In this view, ICT is the medium and its agents are knowledge workers, who are an increasingly important part of the 'knowledge economy'. However, governments are also coming to realise that frameworks which 'externalise' the 'impact' of ICT on the economy and ignore the social and economic context of ICT are over-simplistic and erroneous, and also promote social exclusion. Proof of this are the growing concerns expressed over the digital divide and citizen inclusion, for example.

Finally, in the last part of the chapter we examine the implications of the emergence of the information society in terms of a digital and knowledge divide, together with broadband access, and the effect spatially in the UK.

In examining these issues it is also important to stress that although we are setting ICT within the context of political, social, economic and related factors, we also seek to examine the success of existing policies critically, with particular reference to the UK, and to question the real nature and existence of the information society.

Understanding the role of technological change in society

In Chapter 1 of this book we saw how our socio-technical framework places much emphasis on setting technological change in the context of social, economic, organisational and political factors. Recent work by BT with the Future Foundation (BT 2002) indeed suggests that the technological revolution is just one of four interlocking revolutions within an 'information society' (or what is also referred to as a 'network society'). So the role of technological change is explained by the way in which it interacts with the social and consumer revolutions that are happening at the same time. These are promoting the drive towards greater individuality and self-expression amongst consumers, for example. BT (2002) point out that definitions of families, communities and businesses are all becoming more fluid and so networks are a key feature of society rather than fixed social structures and groupings. The interlocking nature of these four revolutions is shown in Figure 2.1. Therefore ICT provides an essential component within this networked world, offering additional space for interactions to parallel physical meetings and experiences.

This is evidenced by the growth in technology access internationally and nationally. Indeed, it can be argued that the virtual communications

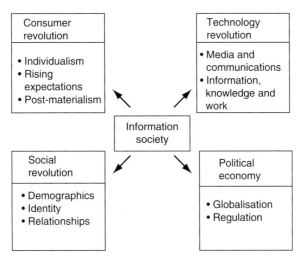

Figure 2.1 Four interlocking revolutions (adapted from BT 2002).

networks and infrastructures have become, in many instances, inseparable from everyday activities. But this also means that social and economic inequalities can also be reflected in patterns of use of technology. It can also be extremely difficult to unravel the impact of technological change from parallel, transforming factors in society. This point is emphasised in research on flexible work practices in Europe (FLEXCOT 2000), where research showed that ICT represented both a threat and an opportunity for firms. ICT can act as a 'push' factor through the internationalisation of markets and the increased competitive pressures stemming from improved information flows. But ICT can also 'pull' firms because it provides powerful tools for re-engineering work and production inside businesses. At the same time, businesses also adopt more flexible methods of working for reasons besides ICT: they may wish to be more cost effective, more efficient or to meet customer demands. Yet the fact remains that ICT can drive flexibility in terms of homeworking or teleworking, for example. It can also make work more standardised and routinised, reducing 'knowledge' needs and perhaps making the employment of part-time or temporary staff more feasible for certain tasks within new production cycles. FLEXCOT (2000) concludes that although ICT is an enabler, it cannot be considered the main driver of change towards more flexible forms of work: that lies in understanding the organisations and their commercial policies focused towards customers.

Research from Eurescom (2001) of teleworking across Europe also found it difficult to isolate the precise impact of technology on the quality of people's lives. In terms of quality of life measures, for example, other social and economic factors were found to be important. For example, although organisation and society can play an important role in providing the context for teleworking, it does not in itself lead to improved quality of life because 'mediating' factors (for example, overtime, flexibility of hours and of place and ability to concentrate) can operate to create the outcomes at work or at home.

It is also difficult to unravel the effect of ICT transformation from other factors such as transport. Teleworking came at a time when personal freedom and mobility had been transformed by the car over a number of decades, and so the role of transport, in alliance with other transformative factors, must not be overlooked (Box 2.1).

In real estate research generally there has been a growing call to look at the 'bigger picture' and see changes in investment and ownership trends in the context of long-term social shifts. Recent work by Investment Property Forum (Barkham 2003) has highlighted the importance of demographic changes in real estate investment patterns. For example, over the next 50 years the UK will see an inexorable rise in the proportion of those aged 60 years or over, because of fertility declines, increased longevity and the post-war baby boom. This could lead to a fall in GDP growth, through a reduction in the total hours worked by the population and the rate of capital formation (as savings reduce). But this could be arrested by increasing the retirement age, a greater improvement in the rate of technical

---

Box 2.1   Transport innovations and urban development

As Schiller (2001) suggests, in technology terms, nothing has had a greater effect on real estate location than the car. Car access increases mobility and offers flexibility and control by increasing the number of trips that can be taken; increasing the choice available to the car user in terms of jobs, leisure and shopping. The car has led to the great mass of movement away from city centres and lies at the heart of the bulk of urban change we have witnessed over the last 40–50 years. Offices, retail, industrial and residential uses have all been transformed by the car. But the car is also the product of the revolution in personal freedom and Western affluence that have also been continuing to drive other types of technological change, including ICT, in more recent years. Technological changes in the mode of transport in the distribution industry have also transformed urban development and resultant real estate patterns. Standardisation of containers and the development of container ships and wooden pallets led to the demise of traditional ports and produced container ports and specialist terminals. Supply chains have shortened, ICT has underpinned the change, and warehousing has become much more concentrated in its location in the UK.

change and improved productivity, all of which have ramifications for consumer demand and investment/pensions activities.

Demographic change is also an important factor in understanding changes in retail real estate. This point has been emphasised by BT (2002) who suggest that older people spend relatively more on eating out, holidays, books and newspapers, cars, education and health, for example. If shopping centres continue to be oriented towards clothing and shoes this will have implications for footfalls, values and rents. This was also highlighted in the College of Estate Management (CEM 2001) research on eCommerce. Currently the UK proportion of over 65-year-olds is 17%, but by 2020 could be as high as 25%, with one-third of those over 80. This has important repercussions for retailers in the UK:

- The proportion of younger people will diminish, with a resultant impact on sales of toys, games, and some apparel/footwear sectors.
- The middle-aged population will take off dramatically.
- The number of single-person households will continue to rise substantially because people marry later or not at all.

In addition, couples are deferring parenthood, so that spending patterns differ further. Government estimates forecast the formation of 4.4 m new households to 2015, of which 75% will be single-person households. Family structures are changing as more women work in the UK, and it can be seen that the attractions of home shopping and convenience shopping are becoming very important.

The CEM (2001) report also suggested that other factors, including changing leisure patterns, were also important. For example, it is true that people still shop for a variety of reasons, and research from the USA (Tauber 1972) suggested that personal motivations for shopping included role playing, recreation/diversion, self-gratification, sensory stimulation and, amongst the social motives, peer group attraction and communication. As Tauber observed:

> As businesses which offer social and recreational appeal, retailers must acknowledge that they are competing directly for the consumer's time and money with other alternatives that provide similar benefits.

This is certainly true today, as time pressures have increased, particularly during the 1990s. Ironically, research also shows that although the time spent on paid work has decreased, the time spent on shopping and childcare and some leisure pursuits (eating out, cinema and pubs) has increased. 'Unpaid work' (which includes shopping) is therefore taking a larger proportion of people's time, perhaps driven by shopping self-service and the greater distances travelled. The trend towards increased leisure is reflected in spending patterns. In general, there has been a long-term shift away from spending on basic necessities such as food and housing towards leisure-related goods. Shoppers' behaviour is also changing and shopping no longer has quite the 'conspicuous consumption' image it had in the late 1980s. Shoppers are increasingly price conscious and perhaps some groups even less brand conscious than they used to be.

We have also seen a decreasing number of shop units and an increasing concentration of sales. The number of small, single independent retailers has fallen in the UK in parallel with their market share. In contrast, multiples have increased in number and have increased their share in turnover. Overall, data from the UK Office of National Statistics show a steady decline in retail outlets over the last decade from around 333 000 in 1990 to 315 000 in 2001. In addition, UK superstores and hypermarkets have increased their number of stores. In 1997 the top five British super-market chains (Tesco, Sainsbury's, Asda, Safeway and Morrisons) traded from almost 4.6 m square metres. By 2002 this had increased to nearly 5.9 m square metres, a 28% increase (Competition Commission 2003). This has led to an increasing consolidation in retail sales: the top 10 retailers combined to account for over 40% of the total retail turnover in 1998/99, for example, compared with 32% in 1986.

Evidence of further consolidation at store level is provided from research by Healey and Baker (cited in ABN-AMRO 1999) which showed that for a retail chain to access 50% of UK comparable goods spend, it needed to trade from 250 stores in 1971. By 1976 the number was down to 75, and by 2010 it is expected to be 40.

Despite these trends towards greater consolidation in the UK retail sector, extensive chains of small shops have also been developed by large retailers, either as new ventures (for example, The Link, a chain of mobile phone stores that are part of the Dixon Group) or through merger. Arcadia, for example, has more than 2000 outlets in the UK trading through eight formats developed as individual brands. These small store formats have a relatively short life cycle of 5–8 years and so require frequent redesign and redevelopment. There is also evidence of falling real sales densities in the early 1990s, deflation and lower margins in retail. Verdict (2000) suggests that from 1990 to 2000 average sales densities in the UK rose by 41%. But neighbourhood shop densities have improved by only 16%, with out-of-town up by 54% and in-town up 39%. However, in inflation-adjusted terms, real sales densities declined for all but out-of-town in the early 1990s, before rising again in the period to 2000.

However, the picture is by no means clear-cut. The sectoral view also varies. Groceries and electricals have the highest sales densities and during the 1990s they have steadily increased. The surge in sales density within the electrical sector can be attributed to the rapid increase in sales of computers and mobile telephones over the period from relatively small retail units. Clothing and DIY have the lowest sales densities, and for some retailers in these sectors sales densities have remained static or have fallen. Price deflation comes at a time when UK retailers' margins are also being squeezed. According to Datastream, over the last 10 years the average net margin of 8.7% for retailers compares with 9.5% for leisure and hotel operators and 12.5% for brewery, pub and restaurant operators. Food retailers' margins are even lower and show a decline over the period 1996–2000. These have come in for even greater scrutiny over recent years with the Competition Commission's investigations into the supply of groceries through supermarkets.

Finally, increasing globalisation has played a role. There has been an increasing trend for retailers to venture beyond the boundaries of their home country. Some of the main drivers behind this have been increased competition in domestic markets, particularly for German, Italian, British, French and Spanish retailers. In order to continue growing, retailers have looked abroad for expansion through self-start, merger and acquisition and franchising (Jones Lang LaSalle 2003). This activity, particularly within the clothing sector, has been dominated across Europe by the Inditex Group, owner of the Zara and Massimo Dutti brands amongst others. In the supermarket sector, Wal-Mart's acquisition of Asda in 1999 was seen by many as an indicator of the structural and global shifts that will impact on retailing over the next decade. The company's operating philosophy of low prices and high stock rates is at the heart of its strategy and its effect is likely to be felt beyond simply grocery sales. Despite the apparent level of increased competition, other evidence suggests that large retailers are growing at a far faster rate than the market as a whole, at least measured by sales volume. In 1998 there were 12 European companies with sales of over US$25 bn compared with eight in 1997. Of those companies with sales of over $20 bn, 17 had increased their sales by more than 100% during the 1990s. Although extensive multinational operation is not necessarily a feature of these companies, low growth companies are characterised by operation in a limited number of countries. In turn, the saturation of domestic markets in the UK and the development of the EU have led UK retailers to develop outlets in other countries (for example, Tesco's expansion in Poland, Hungary, Slovakia and the Czech Republic).

In summary, this example highlights the importance of considering other factors besides ICT in understanding structural shifts in retail real estate. It also shows how changes within society are interlinked and interconnected. The next section explores particular concepts of the information society and new economy in more detail, picking up some of the key themes already identified in Chapter 1.

Towards an information society and the new economy?

The term 'information society' was first used in Japan in the 1970s (Miles 2000), and during the 1990s the concept was widely incorporated into the official discourse of the European Union and its member states. The work of Masuda (1990) was seminal here in suggesting a transition from a highly mass consumption society through a high welfare society (based on consumerism, social welfare and leisure), to a high mass knowledge creation society, based on computerisation, voluntary community and self-actualisation.

The term also had resonance with the need to foster 'knowledge-based' economies, which saw economic growth based on the need to encourage both the technology and service sector industries. The term 'information society' engenders a vision of a society where information is the thread that binds people together, and in this sense promotes perhaps a more 'socially oriented' and 'socially aware' perspective than, for example, the term 'new economy'. There are numerous definitions of 'information society' but IBM encapsulated many of the common characteristics:

> A society characterised by a high level of information intensity in the everyday life of most citizens, in most organisations and workplaces; by the use of common or compatible technology for a wide range of personal, social, educational and business activities, and by the ability to transmit, receive and exchange digital data rapidly between places irrespective of distance. (IBM 1997)

The DTI/Spectrum report (1996: 1) suggested that the term 'information society' could not be precisely defined, because it was still evolving and carried different meanings across Europe and elsewhere, but it conveyed a society that:

...uses information intensively and in a way that is not constrained by time or space, a society where transactions of all sorts can be processed electronically, a society whose working and living practices have been modified fundamentally by technology.

In simple terms, therefore, 'information society' stresses the societal, inclusive transformations of technology, whereas the term 'new economy' emphasises narrower, economic aspects. The term also stresses inclusivity: an information society is supposed to be enjoyed by all, and not just a particular group(s).

Similarly, the history of the so-called 'new economy' is a very recent one, but one that many argue has created large-scale impacts on economic growth. In many ways, however, we have struggled to pin down what this new phenomenon actually comprises. Nonetheless, economic experts have identified a sea change in the way that economies, built on older industries, have been transformed into knowledge and information-based economies based around ICT. In his speech to the US House of Representatives, economist Alan Greenspan (1999) saw 'a deep-seated [and] still developing shift in our economic landscape' caused by an 'unexpected leap in technology'. This raised awareness of a concept which is referred to by a variety of names; for example, a 'new economy'; a 'post-industrial society'; an 'innovation economy'; a 'knowledge economy'; a 'network economy'; an 'e-economy' (Cohen *et al.* 2000).[1]

But what does the term 'new economy' really mean? A number of authors have wrestled with the problem of defining the phenomenon. For example, Coyle and Quah (2002) suggest that definitions of the new economy can be divided into two main groups: those equating the new economy with ICT and its sectoral consequences (either on core industry sectors, such as services, or the wider economic effects on all structures, through cost reduction and networking impacts) or definitions which equate the new economy with the post-industrial economy as a whole. In contrast, Beyers (2002) cites Norton (2000), who distinguishes three perspectives on the new economy: macro, micro and digital. The macro perspective, in Norton's view, incorporates several key dimensions, including a recognition that the fast rate of productivity increase is caused by the introduction of ICT. This has led to strong performance in the US economy alongside jobs growth in key sectors. At a micro scale, Norton argues that the greatest wealth in the US tends to be found within ICT, media and retailing sectors, although this was written before the relatively recent dot.com crash. Finally, he sees the new economy as a digital perspective, with the emphasis on the consequences for society of ICT development (PCs, processors and the Internet). Similarly, the European Commission (2000) pointed out that the new economy emerges from the parallel and fundamental shifts in technology and international economic environment: technology is digital, and the international economy becomes a global economy, accompanied by rapid changes in economic and social frameworks and alterations in institutional structures. In the Commission's view there is no universal definition of the new economy, but it would seem to possess four main characteristics:

- New value-added services or knowledge. Alan Greenspan made an interesting observation in 1996: the economic output of USA weighed the same (measured in physical weight) then as it did 100 years ago, yet economic output has increased a hundredfold. Intangibles such as knowledge and information in the service sector are becoming very important (see Chapter 3).[2]
- Agile enterprises. The new economy is becoming 'molecular' with economies of scale being driven by networking amongst 'weightless' corporations.
- Virtual communities. The new economy exhibits virtuality and new online or virtual communities are being created.
- Excluded middleman. Everywhere the middleman is being excluded and intermediaries being by-passed in the supply chain.

We use the terms 'information society' and 'new economy' mutually exclusively in this book (the latter is dealt with in more detail in Chapter 5), although there are clearly elements of overlap and interaction between the two terms. In hierarchical terms we might see a new economy therefore as part of the information society, which was a theme identified in Erkki Liikanen's speech on the 'Enterprise and Information Society' in 2000 (Liikanen 2000) (Figure 2.2).

The first aspect to be noted about theoretical frameworks for the information society is their extent and variety. For example, as Alvarez and Kilbourn (2001) suggest, both the literature and the overall views on the information society are fragmented, with some 30 different labels attached to the term in 2000. Some labels appear to be different labels for the same phenomenon, and others clearly emphasise different features of the same phenomenon. Another source of fragmentation is the variety of views about the nature of the information society: for example, what are its boundaries and what counts as evidence of change? Finally, there is also debate over the significance of the information society. On the one hand there are those who argue (Berger 1999) that the information society is more apparent than real, whilst others (see, for example, Castells 2000)

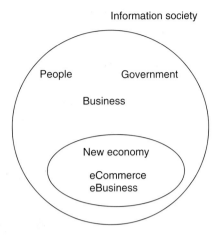

Figure 2.2   The information society and the new economy (adapted from UNCTAD 2003a).

argue that the information society engenders a massive and fundamental shift in our current frames of reference across society. The fragmentation or shifting nature of these arguments is typical of what Kuhn (1962) refers to as 'state revolutionary science' (as opposed to 'normal science'). Lack of agreement is therefore to be expected in a field that is developing, and is in its relative infancy.

Alvarez and Kilbourn (2001) suggest therefore that the information society literature can be seen as a three-dimensional map (or 'sketch' in their words). Varying perspectives (technological; socio-economic; social and educational) are used to examine particular topics: location; interaction; information; individualisation and globalisation. In turn, this matrix is given a third dimension of 'philosophical (or 'root') metaphors' (a concept based on the work of Pepper 1942). These comprise views which are 'formist' (i.e. a view fixated on conceptual and physical types); 'mechanistic'; 'contextual'; 'organic'; 'insight based'; and 'authority based'.

Information society models and ICT models also frequently fail to include an inclusive focus on political, economic and social perspectives.[3] The information society models developed have also paralleled specific technological developments in the information society itself (Steinmueller 2003). For example, the early work of Freeman and Perez (1988) on the importance of inter-sectoral differences in technology diffusion came after the PC revolution had first gathered momentum in 1984, just as Castells (2000) and Mansell (1998) developed the theme of exclusion from technology, after rapid acceleration and economic growth in the 1990s in developed countries had created an increased divide with less developed nations.

In essence, as with ICT transformation generally, theories of the information society seem to suggest that increasingly ICT development should be viewed as internalised within a social system (see, for example, Steinmueller 2003; Mansell 2002), rather than being externalised and impacting from the outside. This reflects an increasing complexity of infrastructure and systems in the information society.

Webster (2002), arguably a sceptic of the 'information society' concept, provides a useful classification of the theory of the information society:[4]

- **Technological**. This view suggests that the sheer extent of ICT must lead to a reconstitution of the social world because of the profundity of its impact. Authors such as Toffler (1980) write of the waves of technological evolution, yet Webster (2004) questions the absence of empirical measures of the information society and also highlights the determinism of much of the writing in this school.
- **Economic**. This approach charts the growth in the economic worth of informational activities, and attempts to link the proportion of gross national product accounted for by the information sector. Webster (2002) cites the work of Machlup (1962) and Porat (1997) here, but again he questions the empirical rationale of their work. For example, is it really the case that R&D in a petrochemical industry should be detached from the manufacturing element and defined as an 'information activity'?
- **Occupational**. This, according to Webster (2002), is the approach most favoured by sociologists, and is the approach most closely associated with Daniel Bell (1973) who wrote at length about the concept of the 'post-industrial' society, a term synonymous with the information society. Here occupational structures are examined over time and changing patterns identified. The thesis is that we have reached an information society when the majority of work is based around information. Others such as Leadbeater (1999) and Coyle (1997) have alluded to a new, 'weightless economy' based around information.
- **Spatial**. This perspective draws on sociology and economics but is strongly based in geography, with the emphasis on information networks which connect locations and can therefore transform time and space relations. The work of Urry (2000) and Castells (2000) are exemplars of this school of thought.
- **Cultural**. The final perspective stresses the importance of media-driven change in society through TV, radio and film, for example (Baudrillard

1983). This creates an 'informational environment' which reflects society and influences behaviour and social relations.

Webster (2002) goes on to suggest these need not be mutually exclusive, although theorists emphasise one or other of the above factors in presenting the scenarios. As he suggests, the concept of the information society should be viewed as a tool to think with, and to provide an 'organised way of seeing things'.[5]

The various and differing approaches to the information society and its evolution and transformation therefore offer us a helpful lens on the importance of social and economic aspects of technological change. There is a clear parallel here with the lessons learned from the perspectives which deal with ICT transformation, and which were examined in Chapter 1. Theoretical visions of both ICT and the information society have therefore been characterised by continued debates over 'continuous change v radical transformation' and 'determinist v socially engaged relations'. Proponents of the information society such as Masuda (1990), Leadbeater (1999) and Dyson *et al.* (1996) are therefore lined up against critics such as Winner (1996), Roszak (1986) and Robins and Webster (1999).

Charles Leadbeater's work (1999), for example, emphasises the importance of 'knowledge' in the 'information society'. In a sense, technology is seen as being less important than 'thinking smart' or being intelligent, enterprising and adaptable to change (Webster 2004) in a world which is living on 'thin air' (or ideas). 'Software' is seen as more important then than 'hardware' to Leadbeater, in a world where human capital is paramount. In contrast, writers such as Winner (1996) argue that historically, people rather than technology have always been at the centre of change, whereas Robins and Webster (1999) argue that today's information society continues and strengthens a long-established age of information (Beniger 1986) and must be seen in the context of changing social relationships.[6]

Perhaps there is room for a degree of eclecticism here, but whatever the merits of the contrasting views, there are strong arguments for viewing the information society, and ICT as part of it, inside a framework that deals explicitly with social and economic relationships. This view is supported by Mansell (2002), for whom 'mediation' in the ICT landscape is a vital process to understand because of its power to alter social and economic relations and networks. In other words, complex, virtual electronic networks are co-existing and fully interwoven with real networks, so that the processes of communication are technologically and institutionally driven and embedded (Box 2.2).

In many ways, the resultant policy response to the emergence of the information society has attempted to echo, and come to terms with, the key elements of this re-emphasis in the theory of the information society. In particular, policies have frequently focused on knowledge and innovation as assets of production.

The role of knowledge and innovation in policy

As the world economy has grown more competitive and globalised, nation states have seized on apparent opportunities to bolster productivity and output using new technology as part of the 'new economy' within the 'information society'. This trend is set against a backdrop of a general movement towards service industries, as manufacturing industries have declined, and a new international division of labour has developed (Begg 2002). Similarly, developed nations have had to consider in which sectors they wish to retain and sustain competitive advantage.

ERICarts (2001) suggests that the work of Machlup (1962) was one of the first major attempts to explore the importance of information and knowledge production to the economic development of a country. Daniel Bell (1973) later developed the concept of the 'knowledge society' and this gradually evolved in popular writings into the concept of the 'information

---

Box 2.2   Real estate networks

In the case of real estate services, especially in terms of residential real estate, there has been much discussion about the pervasiveness of ICT and its potential transformation of the industry. The emphasis has been very much on 'disintermediation' (Tapscott 1996), or the potential for buyers and sellers to reach each other directly, rather than through an intermediary. Frequently, commentaries have adopted a deterministic stance, but research by Sawyer *et al.* (2003) shows that transaction cost and social capital perspectives, both of which emphasise the role of social networks, can explain much of the structural change in the real estate industry brought about by ICT transformation. Indeed their research showed that disintermediation is less of a threat to agents than 'reintermediation', where new types of intermediaries are entering the market (for example, local real estate franchises and web-based service providers). Moreover, the complexity of social networks or personalised contact is actually increased as a result of ICT. For further information on disintermediation and real estate brokerage networks, see Chapter 8.

society', incorporating the development of mass technology infrastructure during the 1990s. Moreover, the Bangemann report (1994) had also promoted liberalism in the information sector and echoes the rhetoric of ICT-driven growth:

> This sector is in rapid evolution. The market will drive; it will decide winners and losers. Given the power and pervasiveness of the technology, this market is global...the prime task of government is to safeguard competitive forces....

More recently the importance not only of social factors but also setting ICT into the context of socio-economic frameworks has been recognised by the EU and OECD. The 'New Labour' government in the UK, for example, has sought to follow the thrust of the OECD Growth Study which had earlier concluded (in 2000) that technological innovation needed to be linked not only to wider social investment in education at all levels, but also to the development of entrepreneurial culture and economy-wide changes in business and management practice (Local Futures Group 2001). Innovation, skills and enterprise are therefore seen as key in current UK government policy underpinning the knowledge economy. For example, in the UK government's White Paper *Our Competitive Future: Building the Knowledge Driven Economy* (DTI 1998: 6)[7] it was argued that:

> ...all businesses, large and small, new and established, in manufacturing and services, low and high technology, urban and rural located, will need to marshall their knowledge and skills to satisfy customers, exploit market opportunities and meet society's aspirations for a better environment.

In a support document to the same White Paper (Analytical 1998), it was also suggested that four important structural changes had transformed the economy and underpinned the knowledge economy. These were:

- revolutionary changes in ICT;
- rapid scientific and technological advance;
- globalised competition; and
- changes in tastes, lifestyle and leisure from increased incomes.

During the 1990s in the UK, the Department of Trade and Industry (DTI) therefore gave priority to building a 'knowledge economy' or 'digital economy'. In the USA, similar hopes were expressed for the 'new economy', and the World Bank's Development Report (World Bank 1998) made a strong case for investing in knowledge to tackle poverty and development problems (Mansell 2003). Nor was the vision peculiar to the developed world: developing nations in Africa (for example, the Africa Information Society Initiative (AISI)) and in Asia (for example, Singapore's Intelligent Island Vision) have also subscribed to these concepts.[8]

The term 'knowledge'[9] as used in such policies has been defined in different ways (Lever 2002) by, for example, OECD (1995) and DTI (1998). Indeed, Lengrand and Associates (2002), in research on innovation for the EU, suggest that the 'knowledge-based economy' can be seen as an 'empirical hypothesis' or as a 'policy goal' or 'vision'. 'Technical knowledge' contributes to the development of new products and processes, and 'customer-base knowledge' engenders new markets, consumer choice, and changing tastes and fashions. Knowledge can also relate to financial inputs to the production process, and can also exist in the form of human capital or skills. Government policies have therefore sought to increase and improve the knowledge base of economies through the encouragement of research and development (R&D) processes, but such policies frequently take a linear view (Malecki 1997), based on the idea that knowledge is generated through research which advances concepts and findings through scientific methods of induction and deduction (Lever 2002). However, if R&D increases, it does not automatically follow that innovation will increase as a result. In fact, such deterministic, linear views have been challenged in the same way that deterministic views of technology have been challenged. For example, work by Myers and Rosenbloom (1996) and by Malecki (1997) show how important it is to consider feedback loops and circuits in the innovation process, where all are part of the larger knowledge creation process. 'Knowledge' and 'innovation' (and more generally, information) have therefore become enshrined as factors of production in the new economy, which drives the information society.

Information society policy development in the UK

The concept of an information society therefore became an important part of policy development in the UK and elsewhere in Europe during the mid-1990s. The emphasis was on the fact that the applications and development of information infrastructures would have significant social and economic impacts (DTI/Spectrum 1996). Essentially, in a society where people use information intensively, usage is enabled by the convergence and integration of three business sectors: the IT sector, the telecommunications sectors and the information and entertainment sector. Figure 2.3 is typical of the policy frameworks envisaged during the 1990s.

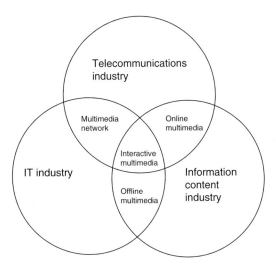

Figure 2.3 Convergence of ICT (adapted from DTI/Spectrum 1996).

UK policy has tended therefore to highlight the connections between the evolution of the information society (driven by the new economy) and a nation's competitiveness and economic growth. This linkage is based on the principle that a nation's progress towards an information society would determine its success relative to other competitors, and is based on three main hypotheses (DTI/Spectrum 1996):

- Effective use of products and services in the information society will enhance and change many business processes, increasing business (and government) productivity and efficiency.
- Adoption by the consumer market of the information society will eventually stimulate uptake in the business market.
- The information society will be one of the fastest growth areas in the developed world, potentially stimulating the growth of indigenous industries.

Early examination of the information society by DTI/Spectrum (1996) suggested that there were various paths to the information society: via increased mobility (the mobile path), via the PC (the IT path) or via the television (the TV path). These reports also stressed that the most important driver of uptake in the information society is the enhanced utility that products and services deliver to consumers, and the extent to which the supply side is able to provide these benefits. Other demand and supply side drivers are shown in Table 2.1. Government's role was also seen as one of

Table 2.1   Key drivers in the information society (adapted from DTI/Spectrum 1996).

Demand	Supply
Access to infrastructures	Strong existing supply base
Macro-economic environment	Access to capital/willingness to invest
Competitive pricing	Access to skills
Access to skills	
Culture, understanding and acceptance	

not only regulating and facilitating these initiatives, but also creating legislative and administrative frameworks.

Current UK government policy on ICT within the information society can also be traced to the 1998 White Paper *Our Competitive Future* (DTI 1998). In addition to highlighting the emergence of the knowledge economy, this document also stressed the importance of developing the skills, innovation and infrastructure needed to underpin its development. The White Paper therefore sketched out a strategic direction and an initial policy framework. This included (Kearns 2002):

- clarification of the legal position and status of eCommerce;
- development of a deeper understanding of the new economy through measures such as ICT promotion in small and medium enterprises (SMEs);
- ensuring a competitively priced network access in converging communications markets; and,
- fostering IT and science cluster development around the UK.

This was closely followed by the Performance and Innovation Unit's report, *e-commerce@its.best.uk* (Performance and Innovation Unit 1999), which focused closely on the steps needed to develop eCommerce in the UK. Further legislation in the form of the Electronic Communications Act 2000, allowing the recognition of electronic signatures, also removed a major barrier to eCommerce.

The emphasis on engendering private sector electronic commerce was also mirrored in the UK government's efforts to develop eGovernment. A key document here was the *Modernising Government* White Paper (Cabinet Office 1999), which placed IT at the centre of the government's strategy to engage more closely with UK citizens. Further detail was provided in a follow-up White Paper, *E-Government: A Strategic Framework for Public Services in the Information Age* (Cabinet Office 2000), which declared the intention to make services more accessible for citizens, suppliers and businesses using a range of new channels including PCs, interactive digital

TV and mobile phones together with new IT-supported one-stop shops. Further policy briefs were produced before, in 2000, the Prime Minister declared that all eGovernment services should be online by 2005.

On the face of it, UK policy has increasingly emphasised that the social considerations of technology-led transformation are as important as the economic dynamics of emerging information societies. But as Mansell (2003) points out, policy frequently puts technology-led diffusion and the dynamics of ICT-related markets first. This is revealed by the tone and substance of much of the content of the UK Cabinet Office Strategy Unit Report on *Electronic Networks* (Strategy Unit 2002), which stresses:

- how digital networks can contribute to productivity gains;
- the importance of the structure of national and global ICT-related markets; and
- the type of regulation that will stimulate innovation.

The emphasis here therefore is still very much on technology as a 'push' factor set within a technological landscape, and this has been promoted in the context of wired and wireless networks and a variety of digital platforms (Mansell 2003).

More recently the emphasis in UK government policy has shifted towards 'electronic networks' (Strategy Unit 2002), which are defined as:

> All the different networks in the UK that offer connectivity, so that information (voice, data, video etc.) can be transmitted to and from multiple points, including a return path from the end user to the originator.

This definition includes traditional telephone and cable networks, data networks for Internet traffic, mobile phone networks, wireless data networks and interactive TV, but excludes traditional broadcast TV, non-interactive digital TV and broadcast radio since these technologies do not offer a return path to the user (Figure 2.4).

Supporting evidence for the Strategy Unit document (Mansell & Nikolychuk 2002) also highlights the importance of social and economic factors in usage:

> The impacts of use [of electronic networks] in terms of perceived effectiveness and efficiency depend on social, economic, political, cultural and organisational issues.

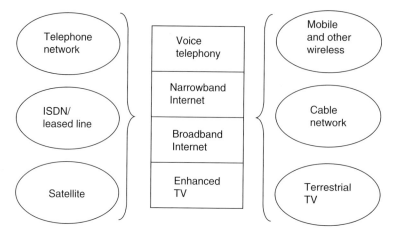

Figure 2.4   Main electronic networks and services (adapted from Strategy Unit 2002).

This point is emphasised in Table 2.2, and the report also suggested that the most important goal should be to move businesses, consumers and governments further up the 'e-adoption ladder', as critical mass builds up. However, Mansell (2003) suggests that simply increasing the level of infrastructure in ICT will not lead automatically to social and economic

Table 2.2   Key determinants of the effective use of electronic networks (adapted from Strategy Unit 2002).

Use	Key determinants of success
Business-to-business eCommerce, for example in supply chain management	• Development of appropriate skills among individual employees • Acceptance of the need for organisational change • Management of cost (especially among SMEs)
Government-to-government eGovernance, for example in policy co-ordination and delivery	• Awareness and acceptance of the benefits of organisational change • Availability of highly secure electronic environments
Business-to-consumer eCommerce, for example marketing and sales	• Recognition and dissemination of user benefits • Provision of a secure and private electronic trading environment • Development of effective and widespread user interfaces
Consumer-to-government transactions	• Recognition and dissemination of consumer benefits • Reduction of the costs of transaction onto new ways of accessing government information and services • Provision of secure and private transacting environments

improvement, and this marks a shift in emphasis from the greater certainty and systemic linkages between drivers and barriers seen in early information society benchmark documents (see, for example, DTI/Spectrum 1996). The complexity of social and economic relations therefore needs to be recognised, and this is influenced by three main features of the information society (Mansell 2003):

- **Systems features of ICT**. The pathways along which ICT demand can develop are numerous and time is always needed for adoption and adaptation. Because of inter-linkages the speed of diffusion may be affected: for example, the way the market develops for broadband depends on other parts of the ICT system, and on the social system in which the services are embedded.
- **Digital information exchange models**. During the Internet's initial growth it was frequently assumed that 'peer-to-peer' networking would favour the democratisation of content and information provision so that everyone would have the power to provide content and this would drive demand for higher bandwidth. The reality in developed countries is that 'point-to-multipoint' models are prevailing, and copyright protection issues are preventing 'peer-to-peer' models of exchange.
- **Quality of learning**. If there are deficiencies in the ICT skills base then the diffusion process can be slowed (see, for example, Gareis & Mentrup 2001; Millar 2002), and this is reflected in increasing concerns over skills shortages and the quality of graduates available to meet demand. The quality of learning is essential not only for encouraging the safeguarding of personal privacy and security but also for building trust in digital networks and services.

In turn, this trend towards increased complexity means that the roles of various stakeholders or actors (i.e. businesses, governments and citizens) in the information society also require careful examination (see, for example, Mansell 2003; Mansell & Nikolychuk 2002; Alvarez & Kilbourn 2001). Table 2.3, for example, shows the way in which electronic networks, including the Internet, are transforming the information society.

Table 2.3 Network connectivity and new services (after Mansell & Nikolychuk 2002).

	Government	Firms/businesses	Consumers/citizens
Government	G2G e.g. co-ordination	G2B e.g. information	G2C e.g. information
Firms/businesses	B2G e.g. public markets	B2B e.g. eCommerce	B2C e.g. eCommerce
Consumers/citizens	C2G e.g. tax	C2B e.g. price comparison	C2C e.g. auctions

In most Western countries, business-to-business sales still continue to dominate, with financial services in the lead, whilst eCommerce transactions lag (Table 2.4). Mansell (2003) suggests that although the majority of countries in the developed nations are adopting basic uses of ICT, relatively few have reached sophisticated levels of usage. There is also an industry sector influence, although the benefits of ICT use in business are being promoted. These include:

- cost reductions;
- increased transaction speed and reliability;
- improved management capabilities
- improved collaboration capabilities;
- stronger interdependencies in upstream and downstream markets; and,
- better customer relationship management.

Those companies which have reaped the benefits have generally invested heavily in education and training and organisational change strategies, and improved trust and safety/protection in terms of secure online ordering are other factors that are also important. There is therefore also a growing body of evidence on the role that digital networks are playing in democratic processes or what is increasingly referred to as 'eGovernment'.

All European Union countries (except Greece) have been classified in the UN 2001 global benchmarking report as having 'high e-government capacity' (United Nations 2001), and the USA was rated the most e-enabled country. Experience suggests (Siegfreid 2001) that smaller developments, in parallel with regulatory changes, are likely to be more successful. Generally speaking, government-to-business transaction services remain less common than government-to-government and government-to-citizen services. Citizen disillusionment and lack of access by many suggest that barriers to eGovernment are still therefore common (Mansell 2003).

Citizens' or consumers' use of ICT also differs markedly across the EU. For example, in the UK one study (Nafus & Tracey 2002) of mobile telephony has shown that it is frequently associated with morality, greater efficiency and increased productivity whereas in Finland, research has shown that the mobile phone is used in a more anarchic and disruptive way to challenge Finnish linguistic culture and existing social environment (Katz & Aakhus 2002). Moreover, other research has suggested that new technology rarely changes lifestyle radically (Livingstone & Bovill 1999) but rather that ICT affects the social environment by redefining private and public consumption patterns (Livingstone 2002).

Table 2.4 Official estimates of web, Internet and electronic commerce transactions: 2000 or latest available year (adapted from OECD 2002).

Broader →

Percentage of total sales or revenues

	Web commerce	Internet commerce	Electronic commerce
Business sector	2.0% Sweden	1.8% United Kingdom 1.4% Spain 1.0% Austria 0.5% Luxembourg 0.4% Portugal 0.5% Canada (2001) 0.7% Australia (2000–2001) 0.3% New Zealand (2000–2001)	13.3% Sweden 7.9% Finland 5.2% UK 4.0% Spain 2.5% Austria 1.8% Portugal 0.5% Luxembourg
Business sector (excluding financial sector)	0.9% Denmark (2001) 0.7% Finland	2.0% Norway (2001) 0.9% United Kingdom 0.4% Italy	10.0% Norway (2001) 9.1% Finland 6.0% United Kingdom 6.0% Denmark (2001) 1.1% Italy
Retail sector	0.1% France (1999)	1.0% United Kingdom 0.6% Canada (2001) 0.4% Australia (2000–2001) 0.2% Austria	1.4% United Kingdom 1.2% (United States, 2nd qtr 2002) 1.3% (United States, 4th qtr 2001) 1.0% (United States, 2nd qtr 2001) 0.2% Austria

Broader →

The main message emerging from this brief overview of ICT diffusion in stakeholder groups is that its use depends on social, economic, political and cultural factors (Slevin 2000; Tuomi 2001). As Ducatel *et al.* (2000: 9) suggest:

> The relationship between technological change and social transformation is now acknowledged to be a complex one, and the simple notion of technological changes having social [and economic] effects, which in turn can be simply controlled by appropriate policies, has now been shown to be false.

As Mansell (2002) points out, if new technology systems are not to be simply regarded as autonomous (or as new 'megamachines', to coin Mumford's (1964) phrase), the nature of mediation processes giving rise to the values and social processes that are embedded in the new technical systems, and the new power structures influencing participation, need closer examination. Further work by Mansell and Nikolychuk (2002) and Mansell (2003) also suggests that three priorities remain for UK government in terms of ICT:

- investment in learning for skill and competency development;
- initiatives to stimulate digital content and information provision, especially within the 'peer-to-peer' model; and,
- increasing the security of networks to build increased confidence.

Indeed, Mansell (2003) suggests that although policymakers are becoming more receptive to these messages, policy frequently continues to maintain a deterministic slant. This theme has often also been reflected in the type and nature of metrics and measurement statistics that are collected.

Measuring the information society

As policies have developed to promote the concept of the information society so have efforts to measure its characteristics also been developed. For example, early work by DTI/Spectrum (1996, 1998) highlighted the importance of benchmarking progress towards the information society. Measuring Internet access and use is relatively straightforward, and it can be argued that reasonable levels of Internet access within a country is a necessary, though not sufficient, condition for the development of eBusiness (UNCTAD 2003b). For example, recent data from UNCTAD (2003b) show that the number of global Internet users continued to grow in 2002, reaching 591 million people, but the rate of growth slowed from 27.3% to 20%. Developing countries actually experienced faster growth because of their demographic profile (younger populations and faster population growth) and at the end of 2002, these countries had 32% of the world's Internet users, an increase from 28% in 2001.[10] If current trends continue it is estimated that Internet users in the developing world will constitute 50% of users by 2008, but still only 10% of the world's population has access to the Internet. In the developed world there are 3262 users per 10 000 people and in the developing world, 391 users per 10 000 people. Similar patterns between the developed and developing world are also present in relation to the number of Internet hosts.

Quantitative data such as Internet users and Internet hosts are relatively easy to source. However, a country's ability to take part in the global information society is an issue that governments now take very seriously indeed, and indicators that capture information about the more qualitative aspects of countries' economic legal and policy frameworks are also vital to consider. The concept of 'e-readiness' therefore has evolved as a precursor to intensity of use, and ultimately the outcomes and impacts on national economies and business interests. As with government information society policies globally, there is a strong emphasis on 'technology push' and 'impact' in the rationale behind such measures.[11]

The UK government's ambition to be the best environment in the world for eCommerce led the government's office of the eEnvoy and the DTI to commission Booz Allen Hamilton and INSEAD business school to develop an international benchmarking framework and benchmark the e-economy of the UK against those of the other G7 countries (Canada, France, Germany, Italy, Japan, and the US) plus Australia and Sweden (Booz Allen Hamilton/INSEAD 2002). The report defined the term 'e-economy' as the 'dynamic system of interactions between a nation's citizens, the businesses and government that capitalise upon online technology to achieve a social or economic good'. The report assessed the e-economy in terms of four layers or sub-indices:[12]

- 'Environment', or the fertility of the environment for eCommerce and eGovernment, encompassing level of political leadership, regulatory openness, innovation, IT skills capability in the population and the cost and availability of access.
- 'Readiness', or the ability of the country's economic actors (citizens, businesses and governments) to capitalise on the information society. Readiness requires an appropriate device together with the skill and will to use it for eCommerce.
- 'Uptake and use' describes the uptake of online services and the volume and sophistication of use.

- 'Impact' is the degree to which adoption of online services has changed the behaviours of citizens or transformed businesses. For citizens this may be a shift towards teleworking or spending habits; for businesses through transformed business processes: using ICT to market, recruit, order, sell or provide customer care.

Booz Allan Hamilton/INSEAD (2002) use the term 'e-maturity' as a holistic concept describing the overall score from these four layers. The report found that the UK has the second best environment for eCommerce amongst the benchmark group of nine, behind the USA. Although the UK has not yet reached its target of being the best environment for eCommerce, progress has been made since 1998 and the UK has a number of strengths (Table 2.5). In summary, the findings were:

- the US, the UK, and Canada have developed the best environment for eCommerce, through a combination of policy decisions and other factors;
- the citizens of Canada, Sweden, and the US are the most involved in the eEconomy, combining high levels of readiness with high uptake and emerging impact.

Table 2.5   UK strengths and weaknesses (adapted from Booz Allen Hamilton/INSEAD 2002).

UK relative strengths	UK relative weaknesses

- **Market environment**
  - Strong educational infrastructure (ICT in education, PCs per pupil, ICT graduates)
  - Strong venture capital centre
  - Large and fast growing ICT sector
- **Political/regulatory leadership**
  - Dedicated cross-departmental organisation
  - Legal foundations for eEconomy largely built (e.g. consumer protection, digital signatures legally recognised)
- **Business readiness**
  - High IT spending / GDP
  - High % of businesses with a PC
- **Government readiness**
  - Strong IT core: Government Gateway
  - Comprehensive eGovernment programme with explicit high service delivery target
	- **Citizen uptake and use**
	  - Low household broadband penetration
	  - Low frequency and duration of Internet use
	- **Government uptake and use**
	  - Low % of services available online
	  - Low % of citizens using eGovernment
	  - Low % of healthcare workers with access to Internet
	
	and to a lesser degree . . .
	
	- **Infrastructural environment**
	  - Low availability of broadband (both SDL and cable modem)
	  - (note: SDL broadband availability is now improving)

- Business e-maturity, the adoption and use of online technologies to change the way businesses work, is most developed in the US and Sweden.
- Sweden, the US, Canada, and Australia have the strongest eGovernment development, driven by their early initiatives, and a sustained commitment to the process.

Implications of the development of an information society

So far in this chapter we have examined how ICT should be viewed within the context of emerging social, economic and political factors in an 'information society', with the new economy as the engine for economic growth. But there are also ramifications and implications of the emerging information society for society as a whole. Three facets of the information society, in particular, warrant further examination. These are the digital divide; broadband; and the knowledge divide.

Digital divide

The debate over the emerging digital social divide, and whether action should be taken to reduce the divide, has existed for a number of years. Neice (2002) points out that some descriptions refer to the divide as digital 'haves' and 'have nots' (see also Wresch 1996), other descriptions to 'included' and 'excluded' and a third group to 'digital citizens' or 'the wired', and the rest of the population. This has led to a plethora of policy guidance from national governments and international agencies and may even suggest that the digital divide metaphor reflects its cultivation by state-appointed bodies and governments. For example, Selwyn (2003) sees the digital divide as the practical embodiment of 'social inclusion' policy initiatives in centre-left governments throughout Western nations. In the 1990s, the UK, France and the USA (during the Clinton/Gore era) saw a shift towards this socially inclusive policy agenda. Selhofer and Husing (2002) also see the roots of the digital divide metaphor in the 'knowledge gap' debate of the 1970s in the USA, which suggested that education level and socio-economic status made a difference in acquiring information.

At first, the issues of social inclusion and the digital divide emerged from the clear disparity between developed and developing nations, but very soon the emphasis shifted towards disparities within individual countries. The term 'digital divide' emerged from a number of documents during this period (see, for example, US Department of Commerce 1995) and sought to justify policies that could deal with the divide. For example, the OECD (2001:5) define the term as:

> ...the gap between individuals, households, businesses and geographic areas at different socio-economic levels with regard to both their opportunities to access information and communications technologies and their use of the Internet for a wide variety of activities.

The policy justifications for treating the digital divide as a threat were that employability needed to be improved and secured; that citizens needed to participate and benefit from ICT access; and that bringing all citizens online would promote economic growth. For example, the digital divide became a political priority in Europe with the launch of the eEurope Action Plan in 2000 (Digital Europe 2003), and a commitment from the highest level to create a cheaper, faster and more secure Internet. In Internet access terms the socio-economic contours of the divide at EU level are shown in Figure 2.5.

Within the EU, including the UK, therefore, government policy has evolved to focus on the issue of the digital divide. In the UK, BT (Forstater *et al.* 2003) sees the digital divide in multidimensional terms and the measures needed to close it in terms of connectivity (being able to get online); content (the type and nature of information online and the way it can be used); and capability (or the ability of different groups of people to use technology).

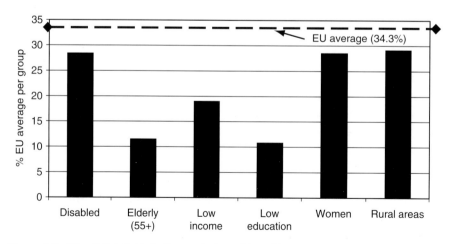

Figure 2.5 The digital divide in Europe (adapted from Digital Europe 2003).

The empirical evidence for the digital divide is based on inequalities distributed along social and spatial lines (Warf 2001) with further inequalities by socio-economic status, income, gender, level of education, age, geography and ethnicity (see, for example, Foley 2000). Clearly, therefore, much of the evidence for this divide comes from the results of statistical analysis of the general public's access to the Internet. However, Selwyn (2003) attacks the concept of the digital divide in current policy terms for being over-simplistic and deterministic. For example, he argues that access does not automatically lead to use, and that much of the digital divide literature is couched in terms of an 's-curve', with an 'early adopter' phase leading through to a majority online at a later date, and the ultimate elimination of the digital divide. This view is also supported by Crabtree *et al.* (2002) who suggest that the future of technology is divided between the 'techno-utopians' and the 'doomsayers'. Both viewpoints, however, promote a 'technology-push' view of the world, or that technological progress is the main driver of social change. But the reality is very different: actually only about 7% of the UK population can be classified as 'early adopters' in technology terms: that is, seeking out technology shortly after launch, with little regard to cost. The majority see ICT as a tool in everyday life and are termed 'quiet pragmatists'.

Based on work by Murdock (2002), Selwyn (2003) also suggests that there are three categories of users: 'core users' (continuous and comprehensive use); 'peripheral users' (spasmodic and limited use); and 'excluded users' (non-existent use). Moreover, use is not determined simply by technology or psychology, but rather by a complex mixture of social, psychological, economic and pragmatic reasons. As Heller (1987) argues, technology offers options or choices based on particular contingencies which determine the impact of technology on people. Selwyn (2003) therefore sees people's engagement with ICT as dependent on the mix of 'capital', in economic, cultural, social, and technological terms. In this way, the digital divide is more accurately formulated as 'stages', which may overlap and interlink:

- Stage 1: Formal and theoretical access leading to effective access.
- Stage 2: Use of ICTs and engagement with ICTs and contents.
- Stage 3: Actual and perceived outcomes and actual and perceived consequences.

In addition to this focus on the existence of the digital divide in a generic sense, there is also much debate over the issue of the 'broadband divide', which is also taxing the minds of governments globally.

Broadband

As the CSTB (2001) points out, the term 'broadband' has become common-place for describing the future of digital communications, and is widely used to refer to a range of high-speed transmission technologies being offered for data communications.

Dutton *et al.* (2003) provide a concise summary of the main technologies currently employed for broadband pipelines (Table 2.6). The issue of broadband access is of course also linked with the wider issue of a digital divide. As with narrowband access, Dutton *et al.* (2003) suggest that the initial perception of the digital divide was based on ICT access in terms of the 'haves' and the 'have nots'. But from the mid-1990s, access to digital networks became an increasingly important component of the digital

Table 2.6   Broadband types (adapted from Dutton *et al.* 2003).

Type	Technology	Typical supplier
DSL (digital subscriber line)	Boosting the bandwidth of traditional copper-wire telephony networks	Traditional incumbent 'telco' telephony suppliers; ISPs offering competitive service using the telco's infrastructure
Cable	Coaxial cables, which have a higher bandwidth than copper wires but lower than optical fibre	Cable TV suppliers offering an expanded range of services including telephony and broadband
Fibre-to-the-home (FTTH)	Optical fibre directly to the home	Telco, cable and other telecom infrastructure players
Satellite	Wireless links to geostationary satellites, currently at lower broadband speeds; Very Small Aperture Terminal (VAST) technology enables small satellite terminals to be used to offer lower-cost and more flexibly located links	Specialist satellite communications companies
WiFi (wireless fidelity)	Wireless local area networks based on the IEEE 811 Ethernet protocol	Commercial Wireless Internet Service Providers (WISPs); not-for-profit communication networks
Fixed wireless	Microware line-of-sight links to fixed lower broadband speeds	Specialist telecommunications suppliers
Third-generation (3G) mobile	Mobile cellphones, likely to be limited to lower broadband speeds	Mobile telephone companies with G3 licences (which required very large investments in some countries)
Powerlines	Electric powerlines adapted to carry broadband	Electric utilities; intermediate service agents

divide, and more recently there have been calls for greater focus on proficiency in use rather than simply access. Broadband is often seen as a transformative technology which can reconfigure access to people, services, information and other technologies and so affect the relative power of different actors involved in the production, use and consumption of content and services.

Related to the growth of broadband is 'wireless fidelity', or WiFi. The number of WiFi hotspots, where users can access broadband infrastructure wirelessly, has grown rapidly since 2001 (Johnson & Sinder 2003). A WiFi antenna, for example, can enable signals to be transmitted to laptops over distances of up to 300 m. Auray *et al.* (2003) see WiFI as a 'hybrid' mixing technical characteristics of networks and social characteristics of use within economic strategic and institutional frameworks, and they point to the growth of grassroots online communities (led by 'lead users'), which use hotspots for their focus, driven by the open characteristics of the technology and by the current fragile state of the telecommunications technology (Box 2.3 and Figure 2.6).

In terms of broadband availability and deployment, the most visible divides are revealed by statistics which map availability of broadband access or deployment/take-up. At the end of 2002, for example, broadband services were available in 82 out of over 200 economies worldwide and since 2000, global broadband numbers have increased fivefold and currently stand at over 60 million (ITU 2003). At the end of 2002 the total number

---

Box 2.3   WiFi communities

Recent research by Socio-economic Trends Assessment for the Digital Revolution (STAR) (Auray *et al.* 2003) has highlighted the growing importance of WiFi (a wireless broadband technology for local networks), but it has stressed that the appearance of communities of WiFi users is not technologically determined. Instead, the communities are the product of co-operation between the developers of the technology and 'lead users', many of whom are technical enthusiasts. The essence of WiFi communities lies in their simple structure: they focus on efficient sharing of equipment and existing local knowledge rather than on knowledge production. The STAR research has enabled a typology of these to be developed on the basis of an analysis of seven European WiFi community case studies, based on their 'ideology', or strategic positioning in relation to the Internet, and their topology, or choice of technical operating mode. Therefore a community such as Consume in London shares transmission band, whereas the Citizen's Network in Brussels favours a self-contained system. *Ad hoc* structures (or 'rings') are also contrasted with more formal structures ('stars') (see Figure 2.6). WiFi communities may offer opportunities to bridge the digital divide.

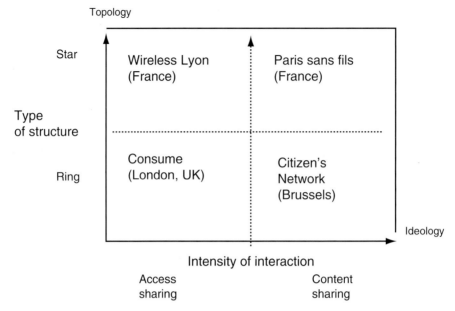

Figure 2.6   Wireless communities (adapted from STAR 2003).

of broadband subscribers in all OECD countries was 55 million (Ismail & Wu 2003), the equivalent of 5 subscribers per 100 inhabitants (in comparison with 0.2 per 100 in developing countries), with 18–25% of all fixed network Internet subscribers having broadband (Paltridge 2003).

Data from the OECD show that the UK was 18th out of 30 countries in 2002 (Figure 2.7) with a definite split between the richer and poorer countries, and evidence from ITU (2003) shows a strong correlation between gross national income per capita and penetration rate. Similarly, Crabtree and Roberts (2003) point to the fact that the UK had hitherto lagged behind comparable countries: in 2003 the UK had 2.5 million broadband users, set to double by 2005, by which time UK will have overtaken France as the second largest broadband market in Europe. They also suggest that the supply side is working well, but that the demand side is problematic. To address this deficiency, and basing their research on ethnographic studies of 12 UK households over a period of a year, they suggest that the uptake process needs to be understood to further promote the diffusion of broadband. In this sense, broadband is not therefore simply concerned with speed and content. Their research showed that the following stages are vital to consider in understanding broadband uptake:

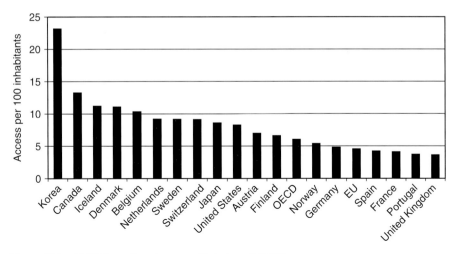

Figure 2.7 OECD broadband access (data from OECD).

- **Adoption**. Microbarriers are more important than macrobarriers in broadband adoption. Availability, understanding, cost and customer service were found to be less of a problem than issues which strengthened the 'status quo' basis. So questions such as 'Will I use it enough?' or 'I'm worried about viruses' were found to be important.
- **Adaptation**. How people change their habits of online use as a result of broadband was found to be an important issue. For example, broadband users may use discovery mechanisms to explore and initiate new ways of surfing by creating and sharing content and using community-based applications.
- **Absorption**. Weaving broadband into everyday life is the final stage that requires better understanding. This is best understood not in terms of content but rather in terms of how the technology gets embedded in households through a dynamic social process of creative interaction between families, friends and work colleagues.

In contrast, Wilsdon and Stedman Jones (2002) take a more critical view of broadband supply in the UK. They pose the question, will broadband growth in the UK be limited by regulatory and structural restrictions, especially the control BT has over local copper wire infrastructures? The starting point for their analysis is the need for electronic networks to foster innovation. They use the concept of 'innovation commons' where infrastructure and governance are shaped in such a way that allows innovation rather than preventing it. The term 'commons' refers to a concept developed by Lessig (2001), who had suggested that the shared resource and open access nature of the Internet and the web, or a non-rivalrous 'commons', was under threat. Lessig went on to point out that digital enclosure was undermining the open access of the Internet through a combination of companies restricting access, lack of reciprocity in data transmissions upstream and downstream, and the defensiveness of dominant firms. Essentially, where a disruptive technology such as the Internet exists, then extending power to existing interests will cause problems in the continuation of open access. Wilsdon and Stedman Jones (2002) build on these ideas to define innovation as (2002: 10) 'an evolving open ended process based on experimentation, resulting in real products and accessible practices that fundamentally alter the way people live'. Innovation therefore consists of two main types:

- Incremental innovation, where business and organisations innovate at the margins of their focus, providing new products and services.
- Disruptive innovation, where innovation upsets and supersedes established models of business, user certainty and frameworks of governance to create wider possibilities in a given field.

They argue that the most important forms of technological innovation are disruptive, driven by a process of social and economic factors underpinned by government and public sector rules. Regulation has to therefore balance the needs of encouraging innovation without compromising the public good. However, in the UK, the authors suggest that tighter regulation is in danger of stifling innovation and simply entrenching existing monopoly interests. This may therefore require not only separation of BT to free up the local loop to increased competition, but also freeing up the spectrum allocation mechanism of WiFi to further competition, and a greater role for Ofcom in 'adaptive regulation'.

Knowledge divide: a spatial perspective

The spatial focus of the digital divide and broadband access has already been alluded to in this chapter. This occurs internationally, nationally, regionally and sub-regionally. Indeed this coincides with a period when governments and policy makers have 'discovered' regions (Martin 2003). Driven by a zeal to kick-start new economic activity through the promotion of innovation, hi-tech industries and entrepreneurial activity on the one hand, and what Martin refers to as 'neo-liberal' policies to maximise policy flexibility cost-effectiveness and market involvement on the other, governments have been decentralising and devolving policy measures and programmes down to a regional level. In the EU, UK and USA (Box 2.4) there has been a clear focus on analysing the regional foundations of

---

Box 2.4   Silicon Alley, New York

During the late 1990s, huge amounts of venture capital poured into a part of New York's Lower Manhattan that came to be called colloquially, 'Silicon Alley'.[13] Based around an emergence of new media companies in what was formerly an old industrial neighbourhood, the transformation was championed at its height as a prime example of how technology and cultural production could revitalise inner city areas. Subsequently the dot.com crash and World Trade Center attacks dissolved the dream of post-industrial regeneration. Yet, as Indergaard (2004) points out, Silicon Alley offers some valuable lessons on how real estate patterns can be transformed not only by technology but also by networks of organised interests. The growth of Silicon Alley was really promoted by the magnet of physical and human resources for the new media companies locating there, which also promoted social networks and relations between start-up companies. A variety of interests mediated the expansion of the district, based on what may be termed a 'neo-liberal' regime (Indergaard 2003), and these included landlords and telecoms companies who competed to supply tenants with digital services. New telecoms companies offered to wire buildings if landlords granted access to tenants, offering revenue cuts and warrants to buy stock, and landlords were invited to differentiate their buildings with websites for tenants. From 1998 to 2001, five million square feet in New York was leased or purchased for telecoms hotels, and rents rose more than fivefold, as manufacturers in the area were displaced.

---

competitiveness (see, for example, DTI/Spectrum 1998). In UK policy, the emphasis has been on a 'knowledge-driven economy'. For example, in the introduction to the 1998 Competitiveness White Paper, Tony Blair, the UK Prime Minister, stated:

> ... We will only compete successfully in future if we create an economy that is genuinely knowledge driven.

Therefore there has been an increasing focus on employment and skills, which carries resonance with the Lisbon European Council's commitment that by 2010 Europe should become:

> ... The most competitive and dynamic knowledge-based economy in the world capable of sustainable economic growth with more and better jobs and greater social cohesion.

In this book we use the term 'new economy' to convey the same meaning as 'knowledge economy'. In fact, in UK policy, there is only a rather imprecise definition as to what comprises an economy that is 'knowledge driven'.[14] However, the World Bank Report Report on the *Korean Knowledge Economy* (Dahlmann & Andersson 2000) defined a 'knowledge economy' more explicitly as one:

... that encourages its organisations and people to acquire, create, disseminate and use (codified and tacit) knowledge more effectively for greater economic and social development.

The report went on to suggest that four pillars underpinned this, which comprised:

- an economic and institutional regime to provide incentives for existing knowledge use;
- an educated and skilled workforce;
- a dynamic information infrastructure; and,
- a system of research centres, universities, think tanks, consultants, firms and other organisations that can tap into the knowledge.

Recent work by Hepworth and Spencer (2002) for the DTI has attempted to use these concepts, and to describe the regional architecture of the knowledge economy (or new economy) in Britain. Building on previous work by Christie and Hepworth (2001) and the Local Futures Group (2001), they use a Regional Economic Architecture to map the knowledge economy in Britain by identifying knowledge-intensive industries (having more than 25% graduates in their workforce) and the skills levels of people in the same areas. This shows:

- a clear metropolitan dominance with larger cities dominating at regional and national levels (for example, London, Bristol, Birmingham, Edinburgh and Leeds);
- a very clear north–south divide in Britain in the knowledge economy, with certain growth poles standing out in the North West;
- local divides, with much lower numbers of knowledge workers in the rural areas;
- a mismatch in many areas between skills levels and the type of jobs available.

In short, their analysis shows that knowledge is based in and gravitates towards existing areas of economic dynamism and follows the existing landscape of economic development.[15] Historically, property development and ownership and occupation have tended to be associated with the regional balance of UK economic growth, as might be expected. Figure 2.8 shows that regional differences in income, Internet access, and the knowledge economy in England are closely related with the distribution of office space, in volume terms, thus reinforcing existing regional disparities. London, for example, dominates in terms of the indices shown.

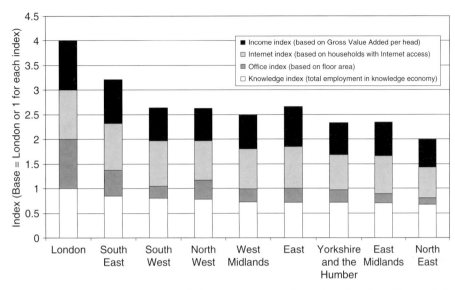

Figure 2.8 The regional divide in England in 2000-2001 (based on data from Hepworth & Spencer 2002, and National Statistics).

Schiller (2001) also suggests that hi-tech estates, housing ICT-related companies, are predominantly located in the Thames Valley and in the south as a whole (Table 2.7). However, there is an exception. As Schiller (2001) shows, drawing on previous research by Henneberry (1987), 'science parks' (Box 2.5) are skewed regionally away from the South East, because they were built with a 'missionary' objective promulgated by policy incentives. Westhead and Batstone (1999) suggest that the policy aim of science park promotion and development, although not specifically formalised, was to use science parks as growth poles in the more marginalised regions of the UK through tax incentives and other fiscal devices. Universities, higher education institutions and financial institutions were also instrumental in their development. This shows that there are exceptions to the

Table 2.7 The spatial distribution of science parks and hi-tech estates in the UK (adapted from Schiller 2001).

All figures (%)	Science parks	Hi-tech estates	Conventional estates
Thames Valley	17	53	36
Rest	83	47	64
Total	100	100	100
South (SE, SW and East Anglia)	33	67	57
North (rest of UK)	67	33	43
Total	100	100	100

Box 2.5   Science parks

The growth of the science park concept in the UK can be traced to Harold Wilson's 'white heat of technology' policies during the 1960s (Edmonds 2000). However, the first UK science parks were set up by universities without external aid, and this happened later, during the 1970s. The role model for these were US successes, such as the parks based at Stanford University in Palo Alto (developed during the 1950s) and Massachusetts Institute of Technology in Boston (Westhead & Batstone 1998). However, US science parks are much bigger than their UK counterparts (200 ha compared with 20 ha). UKSPA (2003) define a science park as a cluster of knowledge-based businesses, where support and advice are supplied to assist in the growth of the companies. In most instances, science parks are associated with a centre of technology such as a university or research institute. Cambridge and Heriot Watt were the first to be developed and a second wave occurred during the 1980s. This was driven not only by policies designed to promote stronger economic growth through clusters of SMEs and the development of new technologies, but also keen interest from the academic world. In 2002 there were 54 science parks in the UK with some 1827 tenants, employing nearly 43 000 workers (UKSPA 2003). The majority of tenants are ICT related but biotechnology is also important (Edmonds 2000). Science parks also provide incubator or innovation services to help smaller businesses on campus plan and develop their growth. In addition, they provide an environment where larger, international businesses can develop specific and close interactions with a particular centre of technology for their mutual benefit and usually have a formal and operational link with such a reservoir of technology (UKSPA 2003). They therefore differ from business parks, which are property development oriented.

UK economic growth doctrine of 'north v. south', and science parks provide an example of how a highly technology-driven real estate use can be steered by policy rather than simply technology alone.

In general, however, the knowledge economy continues to cluster within and around cities, and largely deflates the thesis of the 'death of distance', because personal contacts do still matter and tacit knowledge is locally based. There therefore continues to be a high degree of clustering, because of the presence and strength of pre-existing markets, industries and labour pools. But we also need to dig deeper and see what is happening in individual cities and at the real estate/firm level as a result of changes brought about by the transformative nature of the new economy in the information society. This theme will be picked up again in more detail in Part 2 of the book.

Summary

This chapter has provided a review of the social economic and political factors against which ICT transformation must be viewed. Although some sceptics argue that the empirical evidence for the information society is still unproven, this view ignores the very real attempts being made by researchers and governments to provide indices and measures for the information society. The relationship between the new economy and the information society is a strong one, and government policy in Western countries, including the UK, has been designed to foster the transformation of society through ICT. Conceptually there are also strong arguments for suggesting that the information society and new economy provide a lens for us to see more clearly the changes that are occurring to real estate and, as Abrams (1982) suggests, as a way of organising the phenomena so that further research questions can be posed.

It is also clear that the information society's relationship with the new economy is a complex one. On the one hand we argue that the new economy is the engine for growth within the information society, but on the other hand we must set this in the context of political, social, and economic factors which shape technology use and are shaped by it. In this sense the concept of an information society is also useful for highlighting the changing social dynamics of ICT usage.

We have also seen that the policy frameworks that have been implemented have frequently adopted a deterministic stance, although increasingly, governments have begun to realise that ICT must also have a socio-economic context. Arguments for political expediency have also frequently framed policy initiatives in simplistic ways to deal with regional problems by divorcing 'knowledge' and 'innovation' as concepts from their social and political context. Nonetheless, there is an increasing realisation that government policy needs to focus on the socio-spatial dimensions of ICT transformation, and this is exemplified by growing concerns over such issues as the digital and knowledge divides within society.

Notes

1 Daniels (2003) shows that in 1996 there were 1000 references to the term 'new economy' in the US business press in 1996; by 2000, there were 20 000 mentions.
2 This view has been supported by other studies (see for example Meyer 1999, who calculated that the value-to-weight ratio of a pound of US GDP went from $3.64 in 1977 to $6.52 in 1999, a 79% increase, and Sheerin 2002, who found that in the 1990s, UK real GDP increased by 25% but the weight of the economy by only 2%).

3 Moreover, in social science terms, as Steinmueller (2003) points out, discussions about the information society are frequently cast in the language of 'impact', which lends a rhetorical bias because of the connotations of the inevitable effect of ICT as an agency for change. This parallels the critique of technological determinism in ICT revealed in Chapter 1, although in the current book we use the term 'impact' interchangeably with 'transformation'.

4 The current chapter aims to provide an overview of the theoretical frameworks and themes emerging from the literature, as relating to the concept of the 'information society', and to show relevant linkages and synergy between this literature and the literature covered in Chapter 1, which focused on ICT transformation in a 'new economy' from different perspectives. Chapter 5 deals with the concept of the new economy in more detail.

5 Miles (2000) takes a different approach, and suggests that the evolution of the information society can be broken down into four phases, which are intended to convey fluidity rather than fixed points: 'Islands'; 'Archipelago'; 'Continent'; and 'Ecosystem'. The early years of the twenty-first century are characterised by further consolidation of the Continent phase. Miles likens the Ecosystem phase to an all-embracing 'ecosystem' where ICT is a general-purpose technology and the accepted norm.

6 Woolgar (2002) suggests that five 'advisory', non-prescriptive rules for evaluating claims made about the information society should be defined:

   - Rule 1: The uptake and use of the new technologies depend crucially on local social context.
   - Rule 2: The fears and risks associated with new technologies are unevenly socially distributed.
   - Rule 3: Virtual technologies supplement rather than substitute for real activities.
   - Rule 4: The more virtual the more real (i.e. virtual activities stimulate real activities).
   - Rule 5: The more global the more local (i.e. the more global the impact of technology the more we need to refer to local context to understand its implementation).

7 Webster (2004) suggests that Charles Leadbeater (author of *Living on Thin Air: The New Economy*, 1999), who works for the influential British think tank Demos, was reputedly behind the development of the 1998 White Paper. The linkage between thought leadership and policy development has also been stressed by Webster (2004), who suggests that Manuel Castells, Daniel Bell and Anthony Giddens have all been major social thinkers and 'theorists', and have all influenced policy directly or indirectly.

8 The policy of nurturing and growing a knowledge-based economy in the UK is seen as being key to what 'Third Way' advocates argue is a balance between neo-liberalist deregulation and market liberalisation, and old-style social democracy, focusing on industrial policy and Keynsian demand measures (Giddens 2000). Critics of New Labour, on the other hand, see the threads of neo-liberalism in such knowledge-driven policies, which continue to rely heavily on free

market economics to implement technology-led change (see, for example, Peters 2001; Jessop 2000).

9   In theoretical terms, the work of Castells (2000) builds directly on that of Bell (1973). Castells, for example, defines knowledge as:

> A set of organised statements of facts and ideas, presenting a reasoned judgement on an experimental result, which is transmitted to others through some communication medium in some systematic form.

Indeed, in quoting Bell directly, Castells remarks that he had no compelling reason to improve on the definition. Allen (2000) describes this view of knowledge as 'cognitive' in form, and therefore formal, systematic and rooted in abstract theory.

10   To put this in perspective, in 1999 the OECD reported that more than 50% of the world's population had still not made a telephone call.

11   Two examples of recent, global-wide e-readiness indices are the Global Information Technology Report (GITR) 2002–2003 (World Economic Forum/ INSEAD 2003) and the Economist Intelligence Unit rankings (EIU 2003). GITR ranks 82 economies according to a Networked Readiness Index (NRI), which is defined as the 'degree of preparation of a nation or community to participate in and benefit from ICT developments' (Dutta *et al.* 2003). The NRI measures environment, readiness and usage. The EIU index follows a similar approach with more emphasis on economic factors and its Economic Rank Index (ERI), which includes 65 economies, measures the extent to which a market is conducive to Internet-based opportunities (EIU 2003). Six of the first 10 countries in both rankings coincide and 11 of the top 15; in both cases they are high or middle-income countries. For a description of other measurement systems see UNCTAD (2003b).

12   This framework is based on the Information Age Partnership framework (see http://www.iapuk.org/), but is also based on the 'best elements' of 10 other international framework measures, including work by UK Office of National Statistics.

13   Other new media districts in Los Angeles (Digital Coast) and San Francisco (Multimedia Gulch) also developed in a similar way during this period.

14   For example, the 1998 White Paper on Competitiveness defines a 'knowledge-driven' economy as one in which the generation and exploitation of knowledge has come to play the predominant part in the creation of wealth. It is 'about the more effective use and exploitation of all types of knowledge in all manner of economic activity'.

15   Clustering and dispersion issues are covered in more detail throughout the remainder of the book.

3

Technological Change: Diffusion and Adoption of ICT by Consumers, Businesses and Government

Introduction

In the previous chapter we saw how ICT needed to be understood in the context of a range of social, economic and political factors. In the current chapter we focus on the issue of technological change, and how technology diffusion operates over the lifecycle of adoption, take-off and maturity. We also show that it is important to consider technological change from the point of view of our three key stakeholder groups:[1] consumers (or citizens), businesses and government.

As we saw in Figure 1.4, these three groups are not only ICT users and stakeholders but also real estate users and stakeholders, and their relationships with both production/consumption processes and the real estate that 'houses' these processes are important to understand as part of our framework for analysis. The current chapter therefore also considers the implications of three Internet-driven activities (eBusiness, eCommerce and eWork) for these stakeholders, by examining their nature and the relative size of their markets. Finally, the chapter concludes by highlighting some key ramifications of technological change for real estate.

Technology diffusion

Technological evolution is a complex process because technologies are interconnected in systems which are interlinked and interdependent, not only between themselves, but also with the physical, social and institutional environments within which they are situated (Perez 2001).

Moreover, technological evolution is frequently subject to both continuous change and discontinuity. This point is acknowledged by Mansell and Steinmueller (2000), who suggest that, from a user point of view, the time taken to become accustomed to new technological opportunities, and to develop the skills to use them, makes it unlikely that the precise technical specifications for infrastructure are available in advance. In this sense, they argue that the unevenness of technological advance results from the uncertainty of discovery processes, and experimentation with untried ideas. Progress in technology can also be uneven because of the different rates at which new technologies are adopted and deployed, and because of variations in acceptance and resistance amongst users.

There is therefore much uncertainty associated with the process of technological change, which also produces a number of human responses. Theoretical approaches in both economics and sociology have sought to analyse the adoptive behaviours of those who employ technologies therefore, and, in both schools of thought, technology diffusion is seen as the aggregate outcome of individual choices to adopt new technologies. Rogers (1995) and Stoneman (1983) both offer examples of these approaches. For example, Rogers (1995) defines 'diffusion' as the 'process by which an innovation is communicated through certain channels over time amongst the members of a social system'. An 'innovation' is (Rogers 1995: 11): 'an idea, practice, or object that is perceived as new by an individual or other unit of adoption'. Rogers is therefore not concerned with the context of an innovation, and communication is seen in terms of a simple 'sender–receiver' model.

Mansell and Steinmueller (2000) produce a useful overview of the varying theoretical constructs of technology diffusion. They use a fairly wide definition of technology in their analysis, encompassing all forms of innovation (including new ideas and products), and they suggest that market, technological and institutional considerations, as well as the needs and preferences of individual adopters, shape the adoption choices of actors. They also suggest that economists tend to analyse social processes in terms of their effect on individuals, and hence emphasise the importance of relative profitability in driving adoption. In contrast, sociologists regard innovation as an 'uncertainty reduction' process influenced by cognitive processes and access to information. Frequently, diffusion models have also been the subject of criticism because they have often overlooked the interrelationships between key actors such as producers, suppliers and other users, but also because they overlook the process of learning and negotiation within the context of power relationships (Sorenson 1998). Rogers' (1995) work can therefore be viewed as a 'bridge' between the economics and sociology schools, but even so his work does not include important contextual issues such as governance (policy and regulation) and the cultural context of learning (Bijker & Law 1992).

The classic 'S-shaped diffusion' curve lies at the heart of much of diffusion theory. For example, Figure 3.1 shows how the diffusion curve may be divided into three phases:

- Phase I: Early adoption
- Phase II: Take-off
- Phase III: Maturity

Perez (2001)[2] refers to this process as a 'technological trajectory', and sees this in the context of evolutionary economics. She suggests that after a radical innovation gives birth to a new product capable of creating a new industry, there is an initial period of further innovation and optimisation leading to general acceptance of the product in the appropriate market. Soon after, this leads to market interaction and improvement of design (Arthur 1989; David 1985) and, as markets grow, there are further innovations as the quality of the product and productivity of the process are improved. Eventually maturity is reached, as further investment in

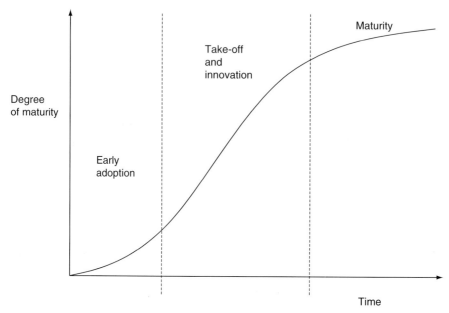

Figure 3.1   Typical 'S-shaped' diffusion curve.

innovation brings diminishing returns. The whole diffusion process can take a few years or many years to occur and in the latter case, improvements usually involve successive models. Within the process, early adopters also acquire competitive advantage, which can also lead to 'lock-out' for later entrants.

The early adoption phase can also be a relatively long period and this can be due, in part, to the quite time-consuming and complex processes needed to adapt the innovation to particular applications and the adaptations that users have to make to adopt the new technology. Cost reduction will therefore play a vital role in promoting general-purpose technologies during this phase, and it is likely that 'near future' technologies are already available in the market in one form or another. For example, the rapid growth of the Internet during the 1990s was based on a technology that had been in the research community since the 1970s. The second phase of take-off is characterised by much more rapid adoption, as the technology comes into widespread use: here adoption rates rise from 20% to 80% and finally during maturity nearly all individuals have the technology. However, 100% adoption is normally never reached because there will always be some non-adopters.

Implications of ICT diffusion for consumers, businesses and government

The diffusion of different technologies has implications for the three user groups, or stakeholders, that we identify in this book:

- consumers;
- businesses; and
- government.

However, consumer demand in technology has often been overlooked. As Coyle and Quah (2002) point out, understanding the new economy means understanding changing consumer patterns and the interaction of both demand and supply for products and services, not just supply and productivity alone. The next section of this chapter therefore examines how the three groups of stakeholders, including consumers, have reacted in their adoption and adaptation strategies to new developments in ICT.

Consumers

The slope, or trajectory, of a technology diffusion curve can vary, and this is dependent on a range of factors: cost, simultaneous awareness amongst users, or the extent to which others have adopted the technology (positive network externalities). Hamill (2003) offers an interesting perspective on how and why households and consumers adopt new technologies. As she points out, there is something of a paradox here. Over the last 50 years there have been significant changes in both work patterns and domestic technologies. Before the 1950s, many women did not work outside the home, but now the majority do. We might therefore logically expect to observe a large rise in the ownership of labour-saving devices, especially as over the same period consumer durable spending doubled. However, labour-saving devices have not dominated the typical UK household. Bowden and Offer (1994), for example, noted that home entertainment devices such as radio and television diffused faster than kitchen and household appliances. As Table 3.1 shows, based on the UK 2001 census, the top seven consumer appliances were owned by more than 75% of households and three were 'entertainment' or 'time-user', devices (i.e. colour TV, video recorder and CD player). Indeed, of the 13 appliances listed in Table 3.1, only seven were 'time-savers'. This is supported by the fact that in the UK, since 1998–1999, expenditure on leisure goods and services has been the single largest item of household expenditure (National Statistics 2003a).

Patterns of adoption are also partly created by an income effect, because wealthier households tend to adopt new technology before less wealthy

Table 3.1 Ownership of domestic appliances in UK (data from Hamill 2003; National Statistics 2004).

	Economically active households: 2003 (%)	Year introduced to UK	Year reached 50% penetration	Half life (yrs)
Colour TV	98	1967	1976	9
Deep freeze/fridge freezer	94	c. 1950s	–	–
Fixed phone	93	Pre-WW1	1975	c. 60
Washing machine	92	1934	1964	30
Video recorder	88	1979	1988	9
Microwave oven	85	Mid–late 1970s	1990	c. 15
CD player	79	Early 1980s	1995	c. 15
Mobile phone	70	c. 1990	–	–
Tumble drier	54	c. 1950	1994	c. 44
Home computer	49	Mid–late 1970s	–	–
Satellite/cable TV	42	1982	–	–
Access to Internet at home	40	Mid–late 1970s	–	–
Dishwasher	28	1957	–	–

households. This income divide, which mirrors the digital divide, is shown in Figure 3.2. This plots data as lines for each technology: the top of the line represents the proportion of wealthiest households owning the technology and the bottom of the line, the poorest households, with the square representing the proportion of all households using the technology. The longer the line, the greater the divide in ownership level therefore. Thus richer households tend to substitute capital for labour and can afford to buy dishwashers and PCs; they will therefore spend more time on leisure activities, other things being equal. Moreover, as societies become wealthier in the long term, households have more income to spend on time and leisure, which may also explain the increase in 'time-using' devices over time (Hamill 2003). Other factors influencing domestic demand for new technologies include:

- positive feedback from network externalities: the bigger the network the greater the benefits of being connected to it (Shapiro & Varian 1999);
- infectious disease model (Douglas & Isherwood 1979) or the habit of 'keeping up with the Joneses';
- shifts in 'time-budgets' or how people spend their time over a 24-hour day will also influence the varying demands for different kinds of technology. There is an opportunity cost for carrying out any activity within a 24 period, for example, and leisure time is an increasingly important part of individual lifestyles.

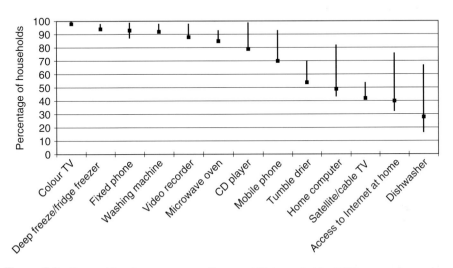

Figure 3.2 Ownership of consumer appliances, UK households, 2001: range by socio-economic group (hi = large employers and higher managerial: lo = routine; average = square) (data from National Statistics and updated from Hamill 2003).

The diffusion curves for selected technologies also make interesting comparison. In general, consumers have become less wary of new technology in recent years, giving rise to steeper adoption curves (Pragnell *et al.* 2000). As Figure 3.3 shows, the past few years have been characterised by rapid growth in mobile phones and home access to the Internet. Mobile phone ownership quadrupled from 17% of households in the UK in 1996-1997 to 70% in 2002-2003 (Box 3.1), while access to the Internet at home rose at a similar rate between 1998-1999 and 2002-2003 and had reached 46% of UK households by 2003 (National Statistics 2003b). In the e-Envoy report (e-Envoy 2003) it was also reported that regular Internet use had grown rapidly, rising to 56% of adults in 2003, a year-on-year increase of 5%. Some 61% of the adult population also reported that they had used the Internet at some time, so although the PC remains the most common way of accessing the Internet, recent years have also seen an increase in the expansion of the use of mobile phones and digital TV as a way of accessing the Internet. In 1999, just 2% of UK households had digital TV; today the figure is 44%, with the UK recognised as a world leader (Booz Allen Hamilton/INSEAD 2002).

Consumer broadband growth is also seen by the government as fuelling demand (e-Envoy 2003) for ICT. Low-cost, flat-rate Internet access and broadband access are leading to longer periods of time spent online: for example, an average of 10 hours a week online compared to six hours in the UK in May 2000. Other data (National Statistics 2003b) show that more than half of adults (53%) had used the Internet for buying tickets, goods and services. The most popular goods and services are shown in Figure 3.4.

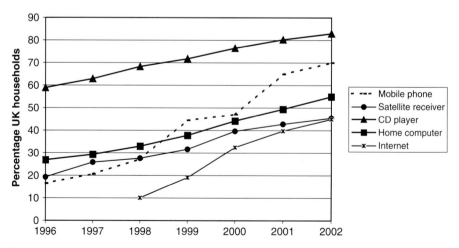

Figure 3.3   UK households with selected durables (data from National Statistics 2004).

Box 3.1   Mobile technologies

The use of mobile phones during the riots at the 1999 World Trade Organization meeting in Seattle showed the real potential for using mobile devices to co-ordinate political action, allowing activists to outwit the centralised radio system of the security forces. Text messaging was also instrumental in organising the public demonstrations that forced Philippine President Joseph Estrada from office in January 2001 (Harkin 2003).

New technologies are driving this activism, and today more than 90% of people aged 15–34 in the UK own or have used a mobile phone (National Statistics 2004). For example, 3G (third-generation) technology is one of a number of mobile technologies which provide locational flexibility for users (McCarthy & Miller 2003). 3G enables text, image, voice, video and music services to be delivered to a variety of portable devices including mobile phones. Other technologies include:

- WiFi (or 802.11b protocol), which allows users with compatible hardware to connect to a network without wired connections within a range of tens of metres; and
- Bluetooth, which is a standard used to allow any electronic device to communicate with others and make wireless connections over a range of approximately 10 metres.

Research by Harkin (2003) suggests that the 'location-awareness' of mobile technologies has immense ramifications for cities and their 'metabolisms'. Mobile technologies such as 3G enable us to say not only 'who' we are but also 'where' we are. These new location-based technologies have the potential to revolutionise the interactions and relationships between physical and information spaces; it is much easier now to access information about a place using these technologies when you are there. 'Hanging data' such as this is already being demonstrated by the London Tourist Board, and is likely to form the basis for conceptualising enhanced, 'connectivity hotspots'.

As Figure 3.4 shows, the most popular were travel, accommodation or holidays (52%), books/magazines (38%), tickets (36%) and music or CDs (34%). Excluding shares or financial services in the three months prior to interview, 40% of individuals had spent a total of £100 or less, but 24% spent a total of over £500 online.

But the way in which people adopt and adapt to this new technology is important to consider. Government policy and guidance, for example, have identified three critical barriers to the uptake of ICT: access, understanding and trust (Performance Innovation Unit 1999). Some consumers had frequently been unable to gain access; others did not understand the new technology, and others found it unsafe or unreliable. In reality, other barriers may be more important (Crabtree *et al.* 2002), and appropriateness and cost may also be critical issues to consider. This is shown by data from National Statistics (2003b), which revealed that the key barriers to Internet use included the fact that consumers preferred to shop in person (28%)

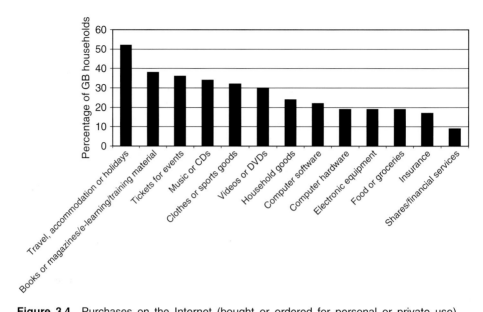

Figure 3.4 Purchases on the Internet (bought or ordered for personal or private use) October, 2003 (GB) (data from National Statistics 2003b).

or that they had security concerns over ordering (25%) or that they had no need (25%). The biggest barrier for not accessing the Internet by non-users was the perceived 'irrelevance' of the technology (Mansell & Nikolychuk 2002). 'Irrelevance' here seems to be associated with non-users' lack of interest: users have frequently reported being too old, not wanting to use it, or not having got round to it. Indeed, taking the argument further, Crabtree *et al.* (2002) suggest there is a mismatch between the 'need' perceived by governments for ICT and the lack of 'need' perceived by users.

One can also argue that if 46% of households have Internet access then 54% of households do not. Also, the most frequent Internet user is young, single and in a higher socio-economic grouping (Mansell & Nikolychuk 2002), and the least frequent user tends to be older and poorer. However, Internet access in the UK is available to much more than 46% of households through a combination of work and public access points. Research by the Oxford Internet Institute (2004) found that 96% of the population are aware of a place where they could get online. It also found that most people have Internet access in at least two out of four places: home, work, school or library. New work by Birkbeck College (e-Envoy 2003) also suggests that 99% of all households are within 10 km of a public access point, and this has been underpinned by a large government programme to develop 6000 UK online centres between 1999 and 2003 in a range of public access locations. So the Internet has become very much a pervasive technology.

The implications of this overview of Internet access statistics in the UK are twofold: first, that consumer demand for online has increased, and second, that consumers are using the Internet to buy a range of goods online. Taken further, if consumers start to move their custom away from conventional stores then this has ramifications for real estate use and demand. But it is important to note that the range of new technologies does not 'push' people into new ways of living (Crabtree *et al.* 2002): rather there is a technology 'pull' going on as people draw the technology into their lives based on their perceived needs. It is more accurate to think in terms of consumer 'clusters' of new technology users and Crabtree *et al.*'s research shows that three main groupings occur:

- **Enthusiasts**. This group represents 27% of the UK's population and have taken up technology enthusiastically.
- **Aversives**. Representing some 31% of the population, this group is not convinced by ICT and may be averse to using it.
- **Quiet pragmatists**. This group makes up the majority of UK users (42%) who see ICT in a practical way, using it as a tool.

Such a typology is helpful in explaining adoption of new technologies. If 'quiet pragmatists' prevail, this may explain the steady growth of new technologies in some sectors but resistance in others. What is clear is that consumers are certainly using mobile technology much more, and this increasing level of technology advance in the domestic sphere has led some to highlight the concept of smart home technology (Box 3.2),[3] although currently, applications such as this are some way short of wide-scale implementation.

Businesses

UK government policy has been designed to encourage ICT adoption (see Chapter 2). This led to targets for take-up of ICTs being developed in the government's 1998 Competitiveness White Paper, which set the overall policy aim of making the UK the best place in the world for eCommerce. The strategy to achieve this goal was then developed in the report, *Ecommerce@Its.Best.Uk* (Perfomance Innovation Unit 1999). From this, three specific targets were set:

- 1.5 million micro, small and medium-sized businesses going online by 2002;

Box 3.2   Smart home technology

The term 'smart home' was first used by the American Association of Housebuilders in 1984 (Harper 2003), although the first 'wired homes' were built in the 1960s. Aldrich (2003: 17) defines a smart home as 'a residence equipped with computing and information technology which anticipates and responds to the needs of the occupants, working to promote their comfort, convenience, security and entertainment through the management of technology within the home and connections to the world beyond'. Examples of smart home projects from around the world include The Adaptive House (University of Colorado); ComHouse (Interactive Institute, Sweden); and The Aware Home (Georgia Institute of Technology). As Barlow and Gann (1998) point out, the development of consumer electronics and electrical equipment systems, and communications equipment with wireless networks, have all contributed to the interest in the smart home concept (see also Chapter 7).

- 1 million micro, small and medium-sized businesses trading online by 2002; and
- the performance of the UK's micro and small businesses were to match the best in the world.

The government's first target was exceeded in 2000 (Booz Allen Hamilton 2003), but the other targets have proved more challenging, and the 2002 International Benchmarking Study (DTI 2002) suggested, for the first time, that there had been a marked slowdown in the uptake of ICT, and for some types of business, a reverse. Businesses are taking time to adopt a more strategic approach to ICT implementation, by considering how they can integrate the new technology into their overall processes. A watershed has apparently been reached, where the 'dash for access' has tailed off and the need to unlock value in businesses through ICT transformation has risen up the corporate agenda. In addition, the report identified the following themes:

- **More cost-focused approach to Internet access**. The demise of dot.coms, and a more competitive business environment, have led businesses to question the bottom-line impact of ICT. The Internet is not seen automatically as boosting revenues, and many smaller businesses are looking at the hard costs of web maintenance and some are even 'disconnecting'.
- **Emphasis on delivering business value**. After several years of heavy ICT investment, many firms are now taking a more considered, strategic view of how ICT can unlock value and transform business processes through supply chain efficiencies.

- **Smaller businesses are struggling with ICT**. In many respects, a clear digital divide has emerged at a firm level, with smaller and medium-sized enterprises lacking the scale and scope to buy into high-level broadband access (Figure 3.5). For example, only 45% and 69% of micro and small businesses were connected in 2003, compared with 90% medium and 98% large businesses.

Despite this, the 2003 survey also included signs of greater diffusion in ICT. The government view is that UK businesses are making more sophisticated use of ICT than ever before, and more are connected at higher speeds. Traditional barriers such as security and trust, skills shortages or lack of clarity over regulation are seen as reducing in importance. For example, in 2003, only 11% of UK businesses viewed regulation as a hindrance to ICT adoption. Reduced costs are a vital driver for ICT adoption in businesses: this was the most important factor for 42% of businesses (Figure 3.6), followed by improved customer communication (16%). As the figure also shows, 37% of those businesses citing this factor felt that they achieved this goal, and 5% did not.[4]

Data such as this can give an overview of the macro level but what is happening at a firm level? ICT is conventionally linked with four types of change (Nathan *et al.* 2003):

- New forms of work organisation and management structures inside firms.
- New work styles and workplaces for individuals, the employed and the self-employed.

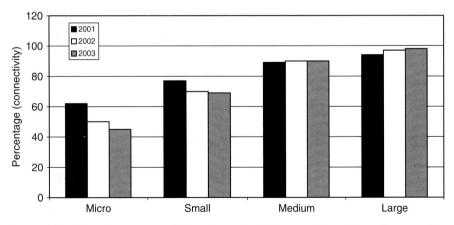

Figure 3.5 UK business connectivity by firm size (%) (adapted from Booz Allen Hamilton 2003).

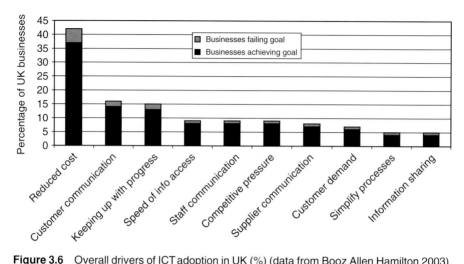

Figure 3.6   Overall drivers of ICT adoption in UK (%) (data from Booz Allen Hamilton 2003).

- New physical distribution of economic activity in industries, regions and sub-regions, countries and internationally.
- New forms of economic activity, such as ICT sector and business sectors dependent on ICT.

Sceptics tend to downplay these impacts, arguing that any effect is limited to key sectors, and that the nature of technological change is slow and uncertain. However, the use of ICT in UK industry has made substantial progress during the 1980s and 1990s. Research at a firm level in Britain by Felstead *et al.* (2002) has shown that in 2001 nearly 75% of employees in Britain used ICT at work, compared with less than half in 1986 (Figure 3.7). There has also been a marked increase in the proportion of jobs in which computing is considered to be an essential or very important component of the work: in 2001 some 55% of employees reported that ICT was essential or very important in their work.

Furthermore, the same study also showed that both ICT penetration and complexity of ICT use vary according to a person's occupation and by industry sector. For example, users of ICT are most concentrated among professionals, managers, associate professionals, and administrative and secretarial. Although personal service workers and unskilled workers tend to use ICT less, the growth in use over the period 1986–2001 has affected all sectors. Higher level occupations also tended to use ICT in more complex ways (i.e. analysis, design and modelling). Sectorally, ICT was found to be relevant to the jobs of more than 85% of employees in finance, public

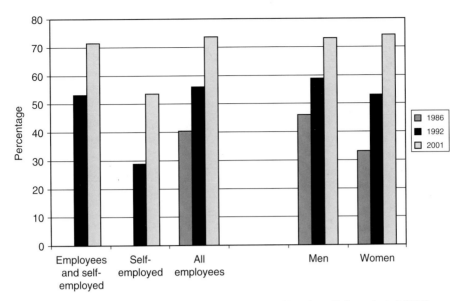

Figure 3.7   Users of new technology at work in Britain (data from Felstead *et al*. 2002).

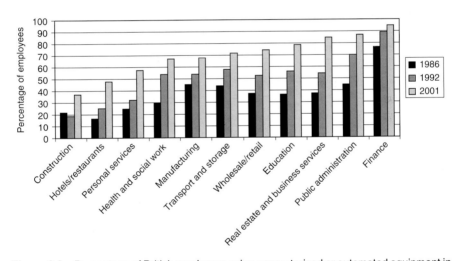

Figure 3.8   Percentage of British employers using computerised or automated equipment in their job by industry, 2001 (data from Felstead *et al*. 2002).

administration and real estate and business services (Figure 3.8), but in construction and hotels/restaurants it affected the work of less than half of employees. Real estate and business services also saw rapid increases in the level of technology since the 1980s, and the level of complexity of use in 2001 was again highest in real estate and business services in 2001 (43%).

This suggests that ICT has become a key technology in business. But how are organisations adopting to new technology, and how precisely is ICT impacting on business? These are important questions to address, given that the aggregate decisions of businesses shape the macroeconomic trends within a new economy.

New evidence (OECD 2003) on productivity gains[5] arising from ICT suggested that, during the late 1990s, productivity in the USA in key sectors (such as retail) had been improved by ICT. New research in the UK (London Economics/CISCO 2003) also suggests that productivity in the UK has been increased by ICT. Moreover, Oulton (2002) shows that ICT accounted for a quarter of the growth in UK labour productivity since 1989 and almost 50% since 1994. In total, ICT has contributed something like 20% of UK GDP growth between 1989 and 1998. Nonetheless, UK firms have tended to lag behind their US counterparts, by investing later.

Transition in any new technology is only to be expected, however, and there is growing evidence that productivity lags can be explained by 'people' factors, either the working practices in organisations or operating systems with poorly designed technology. In their analysis of growth and technological change in OECD countries, Bassanini & Scarpetta (2003), for example, suggest that the diffusion of a general-purpose technology is affected by institutional and related human capital issues, and involves much trial and error.

However, a more sceptical view of ICT within organisations in the UK is provided by Nathan *et al.* (2003). Their work, based on detailed ethnographic studies of eight companies for the Work Foundation's iSociety programme, suggests that UK firms are 'getting by, not getting on' and that a 'low tech equilibrium' may end up as the fate of many companies, which is frequently the result of unskilled users, poor management and disconnected IT teams. Often, organisations therefore do not use IT effectively, and do not reap productivity gains. However, when ICT is implemented well, it can create real value for organisations, delivering between five and seven times normal returns on investments. Nonetheless, they argue that style of management appears to have changed more as a result of ICT than the shape of organisations. The sceptical view is also promoted by Carr (2003), who argues that ICT investments are less likely to achieve a competitive edge now that ICT is so common. However, others such as Betcherman and McMullen (1998) and Murphy (2002) suggest that fundamental organisational change has occurred through structural changes brought about by changes in work process, innovative human resource sharing, new industrial relations practices, and new business practices, such as Total Quality Management, Enterprise Resource Planning, and Customer Relationship Management, all of which have been driven by ICT.

What is also clear is that organisational learning experiences are important to consider in explaining adoption in businesses. This means an emphasis on the 'softer', more human aspects of technology adaptation and adoption. For example, Brynjolfsson and Hitt (2002) found, in an examination of 527 US firms, that simply 'dropping' ICT into an organisation did not work. The firms that saw the greatest productivity increases were those that complemented ICT investment with organisational capital investments; this means altering business processes and organisation structure and creating innovations in customer and supplier relations. Nathan *et al.* (2003) confirm this view by arguing that understanding the firm's adoption of ICT requires an understanding of the 'social context' of ICT within a 'socio-technical' framework. Furthermore, they suggest that the firm must be seen as an 'organic entity', in which there is a complex set of relations between groups, individuals and teams, and where physical and social characteristics influence and are influenced by behaviour.

Understanding the 'ecology' of organisations (Nathan *et al.* 2003) and how these power relations are played out is very important therefore. In this sense, organisational change, and its interaction with ICT, bears close similarity with consumers and ICT: technology does not directly impact on society and simply push change; rather change is uncertain and discontinuous and society itself also pulls technology, with social, economic and political factors intervening and intertwining to determine the path(s) of transformation. Simplistic models, which deal with ICT in linear way, are therefore open to criticisms of determinism. Indeed, the 'e-adoption' ladder promulgated by the UK government is perhaps also open to criticism (Box 3.3). Therefore, as Chapters 1 and 2 of this book showed, understanding the context of ICT is vital if we are to understand how real estate patterns are also changing as a result. The theme of ICT and productivity change and the impact on real estate is examined in more detail in Chapter 5.

Government

The third main stakeholder group is government (central and local). The concept of eGovernment was originally developed as 'digital government' in the USA by the National Service Foundation in 1997, and this became re-branded as 'e-government' during the dot.com boom years, following

Box 3.3   The e-adoption ladder

There is general agreement that ICT was a key facilitator in the emergence of new organisational forms in the 1990s. For example, Davidow and Malone (1992) suggest that the virtual organisation has no clear physical form, and that it is defined and limited only by the availability of IT. Charles and Lever (1996) suggest that ICT can create 'dynamic flexibility' in organisations, where short-term flexibility is combined with wider productivity gains from product and process innovations. This is carried out through three main processes:

- As a productive force, through the application of ICT in improving production, administrative savings, higher quality and lower costs.
- As an interface with the market in which ICT captures market information and adjusts production levels.
- As an integrating force where ICT is used to link functions and productions in a managed supply chain.

As a result of such theoretical constructs, an adoption ladder (DTI 2001) has frequently been used in UK government policy to map the change of ICT from basic technology to more sophisticated use (Figure 3.9). So, as organisations evolve and change, they adopt more sophisticated technologies. This is said to be true of both SMEs and large companies, but such a view masks complexities and the role of cultural, social and other factors at a firm level. Moreover, technological change can be discontinuous, disruptive and chaotic rather than linear.

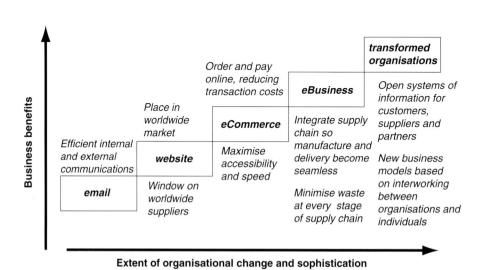

Figure 3.9   Model of e-adoption ladder (adapted from DTI 2001).

rapid growth in eCommerce and eBusiness methods. The first major eGovernment portals were developed in the UK, Australia, Singapore and Canada and from 1999 onwards the UK government began to link the development of eGovernment to a series of targets for online service delivery, for example stating that by 2005 all government services would be online.[6]

There is a growing amount of literature on the contribution of digital networks and services to democratic processes, and much interest focuses on the way governments interact across departments, as well as with businesses and citizens (see Mansell 2003, for example). In the UK, the seminal document *E.Gov: Electronic Government Services for the 21st Century* (Performance Innovation Unit 2000) highlighted the strategic importance of ICT in the provision of government services, which can be defined at three levels as:

- publishing: providing users with information
- interaction: allowing users to search for and obtain information based on criteria;
- transactions: allowing users to search for and purchase products and services and submit information to be processed.

Policy in this arena has therefore been driven by the recognition that the government has a key role to play in the provision of eGovernment services through public investment in infrastructure, encouraging enterprise and innovation in services and generally raising productivity in the public sector. eGovernment in this sense is defined as (EITO 2002: 288):

> The use of Internet technologies to conduct, enhance and support relations with, and transactions between, different government bodies and citizens, businesses and other government bodies.

However, eGovernment has also been taken to mean more widely webbased systems used in conjunction with other communication channels, for example, 'one-stop shops', telephone call centres and digital television services as well as the digitisation of internal government information, such as archives and accounts (EITO 2002). eGovernment can bring particular benefits to businesses who transact with governments electronically, leading to lower transaction costs, opportunities to re-engineer services, by creating costs savings and process improvements. In total spending terms, this is substantial in the EU member states: in 2002, for example, total public administration spending (i.e. central, regional and local government) was 28 bn euros, or nearly 50% of total public ICT expenditure. As with overall ICT spending, the markets in UK, Germany and France are the largest in Europe (EITO 2002) followed by Italy, Spain and the Netherlands (Figure 3.10). For example, Bastow *et al.* (2003) estimate that by 2006, the UK state will have spent around £6 bn on promoting eGovernment at central and local government levels since the launch of the national eGovernment strategy in late 1999. Expenditure on eGovernment is controlled by the Office of the eEnvoy (OeE), whose head reports to the Prime Minister, and estimates suggest that from 1999 to 2004, over £1 bn will be spent directly on eGovernment by this agency.

The emphasis on eGovernment by the current UK Labour government is driven by its twin reform agenda of the renewal of public services and delivering services electronically (Curthoys & Crabtree 2003). In political terms, therefore, new technology is seen by its advocates as a way of improving services, and enabling the improvement of government as a whole, where distrust in government generally and declining citizen participation are increasingly problematic. Indeed, Curthoys and Crabtree (2003) see the latest drive towards eGovernment (Table 3.2) as one of three major post-war realignments of public services (following nationalisation under Clement Atlee during the period 1945–1955 and privatisation under Margaret Thatcher during the period 1979–1990).[7]

In many respects, the UK has a strong track record in eGovernment, as evidenced by its level of ICT spending, and the UK was one of the first

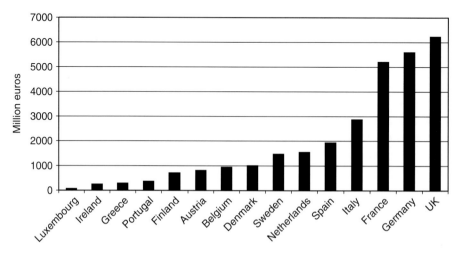

Figure 3.10 Total public administration ICT expenditure by EU member states: 2002 (data from EITO 2002).

Table 3.2 An eGovernment theory (adapted from Curthoys & Crabtree 2003).

	1945–1955	1979–1990	1997–present
Political leader	Atlee	Thatcher	Blair
Theorist	Keynes	Hayek/Friedman	Castells
Approach	Bureaucracy	New Public Management	eGovernment
Mechanism	Nationalisation	Privatisation	Various
Power shift	State centralisation	Market freedom State centralisation	Technological innovation, decentralisation
Purpose	Social security	Enterprise creation	Renewed public service

countries to dedicate substantial resources to establishing a centralised, high-level government unit for advancing ICT use (Office of E-energy), and a variety of government-to-business (G2B) services are now in place including: tax, company registration, statistical data submission, customs declaration and public procurement services (EITO 2003). In their International Benchmarking Study, for example, Booz Allen Hamilton (2003) suggest that although the most advanced eGovernments are in the USA, Canada, Sweden and Australia, the UK is seen as having strong eGovernment 'readiness'. The UK government's Gateway[8] is seen as a particularly good example of a secure interface which enables departments to offer services and use it as an 'authentication engine'. The project was launched in 2001 at a cost of £16 mn and five pilot projects were completed by the end of 2001.

However, Mansell and Nikolychuk (2002) suggest that evidence from Germany, Italy, Belgium and Finland shows that successful eGovernment projects are more likely to develop from small-scale innovations driven by local administrations, and that the more successful projects are developed in parallel with new regulations and policies. The learning curve for eGovernment may therefore be long, and it can be difficult to transfer knowledge between localities. It is also the case that ICT infrastructure is seen by policymakers as following an 'e-adoption' ladder pattern, as users move from an official website. If the e-adoption ladder is accepted as a model[9] then most governments, including the UK, are on the first steps of the ladder (National Audit Office (NAO) 2002).

Research by the National Audit Office (2002) also highlights two main issues if the benefits of eGovernment are to be achieved. First, citizen take-up needs to be encouraged because the public will really only interact with departments if they see real benefits in doing so. For example, in a supporting paper to the NAO research, Margetts and Dunleavy (2002) suggest that citizens' perceptions of departments colour their attitude to eGovernment, and therefore departments may need to provide access through alternative routes such as banks, building societies and post offices, where trust and experience have already built up. Second, supply-side issues are important (for example, the risk that departments may not provide the right services electronically or fail to take advantage of new technology). This may require a re-engineering of working methods, greater user focus, and better incentives for departments to switch to eGovernment delivery.

Moreover, the different culture of government also needs understanding if adoption and adaptation are to be clearly understood. Margetts and Dunleavy (2002) suggest that governments are, to a varying degree, different from other organisations. These differences are reflected in their size; lack of a 'bottom line' in terms of threat of bankruptcy; accountability; separation of policy and administration; public visibility; and monopoly of some functions. They suggest that these differences could lead to distinctive barriers in supplying eGovernment, and that some governments have adopted a negative attitude to eGovernment underpinned by 'technological myths' (Figure 3.11). Margetts and Dunleavy (2002) build on the work of Thompson *et al.* (1990), and suggest these myths comprise the following:

- **Technology benign**. This myth suggests the technological world is forgiving, and no matter what system 'knocks' are introduced, the 'ball' (conceptual shorthand for the 'system') will always return to an equilibrium state. Therefore, managing organisations can adopt a laissez-faire approach, which encourages trial and error.
- **Technology ephemeral**. This is the opposite of the first myth, and suggests that the technological world is very unforgiving and that the least jolt could trigger complete collapse. Thus the managing organisation must treat technology with great care, and this argument is used as a justification for resisting technological change modestly, and in a decentralised way.
- **Technology perverse/tolerant**. Here technology is forgiving in many ways, but is vulnerable to occasional knocks of the 'ball' over the rim of the 'saucer' (Figure 3.11). Managing institutions must therefore plan for unusual events, without the extremes of either 'experimentation' or 'tiptoe behaviour'. Technological expertise is therefore vital in planning, and the strong growth of the Private Finance Initiative in the 1980s and 1990s in UK government led many departments to strike up strong relationships with external ICT suppliers, and these relationships still continue to shape the context within which departments attempt to develop eGovernment.

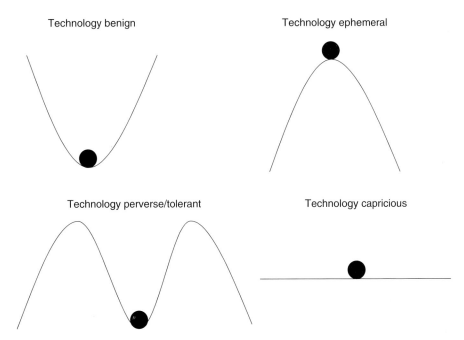

Figure 3.11   Technology myths (adapted from Margetts & Dunleavy 2002).

- **Technology capricious**. Here the world is random, and the ball can move anywhere, so that institutions cannot plan and must cope with erratic, technological events. For example, many UK NHS managers were scared off entering into ICT contracts in the 1990s after a series of high-profile failures, and the poor reputation at that time of NHS computing led to continuing problems.

Despite these issues, however, governments have come to realise the benefits of eGovernment. In the UK, the National Audit Office (National Audit Office 2002) lists these as:

- greater choice;
- improved accessibility;
- improved convenience;
- faster delivery; and,
- improved efficiency.

Cost reduction is an implicit thread in these benefits, and the England and Wales Land Registry initiative shows how cost per unit of work can be reduced (Box 3.4). Nonetheless, Curthoys and Crabtree (2003) adopt a fairly critical view of the concept of eGovernment in the UK. Arguing that eGovernment needs to refocus on reforming government generally, their research suggests that often there is a mismatch between citizen needs and state provision, underpinned by the digital divide issues already discussed in Chapter 2 of this book. Those most likely to need services may not have access, therefore. Often there is also a gap between capability and delivery so that local government, for example, which is delivering most services, may have insufficient resources to deliver eGovernment. Success stories are often overlooked, therefore, and there seems to be some strength in the argument that the 'e' needs to be removed from eGovernment to enable transformative change to occur across government as a whole.

Despite such criticisms, however, government continues to be a very powerful and important stakeholder in ICT transformation. Given that government at local and national level is also a major occupier of real estate, and has also been a major client in outsourcing projects during the 1990s in the UK, the changes brought about by government adoption of ICT also have important ramifications for the use and location of property. An example of the scale of government real estate use is provided by the Lyons Review of public sector relocation[10] (Lyons 2003, 2004). For example, some 230 000 civil servants and other national government workers are currently based in the South East region of the UK (Lyons 2003), and 52 government call centres (out of a total 206), are based in London and the South East. Labour and accommodation costs are also higher in this part of the country. But allied to this, as the Lyons report suggests, is the fact that

---

Box 3.4   England and Wales Land Registry (adapted from National
Audit Office 2002)

The Land Registry (http://www.landreg.gov.uk/) was established under the Land Registry Act 1862 (repealed by the Land Registration Act 2002, which came into force in October 2003). The Land Registry's main role is to provide a register of title to freehold and leasehold land throughout England and Wales. The website provides a range of information online, including property prices by geographical area; information on how to determine property ownership; and forms for lodging applications to register for land. The general public can therefore view computerised land registers, view details of pending applications and searches, and apply for copies of any register or search. Cost reductions have been achieved in real terms from £27 per unit to £22 per unit. The 2002 Act laid the foundations for 'electronic conveyancing' to be implemented, and streamlined the registration and conveyancing processes generally.

modern communication technologies and the government's developing agenda on devolution and regionalism have 'changed the debate about the geographical distribution of state activity' (Lyons 2003: 4). The interim report suggested that the relocation of up to 20 000 of these government workers is possible, and that departments should consider the opportunities for relocation that may arise in the context of joining up processes, and by exploiting ICT to streamline service delivery (in short, to consider process re-engineering). A report on the implications of the Lyons Review for regional development agencies by the CURDS (2004) also suggested that ICT is being used to underpin certain functional and locational configurations in government which include:

- a reduction in customer-focused local offices with remaining offices combining customer service and increased sales activities;
- removal of back-office functions to specialist sites involving relocation to large centres with high numbers of staff;
- development of specialist back-office functions (or 'shared service centres') brought together to serve national and international markets;
- creation of large specialist call centres to deal with customer queries, although 'multi-media contact centres' are supplementing call centres by using email and internet channels; and,
- development of 'virtual single offices' (call centres or back offices) using ICT to integrate sites in a semblance of single office mode.

The increasingly important role played by ICT is therefore recognised as a key driver and enabler of potential relocation[11] (see Box 3.5).

Internet-driven business activities: eBusiness, eCommerce and eWork

The development of the Internet, in conjunction with other factors, has transformed the way in which much of business and commerce is undertaken, as well as work practices, and this has had implications for consumers, businesses and governments. eBusiness is frequently used as a term to encapsulate the changes in business process, brought about by the web and the Internet. In this book we adopt the definition used by Digital Europe:[12]

> The eBusiness sector comprises companies which deliver digital technology products and services as a significant part of their core business or use digital technologies as their primary channel to market. eBusiness as a concept refers to

---

Box 3.5   Lyons Review: *Well Placed to Deliver? Shaping the Pattern of Government Service*

The business case for relocating government departments away from London and the South East is partly driven by cost issues (Lyons 2004). The review quotes work by Actium Consult (City University Business School 2002), which revealed that the average cost of a workstation in London was £13134 compared with an average outside London and the South East of £7934. The Lyons report (2004) cites the example of British Telecom, which began a programme of estate rationalisation and modernisation in 1993 to reduce the inefficiencies of maintaining its portfolio of property. Using flexible working and hot-desking enabled BT to reduce its London desk space by two-thirds and improve its absenteeism rate. Business continuity planning to cope with disasters was also flagged as an important issue in relocation from London. The example of the Department for International Development (DFID) was also highlighted. DFID had used ICT innovatively, with about 100 videoconference suites and half of those in the UK, with the rest overseas. The cost savings from this technology included £250 in air fares between London and Scottish offices and four hours of travelling time, together with further savings on overseas travel.

---

transactions using these technologies such as eWork, eCommerce and eGovernment.

In this sense, the term 'eWork' is a recent phenomenon (Fulton *et al.* 2001). The European Commission replaced the term 'telework' with 'eWork', following the European Commission report (2000) on telework in which eWork was defined as:

> All work enabled or supported by ICTs, in which individuals become simultaneously both more independent (by being responsible for planning their own work and time, and for balancing work and private life), and more dependent (upon management and colleagues) through team and group work where trust and cooperation are necessary.

eBusiness is therefore a wider concept than eCommerce, and the term incorporates eCommerce as one of a number of related, transaction processes.[13] eCommerce, or electronic commerce, on the other hand, is the buying and selling of goods and services on the Internet, especially the World Wide Web (Percival-Straunik 2001). The term has evolved from a fairly limited notion to mean all aspects of business and market processes enabled by these technologies. The web's impact is global, and affects processing within businesses, between businesses, and between businesses and consumers. The UK Cabinet Office (Performance Innovation Unit 1999) defines eCommerce more formally as:

> The exchange of information across electronic networks, at any stage in the supply chain, whether within an organisation, between businesses, between businesses and consumers, or between the public and private sectors.

The OECD (2002: 89)[14] distinguishes transactions carried out over computer-mediated networks (the 'broad definition of ecommerce') and those carried out just over the Internet (the 'narrow definition'). Both definitions, however, stress the transactional nature of eCommerce as being the 'sale of goods and services between businesses, households, individuals, governments, and other public or private organisations'.

eCommerce can be further subdivided into a matrix (see Table 2.3 in Chapter 2). For example, the largest amount of trade online tends to be business to business, typically for suppliers such as Ford or General Electric. Most commentators believe this category (B2B) will continue to dwarf B2C trade in the foreseeable future (College of Estate Management 2001). The other three sectors (excluding government commerce) are as follows:

- B2C, or business to consumer, including online 'etailers', such as Amazon and Gap;
- C2B, or consumer to business, where consumers bid for goods and services, leaving the company to decide on which bid to accept (for example, eBay); and
- C2C, or consumer to consumer, where consumers get together to participate in auctions of goods.

In terms of consumer benefits, the two key advantages of the web are ease of price comparison, allied with greater choice (College of Estate Management 2001). The former has been made even easier with the development of price agents on the web, which can compare prices so consumers, businesses and governments have much greater negotiating power. However, although the web's reach is global, in retail terms, it is not as good at:

- reproducing the social function of shopping, for example;
- producing 'serendipity' or impulse purchases that could come from a shopping visit; and,
- providing the instant 'buzz' that many shoppers expect.

Furthermore, the web seems to work better at replacement purchases than for new purchases. It also seems to work less well for goods that are 'high touch' (for example, clothes and shoes) than for those that are 'low touch' (for example, computers, CDs and books). In general, low-touch items have tended to dominate web sales so far in eCommerce terms. De Kare-Silver

(2000) used an 'Electronic Shopping' (or ES) test to provide a simple guide as to which products can be readily sold on the web. The three steps in the test are:

- product characteristics: the innate set of characteristics that appeals to the consumer's senses through sight, sound, smell, taste and touch;
- familiarity and confidence: the degree to which the consumer recognises and trusts the product, has tried it before and is confident about repurchasing it (i.e. branding);
- consumer attributes: the underlying motivations and attributes towards shopping of consumers (i.e. receptive or not to electronic shopping).

He suggests that books, household goods, insurance and banking all have a high ES potential.

This section now draws out the key activities of eBusiness, eCommerce and eWork by examining the size of the markets and their characteristics, previewing their importance for real estate.

eBusiness

Examples of typical business processes that can be carried out in electronic form include customer support, marketing, advertising and public relations, recruitment of new employees, information resource sharing among employees, strategic and tactical planning, distributed inventory control functions, payroll and benefits management (European Commission 2003). In fact, these tend to address such processes as quality, flexibility and availability, rather than involving direct buying and selling. The role of the Internet is seminal in acting as a support medium for a variety of practices, including supply chain management and online procurement, and Kling and Tilquist (2000) refer to eBusiness processes as 'ICT-enabled organisational change'. Table 3.3 provides some key examples of eBusiness processes.

Research by e-BusinessW@tch (2003) shows that particular sectors across Europe (EU) use ICT in eBusiness in different ways, and therefore are at different stages of evolution. For example, the sector that makes the most intensive use of ICT and eBusiness applications is, not surprisingly, the ICT sector itself (Table 3.4). 'eIntensive' sectors include financial services, which have made substantial investments in ICT networks and deal with large numbers of customers, often making intensive use of CRM software. Internal processes (such as handling insurance claims) are

Table 3.3 Examples of key eBusiness processes (adapted from European Commission 2003).

Process	Summary
Enterprise resource planning (ERP) or enterprise systems	Consists of a software package using database technology to control all company information (including customer, supplier, product, employee and financial data). Connects organisation and customers across product lifecycle. Can lead to flatter organisations but with more centralised control over data
Supply chain management (SCM)	Linked to ERP, SCM covers all aspects of corporate supply chain from raw materials production to customer relations
Customer relationship management (CRM)	Linked to ERP, CRM provides companies with better knowledge not only of their customers but also individual relationships with the customer base
eProcurement and eMarketplaces	eProcurement provides information on goods and services to company personnel. Many eProcurement systems are linked to ERP systems. Includes B2B auctions and market exchanges. A key benefit is reduction in transaction costs. eMarketplaces are digital meeting places that provide aggregation of buyers and suppliers and facilitation of transactions

Table 3.4 Typology of sectors according to 'e-proximity' (adapted from European Commission 2003).

e-champions	e-intensive	e-specific	Late e-adopters
ICT services	Electrical machinery and electronics	Tourism	Transport equipment
	Banking/leasing	Real estate	Metal products
	Insurance and pension funds	Machinery and equipment	Food, beverages and tobacco
	Media and printing	Chemical industries	Retail
	Business services		Health and social services

another important ICT application area where potential cost savings are substantial.

Real estate services[15] provide an interesting example of an 'e-specific' sector (Box 3.6). As with tourism, the Internet is an increasingly important marketing channel, which can inform customers about potential offers. Property, however, is still not typically 'sold' online, although moves towards electronic conveyancing (see Box 3.4 and Chapter 8) are making this more likely. In the real estate sector, about one third of enterprises

---

Box 3.6 Real estate services (adapted from e-BusinessW@tch 2003)

The real estate sector in the EU comprises more than 750 000 companies, employing 1.7 mn, or 1% of total EU employment. Sweden, Denmark and the UK have higher than average numbers of real estate employees, in a sector characterised by a high number of small companies (75% are self-employed single person companies, compared with an average of 50% in the service sector). Some 98% of companies in the sector have less than 10 employees. A lack of information transparency pervades the real estate service sector and therefore ICT has potential benefits in terms of greater information on prices, financial services and legal information. ICT innovation in the sector has lagged behind other sectors because of heterogeneous products, high transaction volumes and long innovation cycles. Barriers to ICT include lack of Internet access, security issues and compatibility issues. Specialist uses of ICT are low in the sector, such as Intranet and Wide Area Networks (WAN), and SMEs frequently lag behind larger companies in the introduction of ICT. However, there are potential benefits in SME growth in this sector through further Internet adoption to reach a wider customer base at low marginal cost.

---

across Europe (EU) believed that eBusiness had changed organisational structure, internal work processes, customer relationships and the offer of products and services (e-BusinessW@tch 2003). Research by the European Commission (2003) on the same data found that for large businesses across Europe, in all sectors, changes in organisational structure and changes in internal work processes were closely associated with one another. This suggests that eBusiness does tend to change organisational structure, responsibilities and internal power structures simultaneously.

Importantly, more than 50% of all EU companies in the survey (e-BusinessW@tch 2003) said that eBusiness constituted a 'significant part' or 'some part' of the way they operated. Again, the impact is perceived as highest in those sectors such as manufacturing or operating IT and electronics, and in sectors with a high potential for digitisation of service delivery (publishing and business services) (see Table 3.4).

eCommerce

As Percival-Straunik (2001) points out, eCommerce is nothing new. The origins of eCommerce date back some 30 years and are based in Electronic Data Interchange (EDI), a standardised way of exchanging data between companies in the trucking industry in the 1970s, and subsequently in food and car manufacturing, which in simple terms involved automating purchasing. However, EDI suffered from flexibility problems and the Internet, with its low cost, ubiquity and global reach, allowed eCommerce to flourish and surpass EDI. Research by the OECD (1999) showed that eCommerce can impact on social and economic structures in five main ways:

- **Transformation of marketplace**: intermediary functions are threatened and with the development of new markets and products, new relationships are built between buyers and sellers. Costs are reduced (Table 3.5).
- **Catalytic effect**: increases existing changes already underway in the economy, such as regulatory reforms, globalisation of economic activity, and increases in demand for high-skilled, knowledge workers. Travel and banking, which are experiencing structural changes, are also transformed by the impact of eCommerce.
- **Interactivity effect**: increased linkages extend to small businesses and households, and reach out to the wider world.
- **Promotion of openness and transparency**: the economic power that stems from the promotion of an open network is substantial, and consumer power has therefore increased as a result of eCommerce and the Internet.
- **Time-shift effect**: eCommerce helps to reduce the importance of time by speeding up production cycles and allowing firms to collaborate more effectively, as well as allowing markets to operate 24-7. As the role of time changes, so the structure of business and social activities changes.

However, as the e-BusinessW@tch (2003) survey points out, from the demand side perspective, eCommerce is still more substantial in overall size in the USA than in Europe. A SIBIS (2003) project, for example, found that on average some 20% of the EU population said they had bought goods or services online: only Denmark, Sweden and the UK, however, where already about 50% of the population does so, came close to the USA figure of some 58%. Moreover, the percentage of regular users was much higher in the USA than in Europe. Cultural differences can explain these findings, together with the fact that the USA adopted Internet technology earlier than Europe (Dixon & Marston 2002).

Table 3.5 eCommerce impact on various distribution costs (US$/transaction) (adapted from OECD 1999).

	Airline tickets	Banking	Bill payment	Term life insurance policy	Software distribution
Traditional	8.0	1.08	2.22–3.32	400–700	15.00
Telephone-based	–	0.54	–	–	5.00
Internet-based	1.0	0.13	0.65–1.10	200–350	0.20–0.50
Savings (%)	87	89	67–71	50	97–99

As a result, the UK's current position in the eCommerce league has also come under close scrutiny. For example, the DTI commissioned MORI in 2001 to carry out a survey which would better inform consumers about eCommerce (DTI/MORI 2001). Based on MORI's omnibus survey, the sample comprised 2013 adults and the survey found that the level of 'e-shopping' is strongly related to Internet access, and that some 26% of the population are e-shoppers (i.e. have bought something on the Internet over the last 12 months). Those on higher incomes, for example, are most likely to be existing and likely e-shoppers, and tend to be Internet users, in social grades AB and broadsheet readers. At the other end of the spectrum, those without Internet, aged 55 or over, in social grades DE or without a credit card are least likely to be e-shoppers. The survey also found that, despite perceived advantages of convenience, saving time and less queuing, 40% of population see the disadvantage of e-shopping to be credit card fraud, giving out personal information and the fact that you cannot see or touch what you are buying.

Other research suggests, however, that 'silver surfers' are the most rapidly growing group of net users in the UK. The number of people aged 55 and over using the Internet in the UK grew by nearly 90% from 2003 to 2004, according to a survey from net measurement firm Netvalue.[16] Two million older people are logging on to the net, accounting for 13% of the total population, and only Sweden and Denmark have a higher proportion of such users in Europe. Online banking is particularly popular, with more than 40% of UK users in this category banking this way. Spare time and home-based access are key drivers in this group.

In terms of market size, data from National Statistics (2003c) in the UK suggest that in 2002 non-financial sector businesses received orders over the Internet worth £23.3 bn, which represents about 1.2% of total sales by the same sectors in the economy as a whole. Of this total, some £6.4 bn was from households, with £16.9 bn from businesses. However, this total includes all non-financial sectors, and not simply retail activities alone. Unofficial data from Verdict (2002) estimated that UK online retail sales (excluding travel and tickets) were worth £3.3 bn in 2002, equivalent to 1.4%. This compares with data from the USA for 2002 (US Department of Commerce 2003), which shows that US online sales during 2002 were worth the equivalent of £24.4 bn ($43.5 bn) or 1.4% of retail sales. So although the proportion of online sales during this period is broadly comparable in sheer volume terms, the USA is much larger than the UK in absolute terms.

For all UK businesses within countries in the 2002 DTI Benchmark Survey, online sales accounted for between 15% and 20% of turnover, although more recent data (Booz Allen Hamilton 2003) have shown a slowing down in eCommerce growth. Furthermore, the B2B market continues to dominate the B2C market: in 2000, for example, B2B accounted for only 0.06% of GDP in the UK and 0.12% in the USA, and B2C was itself only 13–14% of the size of B2C in a range of countries. Nonetheless, more and more businesses are placing orders online, and this frequently reflects sector differences in countries (Figure 3.12). For example, electronics, media and manufacturing are suited to online commerce, and a high percentage of businesses are already online. Paying online, however, is less common than ordering online: in the UK roughly 17% of businesses allow customers to pay online, compared with 30% allowing customers to order online. The ability to carry out B2B transactions is often restricted by the need to employ electronic data interchange (EDI) or, for smaller businesses, online banking or money transfers, although online buying produces structural benefits for buyers through price transparency and comparability, and the reduction of switching costs (i.e. increasing the standardisation of supply chains and redefining existing supplier relationships).

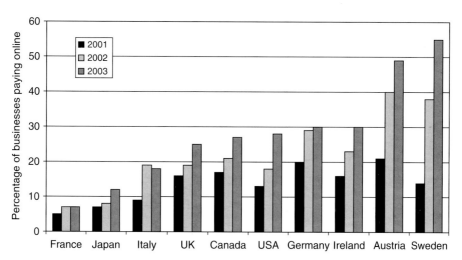

Figure 3.12 Percentage of businesses paying online: 2001–2003 (data from Booz Allen Hamilton 2003).

eWork

To a large extent, the workplace has always been defined by technology. Just as the physical dimensions of the factory are defined by the manufacturing process, so the shape and style of the office are defined by the tools used, and the need to communicate between them (see, for example, Duffy 1997). The fundamental change that has taken place over the last decade is that technology has freed work from some of the consequences of place. With modern networking and information systems it is seldom necessary from the perspective of the work alone to co-locate employees, however desirable it may be socially or managerially (Dixon *et al.* 2002).

The concept of 'virtual workgroups' (Shapiro 1999) has therefore become a practical reality. Virtual workgroups are different from other forms of workgroups because the work is conducted online and the members of the workgroup might either seldom meet face to face or not know one another at all. Many, particularly international, companies now use collaborative software products, so-called 'groupware', such as Lotus Notes, to manage and implement daily tasks.

During the 1990s MIT also examined the impact of ICT on organisations. This research, which built on Zuboff (1988), found that ICT presented four implications for organisations:

- it enabled fundamental changes in the way in which work was done;
- it caused a disintegration of traditional organisational forms;
- it enabled the integration of business functions at all levels within and between organisations; and
- it presented new strategic opportunities for organisations that reassess their missions and operations.

FLEXCOT (2000) point out that much of this literature sees the introduction of ICT as unproblematical, but that much of the research is too 'technicist' or 'technologically determinist'. Organisations do have a political structure and the introduction of ICT requires key roles to be played by the main stakeholders. Moreover, in some instances, the introduction of ICT can constrain institutional change.

What is clear, however, is the strong relationship that exists between ICT, workplace organisation, and output characteristics. In more empirically based work, Bresnahan *et al.* (2000) point out that much of the available case study literature shows that ICT changes authority relationships, decentralises decisions, shifts task content, and changes reward schemes.

Moreover, their empirical work on US companies suggests that it is the combination of increased labour force skills, promotion of education, and greater use of delegated decision making within firms that increases the value of ICT investment. In further work, Brynjolfsson and Hitt (2002) argue that a significant component of the value of ICT is its ability to enable complementary organisational investments, such as business processes and work practices. Such investments lead to potential productivity increases, by reducing costs and enabling firms to increase output quality through new products or other improvements, such as convenience, timeliness, quality and variety.

Telecommunications and computers have been available now for many years, and the emergence of multimedia and the World Wide Web has started to transform work practices. The delocalisation of traditional company locations, brought about by ICT, has led to a range of terms coined for the type of work it promotes. Examples include 'telecommuting', 'flexiplace', 'telework', 'remote work', 'networking', 'digital nomadic work', 'electronic homeworking', and many more.

The general term 'telework' (Box 3.7) first appeared in the mid-1970s as a potential answer to the energy crisis through promoting a reduction in travel to and from work (Nilles *et al.* 1976). In the USA it was branded 'telecommuting'. Research was targeted at the policymaking process as a radical alternative to problems such as traffic congestion and the increasing peripheralisation of economic communities away from the main centres of population and employment. Telework would, it was suggested, allow work to become dispersed, reducing the need to travel (see, for example, Levin 1998). The idea was embodied in the idea of an *electronic cottage* (Toffler 1980), which was seen as the antithesis of the centralisation of function apparent in the industrialised world, using technology to facilitate the integration of work, family and community. A more rounded version of the telework principle appears in late 1980s literature (Kinsmann 1987; Huws *et al.* 1990). By this stage, the idea had been refined into a means of flexible working, which addressed the need to balance family and working life. The role of telework in the improvement of productivity is more recent, with a focus on its role in workplace design (Becker & Steele 1995).

The term favoured by the European Commission and a number of agencies is 'eWork', and this refers to any type of work which involves the digital processing of information and which uses a telecommunications link for receipt or delivery of the work to a remote employer or business client. The emphasis here is on the remote link with the employing body or

---

Box 3.7   Teleworking in the UK

The UK remains the only country which accurately tracks the development of tele-working[17] annually in its Labour Force Survey. In spring 2001, some 2.2 million people worked at, or from, home in the UK for at least one full day per week in their main job, using a computer and telephone (Hotopp 2002). This represents 7.4% of the workforce, compared with 5.5% in 2000. Of these teleworkers, 1.8 million could not perform their job without the use of both a computer and telephone. About two-thirds of all UK teleworkers are men, compared with just over half of all employees. This is because a high proportion are self-employed males. Approximately 75% of all teleworkers in the UK are in the private sector and about 25% work in real estate, renting and business activities. International comparisons show that teleworking in the UK is just above the European average, with Finland having the highest number of teleworkers. EMERGENCE research supports the view that telework (or eWork) is increasing across Europe but the project focused on larger companies. On the other hand, research by ECATT (2000) showed that the penetration of eWork in Europe is distinctly patchy with just 15% of companies using eWorking, 28% in establishments of 10–49 and 73% of companies with 500 or more employees. However, research by Mitel (2000) shows that teleworking is now quite widely adopted in UK companies. Some 59% of the top 1000 companies and 36% of SMEs use teleworking to some degree. One of the key factors restraining further growth, however, is the lack of company policy. In many companies, it simply does not get onto the boardroom agenda. Teleworking is examined in more detail in Chapter 6.

---

business client (Huws & O'Regan 2001; Huws 2001). The definition does not include work that involves dealing with the general public by tele-phone or email (such as call centre work) unless this work also happens to involve the transmission of work over a telecommunications link to a remote employer or business client (for example, an outsourced call centre).

This definition is, of course, very broad and covers a wide range of employ-ment. eWork could also be broken down by occupation, skill, qualifica-tion, or the type of remote workplace involved. The EMERGENCE project,[18] which tracks and benchmarks eWork in the EU, provides a useful conceptual framework for classifying different forms of delocalised work (Table 3.6).

This shows the importance of the legal distinction between work carried out internally (i.e. employees working direct under contract for an organ-isation) and outsourced work, carried out under a contract for the supply of services. A distinction is also made between work carried out on shared premises and work carried out away from 'office' premises. Such workers may be working from home (wholly or partially) or working nomadically from a range of locations.

Table 3.6   Typology of work delocalisation (adapted from Huws 2001).

Type of workplace	Contractual internal/ employees	Outsourced
Individualised (away from 'office' premises) On shared 'office' premises	Employed tele-homeworkers Mobile employees Remote back offices/call centres Employees working in telecottages or other third party premises	Freelance teleworkers or mobile workers Outsourced call centres

Although such a typology is rough and ready it does highlight the choices available to employers as to how they can mobilise the various business services they require. EMERGENCE have therefore developed a ninefold categorisation of eWork:

- Fully home-based working by employees.
- Multi-locational or nomadic working by employees.
- Freelance work carried on away from the premises.
- Remote work carried out in remote back offices, which are not call centres.
- Work by employees carried out in remote in-house call centres.
- Work carried out by employees in telecottages or other remote third party centres which are not call centres.
- Work carried out by employees in telecottages or other remote third party premises which are call centres.
- Work outsourced to business service suppliers which are not call centres.
- Work outsourced to call centres.

The generic business functions carried out in eWork comprise such categories as sales, customer service, data processing, creative/content work (such as R&D), software development, accounting and general management. When combined with the nine categories above, 63 types of eWork are possible.

It is important to note that like many other technology-driven phenomena, eWork is not an isolated event. In its traditional form eWork is one of a number of options that organisations can choose from to adapt to changing circumstances (e.g. market conditions), and individuals can also choose from balancing their working life and personal preferences or obligations. Also many of the major characteristics of eWork (freedom from some of the time–space restrictions that constrain work) are already being integrated in other kinds of work.

Moreover, from a broader perspective, eWork can be seen as one of a number of developments in the way in which paid work is organised. The extent to which this flexibility benefits the employer or employee is subject to negotiation. What is changing is the traditional, post-war work paradigm (ECATT 2000), which consisted of:

- permanent employment with a contract of employment;
- 'life-time' employment;
- standardised working hours ('9 to 5');
- full-time employment;
- state-provided social security provisions;
- workplaces co-located in centralised buildings; and
- strong intra-organisational co-operation based on face-to-face meetings, with external contacts limited to certain gateways.

Changes in the economic environment, together with shifts in social attitude and the impact of ICT, have therefore led to a '21st century Work Paradigm', characterised by:

- spatial dislocation;
- self-employment;
- greater diversity and flexibility in working time patterns; and,
- stronger external boundary co-operation.

This paradigm shift is shown in Table 3.7. The new paradigm is broader than the post-war paradigm as it covers a much wider spectrum of ways of working. However, traditional work practices continue to exist and remain at the core of the labour market, but they are likely to be just one of a number of work patterns that exist in the future.

Table 3.7 Change in work paradigm (adapted from ECATT 2000).

	Post-war paradigm	21st century work paradigm
Time	9-to-5	Flexible
Place	Co-location	Dislocation
Co-operation	Intra-organisational	Trans-organisational
Contract	Employed	Self-employed

Some implications of ICT adoption for real estate

Clearly, the adoption of ICT by consumers, businesses and governments (as our three main stakeholder groups) has helped drive the process changes brought about by eBusiness, eCommerce, and eWork. In turn, these processes will also interact with other social, economic and political factors to influence the demand and use of real estate within cities and urban areas.

In business and commerce terms, the transformational nature of ICT is largely influenced by the nature of the product or service under consideration. This theme has also been explored by Leamer and Storper (2001) in a spatial context. They categorise processes according to the character of the information needed to use them (Table 3.8). For example, mass-produced, standardised products can be codified and shipped separately from the product in the form of specifications, blueprints, standards and so on. This therefore allows geographical distance between buyer and seller. However, if the product is non-standardised it cannot be so easily expressed in a codifiable form: the principal way of verifying the product's qualities is then by touching, feeling or knowing the product. This leads to a much more market-centred focus to the product and thus geographic proximity is important. The Internet has the power to shift these relationships and can lead to both increased 'clustering' and increased 'dispersion' through:

- increases in product variety;
- increases in the fineness of division of labour, or roundaboutness, which is the number of intermediate steps to produce a final output; and

Table 3.8 Messages, transactions and location of standardised and specialised products (adapted from Leamer & Storper 2001).

	Mass-produced standardised products	Specialised, customised and innovative products
Messages	Codified, transparent	Tacit
Degree of intermediate transacting	Low (high scope economies)	High (low scope economies, high roundaboutness)
Degree of agglomeration of supply chain	Remote/low aggregation	Market centred/ agglomerated
Location of production/distribution in relation to markets	Remote	Indeterminate
Examples	Dispersal: consumer banking and finance	Agglomeration: design-driven retail

- the automation of intermediation/co-ordination tasks (disintermedia-tion).

Leamer and Storper (2001) suggest that the ways in which a new ICT, such as the Internet, interacts with production and its geography will be many and varied, and there will be no single business model that is created, but rather complex feedbacks to specialisation and divisions of labour in different sectors will occur. The exact geographies of new mass variety sectors such as designer retail, consumer-driven manufacturing and parts, new consumer services (customised take-out food, Internet-ordered home repair) and knowledge inputs to production will be deter-mined by whether the input–output relations are 'conversations' or 'hand-shakes'. Sectorally, we would therefore expect to see greater changes in businesses associated with the greatest level of ICT adoption, in terms of business/process change, or in terms of the type of product sold (for example, travel, financial services, the ICT sector itself and some retail trades (such as books and CDs).

Kellerman (2002) provides an interesting perspective on the Internet indus-try, comprising production, packaging, authorisation and distribution, in terms of the web-based information industry and encompassing the information production and content industry. He shows that although cities can be ranked in terms of their Internet connectivity (see also Malecki 2002), there is a clear concentration of Internet information in-dustries within the world's top 'global cities', and new types of Internet facilities (e.g. co-location centres and server centres), providing switching facilities (and requiring real estate space), have been developed to cater for the infrastructure needed.

Similarly, changing patterns of work and the trends towards technology adoption by businesses and their employees have changed the profile of demand for buildings. A decade ago there was much focus upon the provi-sion of buildings, particularly in the financial centres, with huge open-plan trading floors to facilitate open outcry trading. Since those systems have been superseded by online trading systems, these trading floors are being converted back into more conventional space. Even within the same envelope, technology has made the use of that space potentially far more efficient by breaking the link between an individual workstation and its function. This has led to new methods of organisation based around transient project or product teams which come together for limited periods of time, determined by the needs of the situation, and then split up again (Dixon *et al.* 2002).

Most studies of the potential impacts of teleworking assume the notion that work has to be based in a physical location, be it the central office or the remote home. With the advent of third-generation (3G) mobile tele-communications, however, even this assumption may be proved false for some types of work. The ability of 3G to provide high bandwidth connections to mobile devices and to identify pretty exact spatial co-ordinates will facilitate genuinely mobile work. It is unlikely to generate many new forms but where there is an element of mobility inherent in a particular function it will allow more efficient use of resources. It is also likely to add to the flexibility with which specific locations can be used. To an extent, even teleworking is subject to the tyranny of tethered applications (Dixon *et al.* 2002). Computers tend to be attached to the power and the phone socket, but neither of these fixed facilities is strictly necessary so potentially the use of space becomes much more adaptable.

Potentially, the growth of telework has significant implications for the way that buildings are used, their location and their value. Using the Huws (2001) definition of eWork, the EMERGENCE study of European employers (Huws & O'Regan 2001) shows the actual participation in teleworking across Europe is much higher than the official figures show, with 49% of all employers using eWork to some degree (Table 3.9). The study also gives a great deal of insight into the structure of eWork. The stereotypical

Table 3.9   eWork (adapted from Huws & O'Regan 2001).

Any eWork	49.0
Within the organisation	
Any eEmployees	11.8
Employees working in remote back offices	6.8
Multi-locational teleworking employees	9.9
Home-based teleworking employees	1.4
Remote call centre in company-owned back office (outside own region)	1.4
Employees working in telecentres, telecottages or other office premises owned by third parties	0.9
Call centre employees in telecottage or telecentre	0.3
Outsourced	
Any eOutsourcing (outsourcing using a telecoms link to deliver work)	43.0
eLancers (freelancers using telecoms link to deliver work)	11.4
eOutsourcing within own region	34.5
eOutsourcing to other region in own country	18.3
eOutsourcing to companies in other countries	5.3
Outsourced call centre	15.0
Outsourced call centre with telecoms link	11.1

Note: Weighted figures; % of establishments with >50 employees in EU (15) plus Hungary, Poland and Czech Republic. Weighted base: 7305 cases employee teleworker based solely at home is in fact one of the least popular forms of eWork. Only 1.5% of establishments in Europe employ people to work exclusively from home in this way. It is much more common to use the new technologies to support multi-locational tele-working by employees, which is practised by approximately one European employer in ten. Some 6.8% of employers have a back office in another region in which its own employees are based. However, less than 1% of establishments make use of telecentres or other remote office premises owned by third parties as workplaces for their remote employees.

These forms of in-house teleworking are heavily outweighed by the use of eOutsourcing as a mechanism for carrying work out remotely. Over half of all establishments (56%) outsource at least one business service (Huws & O'Regan 2001). Restricting the definition only to those that use electronic means of delivery shows that 43% of employers make use of this practice. Much of this eOutsourcing is carried out within the region where the employer is based (34.5%) but substantial numbers (18.3%) outsource to other regions within the same country, whilst 5.3% outsource outside their national borders. Just over 17% of employers use freelancers to deliver some form of information service. When the definition is tightened to include only work involving delivery over a telecommunications link, this drops to 11.4%.

Finally, call centres make up a significant proportion of eWork. Whilst only 1.4% of respondents had an in-house remote call centre (outside their own region with a direct telecommunications link) no fewer than 15% use an outsourced call centre. For 11.1% of establishments, this involves a direct telecommunications link to the main office.

Despite the vagaries of what constitutes a 'region', this spatial dispersion of work cannot but have implications for the existing hierarchy of office centres. An examination of the most important destinations for eWork in the same study suggests a clustering effect, whereby regions build a crit-ical mass on their past reputation for excellence in a given field by attracting more talent and investment in the field, which in turn feeds a continuing cycle of growth. The EMERGENCE study[19] shows that, des-pite the publicity given to the practice of relocating or outsourcing eWork to non-European destinations such as India or the Caribbean, this is strongly outweighed, numerically speaking, by cases where work is re-located with Europe, although recent high-profile cases in India and the Far East have increased fears for call centres in the UK (see, for example, Deloitte Research 2003).

Summary

This chapter has showed how important it is to consider the role of our three key stakeholder groups in the process of technological change. These groups comprise consumers, businesses and governments. Each group has its own set of drivers and barriers, which shape the outcomes of ICT adoption and adaptation. In real estate terms each plays their role in the cycle of real estate investment and development and also in the production/consumption cycle of business and service provision. Understanding how they adopt and adapt to ICT is therefore vital in understanding how real estate patterns are changing as a result of ICT.

Frequently, linear models have been used to sketch out the policy imperative of moving these three groups online in policy terms (see, for example, the UK's 'e-adoption' ladder). However, as was indicated in earlier chapters, such simplistic models ignore key social and economic drivers, as well as cultural factors shaping technology change.

The rise of the Internet and the increased diffusion of ICT within businesses, households and governments has led to the development of three key technology-driven activities: eBusiness, eCommerce and eWork. These activities are growing in importance from a relatively small base, and are shaping real estate functions in a variety of industry sectors. The impact, however, is a differential one and much is dependent on the nature of the sector in question, its level of ICT adoption by key stakeholders and the type of good or service provided.

Furthermore, as we have seen, the impact on real estate also varies, and ICT cannot be treated in isolation from other key structural factors transforming real estate patterns. This chapter has, in part, covered some of the key implications of technological change at an industry level. The next chapter looks in more detail at business process change at an individual firm level and how this impacts on real estate decisions.

Notes

1   See Figure 1.4.
2   This concept underpins Perez's (2002) work on 'technological paradigms', which is covered in more detail in Chapter 1 of this book.
3   The concept of smart homes is covered in more detail in Chapter 7.
4   Interestingly, the study also revealed regional differences in the UK: businesses in Greater London, for example, outperformed all other regions in terms of

connectivity; access to the Internet; website presence; external email facilities; local area network and wide area network. This mirrors the regional productivity differences created by ICT, and which were examined by London Economics (2003), who found that the average ICT contribution to labour productivity growth was 1.16 percentage points per annum (p.p.p.a.) in the London region, followed by 1.08 p.p.p.a. in the South East. These results were largely explained by the fact that sectors such as financial intermediation, transport, post and telecoms had a stronger presence in these regions and had invested more heavily in ICT.

5　For a fuller discussion see Chapter 5.

6　At the end of 2002 some 63% of UK government services were 'e-enabled' (Curthoys & Crabtree 2003).

7　This is another example of how important it is to understand the context of ICT: political factors are frequently important in understanding the adoption of ICT.

8　Other initiatives include (Bastow *et al*. 2003) the UK Online website, which acts as a nodal reference point for citizens and businesses seeking government information; the Government Secure Intranet, which gives secure email and directory services to central agencies; and other initiatives on interoperability and metadata.

9　Bastow *et al*. (2003), in their review of eGovernment at central and local government levels in England (1998–2003), criticise the model, suggesting that development can often be discontinuous and complex, because of changes achieved by strong political leadership, or a one-off receipt of funding may not be sustained or perhaps key staff leave. Linear progress myths may therefore be perpetuated (see Box 3.3).

10　This comes as the latest in a line of public sector relocation reviews (i.e. the Sir Gilbert Flemming Review of 1963; Hardman Review (1973) and a further drive in the late 1980s).

11　The key role played by ICT in public administration is also highlighted in the research conducted by Felstead *et al*. (2002). Some 87% of 'Public Administration' employees, for example, used ICT in their work (second only to 'Finance' with 90%).

12　Taken from http://www.digital-eu.org/aboutus/default.asp?pageid = 40

13　This view of eCommerce as a 'subset' process of eBusiness is distinguished from other views, some of which see eBusiness as a process but eCommerce as the value of goods and services sold over computer-mediated networks (see, for example, Mesenbourg 2001).

14　The OECD member countries have now endorsed these definitions based around communications infrastructure.

15　This includes all those activities in the NACE Rev. 1 classification, which comprises development and selling of property; buying and selling of own real estate; letting of own property; real estate activities on a fee or contract basis; real estate agencies; and management of real estate. In other words, real estate activities are part of the service sector.

16　See http://uk.netvalue.com

17 The UK Labour Force Survey defines teleworkers as people who do some paid or unpaid work in their own home and who use both a telephone and computer (TC). TC teleworkers are a sub-group which includes only workers for whom a telephone and computer are essential to do their job. Both groups include occasional teleworkers.

18 See website at www.emergence.nu

19 An examination of the reasons for choice of a remote back office location or an outsourced supplier in the EMERGENCE study also overturns some popular stereotyped views. Several factors were notable by their absence, including: the availability of government grants or other state incentives to choose a location; a deregulated labour market; the time zone in which the region is located; and low staff turnover. In general, the study shows that by far the most important selling point of any region is the availability of technical expertise. This is followed by low cost, a good reputation and reliability or high quality (Dixon *et al.* 2002).

4

Business Process and Organisational Change

Introduction

Without making any judgement as to better or worse, there is virtually no commercial organisation or individual that has not been changed in some way by the application of ICT. The primary purpose of this chapter is to look at the practical mechanisms through which these changes in ICT affect the real estate industry.

In order to meet this objective the chapter examines how change happens in organisations, and looks at some potential reasons why it never happens as quickly, or as comprehensively, as its proponents expect. We discuss the management context of business processes and some of the high-profile models and techniques that have been espoused for their optimisation. Next, the chapter examines the role of ICT in the design of organisations generally and draws out the scale and nature of the ICT-enabled changes that have already occurred. The chapter then identifies how 'business' is structured, breaking it down into a generic set of business processes that govern how things are done. Further, the chapter analyses how ICT has changed the fundamental business models underlying organisations and identifies changes to property that accrue from them.

Finally the chapter discusses the mapping of these business processes onto real property and the potential impacts that may accrue from changes.

Understanding corporate change

In the 1980s and 1990s planned change at the process level was predicated upon the assumption that structures, processes, ICT, skills and knowledge could all be reconfigured to optimise the achievement of strategic goals. Typically these approaches were given snappy acronyms such as, for example, BPR (business process re-engineering) or TQM (total quality management). As concepts, these were often characterised by strong but heavy-handed implementation and a deterministic, one-size-fits-all approach that saw people configured around systems which attempted to ensure optimal organisational performance, leading, unsurprisingly, to failure in many cases. Business process re-engineering is therefore best seen as the optimisation of organisational processes and structures following the introduction of new information technologies into an organisation.

The concept of re-engineering traces its origins back to management theories developed as early as the nineteenth century. The purpose of re-engineering is to make all of an organisation's processes the best-in-class. For example, Taylor (1911) suggested that managers could discover the best processes for performing work and re-engineer them to optimise productivity, and BPR echoes the classic belief that there is one best way to conduct tasks.

Although the evidence for organisational restructuring to accompany technological change is strong, there are often conflicting views as to the nature of the change. At the top level, the most significant issue is the change in the degree of centralisation of decision making, with attendant questions about the organisational hierarchies that support these.

However, 30 years of research into ICT and organisational change suggest that many organisations encounter difficulty changing their processes and structures to take advantage of the benefits offered by ICT. BPR, for example, has seen a failure rate of 75% (Bashein *et al.* 1994). Also, information systems are widely used in industrialised countries to support an immense variety of organisational activities. But researchers have found that it requires complex organisational work to implement information systems. In addition, there are sometimes major differences between the ways that systems were originally envisioned and how they are used in practice. The body of research that examines topics like these is called organisational informatics (OI) by Kling and Lamb (2001) and OI research has led us to a deeper understanding of IT and organisational change. Kling and Lamb's OI study focuses upon ICT as a socio-technical network rather than a tool for change. In that context, ICT-enabled change is holistic, and it affects every aspect of an organisation from culture through politics to operations, and involves matrices of businesses, services, people, technology and real estate. The lesson from this is that the impact of ICT upon property is similarly complex.

Examples such as the Schwab case study (see Box 4.1) demonstrate the complexity and far-reaching nature of ICT-enabled change. The expectation that ICT increases centralisation of decision making is based upon increases in the information processing capacity of managers, and Pfeffer and Leblebici (1977), Whisler (1970) and Zuboff (1988) all subscribe to this view. However, there is a school of thought (Burton & Obel 1984; Malone & Smith 1988) that expects ICT to decrease centralisation because it reduces the cost of communication and allows decisions to be delegated.

This debate actually shows that ICT itself is a rapidly changing industry. In the late 1970s computing was centralised around large processors with limited local intelligence. The advent of the personal computer in the early 1980s presaged a massive distribution of processing capability and with it a decentralisation of control. While for most users processing power remains available locally, for Internet applications, server-side programming is ensuring that the cycle is moving back towards centralisation of function.

Box 4.1   Case study: Charles Schwab

Charles Schwab and Co. was a medium-sized US stockbroker that saw the potential of the Internet as a sales channel in 1995. Schwab initially set up a small new division to develop the software, systems, and policies for e.Schwab. To compete with other Internet brokerages, Schwab dropped its commissions to a flat fee that was about one-third of its previous average commission. Schwab's regular phone representatives and branch officers were not allowed to help e.Schwab customers. Those customers were allowed one free phone call a month; all other questions had to be e-mailed to e.Schwab. While over a million customers flocked to e.Schwab, many existing customers, used to the higher level of service funded by higher fees, found the different policies and practices to be frustrating. In 1997, Schwab's began to integrate e.Schwab and 'regular Schwab' into one product. This integration required new, more coherent policies as well as training all of Schwab's representatives to understand e-trades. It also required the physical integration of e.Schwab's staff, with their West-Coast, Internet culture, into the offices of regular Schwab staff with a much more conventional expectation. (One side result of all this was a more flexible dress code in Schwab's headquarters.)

The Charles Schwab Corporation is now one of the nation's largest financial services firms engaged, through its subsidiaries, in providing securities brokerage and related financial services for over 7 million customers.

ICT and the design of organisations

Every aspect of property is shaped by the design of the organisations that occupy it. The shape of a building, its size, configuration, location and value are all determined, to a greater or lesser extent, by the processes that take place within.

Changes to the design of organisations have been responsible for dramatic changes in office, retail, leisure and industrial property. They have created new property types and rendered some existing designs obsolete. Changes to business processes have, in turn, changed the way companies communicate with their suppliers, customers, owners and staff, changing the way space is configured internally.

At the heart of changes to the organisation and the business processes that comprise that structure is ICT. In *Future Organizational Design*, Groth (1999) offers three principal contributions of ICT to the design of organisations:

- the ability to process information outside the human mind;
- the improvement of information storage; and
- the ability to communicate.

Above all else it is the impact of these three features upon business processes that defines the space occupied by the organisation. Typically, this impact has been seen as both redesign and totally new design. Robey (1995) expressed the irrational exuberance that often accompanies new technology: 'Each new generation of technology and each major technological advance is invariably ushered in with energetic claims that organisations as we know them today will be radically and fundamentally altered'.

A classic example of this was the technology boom of the late 1990s, where far too great an emphasis was placed upon the capabilities of ICT, in the guise of the Internet, to transform business models, radically change the existing hierarchies and bring about revolution in, for example, purchasing habits. However, it has become clear that this, like most other introductions of new technology, should be seen less as a technological revolution and more as a challenge of organisation redesign (Wang 2000).

Nevertheless, in some types of organisation, the impact of ICT has been revolutionary, creating new ways of working, new lines of business and new types of property to support them. Some types of organisation are more susceptible to change than others. Mintzberg (1979) shows that the structure of an organisation is largely determined by the variety one finds in its environment. For Mintzberg, environmental variety is determined by both environmental complexity and the pace of change. He identifies four types of organisational form, which are associated with four combinations of complexity and change. Figure 4.1 shows these combinations and Mintzberg's environmental determinants of organisational structure. Despite their intimidating titles, anyone with experience of working in a service organisation will recognise these structures and the mechanisms of co-ordination attached to them.

For example, in the 'machine bureaucracy', technocrats rule and co-ordination is organised through highly standardised processes and outputs. Since standardisation is a precursor to automation, organisations with these structural characteristics are likely to see a big impact from ICT. A good example here would be the insurance industry, where vehicle insurance, for example, is available through the completion of an online form. Typically, machine bureaucracies are mature organisations, large enough to have the volume of work needed to justify standardisation.

In the 'professional organisation' it is the skills and norms that are standardised and used as co-ordinating mechanisms. The standards of the professional organisation are formed largely outside its own structure, and in the self-governing association, its operators join with their colleagues from other professional organisations. The professional organisation places great importance upon professional authority, and Mintzberg calls this the power of expertise. As a result, professionals tend to resist rationalisation of their skills because that makes them programmable and thereby dilutes their power.

	Simple	Complex
Stable	*Machine bureaucracy* Standardised processes and outputs	*Professional organisation* Standardised skills and norms
Dynamic	*Entrepreneurial start-up* Direct supervision	*Adhocracy* Mutual adjustment

Figure 4.1   Environmental determinants of organisation structure (adapted from Mintzberg 1979).

Entrepreneurial start-ups that rely upon direct supervision for co-ordination will be much less prone to the automation of existing processes. They may, however, start with automated processes, and the cost advantage that this gives may be the rationale for the creation of the business. Online auction sites would be good examples of this structure.

The 'adhocracy' is the innovative organisation. There is little standardisation of processes or job specialisation and a focus on clients and markets. Communication is the key co-ordinating mechanism (Minzberg calls this mutual adjustment), and advertising agencies would be good examples of this kind of structure.

Typically these different organisational structures have very different property requirements even without any impact from ICT. This revolves around the way space is organised within, for example, an office. Duffy (1997) suggests that, typically, there are four ways of organising space internally: hives, dens, cells and clubs.[1]

'Hives' and 'dens' occur where work is process based and fairly self-contained. 'Hives' are where individual work takes place. 'Dens' involve groupwork, such as the finance teams found in many companies. 'Cells' and 'clubs', on the other hand, engage in knowledge-based work. For example, 'cells' consist of individuals (for instance lawyers and software engineers) while clubs involve a high degree of teamwork, such as creative or multidisciplinary teams.

Applying this taxonomy to Mintzberg's organisational structures gives a clue as to the efficiency with which space is used. It is important to note that there is no necessary correlation here between efficiency in value terms and efficiency expressed as occupational density. Typically, machine bureaucracies are efficient users of space. High levels of automation, standardised processes and limited scope for innovation or creativity suggest open-plan space of relatively high density (i.e. Duffy's hives in action).

'Professional organisations' by comparison are focused far more upon the individual relationship with the client and their space will often reflect this, with much more emphasis upon image, meeting space and personal territory. Inevitably this is less efficient in terms of occupational density. These equate to cells and dens.

Turning to newer start-up companies, the space for entrepreneurial start-ups varies wildly throughout the growth of the company. Usually the requirement is for space to accommodate expansion. In practice this may mean very inefficient occupational densities for long periods. The space organisation will be essentially club-like. Again, adhocracies are creative innovative companies based around small, fluid teams that form and break on a project-by-project basis. Duffy's clubs are the most common implementation in this area.

Of course, many companies will sit uneasily in any particular quadrant of Mintzberg's classification. In larger companies, different departments may well sit in different places. It is clear, however, that ICT enables each of these structures and methods to function. This may be through the provision of automation for the mechanised bureaucracy, through storage for the professional organisation, or by facilitation of communication for the adhocracy.

Similarly, for manufacturing organisations the impact of ICT is very visible in the size and capability of the plant employed. Miniaturisation of components and changes to control systems have reduced the size of plant considerably. Take computers themselves as an example. In the mid-1960s an IBM 360 was a common commercial computer. Typically configured, it would take up around ten square metres of floorspace. Add to that the need for air conditioning and a clean room in which to operate it. Even if their equivalent power were identical, modern computers are a fraction of that size and don't need air conditioning or a clean room. Of course, modern computers are many, many times more powerful as well – Moore's Law in action.[2]

In fact this trend has resulted in computers that are so small and so capable that they have become ubiquitous: almost every device or machine has some kind of embedded processing within it. Automotive electronics is a good example of this. In a wider sense Weiser (1991) articulated a vision of ubiquitous computing that pervaded every stratum of the environment, yet was integrated gracefully with human users. As he wrote, 'The most profound technologies are those that disappear. They weave themselves into the fabric of everyday life until they are indistinguishable from it'.

Ubiquitous or pervasive computing will be explored in more detail in Chapter 6. When our car needs checking, most of us have a mental image of a man in greasy overalls looking under the bonnet at the engine. However, the volume of embedded processing power going into the next generation of vehicles makes the reality very different: that of white-coated technicians analysing the car from a remote control room. This reality reflects three major trends in automotive electronics development:

the increasing number of computers per vehicle; the migration to more powerful processors; and the increasing complexity of embedded software.

Already, some luxury cars have around 50 on-board processors of one kind or another controlling everything from electronic windows, through suspension to engine management. This makes the cars cleaner, more efficient and more reliable. And it doesn't stop there. Mechanical control systems such as steering and braking are being replaced with electromechanical equivalents, improving reliability and maintainability still further. If you have paid enough money for your car, you may find that it has an 'on-board computer' that displays details of your journey, petrol consumption and so on. All the other computers in the car are invisible. You only see them in operation.

But what are the space effects upon the motor industry? Traditionally, car manufacturers have been integrators of mechanical systems. As cars and components become more complex, they need not only an ever higher skill base to effect that integration but they also need to deliver large amounts of complex, safety-critical embedded software. This is compounded by time-to-market pressures as design cycles shorten and cost pressures increase. In future it is likely that cars will be differentiated less by shape or power but by the quality of the services offered by the on-board software. In terms of the type of space required and the use to which it is put, a software production company is a very different organisation to a car manufacturer. Intelligent components may require the same space to be assembled into a motor car, but additional space will be required to develop, integrate and test the software. Facilitated by the need for more ICT, this additional space is not required to be adjacent or even near to the assembly plant.

ICT is equally apparent in the organisation of distribution. The management of stock at the supply chain level has enabled the growth of highly efficient flows of goods between importers and customers. This would have been impossible without sophisticated management systems. Stock selection and picking systems therefore lie at the core of high bay warehouses.

Generic business processes

At its lowest level, a business process is an operational procedure. Davenport and Short (1990) define a business process as a set of logically related tasks performed to achieve a defined business outcome. Later,

Davenport (1993) went on to describe a process as a structured, measured set of activities designed to produce a specified output for a particular customer or market. Processes themselves have customers, who may be internal or external to the organisation in which they operate. Processes may also cross organisational boundaries (i.e. their function may involve more than one internal department, or an external company or companies). At this lowest level, processes are generally identified in terms of beginning and end points, interfaces, and the functions involved. Examples of processes include: developing a new product; ordering goods from a supplier; creating a financial report; raising an invoice.

It should be clear that business processes are the 'DNA' of company activity. To extend the analogy, just as faulty genes can result in illness, so faulty or inefficient business processes can impact upon company profitability. For the purposes of this chapter we are concerned with the impact of changes in business processes upon the acquisition and use of real estate. Whilst aspects such as efficiency or profitability may have secondary impacts upon real estate (bringing about increased demand for space, for example), they are not the main focus. The real importance of business processes in our context is that ICT applications are implemented at the process level. As a consequence, changes to processes often result in changes to the property or real estate space in which they take place. Conventionally, processes are described in what Jacka and Keller (2001) call process maps. Typically these include for each process its owner, the trigger events (beginning and ending), inputs, outputs, risks, key controls, and measures of success. The map also describes the flow of work through the process with timings, volumes, etc.

A simplified example of a process map is shown in Figure 4.2. This describes the development of a website and shows the key procedures, the flows between them and external processes around the edge. Key data for each process have been omitted for clarity.

It is interesting to examine the effects upon the occupation of space inherent in each of these procedures. The process being described is an internal one and is likely to be undertaken within the premises of the company but ICT means that, for many of the procedures, this is not an imperative. The 'develop website' process is typical of one that is locationally independent, as far as the completion of the process is concerned. There is no imperative related to the work involved that dictates that it should be completed in any particular location.

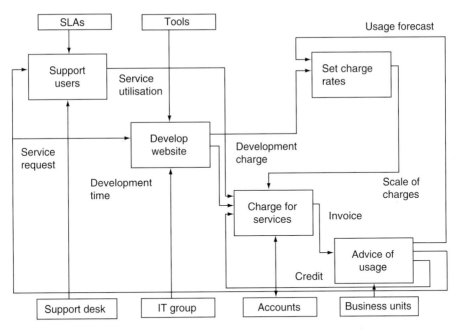

Figure 4.2   Process map: website development.
(Note: SLA is Site Licence Agreement)

'Set charge rates' is an example of a process that is based upon a formula that calculates the scale of charge on the basis of a usage forecast and development recovery, and as a consequence it could well be automated, as indeed could the 'Charge for services' process. Irrespective of automation, however, back-office processes, such as accounting, are prime candidates to be located in lower cost locations.

The 'support users' process, by comparison, is location dependent, requiring close proximity to the business unit users of the website, although interestingly, the external process 'support desk' is often one that is handled remotely. The 'advice of usage' process is essentially the interface between the website and the support process. Again this is likely to be in close proximity to the business units.

Creating a generic model of business processes is not without difficulty, given the difference in the type of operation between manufacturing and service companies. Nevertheless, Figure 4.3 shows a generic structure that links company stakeholders with different generic business processes. Clearly, these processes will have different scope and scale depending upon the type of business. However, even service industries have raw materials stocks of some kind, even if it is only a stationery store.

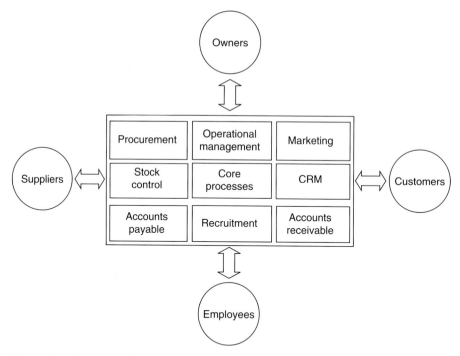

Figure 4.3   Generic business processes.

Typically there are three kinds of ICT-induced changes that can be observed generically:

- **Integration**. ICT here is used to bind adjacent processes together much more tightly, making them much more efficient.
- **Specialisation**. ICT is being used to facilitate a change of focus onto, for example, the customer.
- **Automation**. Here, ICT replaces human action in different parts of a process.

The generic model holds examples of all three types of change.

A practical example of ICT-induced change is seen in research undertaken by the College of Estate Management (Dixon *et al.* 2002, 2003) which showed that, in the City of London at least, firms are already migrating business processes to the Internet. Table 4.1 shows the extent to which the Internet is being used for business processes, for example.

The report examined the extent to which core processes are already under-taken on the web and looked at plans for the next year. By the end of 2002, 70% of companies in the City expected to have their own website, 80% use the web for researching prices and 70% for purchasing. By 2003, around 50% expected to be recruiting, videoconferencing and managing projects online whilst some 40% planned to be training, selling and managing their customers using the web. Procurement therefore remains an important part of the business process landscape.

Procurement

The buying process is one that has seen massive changes, largely delivered by ICT. These changes have been in two main areas. First, in the automation and integration of the purchasing process itself and, second, in the vehicles that may be used to identify and compare products. The internal linkages between procurement and other processes are shown in Figure 4.4.

The purchase of goods can be split into two types:

- capital goods, such as computers or plant; and,
- raw materials, which may include any volume items such as stationery or postage in addition to the materials needed for production.

Table 4.1   Internet use in City of London office (adapted from Dixon *et al.* 2002).

	Now	In 12 months' time	Total
eProcurement	70%	10%	80%
Online price research	80%	5%	85%
Use of online aggregators	4%	9%	13%
Own website	73%	13%	86%
eCommerce to sell	25%	14%	39%
Online CRM	16%	23%	39%
eRecruitment	38%	20%	59%
eLearning	21%	23%	44%
Publication of results online	18%	6%	24%
Publication of transactions	14%	6%	20%
Online share trading	3%	3%	6%
Online project management	27%	21%	48%
Videoconferencing	27%	26%	54%

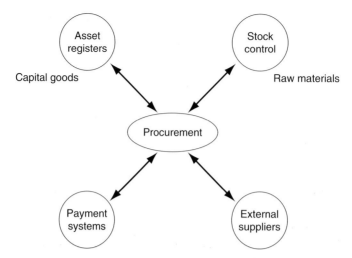

Figure 4.4   Internal linkages.

Internal linkages, procedures and audit trails exist between procurement and the stock control process for raw materials and the asset control and valuation systems for capital goods. Accounting and payment processes are also linked, and ICT has facilitated the integration of these internal processes so that, for example, production systems call forward materials for use, concurrently placing orders for replacements and, once receipt has been confirmed, posting accounting records to generate payment. This level of integration removes layers of documentation and intervention, reducing costs and creating competitive advantage.

Increasingly, the integration is extending to encompass the external suppliers themselves within the same system. This inclusion takes a number of forms:

- electronic data interchange (EDI);
- online auctions;
- specialist exchanges.

EDI is the computer-to-computer exchange of business data in standard formats. In EDI, information is organised according to a specified format set by both parties, allowing a computer transaction that requires no human intervention or rekeying on either end. All information contained in an EDI transaction set is, for the most part, the same as on a conventionally printed document. Although a relatively old technology, it remains in use particularly in the retail area. Some types of data interchange that use

EDI are gradually migrating to Internet-based private information exchanges (see Box 4.2).

Online auctions take place in both public and private domains. Private auctions are used to attract best bids for a particular contract and tend to be held within a closed community of established suppliers. Public auctions use trading platforms such as eBay to solicit bids for particular items. Specialist industry exchanges are also increasingly important (see Box 4.3). These tend to be sector-specific platforms that facilitate communication and collaboration within particular industries, allowing for an efficient bidding process.

Typically, a specialist exchange website allows registered users to look for buyers or sellers of goods and services who may specify prices or invite bids. As for internal solutions, such sites are designed to streamline

---

Box 4.2   Case study: Tesco

For the last decade UK supermarket retailer Tesco has used EDI to communicate orders to the majority of its suppliers. More recently the company has deployed trading information exchange (TIE), an Internet-based private exchange, to improve relationships with key trading partners, control costs, streamline processes and enhance responsiveness across the supply chain. Using Tesco TIE, suppliers can monitor stock levels daily, and make exceptional changes to replenishment plans much more quickly than with simple ordering systems. Tesco, in turn, can view suppliers' service levels in terms of logistics, delivery times and quality of packaging, amongst other criteria. This enables Tesco to monitor its supply chain with an average lag of eight hours, as opposed to the previous two to three weeks on average. Both retailers and suppliers can view stock levels of 96% of the goods Tesco sells in stores via the exchange. Approximately 85% of Tesco's total community of around 1500 suppliers use Tesco TIE. A founder member of the Worldwide Retail Exchange, an online B2B exchange for retailers, Tesco is also co-operating with other retailers on a standardised cataloguing project which 'normalises' data exchanged between suppliers and retailers. Most of Tesco's food products, over 40 000 product lines, run on this product file which is maintained by the suppliers themselves. Tesco is also expert in the use of online auctions. Focusing on high-value transactions and services and with a rigid 20-day bidding cycle, procurement is linked to commodity market movements to ensure the best market price is always available.

Tesco is also one of the biggest supermarkets online with some 110 000 orders per week. In addition to conventional access via a PC, the Tesco.com Pocket Shopper gives the customer access to shopping via a PDA. The application requires an Internet connection to download a product catalogue periodically, and to upload the contents of the selected shopping basket ready for checkout.

Box 4.3   Case study: Covisint

Covisint was formed by DaimlerChrysler, Ford, General Motors and Renault–Nissan. Since its inception, PSA Peugeot Citroen has also joined the initiative. This is a trading exchange for the automotive industry designed to increase the operational efficiency of the whole industry, but the procurement process in particular. Supplier members are able to bid against contracts placed in Covisint by the auto manufacturers. Since its formation in 2000 over 20 000 suppliers have become members and the system has over 92 000 active members. The system has seen over 4500 cumulative online bidding events and more than $82 billion in cumulative transaction throughput.

---

procurement processes by setting standards, placing and approving orders and arranging delivery, thereby eliminating many paper-based procedures and labour-intensive processes. For example, research from Benchmark Research (2002) shows that 63% of high-performing companies in the USA, the UK and Germany saved between 10% and 50% through the use of eProcurement solutions.

Operational management

It is perhaps in the area of operational management that the impact of ICT upon business processes has been the most visible. It is difficult to envisage office life without easy access to word processing or spreadsheet analysis. The day-to-day operation of any business has been revolutionised by the availability of integrated, cross-functional business tools on every desktop and the near universal availability of information. But the downside of this universality is information overload, a significant negative impact of ICT. A significant proportion of information is sent 'just in case it might be needed'. ICT ensures that the marginal cost of sending unnecessary information 'just in case' is negligible, leaving it to the recipient to determine whether or not the information is required.

Another large chunk of information sent is that which is 'out of phase' in some degree (i.e. the information will be needed, but not until later). The recipient files most of the just-in-case information (just in case) and all of the out-of-phase information and this often creates a high-volume, low-density personal information system, that may have additional complexities of multiple formats or media.

'Just-in-time' information, or information on demand, enables individual users to pick the information needed at the right time. However, ICT has frequently failed to meet its potential in this area. Diverse, stand-alone systems with different interfaces and complex interactions have conspired to hold back the principle of information on demand.

The growth of intranet technologies delivers real information on demand. It supports distributed information authoring, publishing and management. Information is authored and managed by those who create it, without having to rely on programmers to create data entry and reporting programs. With standard browsers, a user can retrieve and view information from distributed sources and systems using a simple, uniform interface without having to know anything about the technology being used. This is delivering a real operational impact from ICT and changing the information structure of organisations.

Marketing

ICT has delivered a new dimension to marketing and selling. Technology has driven significant process change in the areas of:

- market information systems;
- online catalogues; and
- eCommerce.

Market information systems

Marketeers have always needed timely, reliable, and relevant information in order to make decisions that enhance the company's ability to compete successfully in the marketplace. In the days of paper libraries and microfilmed records this was seldom achievable. The availability of internal and external business intelligence online has revolutionised this process not only through the offer of better and more timely access, but also through making the data available to more sophisticated modelling and simulation that better informs the whole marketing process (see Box 4.4).

Online catalogues

Corporate brochures have always been beset by issues of quality and timeliness. Paper brochures need to have a sufficiently rich content adequately to promote the company, but not so rich as to make the document unwieldy, thereby making it difficult and expensive to distribute.

Box 4.4   Case study: CoStar Group

CoStar Group is the leading provider of information services to commercial real estate professionals in the United States and the United Kingdom. CoStar's suite of products offers customers access via the Internet to a comprehensive, verified database of commercial real estate information on 50 US markets plus the United Kingdom. CoStar's products provide customers with knowledge to understand market conditions, identify prospects, discover opportunities and conduct transactions efficiently. The market information available includes stock and transaction data, market reports, trend analysis and a news service.

Paper brochures also need to have a long shelf-life, since they are difficult and expensive to update. Evans and Wurster (2000) highlight the process changes wrought by the Internet because it gives companies tremendous 'reach' without sacrificing 'richness' or the quality of the information about products and services. Further, the imperative of timeliness becomes less burdensome since the content of the brochure can be changed regularly at only marginal cost. As far as producers of ranges of consumer goods or services are concerned, online brochures are given added weight by eCommerce systems that give customers the ability to buy direct from the catalogue.

eCommerce systems

eCommerce is an example of a situation where ICT has created a whole new set of processes rather than changing existing ones although purists like Negroponte (2002) argue that it retains the potential so to do.

Experience of online retailing so far is that it is in addition to, rather than instead of, traditional retailing. Despite the growing impact of eCommerce, many of the more dire predictions of the 'death of the high street' have proved wildly inaccurate, and many of the best implementations of eCommerce have been where existing retailers have taken the new format and used it to supplement existing sales (see Part 3 of this book). From the perspective of process change, eCommerce facilitates the integration of the manufacturing, stock control, sales and payment generic processes. This increases the efficiency of these processes markedly but it is just this integration that raises the spectre of disintermediation as an outcome of eCommerce. With an eCommerce system the customer interacts directly with the producer rather than the intermediary, whether they are the retailer, agent or distributor.

Customer relationship management

One of the key differentiators between companies is the speed and level of customer service that they offer. Customer relationship management (CRM) is the generic process by which the totality of the relationship can be managed discretely. Accordingly it will cover all interactions between the company and its customer, be it sales, placing of orders, queries or complaints.

CRM has been affected dramatically by ICT as telecommunications and computing have drawn closer together, facilitating the partial automation of the process and much greater specialisation. The technical integration allows sequences of telephone calls to be preprogrammed, using numbers held in an electronic customer record; details of the conversation with the customer are recorded and appended to that same record. This enables any interaction with the customer to be assessed in the light of a complete record of the interaction (see Box 4.5).

CRM systems both 'push' to the customer, as in the case of sales, or 'pull' from the customer, as in complaints handling or providing technical support. Orders can be taken by phone or, increasingly, the CRM system is linked to an eCommerce system that enables the customer both to view product descriptions and place orders online. Any subsequent queries, changes or complaints will also be handled by reference to the CRM system, showing full details of all transactions. From a process perspective ICT has taken a set of smaller processes embedded in a number of business

---

Box 4.5   Case study: BUPA

When dealing with healthcare issues in the private sector, a patient's relationship with the company providing that service is of paramount importance. To nurture a positive and efficient relationship with a patient, the process often involves the provision of swift, unambiguous and accurate information that relates to a customer's insurance claim. To reinforce that customer relationship, BUPA (British United Provident Association) installed a full CRM system in 1998. Early in 1997, BUPA conducted an extensive study as part of a £50 million investment toward enhancing its existing system to deal with customer claims. These customer claim inquiries, usually asked before a patient undergoes treatment, are often sensitive in nature and require consistent responses. For example, a patient might be anxious before undergoing surgery. If they make a repeat call they want to be treated in the same way with an identical outcome. When a claim arrives, it is pre-authorised in a single telephone call, giving better service and accelerating the payment.

areas and pulled them together into CRM, improving efficiency and increasing the level of customer service.

Accounting

Accounting was one of the earliest implementations of ICT applications. Sales and purchase ledger functions were obvious candidates driven by high volumes of data and requiring formulaic application of arithmetic. Latterly these applications have moved on to become full-blown management information systems, allowing ready access to performance information and detailed analysis of, for example, costs, on demand. Banking and payment systems have evolved in parallel to deliver electronic payment systems, enabling the rapid demise of the corporate cheque.

Recruitment

The recruitment of employees has also seen dramatic changes as a result of ICT. The Internet has created a marketplace in which employers and potential employees exchange information, changing the conventional channel options of direct advertisement or employment agency. Looking for a job on the Internet empowers the potential employee, by enabling them to look in any geographical area for the jobs that they are either qualified for or aspire to. They can ask questions, research their potential employer and apply for a position all at a time of their choosing rather than one dictated by a weekly jobs page in a newspaper (see Box 4.6).

Employers receive a candidate's information in a form they can evaluate, respond to and put into their payroll automatically, thus saving time and money. Many companies now actively solicit employees through their corporate website whilst agencies offer job listings as well as registration of curricula online.

Stock management

Another process that was adopted early by ICT comprises the management and recording of stock (for example, raw materials) and this has been the subject of almost continuous change since the inception of early physical systems. The level of stock needs to be kept in balance with the demands of the manufacturing process, in the case of raw materials, or customer

---

Box 4.6   Case study: Nestlé

Nestlé UK's Food and Beverage divisions are established market leaders and responsible for some of the world's and UK's best known brands. Nestlé's objectives for online recruitment were:

- attracting quality candidates to vacancy adverts published on the corporate website;
- reducing time from advertising to receiving applications by accepting online CV applications;
- management of candidate CVs and applications;
- sorting of applications to determine suitability;
- storage of CVs in an electronic format that could be easily searched;
- response management;
- speedy communication with applicants.

Through the use of online recruitment Nestlé has reduced its recruitment administration for jobs advertised online by more than 50%, and visitors to the Nestlé website have increased by 35%.

---

demand in the case of finished goods stocks. Corporate efficiency is often measured in the size of stockholdings.

Integration with internal production systems from sales forecasts through the manufacturing process and on to procurement and the introduction of manufacturing resource planning (MRP) systems placed stock management at the heart of an efficient business. Better, more available information has also facilitated that integration a stage further into the global sourcing of materials and delivery of goods. Supply chains are now global for many businesses. ICT impacts have also been seen in the identification of units of stock. Just as the unitisation of cargo in the 1950s created the container as the primary unit of goods transportation, for decades the pallet has been the main unit of identification for many manufacturing and service businesses. It is also likely that the introduction of radio frequency identification (RFID) will move the unit of identification down to the product level, changing the process yet again.

Financial management

In addition to the ICT-enabled changes to accounting systems, ICT is also having an impact upon the reporting of those accounts. Company reports and accounts, once just a platform for the formal reporting of data to shareholders and markets, are becoming more dynamic. As legislation on accounting standards makes the figures ever more transparent, so ICT is making them more accessible. Many companies now file accounts electronically, but also make the accounts available to shareholders electronically, either as electronic documents or as data available for analysis on their website.

Mapping processes to property

In deterministic terms, the expectation of the impact of ICT would be that productivity would increase and space requirements would reduce, thereby reducing the demand for real estate (see Chapters 1 and 5). In the light of debates about long-term productivity change, the process level represents that level at which real impacts of ICT-enabled change can be observed on real estate. Typically, these changes take one of the following forms:

- **Reduction in space**. Put simply, a reduction in the amount of space required comes about either through a decrease in the number of people involved in a process or through a reduction in the physical size of plant and equipment. A decrease in the number of people employed in a particular process can be seen as a natural consequence of increased efficiency. The per-capita productivity of the process is improved by reducing the numbers and thereby the physical space occupied by the process. Similarly a reduction in the size of plant and machinery causes it to occupy less space. An example of this would be the physical impact of Moore's Law. Doubling the capacity of a microprocessor every year effectively reduces the space it occupies by half every year for the same level of power. As we have seen, this can be charted in the shrinking size of computers since the 1960s. As ICT-enabled new working practices are adopted (for example, desks shared between several mobile workers), so the number of people using the same space increases and the potential need for space decreases.
- **Changes in property type**. Changes in the type or configuration of property have also been brought about by process change. As a result of management tools such as BPR, specialised, process-focused organisations have been spun out of companies, often requiring new types of property: call centres, for example. Changes in the automation of racking systems within stock management have changed the configuration and nature of warehouses, for example.
- **Changes in location**. A further benefit of the specialisation of processes, allied with ICT-led improvements in communications, has allowed the new process specialists to seek out accommodation in

cheaper locations with access to more labour. Improved mobile tele-communications has facilitated mobile work, allowing the density of office occupation to increase.

Clearly change to a particular process can bring about all three types of transformation and, taking these generic impacts a stage further, Figure 4.5[3] shows our generic process map in the context of individual property sectors and sub-sectors.

Moreover, through the mechanism of process change, ICT has wrought significant changes to all property sectors and created some new ones. However, it should also be noted that productivity arguments in particular are complex and this issue, together with clustering and dispersion, is covered in more detail in Chapters 5, 7 and 9.

Office space

To a greater or lesser extent, offices are affected by process change through-out the organisation either in terms of reorganisation, reductions in the numbers of staff or the need for specialists to become co-located. Offices are all about information work, an aspect that has been grow-ing for 200 years. Beniger (1986) puts the total US employment in informa-tion work at around half the workforce, for example, and ICT, working through changes in business processes and procedures, has changed information work radically. These changes can be categorised as follows:

■ information storage;
■ information processing; and,
■ communications.

	Offices	Call centres	Retail	Industrial	Distribution
Procurement	■			■	■
Operational management	■				
Marketing and sales	■		■		■
CRM	■	■			
Recruitment	■		■		
Accounting	■				
Financial management	■			■	
Stock control	■				■

Figure 4.5 Processes and property.

It is the interplay between these areas of technology and their impact upon business processes that has generated changes in demand for real estate.

Information storage

The University of California at Berkeley School of Information Management and Systems (2003) estimates that some five exabytes (10^{18} bytes) of information were produced worldwide in 2002. The school also estimates that newly stored information has grown at around 30% per annum since 1999. Some 92% of new information is stored on magnetic media, primarily hard disks. Film represents 7% of the total, mainly consisting of photographs. Storage on paper, although substantial, represents a tiny 0.01%, and optical media even less. Figure 4.6 shows these data graphically.

It should be self-evident that the sheer volume of information generated each year requires space for storage. To give an idea of the scale, if we make some simplistic assumptions about the amount of space taken up by just that part of new paper-based information, new office paper in 2002 represented around 106 billion reams of paper. If these were to be stored in a single warehouse with a 10 metre high stack, with no regard to access (i.e. no aisles), the warehouse would need to be 48 million square metres in size.

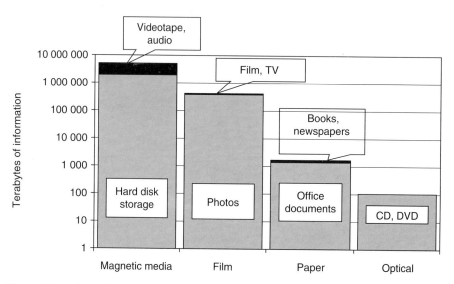

Figure 4.6   Information storage.

Even the relatively dense magnetic storage comes at a price in terms of space. The 1986 terabytes of information created on disk represent 50 million 40-gigabyte disk drives full to capacity (see Box 4.7). In turn, using a standard personal computer footprint, this equates to 5 million square feet of space. This doesn't take into account the other paraphernalia that accompanies the basic computer (i.e. monitor, keyboard, etc.).

Obviously these are statistics relating to the creation of new information. In terms of the overall storage required, destruction of paper files and deletion of magnetic ones would need to be taken into account. Nevertheless the impact of ICT on storage should be apparent.

Information processing
The impact of changes in the power of information processing has been profound at the process level. It is difficult to conceive of an information process of any scale that does not involve calculation or manipulation of data or information. Office property for example, shows in every segment of Figure 4.5. The majority of the impact on space here is through increased automation and reduced numbers of personnel per process. The most visible effect, however, is the arrival of the personal computer (PC). Through the delivery of commoditised processing power and applications to the desktop, this has facilitated the aggregation and automation of office functions.

However, it is difficult to isolate the effect of processing changes in isolation from the revolution in communications or storage.

Box 4.7   Information storage: some powers of ten

Kilobyte (KB)	*1000 bytes* or *10^3 bytes*
	2 Kilobytes: a typewritten page
Megabyte (MB)	*1 000 000 bytes* or *10^6 bytes*
	1 Megabyte: a small novel *or* a 3.5 inch floppy disk
Gigabyte (GB)	*1 000 000 000 bytes* or *10^9 bytes*
	1 Gigabyte: a pickup truck filled with books
Terabyte (TB)	*1 000 000 000 000 bytes* or *10^{12} bytes*
	2 Terabytes: an academic research library
Petabyte (PB)	*1 000 000 000 000 000 bytes* or *10^{15} bytes*
	2 Petabytes: all US academic research libraries
Exabyte (EB)	*1 000 000 000 000 000 000 bytes* or *10^{18} bytes*
	2 Exabytes: total volume of information generated in 1999

Communications

Changes in the scope, scale and infrastructure of communications have been central to the centrifugal effects of ICT on business processes. The growth of Internet Protocol (IP) and, just as importantly, an infrastructure capable of delivering large volumes of data to relatively remote locations have facilitated the dispersal of business processes and processing. This is not to say that remote applications were not feasible before the Internet, but it is IP that has delivered the commoditisation of processing and applications that so boosted the personal computer. The combination of local processing capability and better communications infrastructure makes processes less dependent upon a particular location. Cairncross (2001) refers to this as the 'death of distance'. The principal effects on space are seen in a number of ways:

- First, the ability to split front-office, customer-facing processes from back-office support processes has lead to a massive change in location as support functions are relocated away from expensive, labour-constrained places. This is a long-term trend, particularly in sectors such as insurance and financial services. The provision of much better global communications infrastructure, however, has accelerated the trend and brought many more locations into consideration – in particular low-wage, highly skilled, English-speaking locations in India and the Middle East.
- Second, the growth in new working practices such as home working. UK research by the RETRI Group (2003) found that respondents to a future office survey seem surprisingly sanguine about the prospect of home working, with 56% saying it would definitely or probably happen and a further 32% thinking it a possibility. Only 4% felt that home working would not affect them.
- Third, space is affected by the mobility that is offered by these technologies. The growth of wireless communications offers the potential for information processes to be undertaken away from any fixed point – be it home or office. Public space such as airports or railway stations or private enterprises such as coffee shops can function as a mobile office using wireless connectivity.

Home (or mobile) working does not necessarily reduce the amount of space required in a central office function. Clearly there are examples of mobile workers – perhaps sales representatives – who very seldom use central facilities, but more usually mobile and home working is a part-time activity. However, research by Gerald Eve (2001) into occupational densities found that organisations that do use new working practices such as home working have a higher occupational density than those that do not.

On average, over three square metres per person were gained by the firms that did make use of new working practices.

Retail

Naturally, retail business processes have not been immune to ICT-led changes (Box 4.8). Tagging of individual stock items combined with processing power distributed to till level have facilitated far greater integration of the sales unit within the supply chain.

The impact upon retail space has been the devotion of a far greater proportion of retail premises to display rather than stock. There have also been less obvious changes wrought by the growth of eCommerce systems both by established retailers themselves and by new entrants to the market. One of the best known examples of a new market entrant is Amazon. Amazon sells a range of goods but is best known as an online book retailer. Using its huge catalogue of books it is able to sell from a very low stock base because it has no physical shops.

Although pioneers like Amazon were widely expected to have a detrimental impact upon the high street, in fact bricks and mortar retailers have adapted to the new technologies. The space effects here have not been so apparent in terms of increasing or decreasing demand for retail floorspace; rather they are being seen in terms of increasing specification of space and improved facilities management.

Box 4.8 Case study: Zara

The first Zara store opened in La Coruña in 1975. By 2003, Zara was present in 46 countries, with a network of 606 stores. Zara, and its parent company Inditex,[4] have redefined the vertical retail clothing supply chain with an ICT-based business model that stresses speed and integration of store operations with the design, sourcing and manufacturing operations. By capturing information at the point of sale, Zara quickly identifies trends and items that sell or don't sell at a store level, and then makes appropriate sourcing, manufacturing, and replenishment decisions to maximise sell-through, minimise out-of-stock situations, and drive overall performance. Zara uses small-batch manufacturing and holds strategic inventory in fabrics rather than finished goods which increase their flexibility and speed to market. Using technology, strong design and sourcing strategies brought together by supply chain connectivity, it is not unusual for new concepts to go from the drawing board to the sales floor in under one month, or to have hot selling items replenished to stores the next day, giving a significant competitive advantage.

The real beneficiary of eCommerce has been the consumer through increased purchasing options, more choice and more price transparency (Box 4.9).

Industrial premises

The impact of ICT on the industrial property sector has been seen at all levels. As part of the general trend towards the miniaturisation of machines, the size of plant located in industrial premises has been reducing for 200 years. From an ICT perspective the impact has been seen both in the introduction of better planning through systems such as MRP (manufacturing resource planning) and in the control processes that operate, monitor and control the machines themselves. This is documented by Beniger (1986) in the wider context of societal control. The space impact of these control processes is best expressed by the increasing use of applied robotics within manufacturing industry, taking the automation of processes to an advanced stage. Figure 4.7 shows the penetration of robots into manufacturing industry in selected economies worldwide. Japan shows the highest penetration overall with Germany the highest European country. Typically, robotic processes are very space efficient and require less labour than more conventional manufacturing processes.

Improved communications infrastructure and the growth of eCommerce have facilitated different business models of manufacturing. In particular this has increased the ability to sell direct to customers with better inte-

---

Box 4.9   Case study: Dell

Dell is amongst the world's largest suppliers of computers and has been a pioneer of direct sales, initially by phone and subsequently via the Internet. Launched as a static page in 1994, Dell.com took the plunge into eCommerce shortly thereafter, and by 1997 was the first company to record a million dollars in online sales. In 2002, about half of the company's revenue was coming from the site. A key part of Dell's success is that the site offers consumers 'choice and control'. Buyers can assemble a computer system piece by piece, choosing components like hard drive size and processor speed based on their budgets and needs. The machines thus configured are assembled and shipped to order. To facilitate B2B sales, the Dell site offers each corporate customer an individualised interface. Using what Dell calls a premier page, purchasing managers log on and order using an interface customised for their company's needs. The company's manufacturing is calibrated to respond so closely to orders that inventory is kept to a four-day supply. Systems are built only after they have been ordered, a principle that applies across the product range. With no central warehouse facility, the company ships to customers directly from its manufacturing plants.

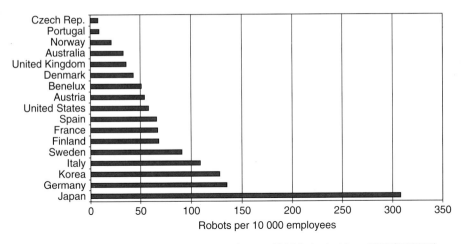

Figure 4.7   Number of robots per 10 000 employees 2002 (adapted from UNECE 2003).

gration of the supply process, and in many cases, making to order rather than making to stock. The space impact of this can be substantial, increasing space allocated to sub-assemblies and work in process, whilst reducing the space devoted to finished goods stocks.

For example, lean manufacturing is a manufacturing philosophy of efficiency which shortens the time between customer order and factory shipment by eliminating waste. Indeed, lean manufacturing documented by Womack *et al.* (1991) is presented as the antithesis of mass manufacturing. It is claimed to use half the human effort in the factory, half the manufacturing floor space, half the investment in tools, half the engineering hours to develop a new product in half the time. It also requires keeping far less than half the needed inventory on site and results in fewer defects.

Whether adopting the 'lean' tag or not, to a greater or lesser extent all manufacturing has changed to adopt at least some of the component identification and planning tools that are embodied in the philosophy. This is an ICT-enabled effect that would not otherwise have been possible.

Distribution warehouses

In many respects, the Dell case study reflects one aspect of the ICT-led changes that have affected distribution warehousing. A direct manufacturing model making to order is effectively 'warehouseless', although Dell is an exception, having started the process without 'legacy' supply networks.

Established companies that seek to gain the clear benefits of the direct model will almost certainly be involved in some kind of channel conflict with existing retailers of their products, and this has held back the widespread adoption of the model (see Box 4.10).

Nevertheless ICT has revolutionised the way goods are stored and how that process is managed. Applied robotics lie at the heart of advanced racking and picking systems that populate the larger end of the high-bay warehouse market. The falling threshold costs of the technology mean that these systems are becoming feasible at ever smaller unit sizes. However, their installation has significant ramifications for the specification of the building, requiring superflat floors and large clear spans to function efficiently.

Stock management has also moved from being a local process to one that is integrated with the entire supply chain from raw materials to customer delivery. In parallel, supply chains themselves can be optimised using software tools to ensure that they are in an optimal location to service a particular customer base and pattern of distribution. This process of optimisation can affect the viability of particular warehouse sites and lead to a change of location.

Box 4.10   Case study: Chivers

Makers of preserves for over 60 years, Chivers is a brand leader producing 60% of all the preserves sold in Ireland and is also a leading exporter to major overseas markets. Additionally, Chivers makes quality jams and marmalades for many private label brands at its Dublin plant and also acts as an agent and distributor for a variety of the leading imported grocery brands. In order to support future business growth and its position of leadership and quality, Chivers invested in supply chain management software that enabled the company to meet its customers' requirements efficiently. One of the key goals of the company was to reduce its stock of finished goods substantially, reducing its manufacturing and inventory carrying costs at the same time as increasing storage capacity for its range of imported goods. Previously all forecasting and planning was done manually, a complex and time-consuming process, and was highly dependent on one or two key individuals. Before installing the software, with over 500 line items, the business was very complex for its size and getting more complex by the day. Using best practice guidelines, Chivers chose to focus initially on forecasting and demand planning before implementing the supply side planning of its imports and manufacturing business. Through the implementation of the planning system alone, Chivers has reduced stocks by 10% and improved its customer service levels by 0.5% to 1%.

Call centres

The growth of call centres as a market sector is entirely ICT led. The convergence of voice and data processing, the development of customer relationship management software and business process re-engineering created demand for specialist processes to handle all interactions with customers (see Box 4.11 and Chapters 7 and 9).

These processes required a very high level of communications provision – initially one phone line per workstation rather than the one line shared between five workstations typical of a conventional office. Additionally they had a very specific labour profile and structure and, being so specialised, could be located away from the corporate core.

Initially the high threshold technology costs dictated that call centres were the preserve of the big financial services users who alone had the scale of operation to make the process viable. As technology costs have fallen however, a call centre operation has come within the reach of all but the smallest company. ICT continues to affect this process. As demand for ever-richer communication has risen and call centres have transformed themselves into multi-media contact centres offering, for example, guided internet browsing around a catalogue of clothes, so the specification of communications has risen much further. Continued growth in global communications infrastructure has rendered call centres equally as vulnerable as back office functions to being moved offshore.

Box 4.11   Case study: Barclays Bank

UK clearing bank Barclays launched Barclaycall, its nationwide telephone banking service, in 1994. Barclaycall telephone banking now has over 600 000 customers. Available 24 hours a day, Barclaycall is now one of the leading telephone banking services in the UK. It provides a comprehensive range of services including bill payment, balance enquiries, transferring funds between accounts, setting up regular payments, ordering statements and ordering travellers' cheques, foreign currency and cheque books. Headquartered in London, the bank has three call centres servicing Barclaycall – in Coventry, Salford and Sunderland. Each of the centres has between 220 and 250 seats. In 2001 these call centres handled approximately 15 million calls from over 900 000 customers.

Summary

Demand for commercial property is shaped by the business processes that take place within it. To that extent property can be regarded as an outcome of technology rather than a driver of it. Impacts and transformations of ICT are rarely simple, even at business process level, and the impact on real estate is often a result of a complex interaction between all parts of a company or organisation as well as ICT acting in unison with other factors.

ICT has played a role in the facilitation of organisational change – through automation, through the provision of storage and through communication – and many changes would not have been conceivable without ICT. Taking a long view, these changes are axiomatic: just as the office 50 years ago bears very little relation to a modern office, nor does a warehouse, nor a shop. They may still retain the same function, but the processes that lead to the execution of that function have changed beyond recognition and changed the use of the space concomitantly.

ICT has also created new classifications of property, engendered reconfigurations of space, reduced demand for space in some areas and increased demand for space in others, all through the practical application of business processes. Of course, these processes are continuing to change. The ability to communicate between processes cost-effectively over long distances is bringing about even more radical change. Rather than relocating processes to cheaper locations within the UK or USA, they are being relocated much further afield with corresponding drops in labour cost. Process management techniques continue to refine and tune businesses, and supply chains are making heavy use of ICT in the process.

To many, the attraction of real estate lies in its enduring qualities of permanence or solidity. To the customer of that property, it represents economic capacity. Business processes provide the mechanism through which ICT has an impact upon space, and the exact nature of the impact is defined by how that space is viewed and operated by key stakeholders in the process. This clearly has ramifications for the role of real estate in the new economy, which is now examined in more detail in the next chapter, together with the empirical evidence that supports the existence of the new economy.

Notes

1   See Chapter 7 for a fuller discussion of Duffy's work.
2   In the 1960s Gordon Moore (1965), co-founder of Intel Corporation, projected that the density (and hence power) of transistors on a silicon chip would double

every 18 months. The principles of Moore's Law have held fast and today's processors have 256 times the density of those manufactured in 1987 and 65 000 times the density of those manufactured in 1975.

3 Note that in Figure 4.5, 'conventional' categories of property or real estate are used. In Part 2 of this book we explore how the distinctions between such categories are becoming blurred and how new types of real estate are being created.

4 See also Chapter 7.

5

The New Economy and Real Estate

Introduction

During the late 1990s many commentators began to refer to the emergence of a 'new economy', built on major structural changes driven by globalisation and ICT. Those companies that utilised these trends to their advantage, it was believed, would outperform their competitors (Pohjola 2002). The stock market boom, ICT growth and the plethora of vibrant dot.coms were seen as evidence of this new economy. In fact, in an opinion poll in March 2000, 57% of Americans believed the USA had entered a 'new kind of economy' that is 'significantly different from the industrial economy' (Business Week 2000).

At the same time, other experts were starting to predict the demise of physical assets in the new economy (Boulton *et al*. 2000). Intangible goods such as knowledge and information were seen as the foundation for a new, 'weightless' economy, and therefore tangible assets, such as real estate, were viewed by some as being 'deadweight'. If ICT could improve productivity, the argument went, space requirements would diminish and the demand for real estate would decline (see Chapter 4). This thesis was strengthened by the concept that real estate outsourcing could provide increased shareholder value, as property was taken off the balance sheet through inventive financial instruments such as sale and leaseback or synthetic leases (Dixon *et al*. 2000). As real assets were considered under threat, then real estate companies providing services to owners and occupiers began to seriously challenge their existence and their *modus operandi*. The whole future role of real estate and related services came to be seriously questioned therefore.

In the light of these trends, this chapter builds on previous chapters to examine the concept of a new economy, critically reviewing its components and providing a formal definition. It also draws together the themes identified under the 'new economy' banner within the theoretical framework in Chapter 1 (and in subsequent chapters) and examines the role of real estate in the new economy. The chapter therefore is designed to provide a bridge with the discussion in Part 2 of the book, which focuses on real estate in more detail, and provides a critical review of previous research examining the link between ICT and productivity at the economy and firm levels. The concept of 'eProperty' is also introduced to underpin the theoretical framework, which runs throughout the book.

The chapter therefore focuses particularly on how ICT is impacting on location of economic activity and the demand for real estate, the intensity of use and the nature of the real estate that is in demand. Building on concepts explored in Chapter 4, it draws heavily on examples from both the retail and office property sectors. In this sense our aim in this chapter is to explore the concepts (and evidence) of 'ICT-driven productivity' and the 'new economy', which have already been referred to earlier. To that extent, and in particular in terms of our discussion of productivity impact, the focus is very much on an overview (and therefore not an exhaustive study) of the most recent empirical research outside real estate, in an area where there are an increasing number of new studies, as new data become more readily available. Finally, we also suggest that there have been a series of 'new economies' over time, and in this chapter we outline the nature of its most recent morphology.

What is the new economy?

In Chapters 1 and 2 the concepts of the information society and the new economy were introduced and their relationship explored. In this book we use the following definition which we believe captures the main components of the 'new economy': 'a knowledge and idea-based economy where the key to job creation and higher standards of living are innovative ideas and technology embedded in services and manufactured products' (Progressive Policy Institute 1998). This seems to us to encapsulate both the potential impact of ICT and the transformational power of knowledge and information-based industries.

But is the new economy really a new phenomenon? Some doubt the veracity of this. For example, Rowlatt *et al.* (2002) suggest there have always been new economies and that the concept is not tied to time or technology. For example, over hundreds of years, periods have occurred when technological change has brought about radical changes to market boundaries, increasing the scope to exploit intellectual capital. Again there have been periods when access to new products and services was created for major sections of society as new consumers or changes in the inter-actions and operating processes of businesses and the redefinition of relationships between customers and suppliers occurred. Examples in-clude printing, steam, power (including electricity), canals, and railways, mass media, and more recently ICT (see also Perez 2002; Gordon 2000 in Chapter 1). Although each innovation changed economic structures and relationships in society, none was purely economic in nature. Each en-abled the commercial exploitation of intellectual capital, brought new products or services to new consumers and changed socio-economic behaviour.

But the new economy of the twenty-first century is different from any other new economy. For example, Rowlatt *et al.* (2002) highlight three main aspects of its current morphology:

- infrastructure to assemble, analyse, communicate and manage infor-mation within 'computer-mediated networks';
- transactions to purchase goods and services carried out through EDI or over the Internet;
- interactions transferring information between enterprises or individ-uals which add to value.

In comparison, Robert Gordon (2000) adopts a more sceptical view. Al-though Gordon sees the new economy as the post-1995 acceleration in the rate of technical change in IT together with the development of the Internet, he is dubious of IT's impact, suggesting it pales in comparison with the great technological advances of the past. In fact, the recent demise of dot.coms and falls in the NASDAQ index in the latter part of the 1990s lend some weight to the argument of sceptics. For example, on 14 April 2000 the Dow Jones Industrial Average saw its biggest ever one-day decline. After rapid growth the global technology market plummeted dramatically and by the autumn of 2000, US start-ups were going bust at the rate of one per day with high-profile failures in the UK (Coyle & Quah 2002). This and the other collapses in the related telecom sectors led to an increased scepticism about the permanency of the concept of the new economy (Pohjola 2002; OECD 2003).

Despite the fallout, however, new evidence suggests (see OECD 2003; Pohjola 2002) that fundamental changes are continuing in the structure of the economies worldwide, and a key reason is technological advances based around the microprocessor. In the 1960s Gordon Moore (1965), co-founder of Intel Corporation, projected that the density (and hence power) of transistors on a silicon chip would double every 18 months. The principles of Moore's Law have held fast and today's processors have 256 times the density of those manufactured in 1987 and 65 000 times the density of those manufactured in 1975.[2]

Most agree that it is this dramatic growth in power (Figure 5.1), and falls in the cost of processing power[3] (Figure 5.2) that have underpinned a range of technologies which are likely to deliver innovative commercial applications over the medium to long run. This technology includes biotechnology, nanotechnology, robotics and advanced materials. Moreover, Coyle (2002) suggests that it is the wide range of applications of ICT in these and other fields that mean ICT is a general-purpose technology (GPT). It therefore has four characteristics:

- **Wide range of uses**. Information processing is a generic description, which includes a variety of uses from authoring movie broadcasts to clothes or car design. Where there used to be one computer for every 100 people, soon there will be one 100 computers for every person.
- **Application across many industries**. Virtually every industry has set up or is setting up online business-to-business supply chains.
- **Complementary to technologies**. Computer technology goes hand-in-hand with other new waves of technology such as biotechnology and robotics.

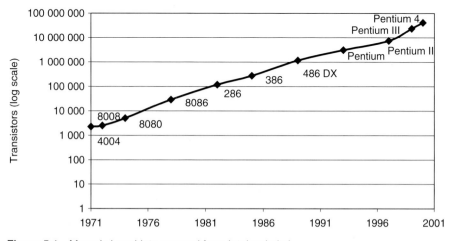

Figure 5.1   Moore's Law (data sourced from Intel website).

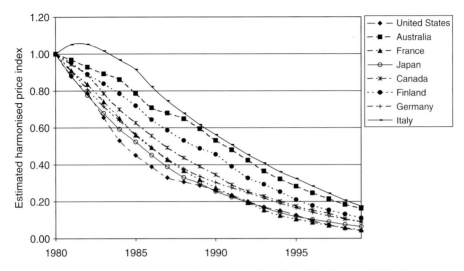

Estimates of 'harmonised' price indices assume that price ratios between ICT and non-ICT products have the same time patterns across countries, with the United States as the benchmark.

Figure 5.2   Price indices for ICT products, harmonised deflators.
Source: OECD, STI/EAS estimates based on National Accounts (SNA93), March 2001.

- **Scope for dramatic improvements**. Building on what has already occurred over the last 20 years, there is likely to be scope for improvements in the speed, power and user-friendliness of computers.

Coyle (2002) also suggests that there are three stages in the development of a new GPT:

- Stage 1. Faster productivity growth in the innovating sector.
- Stage 2. Falling prices leading to capital deepening (i.e. additional investment in new capital goods).
- Stage 3. Significant reorganisation of production occurring around the new capital goods, leading to long-run gains.

However, she also highlights the importance of non-technological factors in affecting the impact of ICT, just as legislative and regulatory factors affected production technologies in the USA in the first half of the twentieth century. These include limited liability; the presence of the stock market; investment banking; and the existence of an anti-trust policy. She suggests that 'hype' is actually important for creating impetus for a step change. Transformation can therefore be highly disruptive and, in her view, adoption can require investments in management, training, infrastructure and other support, which are up to ten times larger than invest-ment in the technologies themselves.

Building on the concept of GPTs, and in contrast to Gordon's more scep-tical view of ICT impact, research by Crafts (2001) also attempts to place the role of ICT in historical context. Using a growth accounting method-ology he compares the contributions to growth (in terms of capital intensi-fication and productivity growth) of three GPTs: steam in Britain from 1780 to 1860; and electricity and ICT in the USA between 1899–1929 and 1974–2000 respectively. His analysis suggests that ICT impact has already outperformed the steam-power revolution and is similar to the impact of electrification. Expectations regarding ICT have been overplayed, how-ever, in his view because of unrealistic expectations and because of short-ages of new varieties of capital.

It can be argued that it is too early yet to draw firm conclusions about ICT impact and the nature of a real paradigm shift. However, despite this, and despite a degree of controversy over its exact meaning, there is growing evidence to suggest that a new economy is developing, driven by techno-logical change in alliance with other forces. The question remains, how-ever, what is the empirical evidence for this new economy and how can it best be measured?

The evidence for a new economy

Problems in measurement

If the new economy truly does exist then this belief needs to be sustained by evidence. Certainly there has been a steady shift away from manu-facturing, as productivity has risen, but measuring the new economy presents problems in itself. A much broader range of indicators are needed to measure the changes that are occurring (Coyle & Quah 2002). Measures such as those suggested by the Progressive Policy Insti-tute (1998) are a helpful foundation in this respect (see Table 5.1). However, Coyle and Quah (2002) argue that understanding the new economy as the dynamic iteration of gradually changing supply, and radically fluctuating demand, offers the way forward. They suggest that businesses need to understand consumer behaviour better if they are to anticipate the changes brought about by ICT. Consumers' experiences with ICT and their evolving tastes and preferences therefore require a clearer understanding. In their view, three challenges should be taken up:

Table 5.1   Keys to the old and new economies (adapted from Progressive Policy Institute 1998).

Economy-wide characteristics	Old economy	New economy
Markets	Stable	Dynamic
Scope of competition	National	Global
Organisational form	Hierarchical, bureaucratic	Networked
Industry		
Organisation of production	Mass production	Flexible production
Key drivers of growth	Capital/labour	Innovation/knowledge
Key technology driver	Mechanisation	Digitisation
Source of competitive advantage	Lowering cost through economies of scale	Innovation, quality, time-to-market and cost
Importance of research/ innovation	Low-moderate	High
Relations with other firms	Go it alone	Alliances and collaboration
Workforce		
Policy goal	Full employment	Higher real wages and incomes
Skills	Job-specific skills	Broad skills and cross-training
Requisite education	A skill or degree	Lifelong learning
Labour-management relations	Adversarial	Collaborative
Nature of employment	Stable	Market risk and opportunity
Government		
Business–government relations	Impose requirements	Encourage growth opportunities
Regulation	Command and control	Market tools, flexibility

- A better analysis of the technological drivers creating structural changes in businesses and working lives, both in terms of case studies and through performance data.
- Better predictive capacity needed in the methods which should also reflect dynamics of the new economy.
- Responsibility to renew business practices and policy prescriptions to reflect the new economy.

Nonetheless, although the empirical evidence for the new economy in the UK is patchier than the USA, structural changes are relatively more easily identifiable. The trend towards services away from manufacturing (Figure 5.3), for example, has occurred more quickly in the UK than in other economies. Coyle and Quah (2002) and Pohjola (2002) also suggest that labour market changes have also been marked: the trend towards flexible working patterns, for example, and changes in corporate structures such as flatter organisations, outsourcing and relocation of production across borders. These have also been underpinned by macro-shifts, including increases in cross-border investment; rapid trade growth; expansion of turnover in financial markets; low inflation led by price decline and

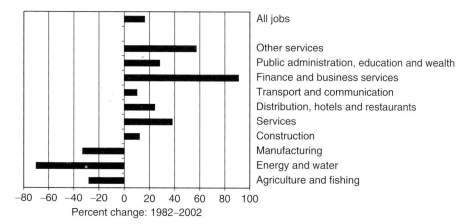

Percent change: 1982–2002

Figure 5.3 Workforce jobs by industry, UK: March 2002 (data from National Statistics 2003).

structural reduction in GDP growth in UK and USA. A common theme in this argument is that the economy is becoming 'weightless' (Coyle 1997): creating value depends less on physical mass and more on intangibles such as knowledge, creativity and information.

Coyle and Quah's (2002) work also stresses the importance of 'belief'. They argue that investments in infrastructure, institutions or processes will not occur unless individuals, businesses and governments 'believe' in the existence of structural changes. In their view if people do not think that there is a reason to spend additional amounts or disrupt their current processes then they will not bother. There is therefore an element of self-fulfilling prophecy in the new economy. Moreover, difficulties in measuring impact are encountered with growth accounting techniques: price indices are difficult to construct and productivity is hard to estimate in many service industries.[4] Indeed, statistics are still designed to measure productivity in the standardised mass economy of the post-war era, and so it is not surprising that productivity impacts may not be revealed in all circumstances. They argue that to better understand the dynamics of the new economy requires better knowledge of consumer demand.

However, such impacts have frequently been difficult to examine empirically, leading to what Robert Solow (1987) referred to as the 'productivity paradox'. In business, he suggested, 'We see computers everywhere but not in the productivity statistics'. Others such as Brynjolfsson and Hitt (1998) have also highlighted the productivity paradox, which meant that computers were not delivering the value promised. This sceptical view has also been mirrored in the work of Robert Gordon in the USA (see, for example, Gordon 2000). Gordon has expressed severe doubts over the validity of comparing the Internet, as part of the ICT revolution, with the great productivity accelerators of the past, such as electricity, automobiles and the railways. Gordon compares the new economy with previous industrial revolutions and examines the impact of new technologies on economic productivity. He suggests that the First Industrial Revolution (1760–1830) introduced inventions such as the steam engine and the power loom, but had little impact on productivity, whereas the Second Industrial Revolution (1860–1900) provided groundbreaking technologies that led to a 'golden age' of productivity growth (1913–1972). In his view, innovations such as electricity, automobiles, and the telephone had a huge impact on people's lives. In comparison the Internet has not had the same impact. In empirical terms he also argues that the case for the Internet is unproven. Breaking economic history into four periods (1870–1913; 1913–1972; 1972–1995; 1995–1999), he suggests that the US economy did experience productivity growth in the post-1995 era in excess of 1913–1972, whereas the other two periods had productivity growth of less than half of these two productive eras. But he also argues that productivity growth is limited to durable manufacturing, especially computer manufacture.

He also argues that the Internet has not increased the growth in demand for computers, and that rapid growth in the early 1990s can be interpreted as the same unit elastic response to the decline in computer prices as was prevalent prior to 1995. A variety of factors also militate against the impact of the Internet and ICT. Market share protection is effectively a zero sum game, where businesses invest in ICT to stay with the competition, rather than on a decision to bolster or increase productivity. There is also a tendency to recreate old activities rather than create new activities with the Internet.

Perhaps the biggest sceptic of all, however, was Paul Strassmann, whose work (see, for example, Strassmann 1997) suggested there was no correlation between expenditure on IT and any known measure of productivity. Using a simple scattergram between return on equity and IT spending per employee, Strassmann suggested that spending more on IT does not in itself boost economic performance. This does not contradict the fact, however, that frequently computers make decisive contributions to efficiency, competitive viability, and value-creation, but high and low spending levels were associated with both inferior and superior results. The same lack of correlation occurred when a single industry was examined. Strassmann (1997) looked at food firms and banking services and again found no correlation. He went on to suggest:

Computers are only tools. They are not an unqualified blessing.... The problem seems to rest not with the inherent capabilities of the technologies, which are awesome, but with the managerial inability to use them effectively....If computer expenditures and corporate profits show no correlation, it is a reflection of the human condition that excellence is an uneven occurrence. It is unrealistic to expect that computerization could ever change that.

These issues create difficulties in measuring the new economy and ICT's role within the new economy. More recently, however, there has been increasing evidence of impact as new research from the OECD (2003) and elsewhere has shown. It is also noteworthy that the productivity performance of the US economy over the latter part of the 1990s has impressed even renowned sceptics such as Solow (Pohjola 2002). Moreover, in 1999 Solow was reported to have shifted his beliefs on the subject and suggested that it had taken time for the impact of ICT to feed through (Lohr 1999). Evidence is beginning to emerge therefore of ICT impact on productivity at both an economy level and individual firm level.

ICT and productivity at the economy level

At the economy level, research by Arnold Harberger (1998) in the USA suggested that technological innovations could be divided into two groups: 'yeast'-like impacts affecting the economy as a whole, rather like bread rising in a warm place, or 'mushroom'-like, where technology increases the productivity of specific industries or processes. Mushroom-like surges tend to be very localised and are independent of each other and are unlikely to create spill-over effects in terms of benefits to other sectors. Harberger's empirical work on pre-1990s US growth suggested that productivity gains were indeed confined to less than half, and sometimes even less, of the manufacturing sector. He therefore concluded that technology-led growth in the 1970s and 1980s was mushroom-like. Coyle and Quah (2002) also support this view and suggest that evidence from the USA lends weight to the 'mushroom' analogy for 1990s growth, especially in certain sectors such as IT.

For example, recent research by McKinsey (Johnson 2002) on the 1995–2000 rise in US productivity suggested that nearly all of the surge in growth in this period was explained by six sectors (retail, wholesale, securities, telecom, semi-conductors and computer manufacturing). All had invested heavily in ICT and this combined with industry-specific factors (managerial and structural factors) was the explanation for the growth. Retail productivity provides an interesting example. Retail productivity growth jumped from 2% (1987–1995) to 6.3% (1995–1999) and explained nearly 25% of the economy-wide surge in productivity. In fact, the McKinsey research showed that more than 50% of the productivity increase in retailing was due to the impact of Wal-Mart, and at least half of Wal-Mart's productivity growth was due to managerial innovations that improved store efficiencies: cross-training of employees who could function in more than one department, for example, was especially important. This is not to suggest that ICT was unimportant; rather that it is not the whole story. Indeed, the McKinsey research also acknowledged that in certain industries which had invested heavily (hotels, banking and long distance data transmission), there had been no commensurate increase in productivity. This suggests therefore that ICT had impacted in only a particular set of industries. But Coyle and Quah argue, once ICT becomes a GPT, 'yeast-like' impacts will be more pervasive. However, they also suggest that the restructuring of organisations requires time and frequently delays diffusion.

More recently, new data from the OECD have enabled further light to be shed on the impact of ICT on productivity at both economy and firm level. The OECD Ministerial Report (OECD 2001) on the new economy concluded that ICT was important and had the potential to contribute to more rapid growth and productivity in years to come. Subsequent work by the OECD in 2001 (OECD 2003) has examined the contribution made by ICT to economic performance in 13 OECD countries to determine the degree to which the empirical findings continue to support the thesis of a new economy. Essentially there are three channels by which ICT can lift potential growth rates (Visco 2000):

- ICT-producing sectors themselves, which contribute directly to overall growth by virtue of their own (increasingly efficient) output;
- higher ICT investment, which raises the capital intensity of production in the economy at large, reflecting sharp increases in quality and a fall in the prices of ICT equipment; and
- spill-over effects, such as the spread of the Internet and the development of eCommerce.

This last channel might deliver significant cost reductions and organisational improvement to firms. In the overall economy, these savings and efficiency gains would show up in the form of faster expansion in the growth not accounted for by the increase in the quantity (and quality) of labour and physical capital used in the production process. This is what economists call multi-factor productivity (MFP) growth (OECD 2003). Nonetheless, as other evidence in the current chapter shows, the new economy must be seen as being driven by ICT in combination with a variety of other forces, thus adding further weight to the argument for a socio-technical framework.

At an aggregate and sectoral level, the OECD research (2003) suggests that ICT has been a very dynamic area of investment because of the steep decline in ICT prices which has encouraged ICT investment, and even shifted investment away from other assets. Growth accounting estimates show that ICT accounted for 0.3% and 0.8% points of growth in GDP per capita between 1995 and 2001. The USA, Australia, the Netherlands and Canada produced the largest increase (Figure 5.4); Japan and UK a more modest one, and Germany, France and Italy a smaller one still. Software comprised about one third of the overall ICT contribution to growth.

These findings have also been supported by results from individual countries. Table 5.2 shows selected results from USA, UK and Finland, for example. The OECD research also points out that the impact of ICT investment on economic growth has not finished: although ICT investment has slowed down, continuing technological progress is expected to reduce the price of computers and microprocessors.

Similarly, ICT manufacturing itself can also contribute to aggregate productivity growth. For example, the OECD found that the largest contributions to growth were made in Finland, Ireland, Japan, Korea, Sweden and the USA. This is as much as 1% of growth in the period 1995–2000 in Finland, Ireland and Korea. Although the ICT-producing services sector

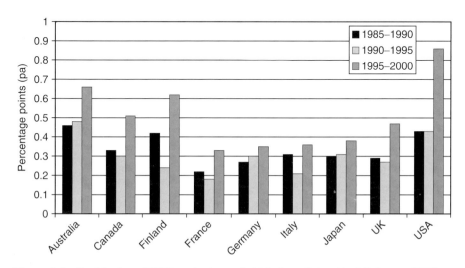

Figure 5.4   Contribution of ICT to output growth (data from Colecchia & Schreyer 2001).

Table 5.2 Impact of ICT investment on GDP growth (% pa) (adapted from OECD 2003).

Country	GDP growth		Labour productivity growth		Contribution of ICT		Notes
	1990–1995	1995–2000	1990–1995	1995–2000	1990–1995	1995–2000	
USA							
Oliner and Sichel (2002)	–	–	1.5	2.3	0.5	1.0	1991–1995; 1996–2001
Jorgenson et al. (2002)	2.5	4.0	1.4	2.7	0.5	1.0	1990–1995; 1995–1999
UK							
Oulton (2001)	1.4	3.1	3.0	1.5	0.4	0.6	1989–1994; 1994–1996
Finland							
Jalava and Pohjola (2002)	–	–	3.9	3.5	0.6	0.5	1990–1995; 1996–1999

(telecommunications and computer services) is a smaller contributor, growth has been fast, driven partly by liberalised telecommunications markets but also by technological change, especially in Canada, Finland, France, Germany and the Netherlands.

Growth appears also to be driven by ICT-using services. For example, research from the USA supports the findings of the McKinsey study. Wholesale and retail trade and financial services tend to use ICT intensively and drive productivity increases. Work by Triplett and Bosworth (2002), for example, found that MFP growth in the wholesale trade increased from 1.1% pa to 2.4% pa from 1987–1995 to 1995–2000. In retail the increase was from 0.4% pa to 3.0% pa and in securities, 2.9% pa to 11.2% pa. In all these sectors the impact of ICT on MFP is due mainly to the more efficient use of labour and capital linked to the use of ICT in the production process.

'Spill-over' effects (where a firm's adoption of ICT has positive impacts on the economy as a whole) can also be important, however, and in countries where the surge in ICT investment started earlier, the benefits to other sectors may be greater. Gust and Marquez (2002), for example, confirm the view that sound macroeconomic policies, well-functioning markets and institutions and a competitive economic environment benefit greater investment in ICT, and they contrast the experience of relatively low ICT investment in European countries with higher levels of investment in the USA.

In summary, the evidence from the OECD (2003) suggests that ICT has had considerable impact on productivity growth during the latter half of the 1990s and into 2001. The impact is threefold:

- In some countries (notably USA, Canada and Australia) with strong growth, ICT investment has supported labour productivity growth, which has continued to be sustained despite the recent ICT slowdown.
- In some countries (i.e. Finland, Ireland and Korea), ICT production has been an important contributor to aggregate labour and MFP growth.
- In some OECD countries (notably USA and Australia) there is evidence to show service sectors (especially distribution and financial services) have invested heavily in ICT and achieved rapid MFP growth.

However, what is clear is that growth is not just the result of single policy or institutional factors. It is also clear that generally Europe continues to lag behind the USA in terms of ICT productivity impact (Daveri 2002), perhaps because of later diffusion. These findings have been confirmed in other research. Work by van Ark *et al.* (2003), for example, shows that Europe continues to generally lag behind the USA in terms of ICT-driven productivity growth. Using shift share analysis in 51 industries they showed that US growth has been faster because of a larger ICT-producing sector and faster growth in service industries that make intensive use of ICT. The difference in growth between the two regions is largely explained by more intensive use of ICT within the wholesale and retail trades, and in the securities sectors in the USA in comparison with Europe. In short, diffusion of ICT in Europe is under way and is following patterns very similar to the USA, but the pace is slower overall (van Ark *et al.* 2002).

Moreover, ICT can help explain growth disparities but does not in itself lead to higher growth (Pilat 2003). Other factors such as innovation, human capital business creation and sound economic foundations are very important in driving productivity growth. As the OECD (2001) points out, a number of factors combined to produce the growth of the late 1990s besides new capital (which included ICT). This included increased use of labour and quality of labour and greater efficiency in how capital and labour are combined (or MFP). A more restrictive market and tighter regulatory frameworks for labour but also falling labour productivity generally may also partly explain the USA-Europe differential (McGuckin & van Ark 2001).

ICT and productivity at the firm level

According to the OECD (2003) the strongest evidence for impact of ICT comes at the firm level. At this level, ICT can impact in the following ways:

- More effective use of ICT can help firms gain market share at the expense of less productive firms and so raise overall productivity.
- ICT can help firms expand product range, customise services or respond better to customers, all of which are examples of innovation.
- ICT can reduce inefficiency in capital and labour through reducing inventories and hence perhaps higher productivity.

However, as we have suggested previously, such impacts have frequently been difficult to examine empirically, leading to what Robert Solow (1987) referred to as the 'productivity paradox'.

Several new studies have pointed to the key reasons why this productivity paradox occurred (OECD 2003; Coyle & Quah 2002). First, productivity benefits may not have been picked up in the statistics, especially in the service sector where most of the ICT investment occurs, and where productivity is harder to measure. Second, it may well be that the benefits of ICT have taken longer to emerge historically. Often technology diffusion is slow and firms can take a long time to adjust in terms of changing organisations, upgrading the workforce and developing and implementing new business processes. It also takes time for ICT networks to develop and impact at an economy level, and it is now becoming evident that there is stronger evidence for ICT impact in the latter part of the 1990s than there was in the earlier 1970s and 1980s. Finally, many of the historic studies of ICT at a firm level were based on small samples drawn from private sources and may be prone to error not only because of size but because of 'noise' from other economic factors.

Productivity can also be difficult to measure because of spill-over effects outside the arena of the individual firm. Connecting firms within ICT networks, for example, can mean that the resultant benefits are transferred, as transaction costs are reduced, which can lead to better matched supply and demand and the growth of new markets. Knowledge creation can also be promulgated by increased use of ICT, which can also lead to increases in productivity (Bartelsman & Hinloopen 2004).

In new research (OECD 2003), therefore, official data have enabled a clearer picture of the impact of ICT at firm level to emerge within 13 OECD countries. This research showed that there is clear evidence to suggest that ICT can have a positive impact on firm performance. For example, evidence from the manufacturing sector in Canada (Baldwin & Sabourin 2002) suggests Canadian firms using one or more ICT technologies had a higher level of productivity than firms that did not use these technologies. The same research also found that communications network technologies were especially important in increasing productivity. Work from the USA (McGuckin *et al.* 1998) has also showed that those firms that use advanced technologies have higher productivity, controlling for factors such as size, age, capital intensity, labour force skills, industry and region. Other evidence from the OECD programme of research also shows that firms using ICT also typically pay higher wages, but that ICT in itself does not guarantee success: for example, many of the firms showing improved performance due to ICT were already above-average performers.

Work in Japan (Motohashi 2001), as part of the OECD research, has also highlighted the importance of computer networks in productivity improvement. This showed that the impact of direct business operation networks (such as production and logistic control systems) was much greater than on back-office supporting systems, such as human resource management and management planning systems. Work in the UK also supports the view that computer networks can benefit firms through electronic publishing rather than through selling. Research by Clayton and Waldron (2003) also suggests that in the UK, financial intermediation is the sector most likely to use network technologies, including broadband, and the sector also most likely to use technologies in combination.

More recently the Internet has also been seen as an important contributor to firm-level productivity. In research funded by Cisco, Varian *et al.* (2002) found that companies implementing Internet business applications were experiencing reduced operating costs and increased revenues sufficiently large to affect the current and projected productivity growth rate in each country examined. For example, the study found that deploying Internet business solutions between 1998 and 2002 had yielded a cost saving of $155.2 bn for US firms, paralleled by revenue increases of $444 bn. In the UK, France and Germany costs savings in the same period were $8.3 bn and revenue increase, $79 bn. In productivity terms, the research suggested that the Internet could contribute nearly half of the expected productivity growth rate increase (0.9 percentage points per annum) in the USA from 2001 to 2010: in the UK, France and Germany the equivalent figures were 36% of the 0.3 percentage point per annum increase in productivity. The report suggests that the Internet represents a new and very flexible way of communicating information cheaply and rapidly. This should therefore reduce transaction costs, enhance the efficiency of producing goods and services and reduce the cost (and increase the effectiveness) of dealing with customers.

However, other related firm-level factors should not be ignored. MFP growth also reflects the effects of competition (Pilat 2003). Analysis of productivity growth at the firm level has revealed, for example, that competition, including the entry and exit of firms, and changes in market shares are important in driving economic growth. New firms tend to use a more efficient mix of labour, capital and technology than existing firms, especially in the ICT sector. Work by Clayton and Waldron (2003) also shows the importance of linking ICT growth with other factors. They found that UK businesses with higher levels of R&D spending relative to turnover in each sector also deliver more new and improved product sales relative to turnover, and that firms with no innovation grow slowest. Firms with moderate innovation perform better, but those firms with the highest innovation levels grow fastest.

Other drivers of productivity

As the OECD study (2003) points out, previous studies of ICT impact have frequently concluded that ICT returns were relatively high compared with investments in other fixed assets, but this has now been explained by the fact that ICT investment is often accompanied by other expenditures which may not count as investment *per se*. This includes spending on skills training and organisational change. Not surprisingly, the other side of the coin is that ICT has the biggest impact in those firms which have improved their skills base and created better organisational structures. 'Co-invention' (Bresnahan & Greenstein 1996), where users adapt, experiment and invent with the technology, has also been found to be very important in driving technology implementation.

Again, the introduction of ICT has also been found to vary with firm size, age of firm and its function. Organisational change, for example, can include new strategies, new business processes and practices and new structures. Very often workers today have to use multiple skills in the workplace and also work in teams. This has led to a variety of work practices which include: teamwork, flatter management structures, and employee involvement and suggestion schemes (OECD 2001, 2003). This places greater pressure on workers to take individual responsibility and a greater linkage between management and labour. This type of management change tends to be firm specific, and empirical studies show a positive return to ICT investment, with substantial variation across organisations. For example, in the USA, research (Black & Lynch 2001) has shown that the introduction of workplace practices such as giving employees greater voice in decision making, profit-sharing schemes and so on can increase productivity. Similarly, in the UK, work by Caroli and Van Reenen (1999) used the Workplace Industrial Relations Survey to examine the relationship between ICT and organisational change, and found that organisational change, technology and skills were complementary. Organisational change tended to reduce the demand for unskilled workers and organisational change had the biggest impact in firms with larger initial pools of skills.

The size of firm is also important to consider as an additional factor influencing ICT impact. For example, research from the UK (Clayton & Waldron 2003) has also shown that larger firms are more likely to use network technologies such as the intranet, Internet or EDI than smaller firms, although smaller firms (10–49 employees) are more likely to use the Internet as their only ICT network technology. This may be partly due to larger firms also using networks to redesign the communication and information flows within a firm.

It is also clear from UK research that the benefits of ICT may only emerge over time. As one would logically expect, the OECD study (2003) showed that in the UK, the firms that had adopted ICT earlier were using eCommerce earlier: for those firms that adopted ICT in 2000 only 20% were using eCommerce, for example, compared with close to 50% of firms who had adopted ICT before 1995. Firms also tend to move towards more complex forms of ICT over time: out of all firms starting to use ICT prior to 1995, only 3% had not yet moved beyond basic use of ICT in 2000. Most firms had developed an Internet site or bought and sold through eCommerce, but of those firms adopting ICT in 2000, over 20% had not extended beyond the simple use of ICT.

Indeed, in the same OECD study, firm-level evidence is stronger than aggregate-level and sectoral-level evidence. There are a number of reasons why this may occur. For example, aggregating data across firms and industries may disguise ICT impact, or it may be that ICT also depends on other factors and policy initiatives which also differ from industry to industry. There are certainly important cross-country differences in firms' use of ICT. For example, new firms in the USA seem to be more experimental with new business models than in other OECD countries, and they also start smaller than in Europe and grow more rapidly if they are successful. This may be caused by lower risk aversion in EU countries such as the UK, linked with more liquid financial capital markets and greater venture capital risk taking. Also, lower burdens in terms of regulations in the USA may play a role and help enable smaller companies to scale up their ICT operations. In the rest of the OECD, firms may face much higher entry and exit costs, however. Other factors were found to be important in affecting firms' investment and the diffusion of ICT, including:

- direct costs of ICT (for example, costs of ICT equipment or telecommunications costs);
- costs and implementation barriers (for example, the presence of skilled personnel, the scope for organisational change or the scale of innovations in ICT);
- risk and uncertainty (for example, the risks of online trading or uncertainty relating to payments);
- nature of the business (for example, ICT is a GPT but is more suitable for some uses than others and may not fit all contexts and applications);
- competition (for example, a competitive environment is more likely to result in a firm investing in ICT).

In summary, as previous research has pointed out, ICT is not the only source of organisational improvement (Momentum Research Group 2003). Productivity increases result from the right combination of worker skills, tools used, environment, and a range of other factors. As Pilat (2003) shows, growth is not just the result of a single policy or institutional arrangement, and ICT does not on its own lead to higher growth. This has important policy implications because governments adopt comprehensive policies linking economic and social frameworks, ICT diffusion, innovation and investment in human capital and new business. Nonetheless there is growing evidence to suggest that ICT can contribute towards productivity improvement in the economy and within firms and businesses.

The role of real estate in the new economy

In Chapter 4 we explored in basic terms how changes in business processes can potentially impact on the space and real estate requirements of organisations. In this section we examine some of the transformations that are occurring in more detail, taking a more critical look at productivity issues in particular.

The relationship between productivity, employment and real estate

If productivity at an economy and firm level is increased then that theoretically changes the demand for space in different businesses and in different sectors of real estate. Put simply, for example, if worker productivity is increased by ICT, fewer workers are needed to produce the same amount of output. Similarly, this will have a knock-on effect in the demand for space occupied by the businesses affected. However, this represents a deterministic and simplistic view of productivity and space impact. As Landmann (2002) points out, employment, productivity and aggregate output are closely linked. If productivity is measured as output per person or output per hour worked then the three variables can be linked as:

$$output = employment \times productivity$$

This shows that any given rate of output growth can be achieved with either high productivity growth and low employment growth, or conversely with low productivity growth and high employment growth. Taken to an extreme interpretation, this has led to an 'end of work' thesis (Rifkin 1994). In fact, as Bootle (2003) points out, a thesis such as this promotes the 'lump of labour' fallacy.

For example, in France in 2001 the government courted controversy by introducing a 35-hour week, not only to promote a better work–life balance but to effectively share work because, the argument went, if people did not work so long there would be more work to go around. However, this assumes a fixed 'lump' of work, which is not the case, because the level of jobs is dependent on aggregate demand: if one person gets a job it does not necessarily mean another loses one.

Similarly, to suggest that technological advance automatically leads to job loss is erroneous (Bean 2003). Although technology may lead to job losses in some firms and some sectors by enabling the same output with less labour, it may not necessarily, because the lower cost of production may allow a firm to lower prices and so boost demand for its product. Whether employment rises or falls therefore depends on how much the demand for the product is affected by price. That is not to say that in some sectors with rapid productivity growth and stagnant demand, employment will not fall (for example, the agriculture sector during the great shifts in industrial economies). Bean (2003) illustrates the fallacy in relation to the UK economy as a whole where the labour force has doubled since the middle of the nineteenth century while productivity has risen sevenfold, whilst unemployment has fluctuated over the same period.

In discussing the relationship between productivity and demand for space, therefore, it is important not to oversimplify the arguments. For example, it can be argued that increased productivity in the use of existing space will lead to reduced demand for space from that user for a fixed amount of production. However, this would only lead to reduced demand for space if the supply and demand for the product remain fixed. This is unlikely. In addition, increased productivity has always been associated with increased affluence and will tend to lead to an expanding economy.

Much will depend, therefore, on the individual real estate or economic sector that is under consideration. This view is reinforced by the evidence of differential productivity impact of ICT on particular industries in different countries (see Chapter 4 and the previous sections of this chapter). However, it is likely that businesses will continue to adjust their space requirements for reasons of efficiency and economy, driven by ICT alongside other factors. Technology can act to transform the workplace in two distinct ways: it changes the way in which people work and the type of work that people do. The dilemma for business is that although distribution and production costs can be reduced through technology, the intellectual or knowledge component of an organisation is much less easy to improve with technology. Recent research by Capital Economics (2002) for the RICS examined the costs associated with property ownership and occupation. This showed how UK businesses could save up to £18 bn pa through more efficient use of their property (boosting trading profits by up to 13%). A further £2 bn could be saved with some changes in government tax policy. If all office workers in the UK were to use 2.1 m^2 less space and assuming 25% of UK workers are employed in London at a higher cost than outside London, the business sector could save £7.8 bn per annum by implementing new working practices, such as hot-desking and hotelling.

Although the findings are based on presumptions of average savings across business they do indicate the importance of the link between technology, productivity and space, even though this still remains a relatively underresearched area. In the broad context of productivity change, one basic measure of assessing occupancy costs is to look at density of occupation. Density can either be dynamic density (the number of staff using a workplace) or static density (the number of workstations). A study by Gerald Eve (2001) examined both measures and compared them with previous surveys in 1997 and 1999. In 2001, for example, the survey revealed an average national benchmark density of 16.3 m^2 per officebased employee, compared with 16.6 m^2 in 1997 and 15.8 m^2 in 1999. In fact, the ICT sector was found to use its space the most efficiently with a density of occupation of 13 m^2 per employee. New working practices, such as hot-desking, hotelling and homeworking, have contributed to this, but much depends on the sector. For example, manufacturing is much less efficient in space terms than other sectors, using some 25.2 m^2 per employee in 2001. However, the same study found that the cost savings from such practices were impressive: the overall difference between those who have and have not adopted them is 2.1 m^2 per employee. The Capital Economics research (2002) also identifies the case of British Telecommunications, which in 2001 sold its property portfolio to Telereal, a joint venture between Land Securities Trillium and the Pears Group, for £2.38 bn. This was one of the UK's largest corporate property outsourcing deals. Although the main reason was to raise cash, the other important factor was to provide the flexibility to move to hotelling, and reduce static density from 1.3 desks per worker to less than one desk per worker.

It is in the light of such evidence that many have questioned the future of real estate assets in the new economy, and these arguments are now critically examined.

The death of real estate?

At the height of the dot.com boom there were those who argued that the revolution brought about by the new economy would lead to the 'death of geography'. As the Internet developed and new technology became all-pervasive, so conventional wisdom suggested, it would no longer be necessary for people to be physically located together. This parallels many of the arguments made for other technologies. A key exponent was Frances Cairncross (2001) who argued the case for the 'death of distance'. In *New Rules for the New Economy*, Kevin Kelly (1998) also wrote that: 'The New Economy operates in a "space" rather than a place, and over time more and more economic transactions will migrate to this new space'. However, he continues: 'Geography and real estate, however, will remain, well...real', although he also suggests that 'People will inhabit places, but increasingly the economy inhabits a space'.

In Richard Florida's view (2002), the death of distance thesis is easy to deflate. He argues strongly that people will remain highly concentrated and that clustering of industries in the new economy is vital to their success. Place and community continue to be critical factors. This view is supported by Joel Kotkin (2001), who suggests that technological transformation is reinforcing the importance of geography and place. It will therefore be increasingly important to consider where information processing companies, related services and skilled professionals choose to locate because this will shape the geographic importance of future cities and communities. This is a trend also identified by O'Mara (1999), who found that economic development incentives are less important in US company location decisions than 'ease of living' and labour market support found in the community.

Authors such as Marshall (1890) and Porter (1998) have also highlighted the importance of agglomeration in industrial clustering, which includes high-tech groupings such as Silicon Valley benefiting from co-location or economic spill-over effects. Others such as Putnam (2000) have suggested that regional economic growth is linked to closely knit communities where firms and the communities in which they are located enjoy strong ties. This is a concept known as 'social capital theory'. Florida, however, suggests that 'creative human capital' theory (building on the work of Jane Jacobs 1961) offers a better explanation for the trend towards knowledge-based clusters[5] in the new economy. This argues that the key to regional growth lies in the 'endowments of highly educated and productive people', and suggests that regional economic growth is driven by the location choices of creative people who prefer places that are diverse, tolerant and open to new ideas. This view is also supported by others, such as Storper and Venables (2002) who argue that face-to-face contact continues to play an important part in the role of cities and their continued economic growth. More recently this view has also gained favour in the UK with the concept of an 'ideopolis' or city of ideas (Cannon *et al.* 2003; Westwood & Nathan 2003), where cities are seen as hubs for international business, centres of indigenous growth and creative dynamic communities.

These views are also supported in other research, which suggests that location is also likely to remain a very important factor for businesses. For example, O'Mara (1999), in the same study referred to earlier in this section, examined the location of the decision-making process of 40 US companies with 'information age' jobs. Ease of living and labour market support in the community were found to be important, together with high-quality infrastructure (including telecommunications). Tayyaran and Khan (2003) also suggest that traditional factors still continue to drive location in an era of ICT (Table 5.3).

Kolko (2002) offers an interesting perspective on the tensions between dispersal and agglomeration in relation to location. He suggests that centripetal forces may act to promote clustering. For example, technological knowledge spills over to other firms, and is likely to be greater the smaller the distance between firms. Firms may also benefit from sharing intermediate inputs, or from sharing access to a common pool of labour. However, a reduction in the importance of the location of production would logically be expected if ICT were making an impact. Kolko studies ICT-intensive industries in the USA and finds that they exhibit slower employment convergence (i.e. the degree to which an industry's employment shifts away from locations in which it is over-represented, or the

Table 5.3 Key factors affecting location choice decisions in the information technology era (adapted from Tayyaran & Khan 2003).

Residential location	Office location
● Household characteristics	● Nature of business
● Housing cost	● Distributed work
● Size of dwelling	● Agglomeration economics
● Availability of information technologies and services	● Land cost and availability/office cost
● Telecommuting	● Availability of human resources
● Intelligent transportation systems	● Availability of enabling information technologies
● Travel time to work and reliability	● Telecommuting
● Quality of education	● Transportation: accessibility, travel time, reliability
● Travel time to school and reliability	● Parking
● Quality of life – outdoor recreational opportunities	● Quality of life
● Intelligent transportation systems	

tendency of an industry to become less concentrated over time) than other industries. However, he also found that it is not ICT in itself that leads to slower convergence: highly intensive IT industries also employ more highly educated workers and once this factor is controlled, ICT appears to lead to more rapid convergence. ICT clustering occurs therefore because of the availability of highly skilled labour.

Finally, Leamer and Storper (2001) combine the perspectives of an international economist and economic geographer to examine how and to what extent Internet will affect the location of economic activity. They argue that most exchanges of physical goods continue to take place within restricted 'neighbourhoods'. Indeed, previous infrastructure changes have had a 'double effect', leading to dispersion of routine activities but also increasing the complexity/time dependence of production. This has also led to agglomeration. Leamer and Storper argue that the Internet will not create the same levels of transformation as in the past, because of the continuing need for proximity which the Internet does not allow: complex, uncodifiable messages are not suited to the medium.

At a finer scale of resolution, the future of real estate which comprises urban areas is clearly under scrutiny. However, in the same way that ICT will not mean the end of cities, it is premature to talk about the 'death of real estate'. For example, changes in technology and lifestyle have driven workplace change and have encouraged dispersed office working. Harrison (2002) provides an interesting perspective on what is termed the 'distributed workplace', driven by the concept of 'matrix living', where individuals' lifestyles include multiple tasks and locations across time. Focusing on DEGW's Sustainable Accommodation for the New Economy (SANE)[6] framework, Harrison suggests that the distributed workplace model fits with a changing perspective of real estate. For example, on the supply side, developers will become more focused on thinking about buildings in terms of the opportunity to deliver high value-added services on a global basis to a customer base, rather than simply as a passive investment vehicle. On the demand or tenant's side there is increasing interest in global solutions that provide flexibility and break down barriers between real estate provisions, building operation and the provision of business services.

This means that companies need to consider different types of real estate to cater for shifting needs and requirements. For example, Gibson and Louargand (2001) suggest that for corporate property managers, the emphasis solely on real estate assets has shifted. Contracts and relationships and workplace infrastructure must also be considered and new ways of looking at managing risk in the real estate portfolio must be developed. They suggest property use can be divided into 'core' assets, used for extended periods of time; 'cyclical' assets used for varying degrees as the business cycle or product cycle waxes or wanes; and 'casual assets' needed on a seasonal basis. They cite the example of a speciality core plant for manufacturing base compounds; cyclical server farms housing equipment that drives Internet applications; and casual assets for short-term vaccine storage. Work by PriceWaterhouseCoopers (2000) has also emphasised the changing nature of real estate in the new economy. For an eBusiness (as opposed to a conventional business) physical capital and working capital may be seen as being less important than customers and company employees (i.e. skills and knowledge) as shown in Figure 5.5. However, even eBusinesses need real estate to run their operations. The emphasis is shifting, but although outsourcing (see the next section) of key operations (such as the management and maintenance of real estate) may seem to be an inevitable consequence of the shift towards intangible assets, real estate has not, and will not, disappear.

What impact is ICT likely to have therefore? Research by Arthur Andersen (2000a) has identified a number of trends in terms of ICT and its impact on real estate. The research is somewhat speculative in nature and lacks a hard evidence base but is paraphrased here to indicate the nature of the trends which the report highlights:

- **Internet**. The Internet encourages growth in worker mobility, securitisation and globalisation. In today's efficient market environment

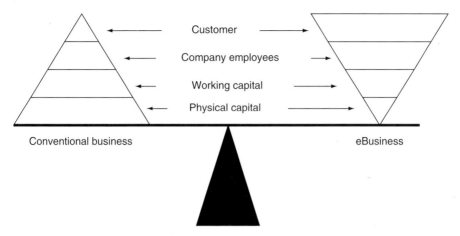

Figure 5.5 Real estate in the old and new economies (adapted from PriceWaterhouse Coopers 2000).

supported by strong growth and expanding trade, the report suggests the Internet has 'generally positive implications' for real estate, and more negative impacts are 'cushioned by an expanding economy'.

- **Location**. The report suggests that location will continue to be central to success, but eBusiness introduces virtual location as a key element in business design and infrastructure. Proximity to transport links remains important but proximity to fibre-optic and cable hubs or to logistics hubs is likely also to be important, the report suggests.
- **Physical structures**. The Internet and eBusiness are encouraging physical changes in product types including automated warehouses and flexible office space configurations. Flexibility in tenant packages and leasing terms is likely to become important, the report suggests. Moreover, the Internet is leading to greater diversity in real estate products as companies redefine their operations: eBusiness purchases require a great deal of support, for example, leading to higher demand for warehouse-based call centres.
- **Capital requirements**. Capital intensity is likely to increase in the real estate industry because of the increasing need to retrofit existing property with new technology. Offices and industrial real estate are likely to be expected to be Internet ready by tenants.
- **New revenue sources**. Internet growth is also likely to generate new revenue sources for all property types (for example, the provision of telecommunications and tenant advisory services).

There are several other trends brought about by new technology which will also have significant impacts on the corporate real estate portfolio

(Kirschbraun 2000). For example, the Internet has enabled the 'networked enterprise' to evolve, based on a variety of possible, outsourced functions ranging from human resources through to IT services and customer services. Inevitably organisations that were formally integrated will require less real estate and some of it will be passed along to the spun-off divisions. Digital telecommunication structures have also tended to reinforce existing patterns of economic activity as telecom companies have sought to provide services in the areas of greatest demand, corresponding to existing growth areas (Table 5.4).

The response of the real estate sector to ICT

The trends in ICT, alongside other social and economic factors, are transforming real estate markets and the provision of real estate services, but do these trends mean that we should consider a new type of property or real estate in the new economy? The term 'eProperty'[7] had not until recently been explored, but Dixon and Marston (2002) define it as: 'property within which the Internet and related technologies are fully integrated and combined to enable owners and tenants to maximise value'. The important point about this definition is that eBusiness and eCommerce are both impacting on physical property and real estate in terms of:

Table 5.4 New business processes and business needs: real estate implications (adapted from Kirschbraun 2000).

Trend	Real estate implication	Comments
Networked enterprise	Less space required. 'Stranded assets'?	Landlords will need to accept a different tenant profile
Access to intellectual capital	Information is a critical asset	Companies need to locate near knowledge workers
	Companies focus on leveraging their intellectual assets	Downtown locations may be more popular
Digital communication	Concentration of telecommunications in growth areas	Further global pursuit of skilled labour and multinationals relocating
Shorter lifecycle for products	Misalignment between planning horizon and real estate assets	Greater flexibility needed in terms of leases
Reconfiguration of supply chains	Warehousing space planning made easier Falling demand?	Back-office functions automated
Customer relations altered	Demand for call centre space increased	Redeployment of workforce

- space requirements of occupiers – a function which once took place in physical space may no longer be needed; and,
- speed of turnover of products – where stock is turned over fast, a lower average turnover time means less need for space.

More specifically, as we have seen in Chapter 4 and the current chapter, ICT is impacting and will impact on the following separate aspects of the supply and demand for real estate:

- financial structuring of space procurement;
- legal arrangements of space procurement;
- intensity of use of space procured;
- configuration/layout of space procured;
- location of space procured;
- amount of space procured; and,
- duration over which space is procured.

However, ICT, including eBusiness and eCommerce, is one of a number of forces impacting on property in the new economy and must be seen in this context. The Property Council of Australia and Andersen (2001) in their Digital Property project[8] suggest there are 10 business rules that constitute a major shift for business models as a consequence of the changing economic environment. Although this study appeared at the top of the dot.com boom, when the new economy was seen as creating almost a separate type of organisation, its findings still carry resonance in what may best be referred to as the most recent, new economy. However, it should be emphasised that the research is not based on extensive empirical evidence and to that extent is speculative in its rationale.[9] The rules, as this study sees them, may be summarised as follows:

- Connectivity – this is fundamental, created by the convergence of ICTs.
- 'Death of distance' – as discussed above, the marketplace is being replaced by marketspace, and corporations demand mobility for their operations.
- Speed – the speed of commerce is a fundamental as project times have shortened and global corporations operate on a '24/7' basis.
- Intangibles – customer service, information and brand value are valued more than physical assets.
- Market transparency – freedom of information has increased market transparency for consumers and margins based on information arbitrage are eroding.

- Contradictions of scale – although consolidation and rationalisation have continued apace[10] through globalisation, connectivity has also resulted in SMEs potentially being able to reach a wider market.
- Drive for efficiency – as the scale of business increases, core business imperatives become more important, leading to outsourcing and disintermediation, but also to reintermediation in business models.
- Human capital – portfolio careers and work–life balance changes are altering the emphasis between employers and employees. The length of time that a corporation can retain its workforce is reducing as churn increases.
- Customer intimacy – greater competition for customers in markets is creating one-to-one marketing. Customisation of products is now very important and has been increased by connectivity.
- Uncertainty – with pervasive connectivity, market cycles have reduced and an unpredictable business environment has resulted, which has led to more flexible corporations with corporations seeking out new alliance partners and collaborating with competitors.

ICT is making organisations more flexible in terms of their structures and their responsiveness to business environment changes, and this in turn is being reflected in changing property requirements and desired lease structures, thereby enabling companies to scale their operations in line with changing demand and the cost and quality profile of global locations. Therefore, the move away from tangible assets towards intangible assets has found further support in the idea of property or real estate outsourcing, and this also illustrates how ICT impact continues to operate alongside other economic and social factors.

A wider perspective on company assets is taken by Boulton *et al.* (2000), for example. They suggest successful companies are making greater use of new 'off balance sheet' assets to create value, including intangible assets, such as brands, relationships and knowledge. This is evidenced by the widening gap between book and market values that first opened up in the 1980s: by 1998 the average book value of publicly traded US companies had gone from virtual parity to just 28% of market value. Although the two serve different purposes, book value can still have a strong impact on market value through investor perceptions, and subsequent decisions to invest in companies listed in the financial markets. Based on a database of more than 10 000 businesses actively traded on the US stock markets between 1978 and 1998, they found that:

- companies with more physical assets used capital less efficiently;

- a minority of companies generated a disproportionate share of value – 29% generated most of the value;
- the top 10% of companies were dramatically more efficient at leveraging assets which were not on their books, measured by their market-to-book ratio which was more than double that of the next 10% of companies;
- highly valued companies were disproportionately represented in high technology, healthcare, communications and financial services;
- organisations low in physical assets produced increasing returns without a commensurate increase in stock volatility, whereas organisations with the most physical assets had the worst ratios of return and volatility;
- most CEOs recognised the importance of intangible assets and ranked 'customer satisfaction' and 'employee retention' as the top two measures of value creation, but few were acting on these factors. They blamed unsatisfactory measurement systems, failed previous attempts and costs as preventing them from doing so.

An empirical study by Deng and Gyourko (1999) in the USA produced similar findings. They compared more than 380 companies' returns with the degree of real estate ownership/investment. They found that within certain industries, particularly electronics, a company's return is lower if it has a relatively high proportion of its assets in real estate, measured by book value. Put another way, companies in high-cost-of-capital industries that own more real estate than their peers have, on average, consistently lower returns to shareholders. For example, a 10% above average concentration in real estate translates into a 1% loss in annual return.

The Boulton *et al.* (2000) study led them to develop the principles of 'value dynamics' and a framework within which assets are defined more broadly than prescribed within existing accounting rules. Because buildings and other physical assets are declining in value relative to intangible assets, managers need to determine carefully how these assets can create or leverage value. No companies maximise physical assets alone, but three examples are used to illustrate how companies are creating additional value from land and buildings:

- Wal-Mart found it could improve performance by renting out in-store snack bars to McDonald's.
- Walt Disney acquired more than twice the land needed for the Florida Disney World: although the unused land has increased significantly in market value, the land is worth more to Disney because it enables the

company to control the setting which underpins the success of its theme parks.

- The Williams Companies Inc. capitalised on a network of gas pipelines to carry fibre-optic cables for the telecommunications industry.

The implications of hidden or intangible value are important therefore. Corporate finance theory suggests companies should not be penalised for investing in real estate per se, so long as they obtain a sound rate of return. However, if investors perceive firms are too 'real estate heavy' (i.e. they want a 'pure play'), and could reap better risk-adjusted return in the core business, then they may be penalising such companies, which leads to lower overall returns. Alternatively, investors may not understand the true risk profile of real estate investments in the company and may be 'mis-pricing' the real estate assets. Some companies may also be evaluating their real estate assets incorrectly by applying an inappropriate rate of return to evaluating real estate investments, because if real estate is lower risk than the core business, it requires a lower return.

In terms of empirical evidence in the UK, research by Donaldsons (2003) has shown a significant shift away from companies owning their property. The level of property held by UK listed companies through operating leases has doubled over the last ten years to £68 bn in 2002 from £34 bn in 1991, and the number of companies leasing all their property increased from 20% in 1991 to 38% in 2001. During the same period the overall level of gross property held on balance sheets fell from £200 bn to £184 bn. The study went on to show that companies that lease all their property have 20% less debt, 25% more cash and hold 40% less inventory as a proportion of their assets than companies owning all their property.

Business models are also therefore changing in response not only to technology but to financial and economic changes as well. A change in business models can be incremental or radical and can relate to a single process or an entire business system. Essentially, the business focus is moving away from supply-driven models to demand-driven models with greater connectivity to customers, more market information and transparency (Property Council of Australia & Andersen 2001). There is a move away from an emphasis on existing characteristics of a product ('service push model') to one based on customer needs ('customer pull').

To take an obvious example, retailing has always been about attaining the right balance and getting the right product in the right place at the right price at the right time. Fulfilling this requirement has changed throughout the history of retailing as a result of 'disruptive technologies', such as department stores, mail order, discount stores and, most recently, Internet retailing (College of Estate Management 2001).

The arrival of the Internet is different because it enables retailers to combine what was previously unattainable by delivering high value (in terms of selection and service) at low cost (and price). In the past it has been very difficult for retailers to do this: there was a trade-off between price and 'service'. Now, however, the Internet provides retailers with an unsurpassed opportunity to provide customers with a highly targeted service at low price. Retailers have adopted a variety of strategies to cope with the impact of eCommerce and to define the relationship of existing real estate assets with the online channel. De Kare-Silver (2000) uses a helpful classification of these responses:

- 'Information only': a limited response and one which provides information, for example, on retail outlets, methods of purchasing and so on (e.g. B&Q website).
- 'Export': again limited, but with an online transaction presence for a specialist sector, for example, overseas sales (e.g. Blackwells).
- 'Subsume into existing business': the emphasis here is not on changing existing retail operations but on integrating or subsuming eCommerce into the existing systems (e.g. Safeway's 'Collect' scheme).
- 'Treat as another channel': retailers using this strategy maintain a separate eCommerce sales channel but keep it as part of the existing business, sharing overheads, systems, back-office functions and personnel with the parent company. Some retailers have also used host 'malls' provided by portal companies.
- 'Set up as a separate business': this model does recognise that a different business can be created without cannibalising existing sales.
- 'Pursue on all fronts': this model rests on the belief that some retailers want to pursue every available channel, meeting all target consumers and being as competitive as possible (e.g. Great Universal Stores).
- 'Mixed system': this combines 'flagship stores with online delivery', with the stores acting as brand name promoters complementing the online direct selling operation. This recognises the importance of showcasing brand strength but reinforcing it with an efficient and fast order and delivery service.
- 'Switch fully': no major physical retailer has switched fully from bricks and mortar to online. Argos is a good example of a high street catalogue retailer which is leaning rapidly that way (Argos was acquired by GUS in 1999). Pure-plays such as Amazon and 1-800-Flowers, of course, are able to switch fully.

In addition, De Kare-Silver suggests there are two other strategies which 'buck the trend' and effectively defend, yet exploit, existing real estate and retail core competencies:

- 'Best of both': this means that all real estate is retained but that it is 'reinvented' to provide products, services, an entertaining environment as well as facilities that consumers want. The new technology is very much a part of this environment, enabling integrated Internet orders and collections/delivery.
- 'Revitalise and buck the trend' ('leisure and retail'): this concedes no ground to the Internet and is designed to defend existing real estate by making shopping an improved leisure experience.

In turn, in other real estate sectors, the impact of greater uncertainty and the changing economic environment is driving corporations to achieve greater efficiencies in their businesses to achieve shareholder value (Property Council of Australia & Andersen 2001). Tenants may therefore alter the nature of their demand for property because of business process engineering, through outsourcing, divesting non-core businesses and changes to workforce practices. This has led to corporations adopting non-conventional property strategies such as:

- working capital – transferring property assets off their balance sheets and using sale and leaseback;
- asset management strategies – aligning property and real estate strategies against overall corporate strategy;
- outsourcing – non-core support functions, such as property and facilities management;
- corporate infrastructure management – ICT, human resources and finance are bundled with property and FM to service total infrastructure.

Offshoring,[11] or the relocation of business functions and processes to lower cost locations in the long term, is also having an increasing impact, especially in the financial services sector (Deloitte Research 2003). Deloitte estimate that some $356 bn of the cost of the financial services industry will be relocated offshore within the next five years, driven by cost savings. This could involve as many as two million workers in the sector, and currently is focused on relocations to India, South Africa, Malaysia, Australia, China and Singapore. Clearly moves 'offshore' would also have implications for jobs but also for real estate demand in call centres, and other support functions in such businesses.

Similarly, tenants are also adopting a range of strategies to optimise their space and office accommodation requirements:

- Changing workplace strategies – hotelling, telecommuting, hot-desking and other approaches reduce floor-space usage.
- Non-territorial space – the creation of open floor-space enables greater flexibility in planning space requirements.
- Head-count reductions – this has been created by outsourcing non-core activities.
- Collaboration agreements – some tenants may enter into agreements to use the excess space of others, especially in cases where there is a complementary business cycle.
- Greater connectivity – ICT connectivity and related technologies can be exploited to substitute for physical space requirements.
- Services decentralisation – relocating corporate support services to lower cost areas can reduce accommodation costs.
- Lease strategies – bundling of lease options to create new pricing structures can create inherent flexibility.

Essentially these tenant strategies all attempt to optimise the effective space usage, based on the existing work functions and need for face-to-face interaction rather than decentralisation. Similarly these elements can be recombined in a range of strategies, underpinned by ICT. The Property Council of Australia and Andersen (2001) give four examples of such strategies (Figure 5.6):

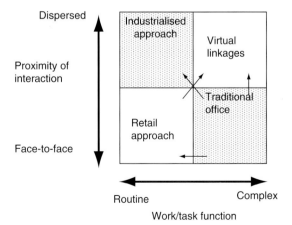

Figure 5.6   Non-traditional workplace strategies (adapted from Property Council of Australia & Andersen 2001).

- Strategy A (Traditional Office → Virtual Linkage). Virtual strategies reduce property and workplace costs.
- Strategy B (Traditional Office → Retail Approach). Customer service is shifted from the office to points of sale to improve customer service, minimise bureaucracy and reduce accommodation costs.
- Strategy C (Retail Approach → Virtual Linkage). Sales and support teams are shifted from retail settings to virtual settings using ICT and so reducing property/overhead costs.
- Strategy D (Traditional Office → Industrialised Approach). Back-office operations and support functions are shifted from high to low cost locations and so accommodation costs are reduced as are commuting distances.

Many corporations are therefore now adopting a portfolio approach to office accommodation provision in order to achieve mobility, flexibility and adaptability in office accommodation. This may take the form of a core–flexible–serviced space split (see also Gibson & Louargand 2001).

Real estate service provision has also come under close scrutiny. A classic case of potential disintermediation (or the elimination of middleman functions between producers and consumers), was highlighted by Tapscott (1996) in the real estate brokerage industry (see Box 2.2 and Chapter 8). Given that commercial real estate brokers or estate agents match property owners with potential buyers or lessees, they can be considered as true intermediaries. However, greater provision of information and transparency of prices through the Internet place the broker's role under threat. To survive demands new ways of thinking and adding value through using new technology to access extensive information and provide new relationships and services for customers. Andersen (2000b) supports this view by suggesting that real estate service providers create value from their employee assets by maintaining the lead role in negotiations: outsourcing some or all of the listing function may be possible, but negotiating skill is likely to be the marker for success. Similarly real estate companies can gain positive benefits from ICT by providing occupancy-based services for tenants that integrate new technology and create new revenue streams by turning tenants into an aggregated customer base of companies and individuals.

Summary

This chapter has examined the concept of a new economy and critically reviewed its characteristics. The new economy, which is the subject of this book, is the latest in a series of new economies but it is clear that ICT and productivity change are at the heart of the latest manifestation.

We have seen how ICT can increase productivity both nationally and at a firm level, acting alongside other factors. New data and research have revealed that the more sceptical views of ICT and the new economy are premature and ill-founded. Despite the fallout from the dot.com boom and bust cycle, structural changes within the new economy are continuing to occur with important ramifications for real estate. However, it is important to take a balanced view and not to oversimplify what are complex arguments, particularly in relation to productivity.

Part 1 of the book (comprising Chapters 2 to 5) has therefore highlighted the importance of seeing ICT within the context of the political, social and economic factors, and we have adopted the socio-technical framework developed in Chapter 1 to illustrate this. Productivity improvement is important to consider from the point of view of real estate, because it has implications for the use of real estate space, but the evidence suggests that prophecies of the demise, or 'death', of real estate in the new economy have been exaggerated. A variety of perspectives have therefore been examined which shed clearer light on both the agglomeration and dispersal effects of new technology. Real estate is clearly not dead, but ICT is changing the demand and locational dynamics of a range of real estate assets and, moreover, creating new types of product and service provision in the real estate sector. Part 2 of the book examines these impacts in more detail, again highlighting how ICT should be seen in the context of a range of other factors within our conceptual framework.

Notes

1 This view has been supported by other studies (see, for example, Meyer 1999, who calculated that the value-to-weight ratio of a pound of US GDP went from $3.64 in 1977 to $6.52 in 1999, a 79% increase, and Sheerin 2002, who found that in the 1990s, UK real GDP increased by 25% but the weight of the economy by only 2%).

2 Coyle (2002) suggests the scale of progress in information processing is startling. Since the 1950s, computing power has increased by 56% pa on average, and this has been promoted by a transformation in technological power. As she points out, the increase in density means that today's computers have 66 000 times the processing power at the same cost as computers in 1975. In ten years, given current trends, computers will be more than 10 million times as powerful as those in 1975 at the same cost, and the past 40 years have seen a billion-fold increase in the installed base of computing power.

3   Metcalfe's Law of Networks (named after Robert Metcalfe, inventor of the Ethernet), which states that the usefulness of the network equals the square of the number of users, also helps explain the related power of the Internet, which is part of the ICT phenomenon. In other words, while the number of users grows arithmetically, the value and impact of the Internet grow exponentially.

4   The UK's National Statistics Office is undertaking a dedicated programme of research into how to measure the new economy (see, for example, Clayton & Waldron 2003).

5   Proponents of clusters as a tool of UK economic policy have not been without their critics, as O'Sullivan (2002) points out. Criticisms focus on limited impact, lack of a critical rationale and the emphasis on limited industries.

6   SANE is a two-year EC-funded research programme which considers the combined impact of the new economy on people, process, place and technology to identify new ways of accommodating work (Harrison 2002).

7   'Digital property' is a term used frequently by Property Council of Australia and Andersen (2001) but it is not formally defined.

8   Website at www.digitalproperty.com.au

9   Indeed, the report suggests that these changes are happening now, hence the use of the present tense in what follows.

10 For example, the top ten UK retailers accounted for more than half of the top 800 UK retailers' turnover in 1999 (CEM 2001).

11 This should be distinguished from business process outsourcing to third parties, where ownership and management of the resource are devolved.

Part 2

REAL ESTATE SPACES AND THE IMPACT OF ICT

6

Real Estate Spaces

Introduction

In Part 1 of this book we examined the ways in which ICT has, in alliance with a range of social, economic and political factors, led to a transformation in the ways that businesses, governments and citizens interact economically, socially and culturally. We saw how ICT cannot be treated in isolation: to do so is to be guilty of technological determinism. We also examined the concept of a new economy (as part of the information society) and highlighted an increasing body of evidence to support the view that such an economy is not only strongly technology driven, but that productivity, organisational structures and consumer demand patterns are also interacting and creating a potent mix of forces for change. We also suggested that any form of technology can only be understood in the context of forces which shape and are shaped by it. Our perspective therefore led us to formulate a 'socio-technical framework'.

In Part 2 of this book we will examine in more detail how ICT is transforming real estate products/assets and services. We will also look at how concepts of space are changing, as ICT transforms real estate markets, and we will see how the concepts of traditional real estate use are becoming blurred through a combination of technology-led change with other social and economic factors. This is creating both flux and change in location; layout and intensity of use; leasing arrangements; value and market patterns and support services. ICT is transforming real estate services such as trading, valuation and management operations, and therefore altering the very nature of the relationships between real estate clients and their advisors.

To begin our analysis, which is based on the 'socio-technical framework' that we developed in Part 1, we examine the changing concepts of space in the new economy. Conventional concepts of space are being challenged, blurring the distinctions between particular kinds of use, and leading to outsourcing opportunities.

At the heart of this transformation is the concept of location. Understanding location, and the reasons for where business and other activities are carried out, is an essential prerequisite for assessing any transformations from ICT. The origins of classic locational analysis are ascribed to Weber (1909), who understood that input resources may be fixed spatially, and this plays an important part in the location of a firm alongside the costs of distribution. Weber's work was focused entirely upon industrial location and this created a strand of thought leading through Predoehl (1928), Moses (1958) and Khalili *et al.* (1974), to McCann (1998).

A more business-orientated analysis is provided by Michael Porter (1990). Location has always played a major role in the determination of competitiveness and Porter described four classic reasons for location of an activity in that context. Firstly, factor cost is important. For example, assembly takes place wherever labour costs are cheapest because a given level of capital is raised in whichever market offers the best terms. Secondly, activities frequently locate in order to tap into specialised local skills or to develop relationships with key groups of customers. Research and development facilities are often classics of this type. Thirdly, activities are often located locally for pragmatic and cultural reasons. The ability to sell in a particular country, for example, is often predicated upon a local presence. Finally, location may be determined by political factors. The location of Japanese car plants in Europe, for example, was at least in part a response to the tariff barriers established around the European Union. Set in this context, ICT is a facilitator, allowing greater flexibility in the choice of location and eroding the importance of distance. Yet location remains something of a paradox in the new economy, as we shall see.

This chapter therefore seeks to address the following issues:

- the paradox of location in the new economy;
- differing concepts of personal, private and public space in the online and virtual worlds; and
- how such concepts can aid our understanding of real estate transformations, brought about by ICT and other factors.

The paradox of location in the new economy

'Location! Location! Location!' is the common cliché espoused by real estate professionals the world over and which has served industry well enough in the past. However, the advent of efficient global supply chains and the ability of consumers to purchase, often with the click of a mouse, from a global entrepôt begin to call into question the rationale for location as a factor. As we saw earlier in Part 1, Marshall (1890) identified the conflicts between centrifugal and centripetal forces in the spatial organisation of the economy over 100 years ago. Castells (2000) also describes an information economy, in which information generation, processing and transmission become the fundamental sources of productivity and power. A 'space of places' has been joined by a 'space of flows'. The latter refers to the technological and organisational possibility of orchestrating social and work practices simultaneously without physical proximity. Building on this, we saw in Chapter 1 of this book how urban and regional perspectives that adopted a spatial dimension could aid our understanding of ICT transformation. For example, Graham and Marvin (1996) use the term 'electronic space' to represent spaces constructed inside ICT networks whilst 'urban places' refers to the built environment or physical space. Graham and Marvin (2001) also show that there is a broad spectrum of writing based around a 'relational' focus (see Amin & Graham 1998; Allen *et al.* 1999). In this perspective, technology and infrastructure only become tangible in relation to organised practices, and so space, place and time do not have any predefined or fixed meaning. There can be many forms of space, because urban areas can be thought of as social processes and multiplexes, bringing together many social experiences of time and place. Therefore it is possible to have highly connected spaces and worlds alongside highly disconnected spaces within the same urban fabric (see the work of Pawley 1997 and Boyer 1996, for example).

Gepts (2001) also proposes a model which suggests that four types of spatial impact flow from ICT (Figure 6.1) and which helps in our understanding of real estate change. We can extend our analysis in Chapter 1 to consider the real estate impacts in more detail, therefore:

- **Synergy**. Here, electronic spaces and urban places coincide. In this outcome the impact of ICT follows current urban patterns. Information intensive business is attracted to network nodes, which are located where there are concentrations of economic activity.
- **Substitution**. In this case, ICT leads to a dispersal of economic activities as work with a high information content becomes less location

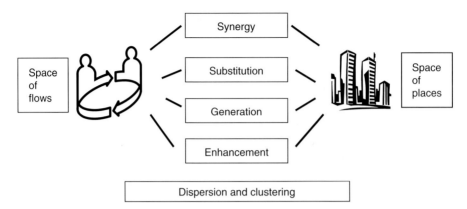

Figure 6.1   A space of places and space of flows (adapted from Gepts 2001).

dependent. Innovative, new processes substitute information flows for physical space, for example online banking replacing physical branches.

- **Generation**. ICT generates demand for new types of space, for example call centres and co-location facilities.
- **Enhancement**. ICT can optimise the efficiency of transport systems through traffic management or spatial planning. So the impact of ICT can both deconcentrate and concentrate activity.

Therefore, depending on the circumstances, ICT can be both centrifugal or centripetal in its effect.

In theory, more open global markets, faster transportation and better communication should diminish the role of location in competition. Nevertheless, potent geographical clusters remain in many industries. It is ironic that much of the advance in ICT over the past decades was generated by Silicon Valley, itself an old-fashioned cluster of industries that grew as a result of specialised local skills. A classic example of ICT as a centrifugal force might be the printing industry in the UK, where the production of newspapers dispersed from the Fleet Street cluster in the space of a decade, a change that was almost entirely attributable to ICT. Equally, there is evidence that ICT acts centripetally, pulling control back from dispersed activities to the centre. Typical here would be the insurance industry where quotations for insurance, calculated locally 20 years ago, are now available online. Moreover, Cairncross (2001) argues that the revolution we are seeing is the third in a succession of great changes in the technology and cost of transportation over the past three centuries. The nineteenth century was shaped by the falling cost of transporting goods; the twentieth century by the falling cost of transporting people; and the twenty-first century will be dominated by the falling cost of transporting ideas and information.

Despite this, localised clusters persist and, in the words of Porter (1990), they: 'are a striking feature of virtually every national, regional, state, and even metropolitan economy, especially in more economically advanced nations'. For Porter, therefore, the competitive advantage of an economy lies in local factors (i.e. knowledge, relationships, motivation) that cannot easily be replicated over distance.

The paradox can be seen in the impact of ICT on real estate every day (Dixon 2003). At the height of the dot.com boom in the retail sector, serious doubts were being raised by some commentators (see, for example, Borsuk 1999) about the ability of conventional retail stores to survive the overwhelming logic of Internet shopping. Yet, despite the ease with which it can be accomplished and the infrastructure in place to cope with the problems of distribution that it raises, shopping online only accounts for a relatively small percentage of retail sales, and the high street remains as strong as ever. Consumers seem to prefer the social aspects, and local accountability, of face-to-face transactions, although certain sectors remain under threat (see Chapters 7 and 9).

Furthermore, retailers are beginning to use the power of ICT to improve the competitiveness of their existing physical network through, for example, making a broader range of stock available to order than can be accommodated in the local store. In this case the store takes on the role of showroom.

In the office sector, the trend towards offshoring of business services is instructive. The business practice of offshoring focuses on the relocation of labour-intensive service industry functions to locations remote to the business centre. Destinations such as India, Ireland and the Philippines have proved popular and this trend reinforces Gepts' (2001) substitution model, where flows of information parallel and in some cases replace or displace physical spaces. This has been enabled by two ICT-led changes. Firstly, an improvement in international telecommunications capacity and, in parallel, a significant reduction in global telecommunications costs. Secondly, the process of *informationalisation* has enabled most business services to become location independent. As a result of these two changes, information can now be transmitted over long distances at very low cost and with little loss of quality.

However, to ascribe offshoring purely to ICT would miss the point. The main motivation for offshoring is that it reduces labour costs. There are very large differences in the wages paid for equivalent skills between the UK and developing countries such as India. In 2002, wage rates in India were 4% of those in the UK and the status of the job is much higher. Clearly, the picture is complex, and McKinsey Global Institute (2004) estimate that, taking into account additional costs of telecommunications and management, the savings from offshoring range between 45% and 55%. Despite the ICT facilitation, without savings of this magnitude, offshoring would not be an issue at all.

Of course, offshoring is only one type of dispersal effect, and the destination need not be offshore. The same technological drivers are responsible for the creation of the call centre as a physical space in which to concentrate upon customer relationship management, and which mirrors Gepts' (2001) 'generation' transformation. For example, in the UK in the 1990s, distressed areas were the destinations of choice with relatively cheap labour in good supply. Call centres still form a central plank of many economic regeneration strategies in these areas. It is ironic indeed that, by touting the benefits of cheap labour, in many cases these regions are being outbid by offshore destinations and may yet see the disappearance of another source of employment.

It is not only at the level of location that there is a spatial impact from ICT. New technologies combine to redefine the way we view space altogether.

Physical form and virtual reality

An important way in which technology also has an impact on physical space is through the delivery of tools for simulation. For example, planners can now model urban environments in three dimensions electronically, using computer assisted design (CAD) or advanced visualisation techniques (Levy 1995). Virtual reality models of entire cities are possible: a model of Bath, produced by researchers from CAD models, is one example of such a large-scale urban model (Bourdakis 1997). Virtual models can be viewed from different viewpoints: both bird's eye views which quickly give survey information about the city, and eye-level perspectives from the vantage point of pedestrians and motorists can be generated.

Batty *et al.* (2000) identify twelve different categories in which these urban simulation models are used:

- **Emergency services**: modelling how different locations can be accessed quickly.

- **Urban planning**: problems of site location, community planning and public participation all require visualisation but detailed design reviews still form the main applications.
- **Telecommunications**: in particular, the siting of towers for mobile and fixed communications is problematic in environments dominated by high buildings.
- **Architecture**: as in urban planning, site location and design review, in particular aesthetic issues and massing, are important factors as well as issues involving conservation and disruption to the urban environment.
- **Utilities management**: water, sewerage, and electricity provision as well as road and rail infrastructure all require detailed data for their maintenance and improvement.
- **Marketing and economic development**: models provide extremely rapid ways of visualising the environment of the city, the locations of uses, and the availability of space for development.
- **Property analysis**: related to economic development but also to the general development of the city. Methods for visualising cities enable detailed data to be computed concerning floor-space and land availability as well as land values and costs of development.
- **Tourism and entertainment**: models provide methods for displaying the tourist attractions of cities as well as ways in which tourists and other newcomers might learn about the geography of the city.
- **eCommerce**: virtual city models provide portals to virtual commerce in that they provide the user with realistic entries to new and remote trading and other commercial domains.
- **Environment**: models enable various kinds of hazard to be visualised and planned for, in particular ways of visualising the impact of local pollutants at a fine scale such as those associated with traffic.
- **Education and learning**: these kinds of visualisation enable users at different levels of education to learn about the city as well as enabling other virtual experiences through the metaphor of the city.
- **City portals**: using models as the entries to urban information hubs.

However, model environments only address half the problem. What are required (Batty *et al.* 2000) are digital tools that can be used to link socio-economic phenomena to physical form and quantitative data and models to qualitative issues. Advances in the power of computing have made the creation of intelligent virtual environments (IVE) a reality. Rudimentary virtual worlds have been a feature of computer games for decades and, it can be argued, also in real estate. Physical models of development have always been the stock in trade for architects to help in the explanations of concepts, and they have been at the forefront in the use of CAD to create simulations of new buildings with walkthrough capabilities.

IVEs give a much higher level of capability, however, encompassing more realistic rendering of objects and the ability to interact via avatars – online personalities – in real time.[1]

This is an area where the majority of the published literature is concerned with technical aspects of the process. However, some papers do give a clue to the kind of applications that are relevant to the real estate community. Farenc *et al.* (1998) describe a simulation of an urban environment, for example, and in fact this paper is about simulating human behaviour in a complex environment. But as an outcome of this kind of research, it is possible to envisage much better simulation tools being available to planners and developers in the physical world in the future.

Such tools can also be used to visualise neighbourhoods as they currently exist and how they might appear after a proposed development has happened, or the system can be used to simulate entirely new developments (see Box 6.1).

Drawing from technologies developed for military flight simulation and virtual reality, a system for efficiently modelling and simulating urban environments has also been implemented at the University of California (Los Angeles) (see Jepson *et al.* 1995). This system combines relatively simple three-dimensional models with aerial photographs and street-level video to create a realistic model of an urban neighbourhood. This can then be used for interactive fly and walkthrough demonstrations. This is a methodology that integrates existing systems such as CAD and geographic information systems (GIS) with visual simulation to facilitate the modelling, display, and evaluation of alternative proposed environments. It is used as the basis for Virtual Los Angeles.

Transactions in space

According to Berne (1972): 'A transaction, consisting of a single stimulus and a single response, verbal or non-verbal, is the unit of social action. It is called a transaction because each party gains something from it, and that is why he [sic] engages in it'. Actually this research is all about transactions between people, but the definition of the transaction holds good for communications between systems and people as well. In the field of environmental psychology, attempts have also been made to classify different types of space in a cultural context. This is defined as 'proxemics', or the study of the human use of space within the context of culture.

Box 6.1   Virtual London

Virtual London is a project undertaken by researchers from UCL's Centre for Advanced Spatial Analysis (CASA). The project, funded by the Greater London Authority, produces a three-dimensional digital map of the whole of London.

The 3D map provides Londoners with information about the impact of planning initiatives, and encourages tourism by providing detailed information about sites of interest. Visitors to Virtual London are able to roam around the site as avatars (digital characters) and take part in interactive simulations.

The objectives of the project are to encourage debate and give Londoners the opportunity to have a say in the way their environment is shaped. The model is being produced using GIS, CAD, and a variety of new photorealistic imaging techniques and photogrammetric methods of data capture. The core model is distributed via the Internet utilising techniques to optimise large urban data sets for broadband distribution. Key to this is communicating the built environment in an innovative manner; to achieve this, Virtual London will be distributed via a multi-user environment. Citizens will be able to roam around a virtual gallery as avatars (digital representations of themselves) and explore the issues relating to London in a game like space.

In addition to its attraction to visitors, Internet access to Virtual London opens up the capital to inward investors and employers looking to re-locate or employ new staff. Virtual London brings planners together from right across the capital – as providers and shapers of content – and links their work more directly with the ICT and new media sectors. The project may also make a contribution to 'e-democracy', allowing Londoners to consider proposals visually and seek answers to 'what if' questions involving placement and visualisation of new buildings, demolitions and changes to transport links.

Hall (1966) developed his theory of proxemics, arguing that human perceptions of space are moulded and patterned by culture. He argued that differing cultural frameworks for defining and organising space can lead to serious failures of communication and understanding in cross-cultural settings. He analysed both the personal spaces that people form around their bodies as well as the macro-level sensibilities that shape cultural expectations about how streets, neighbourhoods and cities should be properly organised.

Hall's most famous innovation has to do with the definition of the informal or personal spaces that surround individuals:

- **Intimate space**: the closest 'bubble' of space surrounding a person. Entry into this space is acceptable only for the closest friends and intimates.

- **Social and consultative spaces**: the spaces in which people feel comfortable conducting routine social interactions with acquaintances as well as strangers.
- **Public space**: the area of space beyond which people will perceive interactions as impersonal and relatively anonymous.

Cultural expectations about these spaces vary widely. In the United States, for example, people engaged in conversation will assume a social distance of around four to seven feet, but in many parts of Europe the expected social distance is roughly half that with the result that Americans travelling overseas often experience the need to back away from a conversation partner who seems to be getting too close.

Wexelblat (1999) considers proximity to be a function of both the physical distance and the cognitive distance between the person and the space. A 'proxemic' space to him is one that is felt by users to be transparent, in that the signs and structures can be easily understood. People feel close to, or part of, the space. Conversely, 'distemic' spaces are opaque to users. Signals go unseen, usually because the people in the space lack the required background or knowledge to translate or comprehend what they experience.

Proxemics teaches us a lot about how personal space is organised physically. From a technological standpoint, Hall's intimate and social spaces adopt new dimensions. In addition to physical space, technology gives an additional virtual layer to interactions, and one in which physical proximity is often not relevant.

Overlaying the concept of virtual space onto Hall's definitions of types of space gives rise to a modified taxonomy. Hall makes a distinction between personal, or intimate, space and social space. Incursions into that space are event driven: a handshake, for example, or a greeting. This differentiation is born of physical proximity, which itself is conditioned culturally. With no culture, virtual proximity does not carry the same weight and, as a consequence, the differentiation becomes less important. Add to this that the cost of interaction can be negligible in a virtual world and it can be seen that there is almost no barrier to continuous event interaction between personal and public space.

Hall's public space is a catch-all in which interactions are seen as impersonal and anonymous. In a virtual environment, however, anonymity may not be as obvious as all that. The initiation of any event other than one in which the individual is purely an observer is likely to ensure that enough information is recorded to enable future events to be initiated outside his/her control.

For this reason it becomes attractive to further divide Hall's public space into 'private space' and genuinely 'public space'. Private space is that space which is under the control of a third party – an employer, for example, or the owner of a shopping centre. Public space is that which is merely administered by a third party – a public park, for example. Simulated interaction in a virtual environment is valuable for planning and analysis, but to make this relevant to physical real estate we need to consider how event interactions take place.

The first thing to note is that events come in two kinds:

- **Broadcasts**: which require no action and are purely for information or entertainment.
- **Solicitations**: which invite further action on behalf of the individual.

In this context an event is a contact of some kind with an individual by a third party. This could be a text message, a phone call, an email or even a personalised message. The initiation of an event can be passive or active as far as an individual is concerned. An active initiation would be a response to solicitation – for example replying to an email. A passive initiation would be location specific, for example driving into a congestion charging zone. The third party responsible for the contact might be the congestion charging authority as in the latter example, but equally might be a neighbourhood retailer, the owner of an adjacent shopping centre or even the owner of a competing centre trying to lure you to shop elsewhere.

Figure 6.2 describes the taxonomy of space referred to in this chapter. These descriptions are to an extent arbitrary and there will be examples of crossovers between the public and private categories. Some types of leisure space undoubtedly exist under both, for example.

Personal space

While proxemics goes a long way towards defining personal space in a physical sense, the same rules cannot easily be transferred to personal virtual space. To begin with, the cultural environment is very different online. Language may still be a differentiator but in the absence of visual clues implicit divisions on the basis of, for example, sex, age or race are

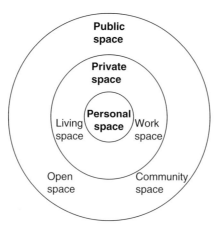

Figure 6.2   A taxonomy of space.

non-existent. Until the era of electric communications media, almost all the cues people used to ascertain social context in communications were physical rather than verbal. In physical space, social conventions are built into the environment and signalled by codes of etiquette and dress, posture, accent, tone of voice, and other cues that describe how to behave in a particular situation.

In virtual space, few of the pre-existing conventions apply and individuals are free to create one or many online personae – avatars – that best suit the transaction in hand. This is useful to know since, unlike physical space, in virtual space everything is recorded. The Internet may be viewed as a communications medium or an information-retrieval tool, but it is also a powerful archiving technology that records everything that takes place in virtual space and stores it forever.

In some respects, this is positive in that individual preferences can be culled from records of sites visited and messages sent and used to personalise virtual space. However, on the negative side, beliefs, habits and indiscretions are also being preserved for posterity.

In physical space, boundaries are generally well-defined entities. Notwithstanding Hall's (1966) identification of cultural effects, the compass of an individual's personal space is usually well understood and is portable to virtual space, with one significant difference. While in physical space conclusions as to preferences may be drawn from appearance, these are often explicit online, and derived from previous behaviour.

The information to personalise can come from different sources. When customers become members or order from websites, or when they sign up for frequent shopper cards, information is collected. It frequently includes name and address. Sometimes salary history, social security, driver's licence, marital and family data are collected. Then, as the customers make purchases, their purchase history is added to the database.

Even websites that may not directly ask for personal data might track the 'clickstream' – clicks, time spent per page, items selected but abandoned, and similar information – all in order to find out more about their customers and their behaviour (Box 6.2). The clickstream data become a useful resource for data mining tools that predict gender, age, income, preferences, and a customer's willingness to purchase.

This ability to identify personal preference allows for solicitations that are tailored to best meet an individual's perceived needs or offer prices tailored on the basis of previous activity. Clearly, in many cases, this can lead to a more informed choice and better prices. However, the downside of this

---

Box 6.2 Amazon.com[2]

Amazon, the world's largest online retailer, is a big user of personalisation. The site both collects information and solicits preferences. At Amazon.com's website, the page entitled 'Your Account' (which is directly accessible via a link on every page on the site) enables customers to choose the kinds of email they want to receive from Amazon. This choice is not just a binary, yes/no decision to receive or not receive Amazon.com emails beyond those related to transactions. Rather, this is a flexible means for customers to personalise precisely what kinds of additional information they want, if any. There are five principal customisation features:

- 'Customer Communications Preferences' allows customers to choose what sort of general emails they would like to receive, if any.
- 'Amazon.com Delivers' allows customers to receive specifically tailored email recommendations, reviews, and interviews on any of over 150 topic areas.
- 'New for You' offers customers broad-based email recommendations based on their purchase history and expressed preferences.
- 'Amazon.com Alerts' notifies customers about very specialised subjects.
- 'Special Occasion Reminder' sends customers email reminders about important events.

Additionally, the site will recommend books or CDs on request based upon previous purchase or ratings history. This history is available for amendment on the site.

data collection is that the initiation of events increases dramatically, especially once mobility is brought into the equation.

Location data are data processed in electronic communications networks which show the geographic position of a customer's mobile phone. In so-called third-generation phones these location data are derived using the global position system (GPS) (i.e. the location of a 3G phone will be known to an accuracy of about three metres). This information could be used to push services to customers when in that area, such as special prices or traffic information.

Mindful of the need to define the boundaries of personal space, the Privacy and Electronic Communications (EC Directive) Regulations 2003 ensure that, within the European Union, this can only be done with the specific consent of an individual. This type of legislation differs in other jurisdictions. In the United States, for example, individuals are assumed to have given consent unless they specifically opt out.

Data protection legislation forms a second plank in the definition of the boundaries of personal space. In the UK there are eight principles put in place by the Data Protection Act 1998 to make sure that individual information is handled properly. Personal data must be:

- fairly and lawfully processed;
- processed for limited purposes;
- adequate, relevant and not excessive;
- accurate;
- not kept for longer than is necessary;
- processed in line with your rights;
- secure; and
- not transferred to countries without adequate protection.

Again, however, this type of legislation varies according to jurisdiction.

ICT has revolutionised concepts of personal space and opened up new horizons of flexibility and personalisation. An individual with a mobile phone, a PDA or even a laptop computer has, in addition to Hall's understanding of physical space, a bubble of virtual space that is portable. From a property or real estate perspective, however, the real impact lies in the way in which that personal space interacts with other kinds of space.

Private space

There are three essential differences between personal space and private space:

- Personal space is mobile, private space is fixed.
- Private space is owned by means of a transaction, personal space is owned from birth.
- Private space is regarded as an asset, personal space as a right.

Private space is defined by the function that takes place within it. A basic taxonomy describes:

- workspace;
- living and leisure space; and
- public space.

Although there are contradictions and crossovers apparent even at this simple level (home-based workspace, for example), this captures the highest level of differentiation between types.

Within the general domain of private space a central issue in the impact of ICT is the extent to which it blurs the boundaries established in physical space. These three types of space are now explored in more detail.

Workspace

The interaction between personal space and workspace has been the coal face for ICT-enabled change over the past twenty years. As we have seen in those processes transformed by eBusiness, trends towards greater organisational flexibility have coincided with more intensive use of ICT (see, for example, McCalman & Anderson (2002)).[3] Similarly, as individuals have been progressively more enabled by ICT so workspaces have changed in application, sophistication and integration of ICT to the extent that it has become an integral part of almost every business. The concept of territory is a long-established feature of physical workspace. Without territory, individuals feel lost and uncomfortable. Marking territory follows established rituals; for example, territory is marked by clearing an area on the table for papers, calendars, and coffee mug. The width of our elbow span, creating 'elbow room', also helps mark the territory. In essence, traditional office design has been 'socio-fugal' in nature (McCalman

& Anderson 2002), with people working in cellular offices at the expense of interaction.

Defined territory is also conventionally an indicator of status. The manager's office is larger and projects a better image than the individual workstation. In addition, it is protected from noise and intrusion by doors and secretaries. Defined territory also bestows status-dependent rights: the higher the status, the more rights the individual has over his and others' territories. A workstation, for example, could be inspected by the manager without invitation, but the manager's office would not be inspected by an individual of lower status.

In many respects ICT has acted as an agent of change in these areas and the interpretation of territory is one of those changes. Organisations have also become less hierarchical and with more open access to knowledge, the workplace has become more project based with greater creativity often required.[4] Such changes have been strengthened and underpinned through the adoption of alternative strategies for workspace, including 'teleworking' or 'eWork' (see Chapter 3).

Because of the generic nature of the term 'telework', different authors have attempted to define it better in different contexts (Figure 6.3). Some have sought to break it down into different forms such as homeworking or alternative officing (Gordon 1988). Others have tried to identify the different groups who might use telework such as central workers, hybrids and nomads (see, for example, Stanworth & Stanworth 1991; Makimoto & Manners 1997). Different terms abound: for example, 'distance working' (Holti & Stern 1986) or 'outwork' (Probert & Wajcman 1988).

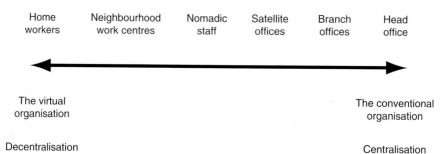

Figure 6.3   A taxonomy of telework (adapted from Moorcroft & Bennet 1995).

One of the most pragmatic definitions, given the practical implementations of teleworking that have been seen so far, is found in *Rethinking Work* (Britton 1994):

> Telework covers a range of new ways of working, using telecommunications as a tool, and for at least part of the time outside a traditional office environment.

Teleworking has also created new forms of real estate workspace and new ways of organising work, which are now outlined.

Telework centres

Telework centres offer an alternative to working in a central office facility or at home. They can be located in urban, suburban or rural areas. They can serve a single corporate client or be multi-tenant facilities. Their distinguishing feature is that those using them live in the same area or, in some cases, share the need for a drop-in work area while moving among work locations. Unlike a branch office, where those working together are part of a group, team or department, typically individuals working in teleworking centres have minimal formal work relationships.

Teleworking centres offer advantages to both the teleworker and the employer. For the teleworker it offers the prospect of retaining the social and professional contact of the workplace and the opportunity to work locally whilst retaining control of his/her private space. From the employer's perspective a teleworking centre offers better resource efficiency, brand maintenance and the ability to specialise easily – a call centre is a specialist teleworking centre, for example.

Teleworking centres may be wholly owned and operated by the employer or they may be general facilities open to all and offering a full range of facilities (see Box 6.3). Examples of the latter format would be the serviced office suite where space and facilities can be booked on an hourly basis. Distance is immaterial as far as teleworking centres are concerned and there are a number of examples of centres based offshore to take advantage of specific skills and lower wage rates. British Airways has a ticketing centre in India, for example, which handles UK transactions.

Home-based teleworking

Home-based teleworking is perhaps the best known of these alternative workplace strategies (see Chapter 3). The principle of using 'spare' space at home as a facility from which to work is one with a long history dating back to before the Industrial Revolution. In those days home work would

---

Box 6.3   Surrey County Council

An ambitious example of the implementation of teleworking centres is that being undertaken by Surrey County Council under its 'Workstyle' programme. This will entail the Council's 3400 office-based employees becoming locationally independent. This is based upon a successful pilot based on an Epsom telecentre, which showed significant benefits.

Call centres, hot-desking, teleworking and working from home are among a wide range of modern working arrangements the Council is exploring with staff. The model being developed under Surrey Workstyle involves reducing the Council's property portfolio from more than 80 buildings to about 30, which is delivering efficiency savings of between £2 million and £3 million a year, to be re-directed to front-line services.

---

be largely craft-based manual work; in the twenty-first century we are talking about more ephemeral work driven by the symbolic economy.

In the past homeworking has been tainted by low wage rates and low job security, being the preserve of the housewife in search of 'pin money'.

The non-territorial office

Conventionally, the office is pictured as a physical space containing desks, telephones, computers. The office of the future is best thought of as a communications space (Hiltz 1984). For many companies, however, this communications space cannot be just virtual, but must have a physical manifestation.

The office also has implications for the individual. The traditional worker has his or her office – part of his or her private space. Conventional employees travel from one private space (home) to another (the office or desk). This space comes at a potentially high price. Prime rents in central London reached £942 per square metre in 2001. With an average City worker occupying seven of those precious square metres, the total rental costs per employee at the peak of the market were around £6600 per head. Add to this business rates, service charges and a contribution to shared space and this figure rises to £15 000 per head per year. For such an expensive asset, office utilisation rates are very low. For example, a report from GL Hearn (2003) found that, on average, workstations were only occupied 55% of the time. At the peak of the market, this meant an effective rent of over £27 000 per square metre per annum.

In a teleworking environment, the territorial office would be utilised even less (see Box 6.4), leading to unsustainably high property costs. In a non-territorial office, however, employees move from a private space (home) to a shared facility with no sense of place. The home-based teleworker even trades control of his/her private space at home, since it becomes part of the corporate workspace.

In practice the non-territorial office acts like a business centre, renting out space on an hourly basis to individuals. All space is public and shareable. All space is connected. Personal files are either stored and made accessible electronically or, where paper is inevitable, stored in portable filing systems which can be delivered to the booked space as required.

Box 6.4   IBM

IBM has been at the forefront of mobile and flexible working, addressing many of the challenges among its own 325 000 employees. It has also worked with many customers as they make similar moves, both in the UK and across the globe.

For IBM, the term 'mobile office' (also referred to as remote working, telecommuting, and teleworking) describes the options now available for employees to interact efficiently with each other, and the rest of the enterprise, from home and on the road. It enables work to be carried out when and where it can most effectively be done. Mobile office is seen as an essential component of creating a flexible enterprise.

IBM distinguishes between different types of mobility; for example, sales teams working with clients on-site have different needs to a buyer working from home. Whether they be executives, knowledge, support or field workers, all have their own specific needs. Even roles that would traditionally be viewed as purely office based can benefit. Often the largest potential cost savings lie in the better utilisation of office space, which reduces the need for real estate and the associated office costs to support each employee. For IBM and many other enterprises the cost of office overheads is second only to that of the employed workforce – the savings from a reduced need for office space can be dramatic. In 1991, IBM allocated 241 square feet of office space for every employee. In 2001, the corporate target was 150 square feet per person. IBM UK achieved approximately 120 square feet per person, mostly due to mobile working practices.

IBM sees benefits across its business through increased morale, productivity and employee retention. Morale is improved, for instance, as employees have increased options around where and when they work, which ultimately reduces stress as they start to feel in greater control of their environment. Reciprocal flexibility between employees and the company helps attract and retain the best employees, potentially reducing recruitment costs.

Virtual teams

Conventionally, the concept of working with someone meant that you were probably co-located with the other members. The definition of a team is a group of people who interact through interdependent tasks guided by a common purpose. A virtual team is defined the same way, but with the rider that it works across space, time and organisational boundaries with links strengthened by webs of communication technologies. These teams may include members located in different buildings, cities or countries and/or members who contribute in different functional roles.

The globalisation of companies expands customers and workforce across geographic boundaries. One of the challenges that this presents is the co-ordination of team-based work chronicled by Solomon (1995). The same technologies that support teleworking also support the operation of virtual teams.

Living space

The crossover between workspace and living space confounds long-established mores but ICT is far more pervasive than just facilitating remote work. Work technologies have been embraced wholeheartedly, in part in order to maintain connections with the workplace, but also because increasingly families organise themselves according to management principles learned at work and with the help of communication technologies they imported from work.

For these families, time is the critical resource. The need is felt for devices that help with efficient time management and that might help them communicate with family and friends.

This blurring of the boundaries between work and home is a double-edged sword: on the one hand, it gives some people the freedom to arrange their lives in a way that fits their needs better; on the other, it overlays an alternative agenda and prioritisation. There is an extent to which flexibility has been traded for loss of control from the individual's standpoint.

Pierre Lévy (1998) refers to the blurring of the distinction between workspace and living space as the 'Moebius effect'. The growth of personal technologies such as mobile phones, PDAs and those technologies dedicated to entertainment such as digital television and electronic games has made virtuality just as much an issue for living space as any other kind.

Communication from living space is increasing. At the end of 2002 research company Jupiter estimated a personal email community of 115 million, 92% of the active online community. The same company estimate that this proportion will rise to 98% by 2008. With this increase in electronic communication comes a rise in SPAM (or junk electronic mail) and some 35% of all messages received were of this kind.

At the end of 2003, research from Ofcom, the UK telecommunications regulator, estimated that digital TV penetration had reached more than 50% of all UK households for the first time. In total the number of households receiving some form of multi-channel television had reached 54.4%. The total number of subscribers to cable television (both digital and analogue) is estimated to have remained stable at around 3.2 million, with digital cable subscribers making up around 70% of the total.

Worldwide, at the end of 2003, 10% (nearly 100 million) of global homes were receiving digital signals. This is nearly triple the 1999 figure and this number is expected to more than triple again by 2010 when 38% of the world's TV households will receive digital signals. Digital TV is about more than the ability to receive better quality pictures and more channels. Alongside these broadcasts comes interactivity – the ability to interact with, and respond to, events in the broadcast.

Watching TV and using a computer are fundamentally different tasks and whilst there are indications of crossover in certain areas – the ability to read emails on the TV for example – the main drivers here are likely to be TV-related applications.

Amongst the most important are electronic programme guides. Potentially digital TV delivers a massively bigger universe of channels and programmes to navigate. Viewers can customise the guide, search for programmes by name, category, actor, director, and so on, and obtain programme information and receive suggestions based on past viewing habits.

Other applications will include the following:

- **Video-on-demand**. Viewers are able to watch any movie, any time and store movies locally to rewatch specific scenes. They can also preview movies by seeing trailers and digests.
- **Reminders and alerts**. The user sets reminders to pop up when a future programme, actor or sports event comes on. Alerts suggest programmes of interest.

- **Simplified video recording**. The user can simply click on a programme in the guide to set recording. There will be no need for complicated menus.
- **Better features**. Better picture control through zoom and pan, change of viewpoint, multiple viewing windows, etc.
- **Interactive advertisements**. Giving the opportunity to purchase a product being advertised.[5]
- **Participation**. Giving the ability to vote on issues or participate in quiz games.
- **Additional information.** In-depth information about a broadcast via the remote control.

Clearly, digital TV offers the opportunity to shop either in response to a particular advertisement or generally using the interactive facilities offered to access online stores. This direct connection between an advertisement and a sale is beginning to change television advertising substantially as direct solicitation replaces more subtle forms of message. The continued popularity of shopping channels also demonstrates the power of the TV channel to deliver customers (see Box 6.5).

From a real estate perspective there is increasingly little difference between workspace and living space save one of scale. Both require high degrees of connectivity and, increasingly, shared ICT facilities. The implementation of networks of shared resources has been a feature of workspace for the last two decades. As the number of shared devices in the home

---

Box 6.5   QVC

QVC Inc. was founded in 1986 by Joseph Segel, founder of The Franklin Mint. The company established a new record in American business history for first full fiscal year sales by a new public company, with revenues of over $112 million.

By 1993, QVC had become the number one televised shopping service in sales, profits, and reputation in the United States, reaching over 80% of all US cable homes and 3 million satellite dishes. In 2002, more than 107 million units were shipped to customers around the world as a result of more than 150 million phone calls, leading to nearly $4.4 billion in sales. QVC is the world's pre-eminent electronic retailer. The service reaches approximately 85 million American homes, over 11 million households through a joint venture with BSkyB in the United Kingdom, 34 million homes in Germany, and over 8 million homes in Japan. QVC's eight distribution centres worldwide cover over 3.8 million square feet and operate in real time with the ordering and programme scheduling system. Live broadcasts are controlled in length by the rate at which the ordering process is taking up stock.

increases, so the incidence of home networks is increasing, facilitated by the wide availability of wireless networks.

Public space

Steven Carr and the authors of *Public Space* (Carr *et al.* 1992) provide a comprehensive definition of pure public space as 'responsive, democratic and meaningful' places that protect the rights of user groups. They are accessible to all groups and provide for freedom of action but also for temporary claim and ownership.

In practice, the main thing that distinguishes public space from private space is ownership. Although public bodies clearly own space, their objective is to manage it for the public domain rather than for private capital. As a function of this type of space there tend to be fewer solicitation events and more broadcast ones.

However, there is a substantial area of overlap between public and private space even using this definition. Publicly accessible areas such as airports or stations are privately controlled yet show all the characteristics of public space (see Box 6.6). Leisure facilities may fall into either domain.

As an individual's personal virtual space moves between public and private space there is little real difference. A wireless network provided by a coffee shop, for example, is as accessible from the street outside (public) as it is from inside (private).

The impact of ICT upon public space falls in three main areas:

- Access to better information.
- Giving the ability to respond better to events.
- Better security.

Information
The availability of targeted information in the public domain has increased dramatically in recent years as a direct result of improvements in ICT. Real-time, event-driven information is available at access points such as bus stops and on motorway signage; news is available via video wall technology in public spaces or via mobile phones; and advertisements are available through any of these channels (see Boxes 6.6 and 6.7).

This has changed the context of public space dramatically. To an extent Carr *et al.*'s meaningful and democratic space is diluted by the overlay of a

Box 6.6 Countdown

Countdown is an electronic information display system that gives people waiting at London bus stops real-time information on bus arrivals. The Countdown system helps take the uncertainty out of waiting for buses, as passengers know exactly when their bus will arrive – taking away some of the worry about how long to wait, knowing that their bus is on its way.

Each Countdown sign features regularly updated, real-time information for the relevant routes, showing the order in which buses will reach the stop, their destinations, and the number of minutes to arrival. All this information helps to provide passengers with the reassurances they need about service reliability.

As well as indicating which routes are running and their arrival times, Countdown can display special messages to passengers regarding information on traffic delays or forthcoming roadworks.

There are a number of sophisticated systems which work together to make Countdown operate efficiently. Technology on board buses allows a central system to receive a regular update from each bus about its exact location. Bus operators can then monitor exactly where the bus is and use this information to control services more effectively.

As the largest system of its kind in the world, Countdown is now being rolled out to thousands of key London locations as part of a £30 million programme of investment. To date 2000 Countdown sites have been installed. In his Transport Strategy the London Mayor has made a commitment to have a total of 4000 Countdown displays in place by 2005, thereby ensuring real-time information for more than 60% of total daily bus journeys will be provided.

Box 6.7 BT Openzone

BT Openzone is a public-access, broadband wireless Internet connection, allowing Internet access at selected public venues or 'hotspots', using a wireless-enabled laptop or PDA. HotSpots are available in around 1400 selected public locations across the UK. These include motorway service stations, airports, conference centres, hotels and cafes. HotSpots extend between 70 and 100 m, enough to cover a large site. The service is available either using pre-paid vouchers or via a subscription, both of which can be set up as needed. Through a partnership with British Airways the service is available in airport lounges in major European cities, such as Amsterdam, Rome, Berlin, Copenhagen and Athens, as well as all the major destinations in the United States and locations in Africa, South Africa and India. BT is also rolling out the service to McDonald's outlets throughout the UK.

context of controlled information; however, from a purely pragmatic standpoint it eases the frustrations of travel through public space.

Response

The ability to respond to events in public space is variable. Improvements in infrastructure such as the increasing availability of wireless broadband access in urban areas broaden the scope for response but these facilities tend to be provided by private space controllers in areas where private and public space overlap – airports, for example.

For the individual equipped with a mobile phone, any ability to respond is governed entirely by the provision of sufficient aerials to give a signal. Until recently, for example, tube travellers were unable to get a signal at all whilst underground. Nevertheless, the provision of response points, public payphones for example, is shrinking rapidly in the face of these alternative technologies.

This is becoming a more important issue for real estate as public concern about the supposed health risk of being in proximity to these aerials continues to affect planning decisions. The rollout of third-generation mobile services relies heavily upon a quantum increase in the number of mobile phone masts.

Security

Currently, the role of ICT in the security of public space revolves around the proliferation of digital CCTV. As well as becoming a useful source of cheap television programming, the wide coverage of CCTV in urban areas and the massively improved quality offered have changed the feel and character of public space as well as creating the fashion for hoods in youth culture.

Digital CCTV images can be transmitted instantly and processed against databases of stored images to assist with identification. Practical ramifications of this include the ability to monitor sites or facilities remotely, to verify identity as a means of access control and the ability to police sensitive areas without intrusion.

From the perspective of personal space this is certainly a passive intrusion and not one that is covered by any boundary legislation. At the current level of technology it is seldom possible to identify as complex a picture as a face with any accuracy automatically – image processing is really restricted to simple constructs such as the identification of number plates.

There are, however, technologies that have the capacity to identify themselves and thereby an individual, remotely.

The third-generation mobile phone with GPS capability goes some way down that road, but is probably not accurate enough to identify an individual in a crowd, for example. Radiofrequency identification (RFID) tags have that potential, however.

RFID tags are very small chips containing a tiny antenna, and can be fixed to physical items. Retailers are interested in using them as a hi-tech replacement for bar codes, as they offer the possibility of improved stock control – allowing a company to automatically count how many items it has in store, for example. Were these to be implemented at the level of individual products – clothing, for example – in theory it would be possible to monitor the location of that clothing once it had been purchased.

Currently RFID is being implemented at the pallet level and costs of the individual tags will have to fall substantially for product-level tagging to become feasible but this has not stopped civil liberties groups campaigning against their use.

Summary

Clearly, the impact of ICT upon workspace dominates this book, but the blurring of distinctions between types and uses of space is an observable outcome of ICT-enabled change. From the perspective of the choice of location, through the definition of personal space to the operation of private and public space (and in alliance with other factors), ICT has had a dramatic impact upon the built environment. It has changed the level of information available, the accessibility of systems and processes and the way that individuals interface with space. On the downside it has increased the vulnerability of personal space to incursion and the ability of private groups to leverage their particular interests. To an extent, the nature of physical space – real estate – has always been an outcome of technology. ICT is another flavour of technology that is continuing to shape how we design, view and use space. The next chapter in this book examines how ICT is interacting with other forces to shape real estate space.

Notes

1 Real-time technology differs from animation, which uses a sequence of pre-determined and pre-rendered images to create the illusion of movement. In real-time technology, the user interacts with the modelled environment at will, controlling movement direction and speed with the mouse or keyboard commands.

2 See also Box 9.1 in Chapter 9.

3 McCalman and Anderson (2002) also highlight the importance of the 'intelligent building' concept during the 1990s in encouraging the view of ICT as a liberating force in future office design. In this sense, intelligence is a collection of technologies able to respond to organisational change over time (DEGW 1992).

4 Van der Linden (2002) suggests that the architecture/construction process has itself evolved to shift conceptualisations of space away from an emphasis on sequential space (constrained by seasons and cycles in an agrarian economy) and parallel space (where construction allows for contextual freedoms) to transitional space (where new types of space are created in virtual worlds).

5 BSkyB Open's first interactive TV advertisement in the UK was broadcast on 27 March 2000, and promoted the cooking sauce *Chicken Tonight*. It allowed viewers to request a coupon for a free jar of the sauce. While the advert is running a red 'Press Now' appears in the top left-hand corner of the TV screen. On pressing the red button on their remote control, viewers are taken to the on-screen 'Creative Kitchen' where they can view recipe suggestions (complete with video clip instructions) or request a money-off coupon.

7

Real Estate Use and ICT

Introduction

In the last chapter we saw how concepts of space can aid our understanding of ICT transformation in real estate. In this chapter, we look more closely at the specific transformations that have occurred in particular real estate sectors. In examining the role played by ICT alongside other factors, we have adopted a different categorisation of real estate space from the 'conventional' one of offices, retail, industrial and residential. Here we examine a more generic taxonomy to include:

- sales;
- processing;
- manufacturing;
- distribution; and,
- leisure and living.

This is because the divisions that have often existed between sectors are blurring, as technology and other factors create more flexible forms of real estate space. In addition, we continue to use our 'socio-technical' framework in this chapter, as we emphasise the importance of ICT acting with other social, economic and political factors to create the transformations we highlight.

Sales

Overview

One of the major public faces of the growth in web-based technologies since the late 1990s has been its use by retailers as a new channel for reaching their customers. An early wave of pioneers dominated this activity in the mid-to late 1990s, as hundreds of small retailer enterprises set up online stores. Some of these have survived and gone from strength to strength (e.g. Amazon, lastminute.com), while others were the subject of acquisition by larger rivals or just went bankrupt. However, technology has a long history of influence over the way goods are bought and sold by both businesses and consumers. The growth of online retailing is the most recent application of technology in this area, and one that has been particularly evident to consumers themselves.

Many of the technological applications in retailing that have occurred over the last 20 years have tended to be in the back-office functions of manufacturers and retailers. Occasionally the evidence of these changes has been visible to consumers themselves (for example, the introduction of bar code scanning in the 1980s). Others are not as obvious and have led to improved efficiency for retailers during a period when their profit margins have been squeezed more than ever before. Indeed a number of underlying factors have impacted on the retailing sector over the last decade that place these technological changes into context, as was discussed in Chapter 1.

Some sectors have been more suited to the move online than others, particularly within the business-to-consumer market, and this can be seen by reference to the most successful online retailers. Broadly, those goods of which consumers have a good knowledge before purchase or whose characteristics can easily be summarised online tend to be most suited to online sales. Such goods include books, music and DVDs as well as travel. Clothing has typically been seen to be unsuitable for online sales due to customers wishing to see and touch the garments before they are purchased. However, some clothing items can be highly successful online, providing they are a unique standard item with a strong brand (e.g. soccer shirts, designer underwear and lingerie). Benchmarking research of retailers and retail property investors and developers has developed a risk spectrum of different types of retail property and the potential risk from eCommerce (see College of Estate Management 2001; Dixon & Marston 2002; Marston & Dixon 2003). Properties occupied by travel agents and banks, for example, have consistently achieved the highest risk ranking in these surveys, and Chapter 9 provides more detail on this and future scenarios in retailing.

The hype surrounding eCommerce in 1999 and 2000 was accompanied by a surge in the volume of statistics claiming to measure this new growth industry. Like many of the dot.coms that failed to survive, many of these metrics have quietly disappeared. Verdict, the British retail analyst, has continued to measure the sector and their data shows that in 2003 UK online retail sales totalled £4.9 bn, accounting for 1.9% of total retail expenditure, an increase of 36% on 2002. The growth has also occurred in the USA and the UK now has a similar proportion of online sales activity. By the end of 2003 data from the US Department of Commerce showed that online sales in the USA also accounted for 1.9% of total retail sales (worth nearly $55 bn for the full calendar year).

Despite the growth of eCommerce the high street retailers and shopping centres are still trading. It is unlikely that there will be any serious impact on traditional retailing locations because of eCommerce as shopping remains a social activity that is of increasing importance as a general leisure pursuit. It may, however, change the way we experience retailing. Physical changes to the configuration of retail units are discussed later, but also of importance are the changes to the overall retail mix of the high street or shopping centre. The growth in the use of technology will affect different parts of the retailing sector to different magnitudes. In this section we focus on three types of goods in particular: retail banking, travel and music. All three have proven to be highly adaptable to an online, digital world. Banking is a service that no longer requires a physical transaction to take place, music can easily be distributed over computer networks and travel can also be experienced after and not during its purchase.

Banking

Over the last ten years there has been a steady decline in the number of bank branches in the Britain. Over the same period there has been a substantial rise in the number of auto-teller machines (ATMs). In 1994 the British Bankers' Association recorded that there were 13 950 bank branches and 14 600 ATMs across Great Britain – almost one ATM for every branch. By 2002 the number of branches had fallen to 10 750 (23% less than in 1994) and the number of ATMs had risen to 25 870 (up 77% from 1994) – now 2.4 ATMs for every branch. As shown in Figure 7.1 one aspect of this growth in ATMs has come from the off-site machines (i.e. those located in places other than a bank branch). ATMs are increasingly being found in supermarkets, petrol stations, railway stations and even pubs. By 2002, 35% of ATMs were located away from a bank branch compared to just 12% in 1994. In some locations bank branches have practically removed all counter services and replaced them with a collection of ATMs.

This is an example of how banking has become more and more removed from the traditional high street bank branch. October 1989 is often seen as

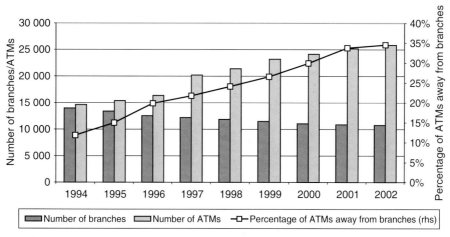

Figure 7.1   Changes in UK bank branches and ATMs (1994–2002) (data from British Bankers' Association).

a watershed, the point in time when telephone-only bankers First Direct appeared on the market. Henderson (1995) argues that the property requirements of retail banks have created an oligopoly within the UK banking sector. Traditional delivery strategies require a bank to develop an extensive branch network, a highly significant barrier to new entrants. The success of First Direct and subsequently a number of online banks (e.g. Egg, Smile, Cahoot) has demonstrated that technology has overcome this long-standing barrier.

Music

The influence of the Internet on the music industry has received widespread coverage in the general media. The principal output of the music industry, recorded music itself, is highly suited to online purchase and, unlike many other goods, can be also distributed online. This can only become more important as computer processor speeds and media storage capacities increase both in desktop PCs and in handheld media players (such as Apple's iPod player). The other important driver will be the move from dial-up to broadband, 'always-on' Internet connections. Downloading of music (both legal and illegal) is now regarded as the only way of accessing music for many people, particularly for younger generations. In 2003 market research showed that 26% of UK Internet users download music, of whom two-thirds are aged 15–35 (British Phonographic Industry 2003). At the time of this BPI survey, 58% of downloaders were using file sharing services such as KaZaa; however, this is likely to change as the music industry as a whole begins to provide online sales of downloadable music. Sales of CDs and DVDs have also been strongly influenced by online sales in similar ways to the growth of online book retailing (see Box 9.1 on Amazon, page 346).

Travel

The sale of personal and business travel services has also shown strong growth patterns. Online purchase has always formed a much larger proportion of the total travel market than in the retail sector as a whole. The European market was estimated to be worth €7.6 bn in 2002 representing 3.6% of the travel market. This compares to €2.5 bn in 2000 (1.2% of the market). The UK and Germany are the main markets for online travel sales and together constitute 60% of the market (UK: 38%; Germany: 22%) (Marcussen 2003). One of the major drivers behind this trend has been the growing presence of the so-called 'no frills' airlines across Europe and particularly within the UK and Ireland. These airlines have taken bookings in very different ways from the national carriers. Bookings have not been taken through retail travel agents and have directed activity online or through call centres. Many other airlines have also increased the importance of the Internet in their routes to market and begun to close the traditional retail booking agencies.

Ultimately the use of technology within retailing has been governed by the search for increased market share and profits. Retailers' margins have continued to tighten so the need to be efficient, as we shall see later in this chapter, with supply chain management, has never been more important. However, technology has also had a role to play in the marketing side of retailing, and not just through the use of the Internet. In the context of the shopping centre a number of different forms of marketing have been identified that together form a 'marketing mix' (Kirkup & Rafiq 1999). Like technology itself, some of these are self-evident (e.g. advertising); others less so. Examples include design, layout and attractiveness of the centre and the maintenance of that image once the centre is trading. The centre operator can also provide services to shoppers ranging from food outlets, through leisure services to providing personal shopper services. Increasingly technology is playing an important role here with centres experimenting with the provision of different types of services online. These include:

- providing exclusive offers online;
- loyalty card schemes operated online;

- shopping support services for customers with mobile telephones or handheld computers.

Some centres are also experimenting with online stores or virtual malls. Meadowhall Shopping Centre in Sheffield has an online gift shop which enables smaller tenants within its centre to offer some goods through an online store managed by the centre owners. The British property company Hammerson has also introduced online shops linked to some of its centres (The Oracle in Reading and West Quay in Southampton), although these are managed by a third party company and rely on individual retailers to have online offers already in place. It remains to be seen whether these initiatives will be of long-term importance to shopping centre operators.

Many of these initiatives have been supported by increased networking within shopping centres. The centres now link together all the individual tenants with the centre's management which can assist with a whole array of operational and management processes, ranging from sending out alerts for missing children to the submission of turnover statistics for individual units in order to calculated turnover rental payments.[1]

Just as the introduction of wireless networks in offices gave the opportunity for companies to put in place new forms of workplace design, so in the retailing sector companies can move away from a fixed store layout (Field 1999). This may be particularly useful for retailers of large bulky goods or department stores where sales staff could be equipped with handheld PCs. Fashion retailers may also benefit by being able to be more innovative with their store layout and allow flexibility over the location of payment desks. Wireless technology and handheld devices have already been useful to retailers, particularly supermarkets, for stock control purposes and more recently some supermarkets have begun using digital display pricing on shelves linked to the store's computer systems, allowing stores to update the price of individual items at any time.

Supply chain issues

As discussed earlier, the other important aspect of technology in the retail and supply sectors has been the growth in automation within the supply chain as a whole. During the 1970s and 1980s this became an increasingly important area for cost control, particularly within the food retailing sector (Wrigley 1998a). Indeed Sparks (1994: 331) sums up this period as one where retailers 'progressed from simply being the innocent recipients of manufacturer's transport and storage whims, to controlling and organising the supply chain, almost in its entirety'. These developments in particular, and the technological developments that enabled them, have had the greatest implications for retail property.

In the 1980s, British food retailers began to develop regional distribution centres across the country to act as hubs within their supply chain network. This in turn enabled shorter and more predictable delivery lead times to be introduced which prevented the need for large amounts of warehousing and storage space at individual stores. Consequently more floor-space within stores could be devoted to the retail space itself. The food sector pioneered this crucial shift to the extent that Wrigley (1998b: 117) states that 'the major UK food retailers were significantly ahead (perhaps as much as ten years) of their North American equivalents at this time, and also in advance of their major continental European rivals'.

This trend, however, has now spread across the whole of the retail industry. Retailers such as Zara now rely on just-in-time supply chains to maintain stock levels within their stores across Europe and can respond to changes in consumer taste and preference (see Box 4.8, page 153).[2] The changing requirements of retailers have also led to a change in the demand profile for retail property. A 'standard' high street shop unit in the 1970s would have been regarded as one with retail space of 75 to 110 square metres. Twenty years later the 'standard' has more than doubled to 240 square metres, and in some prime locations to in excess of 300 square metres (Knight Frank 1996).

Throughout the 1990s a number of different supply chain concepts were introduced to make the business relationship between retailer and supplier more efficient and cost effective. Three concepts in particular have been widely discussed in the literature:

- quick response (QR) (McMichael *et al.* 2000; Perry & Sohal 2000);
- efficient consumer response (ECR) (Duffy & Fearne 2004; Kotzab 1999; McMichael *et al.* 2000); and,
- collaborative planning, forecasting and replenishment (CPFR) (Barratt 2001; Schwarz 2004).

Sparks and Wagner (2003) have neatly summarised these different concepts as shown in Table 7.1.

These approaches towards supply chain management have been popularised by the introduction of increasingly sophisticated forms of stock control technology. In particular, these have been built on EDI infrastruc-

Table 7.1 Summary comparison of QR, ECR, CPFR and retail exchanges (adapted from Sparks & Wagner 2003).

	QR	ECR	CPFR	Retail exchange
Focus	Apparel industry	Grocery industry	Retail industry	Retail industry
Technology	EDI, EPoS, bar coding	EDI, EPoS, bar coding	Dedicated intra and extranet	Internet
Goal	Reduced cycle time Reduced inventory Efficient management of disturbances in supply chain More efficient planning of supply chain			

Prerequisite	Strategic partnering
	Compatible management information
	  systems
	Real-time information management
				Internet access
				Internal and external IT
				  capabilities

Behaviour	Teamwork Continuous improvement Joint problem solving Supply chain transparency			Transactional Promotes co-operation (but not evident so far)
Levels	Strategic – partner selection Tactical – implementation across boundaries Operational – process interface efficiency			Strategic, tactical and operational

Trade-off	Balance between autonomy and control			Loss of differentiation vs
				  efficiency and reduced
				  costs
				Loss of intellectual
				  property vs capability
				  development and
				  innovation

tures and have made use of bar coding and electronic point of sale (EPoS) systems used by retailers. With the Internet new opportunities have arisen for suppliers and retailers to collaborate, this time in online B2B retail exchanges (Sparks & Wagner 2003). Two major international retail exchanges emerged in 2000: Global NetXchange (GNX) and WorldWide Retail Exchange (WWRE).

Across the retail sector, therefore, there has been an increasing hunger for data and consequently the technology that can support and store those data. Hallberg (1995: 233) in particular comments that retailers have been 'eager new recruits to the database revolution'. This need has arisen both on the supply side (records of inventory and stock) and the demand side (records about consumers). In relation to the latter, retailers have introduced loyalty programmes. The most common form has been the loyalty card format used mainly by supermarkets. These have encouraged consumers to part with personal information in exchange for discount vouchers or free gifts. The retailer is then able to collect detailed information about individual shopping patterns and taste which can be used for more targeted promotions and efficient stock control. It is this data-gathering potential of loyalty programmes that is ultimately seen as their greatest advantage (Passingham 1998). The benefits of collecting knowledge and information about consumers are important for many parts of the retailing sector. Retailers and retail property investors choose the best properties for their businesses and investment objectives based on demographic and expenditure profiles of local populations. Traditionally, these data have been characterised by their generic structure, summarising populations over a relatively large geographic area, and their anonymity. The data collected by retailers are now increasingly becoming more local-ised and detailed. Loyalty schemes are therefore one way in which retailers have sought to make their databases more specific to the household or individual. KPMG (2001) have also shown that loyalty schemes can have a positive effect on turnover and profitability. Their analysis of store-based loyalty programmes has shown that they appear to break even when turnover increases by between 3% and 4%.

On the supply side there is also evidence to suggest that retailers are seeking more detailed and precise information. The data stored have tended to be down to the level of specific product lines or a packing crate. Retailers, including Wal-Mart, are now beginning to use technology such as radio frequency identification (RFID) (see Box 7.6) to gather data relating to a single item or component of an item.

Technology and retail leases

With the rise of online retailing the real estate literature has begun to examine implications for the retail lease. In particular attention has focused on the shopping centre lease and various authors have examined possible strategies that shopping centres could activate to take advantage of these new routes to market. Hendershott *et al.* (2000; 2001) have ex-plored the concept of hybrid and virtual malls. Although both papers discuss the issue of eCommerce and store-based retailing from a US per-spective, they also present a theoretical model for how shopping centres can capitalise on web-based sales. This is described by Hendershott *et al.* (2000) as the 'hybrid' model where customers order and purchase online, then collect their purchases at a local shopping centre or store. This could either be led directly by retailers or by shopping centres themselves. Indeed in their second article (Hendershott *et al.* 2001) this idea is taken further. They suggest that large shopping centres and networks of centres[3] have the economies of scale and ability to aggregate information that will allow the hybrid model to succeed. However, for this to work best loyalty programmes should be introduced by the centres.

The difficulty with this model is how shopping centre owners can lead the way with providing an online sales environment which brings in their largest tenants. Many tenants of large shopping centres are not independent retailers. They are part of a larger company with many aspects of the stores being controlled through the retailers' headquarters. In particular this includes online operations. Many large retailers have now invested large amounts into online shops and may be highly reluctant to create online stores for specific use through a shopping centre. This certainly seems to be an unsustainable way of running online sales channels.

The whole issue of capturing web-based sales has also been debated heavily (Baen 2000; College of Estate Management (CEM) 2001; Miller 2000; O'Roarty 2000). In the USA there was a fear that revenues could be lost from stores due to the increased sales online. This is because many shopping centre units in the USA are let on a percentage lease, similar to a turnover lease in the UK. Turnover leases have typically been more common in the USA than the UK (McAllister 1996), where 93% of non-anchor store leases have overage or turnover clauses (Eppli *et al.* 2000). Any reduction in store-based turnover from online 'cannibalisation' would therefore have implications for the shopping centre owner. This prompted initiatives to capture online sales through 'wired leases' (O'Roarty 2000). Similarly Miller (2000) proposed a solution for adding an online element into the rent calculation, and a study by CEM (CEM 2001) found that the impact of eCommerce on a turnover lease in major shopping centres was minimal given the strong existing retail mix.

Processing

Overview

If a fairly 'loose' definition of 'offices' is adopted (i.e. real estate containing basic walls, windows, doors, ceilings and with space to support equipment and workers at desks (Schiller 2001)) then the majority of people work in offices (Duffy 1997). Although Evans (1985) categorised office space as comprising finance, corporate head offices and business services, and the US commercial real estate market refers to FIRE or Finance, Insurance and Real Estate, other office uses have emerged and grown in size over the last

20 years, ranging from media and telecommunications, through to entertainment and government.

One of the key driving forces influencing office space has been the managerial changes that occurred at the end of the nineteenth century, as greater control became exerted over manufacturing and distribution through the accumulation and synthesis of information (Duffy 1997). Paper-based tasks became more common and greater numbers of workers were needed to process the information. 'Taylorism', or the scientific management of people as units of production, operated first in the factory and then in the office, and encouraged an ordered, hierarchical, supervisory approach to office space that is still seen in the legacy buildings of the last two centuries, and was also strongly underscored by a general decline in manufacturing and a flight to the service economy (see Part 1 of this book).

Partly as a result of the changes brought about by ICT and allied social and economic forces, the meaning of the term 'office use' has become increasingly blurred. New kinds of space have emerged which offer greater flexibility and comfort to users and occupiers. Duffy (1997)[4] in fact recognised this in the 1990s with his seminal work, *The New Office*. Duffy suggested that, historically, the dominant mode of the conventional office was the 'office as factory', where individuals processed work under supervision at their own desks. In some instances such work has been outsourced overseas, but in general he characterised such processes as giving rise to 'hives' (Figure 7.2). 'Cells', on the other hand, were characterised by independence and concentrated study (for example, professional and research tasks). In

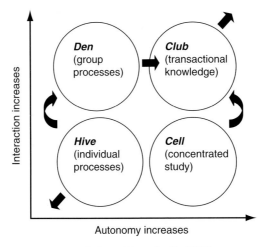

Figure 7.2   Office space concepts (adapted from Duffy 1997).

contrast, where group processes were involved this led to more teamworking and interaction, and Duffy therefore termed this type of space 'dens'. There is also a cyclical dimension to Duffy's typology, because as group processes and concerted study are transformed through organisational and technological change, they may in some instances converge into 'clubs' or spaces for transactional knowledge. This typology can apply to parts of a business or a whole business, and Duffy also suggests that differences in work patterns, space layout, and ICT requirements are all closely related to these types of space.

A similar, yet distinct, typology of office space has also been developed by Myerson and Ross (2003) who identify four themes in twenty-first century office development, again largely driven by organisational and technological change:

- The narrative office – here design and layout are used to develop brand differentiation (examples include Toyota's UK headquarters at Epsom Downs and Reebok's Canton, MA, US headquarters).
- The nodal office – here design is used to encourage new ways of working such as hot-desking and hotelling so that fixed points for networking, coaching, training and knowledge sharing are promoted to complement the more mobile work methods (examples include IBM's Santa Monica HQ in USA and McKinsey and Co.'s Amsterdam Harbour complex in the Netherlands employing 'lounges' and 'cocoons').
- The neighbourly office – this runs against the grain of the 'Taylorist' model and uses design and layout to promote social interaction (examples include Cellular Operations centre in Swindon in the UK).
- The nomadic office – this is characterised by a series of geographically distributed spaces for work (examples include Workspace, operated by Granada and BT, and the Institute of Directors building in London).

On the face of it, the two typologies of office space above perhaps support the view that 'processing space' is a more appropriate term than 'office space'. Flexibility, efficiency and effectiveness in design and use are therefore increasingly powerful mantras, and ICT has played a major role in transforming the shape and form of traditional office use, as business models themselves have changed and adapted to technology and socio-economic factors.

Consumer-orientated services provide the obvious example of how ICT infrastructure allows the remote location/relocation of organisations. A case in point is retail insurance: car, home, holiday insurance and so on. The traditional way of selling retail insurance products was through a chain of hundreds of owned or franchised high street shops. Such outlets would market, sell and process applications and claims, as well as handle customer enquiries. But, today, high street insurance retailers are a rarity and technology has enabled the sale of retail insurance to be undertaken via either telephone or the Internet. The conventional business model relied on a high street presence as a key component of marketing advantage. The company that could afford a unit on every high street would take market share and create a barrier to competitor market entry. The real estate and the shop window it provided were seen as an asset to the organisation.

However, technology destroyed the importance of real estate in the selling of retail insurance. If a car or home insurance policy could be effectively marketed and sold over the telephone or over the Internet, then the high street shop window could be replaced with TV and billboard advertising. The shift would be from tangible brands towards virtual brands. In effect, retail insurance would become a price-led commodity. Commoditisation of consumer and business services and the creation of virtual brands have been made possible by ICT advance, and the development of business models, to take advantage of the technology available. As a result, big brands such as supermarkets, with their trusted customer bases, have been able to enter markets such as banking, insurance, and utilities retailing without having to invest in dedicated high street sales units. Their service shop windows are TV adverts and leaflets at the tills, while the sales are done via call centres or through automated websites.

Today, the real estate footprint of a typical marketer of retail insurance is centralised around one (or several) 'call centres', with associated administration and data centre space, in contrast to the old business model of high street outlets and associated local/regional back offices and HQ space. The same story can be told of retail banking, pensions, credit cards, and other types of consumer savings and lending. Real estate spend (creating and maintaining the shop window) has been replaced with technology and marketing spend, in order to reach and service the same customer catchment. But the principle can be applied to the business processes within many other types of organisations. Human resources, accounts, IT support, data centre management and customer care are all examples of business processes that can be located away from the HQ function, but remain connected and controlled via ICT infrastructure. For example, an investment bank may have its HQ in London, its data centre management in Bristol, and its customer care in Sheffield.

The relocation of back-office operations parallels the vogue for business process outsourcing (BPO). EDS, IBM, ITNet, Accentura, CSC and Xansa are examples of companies that offer BPO services and have grown their businesses rapidly in the last few years. Multi-hundred-million pound contracts to take over and run whole back-office functions for large enterprises and government bodies are not unusual today. In many cases the contract will require the relocation of the business process to the most cost-efficient location.

The next part of this section therefore examines some examples of how ICT is impacting in terms of location, layout and configuration, intensity of use/productivity and leasing in a number of case study examples:

- global city office markets (London and Singapore);
- core space: TMT and dot.com occupiers;
- peripheral space: serviced offices; and
- call centres.

The examples in this section therefore cover what might be termed 'mainstream offices', where ICT transformation is perhaps relatively under-researched empirically, as well as more specialist office types such as serviced offices and call centres, where ICT has clearly grabbed the headlines.

Examples of ICT transformation

Global city office markets

In a survey of City of London office occupiers in the UK, Dixon *et al.* (2002, 2003) found that although technology was an important driver in terms of process change, other factors were equally important. For example, where face-to-face contact was considered important, ICT was treated very much as a tool to be managed and certainly transport and human resources were also highlighted as two key drivers in influencing location. Again, their research showed that larger organisations tend to use eBusiness technologies more widely in their business than smaller organisations, emphasising the digital divide that exists between Small and Medium Enterprises (SMEs) and larger companies. This was particularly true of customer relations, staff training and recruitment, shareholder relations and videoconferencing. For example, some 71% of firms with more than 250 employees had this facility available to customers, but for other organisations the proportion was just 25%. Similarly, over half of the largest firms operated online CRM, with the remainder planning to do so over the next 12 months (compared with 16% firms of less than 250 employees).

Interestingly, in the same study, security and the threat of terrorism also featured as a driver in promoting the greater use of videoconferencing, and larger firms were also more likely to use this technology. However, little support for the view that eBusiness generally can reduce costs or raise profits could be found amongst the respondents. But this view holds true only for today. Respondents believed that in 12 months' time eBusiness would make a difference to the bottom line. Some 28% of respondents did believe, specifically, that broadband has improved profits, and 23% that it has lowered costs. These tended also to be larger organisations, which already had broadband and viewed it as focusing on faster access to data and data transfer.

As far as homeworking is concerned, a relatively large proportion of respondents (62%) in the survey also said that their staff have access to files or email from home, and 42% of respondents said they anticipated a large increase in staff working from home over the next two years. The supporting interviews in the research suggested that transport problems would drive this as much as technology, however. Again, size differences were an important feature of the results:

- All large organisations allow access from home.
- Two-thirds of medium-size organisations allow access from home.
- Just over one-third of micro-organisations allow access from home.
- Moreover, there is a greater tendency for financial and corporate sectors (68%) to allow such access than other sectors (55%).

This supports findings in other research which has highlighted the importance of new working practices such as hotelling, and hot-desking (see Capital Economics 2002; Gerald Eve 2001; University of West of England 2003, for example). Hotelling is the reserving in advance of a workstation with full support and hot-desking means selecting any workstation on a first-come, first-served basis. The Gerald Eve (2001) survey of UK companies showed that some 35% of companies had introduced hot-desking, with 24% of staff in those companies affected. But the same survey found that new working practices (also encompassing homeworking and team-working) tend to be focused on larger organisations. Although the same research has shown that net densities have increased over time and that new working practices (NWP) increase densities[5] (see Table 7.2), the picture is by no means straightforward, and firm size, length of occupation, and whether a property is leasehold are also important factors to consider.

It was clear from both the postal survey and the interviews in the City of London survey (Dixon *et al.* 2002) that the City still has an important pull

Table 7.2 Floor-space per worker ratios and new working practices (NWP) (net floor-space (m^2) per worker) (from Gerald Eve 2001).

Function	Offices without NWP	Offices with NWP
Head office	16.8	15.2
Admin centre	17.2	15.6
Branch office	17.1	14.8
Sales office	17.6	14.8
Sole office	16.8	15.1

on many companies, particularly those that require face-to-face contact with clients. Although technology is leading to process change, transport difficulties and human resource issues were also equally as important as ICT in driving such trends as homeworking. Over the next five years (from 2002), respondents believed that Internet connection speeds would increase, the tasks carried out online would increase, and people would use email even more. Moreover, 41% of respondents believed that their staff would be doing even more homeworking than today. However, business travel would still be an important part of corporate functions.

Some 40% of respondents believed they would require less space per person in five years' time (Figure 7.3). Many were in the SME size range: for example, 46% in the size range 6–50 employees considered they would require less City office floor-space per person overall in five years' time (i.e. densities will increase). This is not surprising, since the density of occupation of SMEs in our survey is lower than larger companies. Given that only 12% of all respondents said they would require less space overall in five years (i.e. the majority of 5–50 size firms would be occupying the same amount of space), the implication of this may be further expansion of jobs in the sector.

Most office occupiers in the City of London are service providers. New technologies have made, and will increasingly make, some of these companies extremely footloose but despite this, many are still based in the City of London. The final questions in the City survey sought to identify those organisations that may consider moving away from an expensive City location over the next five years (Figure 7.4).

Overall, the need for a City location remains very high. A mere 8% definitely said that they anticipated being located outside the City of London in five years' time, and a further 12% said they would still be in the City but would be occupying significantly less space than they currently do. Those that planned not to be in the City were all small companies with less than 50 members of staff. Almost half (49%) said they

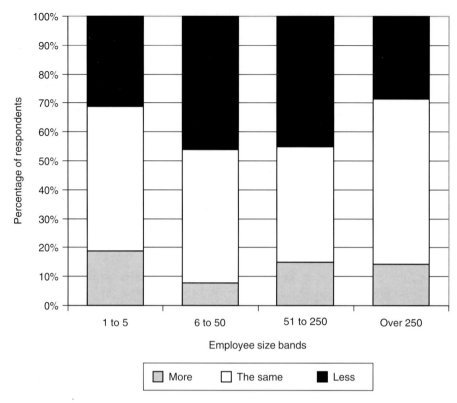

Figure 7.3   Floor-space changes over the next five years, by employee size bands (adapted from Dixon *et al.* 2002)

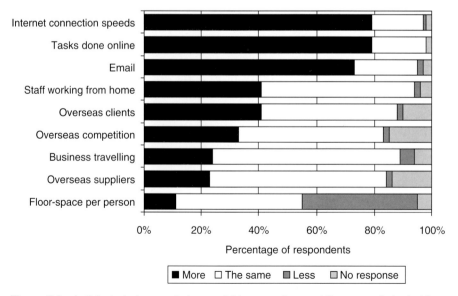

Figure 7.4   Anticipated changes in key variables over the next five years (adapted from Dixon *et al.* 2002)

would remain in the City, occupying the same space, and the remaining 30% said they would be occupying more City office space.

The majority of City companies in this survey appeared to be 'London-centric' in supply chain terms and 'City-centric' in client terms therefore. But, anecdotally, SMEs face particular pressures from rents/rates in the City. For larger organisations and those facing less pressure, the locational pull of the City, particularly in client and face-to-face contact terms, transcends the centripetal forces of technology, although in some sectors ICT is becoming an increasingly important driver for change.[6]

In a study of the Singapore office market, Tien Foo (2002) provides an interesting economic analysis of ICT to suggest the demand function for office space in two main ways. Firstly by the expansion and creation of new firms offering ICT services to other firms; secondly by the new working practices and business reorganisation that may arise leading to structural change. ICT-enabled operations can achieve improvement via efficiency gains in three main areas: business function and configuration; staffing and organisation structure; and locational flexibility. If ICT-induced change therefore impacts on firms occupying larger office space, then aggregate demand for space is also likely to be affected by the increase in ICT investment. This is shown diagrammatically in Figure 7.5.

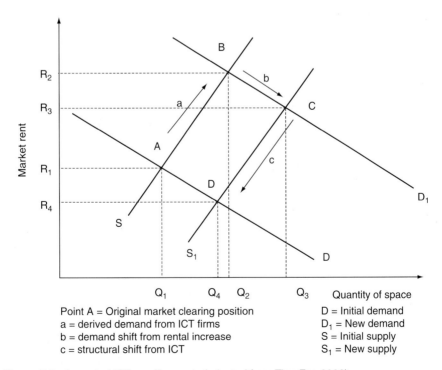

Point A = Original market clearing position
a = derived demand from ICT firms
b = demand shift from rental increase
c = structural shift from ICT

D = Initial demand
D₁ = New demand
S = Initial supply
S₁ = New supply

Figure 7.5   Impact of ICT on office rents (adapted from Tien Foo 2002).

Assuming perfectly elastic supply, new ICT firms would push equilibrium demand from A to B on the new demand curve D_1 leading to a rent rise to R_2. But when new office supply is increased rent is adjusted downwards to R_3 with a new equilibrium point of C. Moreover if ICT-induced effects take place more firms may give up space by downsizing and a new equilibrium point is reached at R_4 with a lower amount of occupied space, Q_4 (point D). The Singapore survey also showed that those occupying firms that tended to be more positive towards ICT generally also tended to perceive that ICT adoption would lead to a reduction in floor-space per worker.

Clearing mechanisms in the market will also affect the rental value of office property and it would logically be expected that 'wired buildings' would carry a rental premium over and above other buildings. Further work by Tien Foo *et al.* (2004) focused on the developer's perceptions of ICT and broadband in office buildings in Singapore and also attempted to measure the value impact of ICT. Building on work by Thompson and Hills (1999), Almond (2001), and Spurge (2002), they studied Suntec City in Singapore and found that in their survey of 24 developers, 71% expected upgrading of buildings to increase marketability and also to be able to attract tenants who are willing to pay a premium for ICT and broadband services. The majority of developers also felt that ICT would impact positively on occupancy rate, rent and running/maintenance costs. Network externality benefits can arise also where the utility of a user increases as a result of growth in the network (Katz & Shapiro 1994), and Tien Foo *et al.* (2004) incorporated a measure of this (based on size of office building as a proxy) in an incremental net present value model to estimate the economic gain of investing in ICT and broadband. Excluding intangible economic benefits such as enhanced landlord–tenant relationships, lower leasing risks, higher market branding and so on, their research showed that ICT/broadband connectivity produced a premium of 3.86% of unit rental value.[7]

Core space: the TMT and dot.com sector

The increasing focus on core business, outsourcing, changing employment patterns and shorter product lifecycles has led to the growth of a core–periphery model in some real estate sectors (Byrne *et al.* 2002), and this has also been driven by ICT growth. Core space is held on a long-term lease (or freehold) forming the main focus for an organisation's activities whilst peripheral space is taken up as the need arises, with the emphasis on flexibility and agility.

In terms of core space, the expanded demand for office space from new Internet or dot.com companies led to a number of empirical studies during the latter part of the 1990s in the UK. For example, Jones Lang LaSalle (2001) found that in a survey of the London Technology, Media and Telecoms (TMT) sector (which included the dot.com sector), public transport issues and levels of connectivity were prioritised as the most important location criteria, and that Internet infrastructure and fit-out were highest ranked on the list of building criteria. This was also true of TMT companies globally. Indeed the research also revealed a strong clustering effect in Central London. This supports the findings from other research (Trends Business Research 2001; Taylor *et al*. 2003), which shows that the new companies associated with ICT cluster because of the need for innovation, the benefits of localised externalities, and the need to locate around key metropolitan markets.

More recently, empirical work in the UK for the DTI (Trends Business Research 2001) identified 154 clusters,[8] representing between 8% and 18% of the UK region. Besides financial services clusters in the City (with significant employment in Westminster, Islington, Tower Hamlets, Camden and Croydon) other City-related clusters include business services (such as market research and management consulting) and property/real estate. Moreover, in the City fringe (Hoxton, Clerkenwell and Spitalfields), new media clusters are evolving based on the ICT sectors and small firms (Local Futures Group 1999), and this relates to the continued growth of the 'knowledge economy' in the UK.

In the USA, research by Gorman (2002) in New York and San Francisco has shown that eBusiness service companies (Internet-related consultancy, software development and IT outsourcing, for example) tend to agglomerate in existing centres of urban growth. Domains, bandwidth and population appeared to be the most influential drivers of regional Internet economic growth (see also Malecki 2002), and downtown and central business areas were the most favoured locations in a hierarchy that matches the most populous metropolitan areas (Table 7.3). Kolko (2002) has also supported this view, with evidence from Silicon Valley, which indicated that high-IT industries need skilled labour and therefore tend to concentrate. Lower-skilled industries using IT more intensively may tend to disperse, however, in the future. In Europe at a national scale Koski *et al*. (2001) also produced similar findings: a central 'banana' of ICT clustering from London via Randstat through industrial areas in Germany and Switzerland to Northern Italy, with a smaller 'Nordic potato' covering Stockholm and Helsinki: again suggesting that processing functions in Internet-based work maps onto existing economic activity.

Table 7.3 Number of web firms in US cities (adapted from Forrester 2000).

City	Web firms
New York	39
San Francisco	33
Boston	23
Los Angeles	20
Chicago	19

The technological infrastructure needed to service Internet industries is also mapping onto centres of economic activity, which also strengthens the clustering effect for many process-based businesses. As the Local Futures Group (2001) report on e-London points out, 'broadband London' has been very much business dominated and shaped by the needs of global companies and knowledge-based industries, located in a corridor that runs from Canary Wharf through the City, the West End and Hammersmith to Heathrow. Jenkins (2001) indicated that London currently enjoys a strong competitive position through the deployment of Internet technology, which suggests that London is the leading eBusiness centre in Europe and has a standing equal to New York and ahead of Tokyo. Indeed, London has more capacity in use in terms of Internet infrastructure than any other world city,[9] and is a hub for three of the five largest Internet city to city connections, including the top two.[10] When web-hosting is included, London is the largest centre in Europe (Local Futures Group 2001), and London to New York (77.7 Gbps) is one of the world's key Internet backbone trunks.

Although the Internet remains US centric (Telegeography 2001), Europe–USA links are growing rapidly, and other UK cities are also seeking to capture new eBusiness-related office occupiers. Leeds, for example, has the largest server farm in Europe and handles 35% of all UK Internet traffic (e-HQ 2003; see also Gore 2001) and Yorkshire Forward have promoted the development of a new Internet quarter based at the Holbeck Urban Village Development (Box 7.1).

Peripheral space: serviced offices

Peripheral space requirements have also grown in importance, and not only in the TMT/dot.com sector. This has led to the growth of serviced offices in the UK, or what are known as 'executive suites' or 'business centres' in the USA (Byrne *et al.* 2002). As we have argued earlier in this book, the impact on serviced office space from ICT is through technology impact interacting with organisational change to drive the demand for more flexible space. ICT therefore does not drive space demand on its own.

Box 7.1   Holbeck Urban Village, Leeds: the Internet quarter

The Leeds e-HQ initiative was launched in 2001 as a partnership of public and private sector organisations to work together to create new eBusiness opportunities in the city. Leeds already had a thriving eBusiness environment founded on a substantial ICT sector (1300 companies employing 12 000 people and the location for two of Energis' UK data centres, with more than 90% of the city's exchanges broadband enabled) (e-HQ 2003). In 2003, work was started on the Holbeck Urban Village, a major new regeneration project in the centre of Leeds based on the former Round Foundry site. This incorporates a dedicated Internet quarter with 2600 m^2 of space for high technology businesses. Yorkshire Forward, the Required Development Agency, will lease an Internet building with incubator units. The scheme also includes residential and leisure use.

Although the serviced office concept has been established in the UK for a number of decades, until the late 1980s the sector was characterised by fragmentation and diversity of ownership and nature of operation. Specialist serviced office providers such as Regus, HQ and MWB offer a combination of flexibility and services to their occupiers and have been the main suppliers. Typically, they provide a full range of business support to their occupiers in terms of facilities management, equipment, IT, catering, secretarial/reception and so on, in addition to flexibility of exit from operational properties. In relation to type of occupier, a survey of the UK serviced office sector (Gibson & Lizieri, 2000) found that 41% of occupiers were IT companies (24% business service firms and 21% financial service firms), and a corresponding US survey by ESA (2000) found that technology firms comprised 29% of occupiers followed by business service firms (17.8%), and financial service firms (12.5%). The increasing expansion of the TMT sector (see above) has therefore also fuelled the growth in the serviced office sector.

Clearly, occupiers of serviced offices require flexible space and lease arrangements, and research by Jones Lang LaSalle (2001) has shown that dot.com companies have been successful in securing a significant degree of flexibility in their property arrangements, ranging from shorter leases (an average of 5.2 years, compared with 15 years typical length in the London office market) to more extensive use of serviced space on a 24/7 basis. The rent package in this sector also differs from 'conventional' office suites: executive suites or serviced offices offer 'virtual space' and firms can use the centre for telephone or mail answering, hiring meeting rooms and so on and the rent chargeable reflects the bundle of services available (Gibson & Lizieri 2000).

Finally, as with other types of technology-driven space, there is evidence from the USA (Byrne *et al.* 2002) to suggest that clustering of executive suites occurs in metropolitan areas (for example, Atlanta, Dallas, Chicago), with the largest populations and with relatively high numbers of financial and business services employment, although there also appears to be a critical size threshold for the urban area, above which it is uneconomic to supply more centres.

Call centres

Call centres[11] and related IT service centres now represent the real estate footprint of many consumer services organisations. In the UK there are some 4300 call (or contact) centres with three-quarters of a million employees, representing nearly 3% of the UK workforce. The South East and London account for some 40% of the UK call centres (Morrell 2003) and fewer than half of the UK's call centres have been set up prior to 1995, reflecting the rapid growth in the sector. However, in other parts of the UK (the North East, for example) some 4% of the working population is employed in call centres, reflecting the substantial losses in employment from heavy industry's demise and the subsequent mobilisation of a 'hidden' female workforce (McConnell 2004). The growth in call centres (ECOTEC 2000) has been fuelled by:

- increasing the role of customer service in many organisations from retail through to B2B supply;
- increase in the number of retail channels to market and therefore contact points required;
- professionalisation of the customer service function, driving the second tier growth of outsourced suppliers;
- rapid ICT development, including voice-over and integrated and neural network databases, and linkages over several functions and businesses;
- drive to reduce operating costs through increased centralisation;
- deregulation of the marketplace in telecoms, utilities, and financial services.

The growth of a 'virtual business model' anchored in a call centre in many parts of the service sector has lowered the barriers to entry, enabling many new entrants who wish to capitalise on their brand strength, operational know-how, and/or marketing funds. For example, Dutch bank ING has entered the UK consumer savings and loans market from a law base. US credit card companies MBNA and Capital One have built a significant share of the UK credit market. Insurance brands such as Direct Line, Admiral and Norwich Union Direct operate without a physical branch sales network, whilst a host of direct banks have won market share with only a telephone and Internet interface with their customers.

For companies seeking to enter direct consumer service markets, the virtual character of the underlying organisation offers freedom of choice as to where to locate the physical operations. The inherent flexibility regarding location is of vital importance to both local government economic development officers and the real estate industry. The location decision-making process for a direct service provider is usually based on a combination of total running cost, availability of labour, real estate and grant aid, and competition among UK regions and among the local authorities within the regions is high, enticed by the prospect of a direct service provider creating hundreds of new jobs. Inducements to secure new employment include training grants, real estate and fit-out grants, assistance with recruitment, and grants towards the relocation costs of key staff.

Without ICT infrastructure and the development of the direct consumer services business model, many UK cities and towns that suffered from the decline of heavy industries would not be natural beneficiaries of the expansion of the services economy. Regional development agencies in the UK have therefore sought to attract call centres to the regions with financial incentives and tax breaks as they offer fast ways of creating jobs in areas of economic decline. The combination of ICT infrastructure, grant aid, local government assistance, and available labour made cities such as Glasgow, Cardiff, Newcastle, Manchester and Liverpool attractive locations for direct consumer service organisations, and has led to the concentration of call centre space in those areas. Leeds, for example, has one of the highest geographic concentrations of call centres in the UK, driven by its good-quality office accommodation, access to large sub-regional labour market and a pivotal location on the UK telecoms network (Gore 2001).

However, as with other back-office processing and software design and development, there has been an increasing number of call centre businesses moving 'offshore' from the UK (and USA). Barrett (2003) suggests that some UK commentators are predicting as much as 2.3 million m² of UK office space could be vacated within the next ten years as companies relocate non-core functions to India and the Far East. Prudential, HSBC and BT have already set up large operations in Malaysia and India. Other functions such as R&D and the pharmaceutical sectors may also be at risk. As a result, Arlington recently announced the development of a partnership to establish business parks in developing economies. Ironically therefore the technology that drove call centre growth in the UK is also now acting as a driver with other factors (low cost/rents; skills shortages; successful overseas experience and globalisation) to move call centres offshore (see ECOTEC 2000; Celner *et al.* 2003).

Manufacturing

Overview

In most mature economies, manufacturing represents a declining proportion of output and employment. Traditional, heavy industries that once dominated the landscape have largely disappeared or relocated to lower cost locations and much of this manufacturing capacity has been lost to alternative land uses. In the UK, for example, nearly half the stock of factory premises was lost between 1974 and 2004 (ODPM 2004). Concurrently the economic share of services has risen. For example, Sauvé and Dihel (2002) reported that the share of services in world GDP had risen by 5% between 1980 and 1998, and the same authors record that nearly 70% of production and employment in OECD countries is in services. This decline has also led to a shift towards hi-tech or laboratory-based manufacturing in the UK, which has also been promoted through policies designed to develop a knowledge-based economy (see Part 1 of this book, especially Chapter 2). In contrast, low-cost locations in India and the Far East as well as Eastern Europe are now important manufacturing economies serving home markets with ICT-enabled supply chains.

The manufacturing sector has always been at the forefront of the impact of ICT on production processes. Since, to a large extent, these production processes determine the nature and configuration of the real estate that houses them, it follows that ICT has had a significant impact upon manufacturing property.

The principal mechanism through which this impact is manifested is that of control. Beniger (1986) describes the history of the control process from early mechanical controls through sophisticated measurement to the 'soft' controls seen today. Interestingly, he puts the modern synthesis of industry and information in the period 1880–1920. Since then, he contends that we have been in essentially the same 'industrial–economic–technological' phase. The advent of computers was obviously very important, but in his view they did not usher in the information society, because we already were one.

However, in the mid-1980s when Beniger was writing, computers were still primarily large, expensive machines used in corporate headquarters. PCs were just beginning to reach the public. The Internet was still a closed system restricted to a few research institutions. Up to that point, the effect of computers had been to support centralisation of control. It seems that Beniger was analysing only the first wave of the control revolution.

Since the mid-1980s, computers have moved out of air-conditioned rooms onto the desk, onto the lap and into the pocket. Each step has been accompanied by an increase in computing power, a decrease in costs, and a proliferation of users and uses. Since the early 1990s the pace at which computers have been connected together has accelerated to the point where a stand-alone computer is now very much the exception, and the Internet has grown into a new channel of mass communication. Shapiro (1999) argues that, taken together, these changes have created a second wave of the control revolution (i.e. that control over information flows has been decentralised and distributed).

This second wave of the control revolution has had a dramatic impact upon manufacturing industry, facilitating changes to the fundamental business models that underpin the sector. Without the need for mechanical control of processes, machines themselves have become dramatically smaller. The degree of control offered by constant, real-time monitoring and measurement has improved the efficiency of the machines themselves and made them cleaner. Automation of handling has also made the machines faster.

The impact of these changes (i.e. smaller, cleaner, faster machines) has been to change the buildings that house them. To many, the very term 'factory' conjures up a picture of the dark, satanic mills of the Industrial Revolution. While there is no doubt that dirty, polluting industries still exist, environmental legislation, improved technology and reduced costs have combined to reduce them substantially. Many such plants are legacy facilities at the end of their economic lives.

Manufacturing has always encompassed two main models:

• build to stock; and
• build to order.

Build to stock

The build-to-stock model is a creature of mass production (Box 7.2). Batches of identical products are produced to stock. This stock is then

Box 7.2 Fordism

Hounshell (1984) catalogues the role of Henry Ford in developing the principle of mass production. Ford is credited with synthesising the various elements constituting the modern model of mass production which bears his name, and which is often said to date from the development of the first moving assembly lines, put into operation at Ford's Highland Park, Michigan plant in 1913–1914. These displaced predominantly craft-based production in which skilled labourers exercised substantial control over their work. Fordist production entailed increased mechanisation, a division of labour into specialisations and the co-ordination of sequential machining operations and converging assembly lines, to achieve a steady flow of production. It also created a shift toward the use of less skilled labour performing specific tasks and the potential for increased control over the pace and intensity of work.

The hallmark of his system was standardisation – standardised components, standardised manufacturing processes, and a simple, easy to manufacture (and repair) standard product. Standardisation required nearly perfect interchangeability of parts. To achieve interchangeability, Ford exploited advances in machine tools and gauging systems. These innovations made possible the moving, or continuous, assembly line, in which each assembler performed a single, repetitive task. Ford was also one of the first to realise the potential of the electric motor to reconfigure work flow. Machines that were previously arrayed about a central power source could now be placed on the assembly line, thereby dramatically increasing throughput (David 1990). The promise of massive increases in productivity led to the widespread imitation and adaptation of Ford's basic model of production through the industrial core of the US economy, and in other industrial capitalist countries.

The past three decades have seen adaptation of the basic mass production models. During this period, the system of organisation of production and consumption has undergone a second transformation. This new system is often referred to as the 'flexible system of production' (FSP) or the 'Toyota production system'. On the production side, FSP is characterised by dramatic reductions in information costs and overheads, Total quality management (TQM), just-in-time inventory control, and leaderless workgroups; on the consumption side, by the globalisation of consumer goods markets, faster product lifecycles, and far greater product/market segmentation and differentiation.

Piore and Sabel (1985) define FSP through a set of key features. Flexible production rests on the presumption that a competitive edge cannot be gained by treating workers like machines and that nobody in the manufacturing process but the assembly worker adds value, that the assembly worker can perform most functions better than specialists (lean manufacturing), and that every step of the fabrication process should be done perfectly (TQM), thus reducing the need for buffer stocks (JIT) and producing a higher quality end-product (Box 7.3). This adaptation is enabled by ICT. Without information processing and connectivity the flow of goods to the production process 'just in time' for them to be used could not function without significant buffer stocks. The types of space determined by the build-to-stock model are clear. Storage space will be required for raw materials, for the production process itself, and for the storage of finished products.

Box 7.3   Lean production

Lean production is a system of production management that was conceived by the Toyota Motor Company in the 1950s. Taiichi Ohno, who is widely credited as a key developer and promoter of this system, stated that its objective is cost reduction (Ohno & Rosen 1988). At Toyota, Ohno focused attention on the need to eliminate inefficiency and waste throughout the manufacturing system by targeting overproduction, waiting time, transportation, processing, inventories, movement and defects. The term 'lean production' was coined by a member of the research team that produced the best-selling book, *The Machine that Changed the World* (Womack *et al.* 1991). This was the result of a major programme of research at MIT (International Motor Vehicle Programme). The concept of lean production has filtered through into the shipbuilding and aerospace industries (e.g. UK Lean Aerospace Initiative, which has produced the Lean Enterprise Model). Essentially the top-level lean principles on which the concept is founded are: teamwork; communication; efficient use of resources and elimination of waste; and continuous improvement. To be effective all five concepts must be linked in the system of lean production. Lean thinking therefore enables companies to remove waste from their processes, dramatically increasing their competitiveness and profitability. Data from the magazine *Technology Century* (October 2001) suggest that compared to conventional manufacturing principles, products manufactured using lean principles have required significantly less resources to produce, and have resulted in:

- productivity gains of 300–400%;
- labour productivity increased an average of 25% a year;
- defect rates reduced from more than 2000 to less than 50 parts per million (PPM) and in many to less than 10 PPM;
- cost of quality cut by over 60%;
- work-in-process inventory reduced by more than 80%;
- revenue per 1000 square feet of factory space was raised 350%.

---

distributed to the end user of the product, issues of consumer choice being predetermined by the production process.

Build to order

The growth of cost-effective marketing and sales channels on the Internet has brought the build-to-order model within the compass of most manufacturers. Mass markets are becoming more and more heterogeneous. Market segmentation strives to identify the segment of one representing the demand for customised products or services for each individual customer, leading Kotler (1989) to declare the death of the mass market altogether.

Traditionally the build-to-order model was confined to high-value, customisable goods with a long lead time: shipbuilding, for example. However, companies in all branches of industry are being forced to react to the growing individualisation of demand yet, at the same time, increasing competitive pressure dictates that costs must also continue to decrease. Companies have to adopt strategies which embrace both cost efficiency and a closer reaction to customers' needs.

Mass customisation meets this challenge by producing goods and services to meet individual customers' needs with near mass production efficiency (Tseng & Jiao 2001). While Toffler (1970) identified the concept as 'de-massing' some three decades ago, Davis (1987) coined the term 'mass customisation' and the idea was developed further by Pine (1993).

The competitive advantage of mass customisation is based on a combination of the efficiency of mass production with the ability to customise products to individual needs. There are three key principles in mass customisation:

- **Differentiation**. The production of goods and services for a large market, which exactly meet the needs of every individual customer with regard to certain product characteristics. At its current level of implementation this does not mean, necessarily, that each product is a one-off since the dictates of the products themselves are that they tend to be very similar with limited customisable options.
- **Cost**. Customisation has to be done at costs corresponding to those of standard mass-produced goods.
- **Relationship**. In the course of the customisation process customer-specific information is collected. This information serves to build up a lasting individual relationship with each customer. Once the customer has successfully purchased a product item, the knowledge acquired by the supplier during the product configuration represents a barrier against switching suppliers. When the information acquired by the company about its various customers is aggregated and compared, customer behaviour becomes transparent (Kotha 1995). New customers can be served better and more efficiently, because they are offered an individual product variation which other customers with a similar profile have already purchased in the past.

Since its beginning, mass customisation has been closely connected with the capabilities offered by new manufacturing technologies such as computer integrated manufacturing (CIM) that have proved able to reduce the obvious trade-off between variety and productivity.

Efficient processing of information can be regarded as the most important factor for the implementation of mass customisation. Unlike the traditional build-to-stock model of mass production, in customised manufacturing every transaction gives information about the wishes of each individual customer. This information has to be translated into a product specification and has to be communicated from the point of sale to the manufacturing and fulfilment operations.

Zipkin (2001) calls this process the elicitation of mass customisation systems, the mechanism for interacting with the customer and obtaining specific information in order to define and translate the customer's needs and desires into a product specification.

The space needs of a build-to-order model have a different configuration from build-to-stock. Storage is still required for raw materials, but the requirement to store finished goods is much reduced. Since the customisation of products will usually apply to the finished specification, this model often generates a need for additional storage during the production process as more sub-assemblies are kept part finished (Box 7.4).

The BMW case study identifies the relative complexity and degree of integration required to implement a build-to-order model. Irrespective of the configuration of the buildings, manufacturing premises require to be in specific locations relative to their suppliers and require high degrees of connectivity to facilitate information flows. Location 'lock-in' and sunk costs, together with the fact that most urban areas are complex systems which change more slowly than technology, therefore frequently militate against dramatic changes (Cortright 2001).

Whichever manufacturing model is employed, getting the goods to the end consumer is of paramount importance. Given the relatively fixed costs of labour and plant, manufacturers seek to reduce the costs of stocking and distributing their goods. To this end, full integration between manufacturing and distribution processes is essential to ensure that the whole supply chain from producer to consumer is efficient and responsive.

Indeed, manufacturing is an area of property where ICT is delivering significant changes at a building level through a reduction in the demands that production processes put upon buildings. The logical consequence of Fordism, which introduced high levels of mechanisation and standardisation, was automation. Single repetitive tasks undertaken by people have

Box 7.4 BMW, Spartanburg

The BMW Group has created a mass customisation concept, which allows customers to design their own 'ultimate driving machine' nearly piece by piece. It has been calculated that the number of possible ways to customise all of BMW's models is 10^{17}. For the BMW X-5 sports utility vehicle built in Spartanburg, South Carolina, for example, there are 1000 bumper variations, 4000 instrument panel choices and 448 different types of door panel.

Build to order in the automotive field creates a big challenge to the supply chain that requires meticulous planning and standardisation of business processes such as logistics. This challenge allows customers change their choices right up until the production process starts, yet ensures that the right parts in the combination the customer wants arrive at the right time in the production process.

BMW leads the automotive industry in build-to-order delivery times. Elapsed time from order to delivery for new models stands at ten days. In addition to allowing customers a wide choice of components, colour schemes and choices (no two cars are alike) such as what dashboard instruments they want and where, BMW attempts to optimise the engineering core of the car continuously. This has become such an integral part of the process, and small components are changed so often, that BMW does not change its actual part number but instead uses 'a change level' number to indicate a new 'version' of a part, in the same way software houses indicate upgrades.

To keep control of this constantly changing, complex and time-sensitive supply chain requires integration of all aspects of the supply chain from production through to final delivery. The planning process involves management of information flow as well and requires sophisticated information technology. With cars that can include as many as 9000 parts combined in a variety of ways, BMW has invested heavily in sequencing technology and developed sophisticated transatlantic communications.

The supply chain management process begins with a very detailed plan for each component. These plans are developed in-house by BMW's logistics department in Munich in co-operation with its manufacturing plants in the US, Europe and South Africa and the supplier involved in making a part. Once the precise plan is developed, the responsibility for implementing it reverts to the logistics directors at the various manufacturing plants.

For major components, that have a high degree of variance, suppliers are required to locate near BMW's manufacturing plants. In Spartanburg all the major component suppliers are within 20 miles.

BMW's suppliers are integrating into the carmaker's IT system in real time. BMW has a long-standing relationship with German enterprise resource planning software producer SAP. BMW's Enterprise Resource Planning system allows data to be entered only once and then automatically sent to all the functional areas within the system that require the information. About 600 personal computers are linked through the global network.

been replaced by single-function robots. To stretch the automotive example further, spray painting vehicles even 30 years ago was a manual process, but nowadays it is almost entirely automated. As a result, there is little waste, the process is highly efficient and quality is ensured. From a real estate perspective, the paint shop of 30 years ago was regarded as one of the dirtiest jobs in the process of manufacturing a car and the buildings reflected that, necessitating containment facilities, massive ventilation and space for employees. The modern paint shop houses a clean process with employees only for monitoring and controlling the flow of vehicles through the plant. The physical building reflects that in its size and configuration. Modern factories, like the production processes they contain, are smaller and cleaner than they have ever been.

Distribution

Overview

Distribution property is amongst the least homogeneous of the property sectors. Its very complexity makes it difficult to classify and equally difficult to measure, with significant crossover in function between warehousing and 'standard' industrial property. This complexity is also set in a context of a rapid pace of change in almost all aspects of the operating environment over the last three decades. Legislative changes controlling many aspects of distribution operations have altered key parameters in its efficiency. Changes in the technology applied to storage and movement of goods have rendered older infrastructure obsolete and caused rapid renewal of the warehousing stock. Moreover, a combination of new technology, better information, demographic changes, increasing wealth levels and consumer spending is influencing warehouse structure in a number of ways (Arthur Andersen 2000). For example, both size and eaves height have increased and the amount of land use has increased. Technology is also making the distribution of goods more efficient as historic inventory-to-sales ratios also fall.

For Mulani and Lee (2002) technology has become a core component of virtually every supply chain innovation. The Internet brings immediacy to almost any supply chain event by enabling the capture of real-time customer demand, and by maximising visibility into asset status, including location of goods in transit, inventory positions, and supplier capacity.

Customer expectation has also risen markedly, and the expectations of the retailer are that goods will be freshly available at any time and a firm delivery window of hours, not days, is the minimum requirement.

The key change is therefore one of philosophy. The supply chain has come to be regarded as one of the main differentiators between companies, offering the potential for competitive advantage. This, and the consequential need to optimise the supply chain, lies behind the implementation of all these changes (Table 7.4).

Changes to the optimum specification of warehousing have continued to make warehouses more complex and more specialist across the whole range of sizes. In the last decade, third party logistics capabilities have become increasingly sophisticated to keep up with market demand, and many larger players have acquired or aligned with consulting firms, technology providers and other logistics specialists to raise ever higher competitive barriers.

UK logistics groups were at the forefront of the development of sophisticated supply chain management techniques and systems. Some of the first businesses to adopt the principle were UK retailers. In the early 1980s a great deal of inventory was held at the level of the individual shop to ensure that products were available for sale. Suppliers were making numerous daily drops to individual stores, creating congestion and ensuring excessive stocks were maintained.

Table 7.4   Changing focus of distribution property.

1970s–1980s	1990s	2000 onwards
Supply chain focused on functional excellence to reduce costs and to improve product quality and customer service	Supply chain focused on linking the extended supply chain to improve productivity and efficiency	Supply chain focuses on flexible, global supply chains that respond quickly to changing market needs
Practice innovations		
● Business process re-engineering ● Total quality management ● Local third party logistics outsourcing	● Build-to-order supply chains ● Collaborative product forecasting and replenishment ● Contract manufacturing ● Regional third party logistics outsourcing ● Buy-side and sell-side e-markets	● Mass customisation/ one-to-one supply chains ● Collaborative product commerce ● Portfolio of strategic partnerships

The retailer's response was to take control of the supply chain, building regional distribution centres and outsourcing the management of the process. The high street store therefore reverted to being a retail outlet rather than a quasi-warehouse, with almost no surplus stock held on site.

In procurement logistics a similar situation evolved as major manufacturers started to outsource the delivery of components. The pressure of manufacturing techniques, such as just-in-time (JIT), necessitated networks of warehouses located to supply within the time parameters defined by the manufacturing process, rather than those dictated by large regional centres.

Increasing competition, decreasing profitability and constant pressure from all stakeholders for greater efficiencies have also therefore begun to change the outsourcing model. Supply chains have, in any event, become more complex as the globalisation of products and brands has taken hold. Logistics operators have increased the productivity of their operations considerably, spurred on by the growth of target-led incentives and aided by the development of sophisticated software, covering the management and optimisation processes.

Today, therefore, distribution real estate covers a range of types. The term 'warehouse' is more aptly defined as a loose description of a building type classified by its use instead of any particular defining characteristic of its construction or location. From observation, much of the UK industrial stock could be classified as distribution property if this singular characteristic were to be applied. At one end of the spectrum small buildings in daily use for distribution abound on industrial estates across the country. At the other large, highly specialist warehouses are clustered together on distribution parks chosen to complement the efficiency of the supply chains of which they are an integral part.

A pragmatic taxonomy for the sector is described in Table 7.5. This is not an absolute hierarchy, since many small companies may operate national distribution from small local storage facilities, but it captures the majority of the market. The trend is for automation, optimisation and specification to be applied to even smaller buildings.

At the lowest end, the local storage category is the relatively lowly specified, multifunctional 'shed'. Although this is not an area in which institutional investors are particularly active other than as part of overall industrial estates, the category is estimated to represent a significant slice of distribution output.

Table 7.5 A pragmatic taxonomy for warehousing (adapted from RETRI Group 2003).

Local storage	$< 500\,m^2$	No automation, fringe urban location, standard specification
Sub-regional	$500 - 3000\,m^2$	Limited automation, fringe urban location, standard specification
Regional	$3000 - 10\,000\,m^2$	Increasing degree of automation, optimised location, highly specified
National	$> 10\,000\,m^2$	High degree of automation, optimised location, highly specified
High bay	$> 15\,000\,m^2$	Totally automated specialist building

Similar comments can be made about the sub-regional category, although increasingly, buildings at the top end of this size range are seeing rising specification. High bay warehouses are every bit as specialist as large-scale factory premises, for example. Because of the physical constraints of working in a 30 metre high racking system they are almost totally automated, and effectively these are racking systems with cladding rather than conventional buildings.

There are four main drivers of the supply chain and distribution property:

- optimisation;
- outsourcing;
- collaboration; and,
- automation.

Each of these areas demonstrates an ongoing impact from ICT and resultant changes in distribution real estate.

Optimisation

Over the last decade, increasingly sophisticated analytical tools have emerged to help companies address optimisation of their supply chain networks. These tools allow companies to model existing and alternative supply chain networks and identify the trade-offs in cost, service and time that must be made in developing a supply chain strategy that optimises their competitive position.

Bearing in mind that supply chains stretch from the provision of raw materials to the delivery of goods to the end consumer, the networks involved are complex. Their optimisation involves the simultaneous determination of the number, location and mission of production facilities, supplier locations and consumers in order to maximise the efficiency of the flow of goods between them. The location and cost of warehousing, whilst important, is therefore only one factor in a complex equation.

Outsourcing

Research by Cap Gemini Ernst & Young (2002) found that the percentage of companies using third party logistics suppliers in any area was 94% across Europe compared with 92% in Asia and only 78% in the USA. The growth of this sort of outsourcing has facilitated the expansion of third party logistics specialists who have invested heavily in ICT and systems as part of the drive to make supply chains as lean and efficient as possible.

Collaboration

As part of the outsourcing process, 'open-book' contracts, in which all costs are revealed, are standard in the industry. This high degree of transparency is also present in the collaborative nature of logistics contracts between parties. It is increasingly common for external logistics managers to be party to the internal inventory and production management processes that generate demand for the service. Different kinds of collaborative models are in operation from a simple sharing of order and inventory information through to systems that are so transparent that the retailer never has to take ownership of the goods being sold until they pass through a checkout. Given the different locations and corporate structures involved in the sharing process, it follows that ICT is the enabler of this process, and without ICT it would not be feasible.

Automation

The concentration upon efficiency in the logistics process extends inside the warehouse as well. The four major functions of warehousing are receiving, storage, order picking and shipping, with storage and order picking being typically the most costly. Storage is expensive because of inventory holding costs, and order picking because it is labour intensive.

Changes in design

Changes in distribution processes have also led to differing requirements by occupiers in the supply chain (see Box 7.5), in terms of building design and layout, which are now explored in more detail.

Cross docking

Cross docking is a logistics technique that minimises the storage and order picking functions of a warehouse while still allowing it to serve its receiving and shipping functions. The idea is to transfer shipments directly from incoming to outgoing trailers without storage in between. Shipments typically spend less than 24 hours in a cross dock, sometimes less than an hour. Cross docks are essentially trans-shipment facilities to which trucks arrive with goods that must be sorted, consolidated with other products, and loaded onto outbound trucks. In a cross-docking model, the customer is known before the product gets to the warehouse and there is no need to move it to storage. Clearly cross docking places constraints upon the design of the warehouse internally and with respect to its footprint.

Box 7.5   Tibbett & Britten and Marks & Spencer Wines

In March 2000, Tibbett & Britten started operating a new contract covering all the UK central warehousing of Marks & Spencer's wines, beers and spirits. The contract is based at a 260 000 ft^2 shared-user, rail-connected warehouse in Daventry, UK, and involves the storage and handling of a complete range of wines and spirits.

Tibbett & Britten is responsible for the planning of intake, physical receipt, storage and despatch of palletised products to seven Marks & Spencer food distribution centres across the UK. As 'warehouse keeper' Tibbett & Britten is also responsible for maintaining the site's bonded status and for liaising with HM Customs & Excise.

The market for wine is highly seasonal, with volumes doubling around Christmas. These seasonal changes impose special demands on the logistics company. It has to arrange additional temporary staffing and equipment; plan receipt and storage areas to cope with the extra volumes; and train the new staff. It also moves to seven-day working (instead of the usual six), with 24-hour operations on weekdays. To help Marks & Spencer achieve vendor-managed inventory, Tibbett & Britten has developed an in-house, web-enabled stock management system. Data are received from both parties and appropriate information is published to a secure extranet, allowing Marks & Spencer and its suppliers to monitor and manage their stock levels across the supply chain. Tibbett & Britten also provides added-value services. These include maintaining a 'wine library' at a constant temperature in a separate section of the warehouse, where samples of every different lot number and vintage are stored, and the re-labelling of bottles. Besides safeguarding service levels to all locations, Tibbett & Britten's support has enabled Marks & Spencer to benefit from a 10% reduction in inventory across the supply chain, coupled with a 30% increase in the number of products held within the bonded warehouse.

Superflat floors
Within the last decade, the use of computer controlled warehousing facilities and advanced racking systems has mandated the need to install extremely flat and level floors in warehouses. Since these systems may well be fully automated using very narrow aisles (VNA) technologies, any unevenness at the base could be reflected in considerable variations in the width of the aisle 15 or even 30 metres further up.[12]

Eaves heights
The internal height to the eaves is important to the capacity of the warehouse since it determines how high racking can go without impediment. Typically, eaves heights for large warehouses are between 10 metres and 12 metres with the trend towards the latter. For larger units of, say, over 25 000 square metres, the height may go up to 15 metres. High bay warehousing can be over 30 metres to the eaves.

Clear spans
The clear span of a warehouse is also important because of the constraints that could be imposed upon racking systems by supporting structures. How wide a span can be achieved depends on a number of factors, not least overall size, but typically this will be 30 metres for sizeable new build.

Security and fire protection
Of increasing importance are insurer-led initiatives to improve security and protection within warehouses. Escalating premiums mean that protection systems such as sprinklers, smoke extraction and smoke doors are becoming a standard part of warehouse specification.

Connectivity
Increased integration with other elements of the supply chain has increased the demand for high bandwidth telecommunications in warehouses. Complex supply chain management systems are now a standard feature of most larger warehouses. These systems require access to large volumes of stock information throughout an entire supply chain from production to delivery.

New technologies such as radiofrequency identification (RFID) tags that allow remote monitoring of the location and details of individual products will add substantially to the amount of bandwidth required by warehouses (Box 7.6).

Change in distribution property has therefore been driven by the imperative to improve the efficiency of the supply chain process. ICT has underpinned the majority of the changes seen at the level of individual warehouses, and has been a facilitating agent in the choice of location and business model. eCommerce and eBusiness in particular seem to have spawned two opposing demand trends (Arthur Andersen 2000). On the one hand, these processes reinforce the trend of falling inventory levels and continue previously established trends; on the other hand, the same processes are generating demand for new types of space: warehouses become stores; they increasingly perform the final stage in manufacturing, and can also act as call centre space. There may therefore be an increasing trend in the future towards 'throughput' warehouses for more flexible use, and for industrial premises with more employee-focused amenities.

Box 7.6   RFID

Potentially automatic identification applications are extremely broad – tracking everything from people to pallets – but the term refers mostly to radiofrequency identification (RFID) technologies with supply chain-related uses (identifying products, cases, and shipments). RFID uses low-powered radio transmitters to read data stored in tags that are embedded with tiny chips and antennas. Proponents of the technology say such 'smart' tags can store more detailed information than conventional bar codes, enabling retailers and manufacturers to track items at the unit level. Compared to traditional bar code-based systems, RFID-based data-capture systems have a number of advantages:

- Simultaneous reads. A bar code reader only reads one code at a time – RFID uses radio waves to examine numerous tags at once. This 'parallel processing' capability has significant productivity ramifications up and down the supply chain – scanning an entire shopping trolley of goods at a checkout, for example.
- Line of sight. The process of reading a bar code is inherently problematic: items must be scanned by an operator or moved past a fixed point. RFID systems can be read in any dimension.
- 'Always on'. (Active) RFID systems are always functional and signal an item's presence all the time. There are two types of RFID tag: active (i.e. with a battery) or passive (without a battery).
- More data. RFID tags hold far more information than a bar code, allowing tracking to be undertaken at a product level.

RFID could well become an important technology, despite concerns over personal privacy (Murray 2003), particularly as the US retailer Wal-Mart is requiring its top 100 suppliers to use RFID tags on pallets by 2005, with its remaining suppliers following suit by 2006 (Quinn 2004).

Leisure and living

Overview

This section of the chapter explores some of the emerging issues arising from the impact of ICT on the use of real estate for leisure and living. The impact of ICT on real estate in both sectors has not, so far, been as directly transformative (for example, in terms of use, location, layout, intensity, and so on) as other sectors. For example, some of the material in this section is necessarily more speculative than the rest of the chapter, where the transformations arising from ICT are more tangible.

Both leisure and living activities are fundamental to a person's well-being, and the close synergy required between the human experience and the tangible consumption of the good (for example, the direct participation in enjoying a cinema or theatre event or sporting activity and living in space that provides shelter, social activities and entertainment) perhaps explains the lack of perceived ICT impact hitherto on real estate uses that include:

- leisure: cinemas, arts and media production, sports clubs, bars, cafés, restaurants, hotels, casinos, and games arcades; and
- living: flats, houses and other living accommodation.

Of course, leisure and living uses do still require space, but the transformative nature of ICT so far, for example, has come through changing or altering the provision of the service (through online ticket/reservation bookings, for example), or redefining the nature of the experience itself (for example, the use of ICT technology in cinemas or theatres), or what might also be referred to as an 'embodied experience' of the world (Hubbard 2003). A key driving force here therefore is the Internet and the increasing pervasiveness of smart access points in the home, at work and in public spaces.

In the case of multiplex cinemas, one can argue that it is the transformative nature of personal mobility, wealth and the growth of leisure activity in general that has primarily driven the change in the nature of the real estate product. Nonetheless, there are examples of real estate use (i.e. arts and film production, hotels, Internet cafés and smart homes) where the primary effects of ICT on space, use and location are as important as in other real estate sectors.

Leisure

Spending on leisure is now the largest single financial outgoing for most families in the UK today (National Statistics 2003). For example, household spending on 'recreation and culture' and 'restaurants and hotels' was some £156 bn in 2002 in the UK. As household incomes have grown over the last 25 to 30 years, spending on non-essential items has increased. For example, spending on food and non-alcoholic drink, as a percentage of total expenditure, has fallen from 25% in 1976 to 16% in 2002-2003 (National Statistics 2003), but over the same period, spending on leisure goods and services has increased from 10% to 18% (Figure 7.6). Typically, today the average UK household spends £72 a week on leisure followed by housing (£67 per week) and food and non-alcoholic drink (£62 per week). About a third of the expenditure on leisure is on in-home entertainment with satellite and digital TV, PCs, videos and DVD technology all providing new outlets for domestic leisure.

Alongside the home as a focus for entertainment and leisure activities, '24-hour' cities have been promoted to showcase urban areas as evening leisure centres attracting visitors to pubs, clubs and restaurants, and cinemas. This trend has also seen shopping centres acting as major new foci for 'shoppertainment' themes, combining the shopping and leisure experience.

Despite flexible working, however, the majority of this form of leisure is consumed at night (Hubbard 2003), and this has led to the development of the 'urban entertainment economy' (Chatterton & Hollands 2003), characterised by 'corporitisation, branding and market segmentation'. This has paralleled a 'return to the centre' (underpinned by PPG6 in the UK) with a renewed focus on knowledge-based working and '24-hour' cities founded

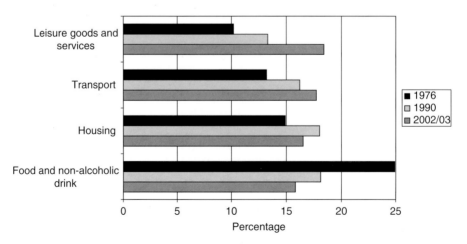

Figure 7.6 UK household expenditure as a percentage of total household expenditure. *Source: Family Expenditure Survey and Food Survey, Office for National Statistics.*

on leisure and culture (Comedia 2003), and has also spawned the growth of urban entertainment destinations in many downtown areas in the UK, bringing together cinema, shopping, eating and other nightlife activities and drawing on anchor tenants such as Warners, TGI Fridays, Starbucks, and Planet Hollywood (see, for example, Chatterton & Hollands 2002, 2003). The Trocadero development in London's Piccadilly Circus, Great Northern Experience in Manchester and Broadway Plaza in Birmingham are all prime examples of this type of complex. Other more residual and marginal 'nightscapes' have also developed in our cities through a range of production, regulation and consumption interactions (Chatterton & Hollands 2003) and which promote alternative clubbing and nightlife cultures.

Directly attributing impact to ICT within real estate for leisure activities is problematic therefore because complex forces are interacting to define the production and consumption of leisure activities and spaces which themselves require personal embodiment or direct experience.

At a city-wide level, however, ICT is being used to promote the urban experience through websites and online service provision (see Virtual London in Box 6.1, page 207), and the UK Core Cities[13] programme (Comedia 2003) has shown how important it is for the cultural capital of cities to be linked with assets in the city knowledge-based economy, including intensity of knowledge workers, accessible business incubators, and start-up facilities and innovative clusters and supply chains. Innovative examples of using technology to promote tourism and culture within a city include the Urban Tapestries project,[14] based at the London School of Economics, which uses wireless technology to access and author location-specific multimedia content and share experience and knowledge of a city.

Leisure production
In leisure production (for example, arts and media)[15] it is perhaps a little easier to find current, concrete examples of ICT transformation on space and location and often, as we have seen before in this book, ICT can reinforce a 'clustering effect'.

Examples of innovation 'hotspots' underpinning the culture of cites include Bristol's animation cluster (based around Aardman Animations, creators of *Wallace and Gromit*), or Sheffield's interactive games industry. Leadbeater and Oakley (2001) provide a valuable analysis of the replacement of the decline of the 'old media' cluster of Fleet Street newspapers with the parallel growth of the new media cluster of the East End in Hoxton, which is today one of the largest concentrations of new media, digital design and Internet businesses in Europe. They suggest that the growth of Hoxton was no accident nor was its growth unplanned. The focus of the cluster was Curtain Road, the site of one of the world's first Elizabethan theatres, and was based around a development of new light warehouses which became home to a new generation of British artists (for example, Tracey Emin and Damien Hirst).[16] The development of 'Britart' also coincided with the emergence of the Internet during the 1990s and many Internet companies gravitated to Hoxton. Deepend (founded by graduates from the Royal College of Art), for example, based originally in Hoxton, became one of the largest independent web design companies, and was joined by other companies: Digit, Lateral and Tomato. Nearby, Vibe Productions (a music company) had become managing agents of the Truman's Brewery on Brick Lane and by 2000, there were 300 small businesses on site, many in eCommerce. Later in the same year, Gorilla Park was opened nearby, as one of the largest business incubators in Europe, and further media and design companies set up base in Clerkenwell. In turn the development of the Clerkenwell–Hoxton–Brick Lane triangle created demand for a number of ancillary services: bars, restaurants, clubs, cafés, the Lux art cinema and the White Cube Art Gallery. Ultimately the cheap space and 'bohemian' feel of the area have attracted media companies and concentrated and focused the clustering effect.

Leisure consumption
On the consumption side of leisure, there are also several types of real estate use that will continue to be affected by ICT through:

- inventory and purchasing management improvements; and,
- advertising and marketing through the Internet.

These changes will impact on cash flows and revenue streams and therefore rental and yield performance in cases where the property is occupied rather than owned, and corporate turnover and value where the business is owner-occupied.

For example, the hotel industry (as just one part of the tourism sector) is in many ways the most advanced real estate sector in terms of technology use: reservations, conference management, inventory control and other facilities have increasingly been computerised over the last 20 years (Arthur Andersen 2000). The Internet can widen market scope and lead to other operational efficiencies, but is also likely to continue to provide stiff competition in pricing, which in locations where occupancy rates remain low will lead to further consolidation in the sector. Research by Knight Frank (2003) in the UK also showed that some 95% of hotels in their survey had websites with more than 25% of all bookings occurring online: in fact, such systems enable yield to be monitored quickly so that price can be adjusted to reflect demand. Other third party websites such as hotelsonline.co.uk and lastminute.com have also been developed and may continue to erode the business of traditional, high street travel agents (see Chapter 7). It is also likely that growing eBusiness and B2B operations will see occupancies weaken in some sectors, especially extended stay hotels (Arthur Andersen 2000). Many hotels have seen this as a competitive advantage, however, by offering eBusiness facilities such as WiFi facilities to customers.

For cinemas, online booking systems and web marketing are likely to enable mass marketing and branding to be reinforced. The growth in UK cinema attendances has been dramatic: nearly two-thirds of people aged 15 years or over said they attended the cinema (National Statistics 2003), with an estimated 176 million cinema admissions in the UK in 2002, second only in the EU to France, and reaching a 30-year high in the same year. The first multiplex cinema opened in the UK in 1985 and by 2002 there were 226 multiplexes in the UK accounting for nearly two-thirds of all cinema screens and 75% of all cinema admissions in just one third of all cinema sites (Mintel 2002); meanwhile town centre-based cinemas have declined. Nonetheless, online ticketing and marketing enable customer loyalty to be rewarded and advertising targeted more efficiently within a 'clicks and mortar' business model where the move towards digital cinema is likely to maintain customer growth. Future threats to the industry, however, include Internet film piracy and the growth of legitimate Internet-based video on demand services (Screen Digest 2002) financed through advertising subscriptions or licensing agreements.[17]

The Internet's power in advertising has also been recognised in the world of sport. Sport is one of the basic items in all search engines and constitutes one of the basic offers of mass media on the Internet (de Moragas Spa 2001). For example, Vancouver's successful Winter Olympic 2012 bid was widely acknowledged to be founded on successful Internet and email marketing campaigns (Wilson 2004). The growth of outreach from sporting institutions (federations, clubs, national Olympic committees) has also enabled them to connect with their fans or communities and create new revenue streams through marketing, online sales, sponsorship deals and other ventures.[18] Church (2001) estimates that publicity in sports websites will rise to $6 bn in 2005 and online sports products sales will increase to $5.8 bn. Clearly Olympic marketing and advertising stimulate interest and participation in the event, and this can lead to business and economic benefits to the host city.[19]

Finally, the arrival of wireless technologies and the associated 'hotspots' where users can use mobile technology to surf the web has attracted the attention of leading café brands. Coffee houses have, since the boom of the seventeenth and eighteenth centuries, been rife with business gossip and the latest rumours (Economist 2003). Today the modern equivalent are Internet cafés, which have become commonplace in department stores such as Debenhams, or on the High Street, as independents or branded chains, or cafés and other food and drink outlets offering wireless access. Ironically, the arrival of wireless may mean the days of Internet cafés per se are numbered (Hargrave 2004). Instead, other real estate users are providing connectivity. Thompson (2003) shows how Starbucks has already connected nearly 60 of its UK outlets with WiFi and Caffé Nero has plans for 120 of its outlets, but competition for custom is fierce with hotspots in hotels, pubs, railway stations and shopping centres. The support that such cafés and other centres provide for mobile workers therefore potentially reduces the need for office space (and blurs the 'leisure–work' distinction), in the same way as home working, although this is likely to have only a marginal impact.

Living: smart homes and teleworking

Changing demographics and household formation are shaping the demand for residential property. In the UK, it is forecast that by 2011 (Cabinet Office 2001) about 16.5% of the UK population will be over 65, and this ageing trend will also be apparent across the rest of Europe and other parts of the developed world. Moreover, it is now harder to speak of the 'average' home (Labour Party 2003): in 1961 50% of homes were couples with children; now less than 40% are, and more than one-third of households are single person. These demographic changes have repercussions for house demand nationally and regionally. At the same time, accompanying technology-led change is transforming the workplace, the home and 'work–life' balance, and there is increasing demand for smaller homes that are safe and secure for a variety of age groups.

It was Alvin Toffler (1980) who coined the phrase 'electronic cottage' to convey the idea of a home as the locus for employment, production, leisure and consumption (Barlow & Venables 2003). In her book *Tomorrow's People*, Susan Greenfield (2003) paints a rather more dystopic picture of the twenty-first century. Although she imagines a future that is free of pain and disease, and one where new drugs and genetic technology will reduce disease and mortality still further, many people will, in her view, increasingly inhabit a virtual world of 'dreams and shadows'. As far as leisure and home space are concerned (and paralleling the concepts of space we presented in Chapter 6), she suggests both work and leisure will have the potential to transcend space restrictions: space in the home is likely to be much more flexible, as home offices blend into individual private areas with workstations, leaving a minimum of natural or real living space. Needless to say, these homes of the future will be ICT-dominated with smart, heuristic devices functioning on an 'if X then Y' basis. Temperature, water, services and other aspects of home life will be controlled by proactive devices. Indeed, William Mitchell (1995) takes a more extreme view still (quoted in Barlow & Venables 2003):[20]

> ... You will begin to blend into the architecture ... so 'inhabitation' will take on new meaning ... Your room and your home will become part of you and you will become part of them.

Such visions of the future might appear to be fantasy or fiction, but in fact there is currently much interest in the concept of 'smart homes'.[21] Although there is no fixed definition of a smart home, it could be defined as (BRE 2003), 'a home where technology has been introduced with the aim of enhancing lifestyle or quality of life'.[22] Research by Pragnell *et al.* (2000) suggests that smart homes use electronic networking technology to integrate a variety of devices found in most homes, together with the building environment systems found commonly in factories and offices. This enables a home to be controlled centrally or remotely rather like a single machine, and can offer a range of services (including healthcare services) and assistive technologies for elderly and disabled people and other groups (Intille 2002). Barlow and Venables (2003) see the concept of smart homes as involving two approaches:

- automation of the material environment and domestic tasks; and,
- informational content, where existing and new information services are used to improve the management of home living.

Many therefore see connection to the Internet as being a key element of the smart home concept and this gives users access not only to online services but also to remote control of home systems, for example, using remote technology to carry out security or heating operations (BRE 2003 and see Table 7.6). Benefits of such technologies include the following (BRE 2003):

- improved and lower cost social care, medical care and property care;
- extended independent living;
- improved personal safety, security and 'peace of mind';
- 'digital inclusion' – access for all to eServices and digital information;

Table 7.6   Smart home technologies (adapted from BRE 2003).

Existing technologies	Smart home technologies
• Wired and cordless telephones • Digital TV (terrestrial, satellite or cable) • A telephone network, with a number of telephone points distributed around the home • One or more PCs • Dial-up or broadband Internet access – but usually from only one PC • A security system • Smoke detectors	• A PC network with broadband Internet access, so that every PC can access the Internet at the same time • A home entertainment network for distributing hi-fi, radio and TV signals around the home • Access control and security featuring CCTV, breakage detection, presence detection, occupancy simulation, central locking and remote control and monitoring • Zoned heating and ventilation control • Automated lighting control with scene setting (adjusting the brightness of a group of lamps to suit particular tasks or moods) • Safety monitoring systems that generate local and remote alarms in case of fire, smoke, gas (e.g. carbon monoxide and methane), water leakage, flood, voltage drop, or a medical condition • Assistive devices for the elderly and disabled, along with access to web-based social and medical services • Electricity, gas and water consumption monitoring and feedback to promote conservation • Remote monitoring and control of home systems and appliances using PCs or remote technology

- reduced energy consumption; and,
- flexible control of electrical devices.

Although smart homes still continue to capture the imagination, their method of delivery comes through technology-push rather than demand-pull (Barlow & Venables 2003), and affordability remains a key issue. However, Pragnell *et al.* (2000) see several drivers, which may stimulate activity in the smart homes market:

- scale economies from the US market;
- better integration of new technologies; and
- increased interest from the consumer electronics industry.

Their research for Joseph Rowntree Foundation in the UK also identifies similar groupings of smart homes consumers to those identified for other, generic ICT (see Chapter 3), namely the 'interested', the 'ambivalent' and the 'uninterested'. 'Safety and security' were also key aspects of appeal for those consumers who favoured smart home technology. Recent technologies such as 'Bluetooth' (Ross & Davies 2003) or its domestic equivalent 'Whitetooth' (i.e. white goods with the ability to communicate with each other) set within 'residential gateways' offer connectivity options and telephony (see, for example, Toshiba's Bluetooth Home). However, as Barlow (2000) points out, integration of systems is potentially easier for new build than it is for retrofitting existing housing stock.

The concept of smart homes comes at a time when the UK government is also promoting the use of ICT as a 'tool' for regeneration through its Policy Action Teams (PATs) and National Neighbourhood Renewal Agenda (DETR 2000; PAT 15 2000; PAT 13 2000), and when 'digital communities' (for example, the UK Communities Online initiative), with open access to the Internet, continue to be promoted as a model for future residential development. As yet, however, the real implications of these potential changes, in terms of digital divide and impact on space requirements, remain uncertain, but if workplace dislocation increases through teleworking, then this will have ramifications for home and office space.

Recent research by SUSTEL (2003), for example, found that 12 of the 30 international case studies in their research would need less office space as a direct result of teleworking, and that people may move or add extensions to their homes in order to create more domestic working space. Moreover, research by DTI (1998) in the UK found that most teleworkers in Britain had 'limited space to undertake teleworking activities', and work by the Department of Labor (2000) in the USA suggests that availability of space at home is an important element of successful teleworking. It is clear therefore that further trends towards teleworking and smart homes will have ramifications for residential property in the following ways:

- **Demand**. As the home increasingly becomes the centre of consumption and production (Priemus 2003), so there is likely to be an increase in demand for housing in attractive residential environments (Stec Group 2000). Hodson (2003) suggests that the USA's 20 million teleworkers require some 2.8 bn ft^2 of home office space, which represents the equivalent of \$14 bn commercial office space, and Johnson (2003) suggests that the 'co-workplace'[23] (a local, neighbourhood-based centre to support collective telework), combining private workspaces close to home with shared facilities and options, provides a viable alternative model to disconnected home work space. Research by Hampton and Wellman (2003) in Ontario, Canada, has also shown that Internet access in communities supports stronger neighbourhood ties, and at a community level there have been moves to create urban areas based around a 'smart community' or 'e-village' concept. Recent examples include Ennis in Ireland (the most wired community in Ireland), and Nortel's 'e-village' in Madera County, California (see Box 7.7). It is also likely that the sustainable development agenda of Western governments will also drive the move towards an increased demand for this type of living/work space (see Chapter 9).

• **Design**. In the early 1990s research by BT (1992) suggested that detached and semi-detached houses were most appropriate for homeworkers because they were not over-occupied and had extension potential; conversely, smaller terraced homes, and houses designed for single persons, were less adaptable. Green *et al.* (2000) suggest that flexible, open-plan space will provide key potential for accommodating these workers, therefore. Similarly, Ahrentzen (2001) suggests a number of design features for teleworking/homeworking including:

  • vertical distancing, characterised by 'shop houses' with business space on the ground floor and living space on the first floor, although there may be neighbourhood compatability issues; and

  • horizontal distancing, where the house plan is 'long and thin' and workspace is separated laterally.

Box 7.7   Wired communities

There is an increasing number of projects globally which are designed as exemplars of what might be termed a 'wired community' concept. For example, the Ennis wired community in Ireland, established by Eircom's Internet infrastructure in 1997, is a prime example of how universal Internet access can transform home and business communities in a relatively remote rural area (Intelligent Community Forum 2000). Eircom (then known as Telecom Eireann) sponsored a competition across Ireland to create a wired community, and Ennis (as the winner) received a £15 million grant to invest in telecommunications infrastructure, education and training, and the integration of information technology into local businesses. By 2000, Ennis had invested £9 million in building a broadband fibre ring and digital exchange; offering a free telephone connection and PC to every resident; and installing IT equipment and providing training in the schools and small-to-mid-size businesses. A further £1 million was raised in the local community, providing £7 million to fund the project until 2002, and the city is already earning revenue by offering itself as a test bed for interactive services (Intelligent Community Forum 2001).

Similarly, in Madera County, California, USA Nortel have teamed with the Property Development Group to build a sophisticated, planned community of more than 30 000 homes on a 15-acre site for teleworkers, together with office, business and hospitality centres (Nortel 2003). Dubbed the 'e-village', the site is based near Fresno and is being developed as a 'green' community that is intended to aid the environment, through reduced traffic, congestion and smog. There are also close links with the local Fresno State University.[24]

- **Social inclusion and community**. The trend towards smart homes and smart communities has implications for social inclusion and sense of community. For example, Graham and Marvin (2001) suggest that there is a danger that only affluent people have access to the networks and infrastructures that are required for these new ways of living. Increasingly, there is a sense that such individuals are seceding from their immediate urban environments (Lorente 1997) as there is an increasing emphasis on security and surveillance (as also evidenced by the recent growth in 'gated communities'; see Minton 2002). As Graham and Marvin point out (2001: 285): 'Increasingly, then, the homes of more affluent socio-economic groups are being transformed into secured sanctuaries and hubs for infrastructurally mediated exchange, communication, work and transactions'.

Summary

In brief, this chapter has examined the following real estate sectors:

- sales;
- processing;
- manufacturing;
- distribution; and,
- leisure and living.

We started our discussion by suggesting that the distinctions between conventional real estate sectors were becoming blurred. We have seen how ICT has acted with a range of other factors to shape and transform these sectors. The first part of Chapter 9 contains a more detailed summary of the main themes emerging from this transformation of real estate space. In the next chapter we will examine how real estate services are also being transformed by ICT and other related factors.

Notes

1 Technology has also assisted in attracting customers into retail spaces through changing approaches to store design. Advances in material and lighting science have enabled new, exciting designs to be used within stores themselves. In particular Din (2000) identifies the importance of advances in lighting technology and its use within store-based environments. The 1980s saw the introduction of low-voltage tungsten-halogen bulbs which were smaller than existing forms of lighting and more energy efficient. Their smaller size

led more attractive fittings to be designed and introduced the ability to use lighting strategically within stores to highlight particular displays or products or to set a certain mood. Other examples include the installation of large video walls into stores, particularly music and some fashion stores. Field (1999) cites the example of sportswear manufacturer Nike and its chain of flagship stores branded NikeTown.

2   Inditex (of which Zara is a part) have successfully made use of EPoS data to inform their whole business. Consumer tastes are analysed and swiftly sent through to the design area of the group. The group actively looks to reduce its inventory levels to a bare minimum, which has required a just-in-time (JIT) manufacturing system to be adopted. Communications and logistics technology are therefore an important element in the successful operation of the group and its rapid expansion across Europe.

3   In the US this is a more compelling model given the ownership profile of shopping centres. Many of the large centres with comparison goods retailers are in the hands of just a few owners, in particular General Growth Corporation and Simon Property.

4   See also Chapter 4 for a discussion of how Duffy's concepts can aid understanding of organisational space.

5   The RICS (2002) study suggested that new working practices could cut the costs of property usage, and if each firm cut space by $2.1\,m^2$ per employee, savings of £7.8 bn would be achieved nationally in property costs.

6   The study by HM Treasury on the location of financial activity and the euro (HM Treasury 2003) also supports this view. Strong economies of scale continue to reinforce clustering although centrifugal forces are also at work.

7   When probabilistic uncertainties are introduced the premium increases to 5.27%.

8   However, there is some controversy over the use of the term 'cluster'. The DTI study suggested that the UK clusters were more akin to 'concentrations', without necessarily the degree of inter-relatedness and inter-firm benefits required for the more formal use of the term.

9   Note, however, the importance of measuring bandwidth per capita (see Thompson 2002). On this measure London would trail other cities such as Geneva.

10 London is in the top four European cities in terms of average and total space for Internet data centre co-location centres (Dixon *et al.* 2002).

11 Defined by the UK Call Centre Association (sourced in ECOTEC 2000) as 'a clearly defined business unit within an organisation of 20 or more seats where the primary role is to make or receive telephone calls, be it for customer service, account handling, billing enquiries, technical support or telemarketing, working to pre-set measurable objectives. Its operation is usually dependent upon the use of sophisticated IT and telecommunications hardware and software'. See also Chapter 4.

12 Flatness and levelness are terms increasingly utilised in recent years to specify finish criteria in concrete floor slab construction. 'Flatness' describes the magnitude of 'waves' in a floor surface. 'Levelness' refers to the relationship

of the floor surface to a horizontal plane. ASTM E-1155 'Standard Test Method for Determining Floor Flatness and Levelness Using the 'F-Number' System (Inch-Pound Units)' describes the 'F-Number' system and a recommended measurement system. The F-Number system assigns a numerical value for both flatness and levelness. A higher number indicated a flatter or more level floor surface. F_F, referred to as the flatness F-Number, defines the maximum floor curvature allowed over a 24 inch (610 mm) length. F_L, referred to as the levelness F-Number, defines the relative conformity of the floor surface to a horizontal plane over a 10 foot (3 m) distance.

13   The core cities comprise Birmingham, Bristol, Leeds, Liverpool, Manchester, Newcastle, Nottingham, and Sheffield (see www.corecities.com).

14   See www.proboscis.org.uk for further information on this project. Urban Tapestries allows people to author their own virtual annotations of the city, enabling a community's collective memory to grow organically, allowing ordinary citizens to embed social knowledge in the new wireless landscape of the city. People will be able to add new locations, location content and the 'threads' which link individual locations to local contexts, which are accessed via handheld devices such as PDAs and mobile phones.

15   This chapter does not cover casinos or online gaming, which are also growing in popularity, driven by Internet marketing and technology convergence, combined with increasing demand for leisure. For a good overview of gambling and casinos see Jones Lang LaSalle (2002). Online gaming has increased market reach and revenue for many betting businesses and its borderless nature presents regulatory and enforcement challenges to governments (for example, money laundering). Estimates put online gaming revenues at $5 bn in 2003 or some 4.3% of all B2C commerce globally (see US General Accounting Office 2002 and Gaming Board of Great Britain 2002).

16   Hackney (of which Hoxton is part) has the largest population of artists per head of population in Britain (Leadbeater & Oakley 2001). The area has recently lost much of its creative talent because of development.

17   We are also seeing how the Internet can impact on existing distribution/ consumption models in music and film. For example, the music industry initially fought Internet distribution to protect its business model, but with the advent of proactive music industry joint ventures, Pressplay and MusicNet in 2001, the industry began to realise that the demand of music customers for downloadable tracks was unstoppable. Data from BPI (2004) show that, in January 2004, downloads outsold physical formats for the first time. The film industry has, in contrast, adapted more readily: the advent of Movielink in 2002 (Levin *et al.* 2003) is a step towards a digital download model, but movies are in any case a less 'portable' product in many ways than music (see also Chapter 7 on high street music sales, page 229).

18   Sports clubs and football clubs are also likely to continue to increase their reach and scope through online marketing. De Moragas Spa *et al.* (2003), for example, show how the top five UEFA clubs for 2002-2003 (Real Madrid, FC Bayern Munich, Manchester United, FC Barcelona and SS Lazio) have used B2C and B2B to link with fans and other businesses respectively. Facilities

included news and information (for example, the 'Lazio Village' site; streaming and webcasting; e-tickets; interactive services and online shops). Again this will have ramifications for additional real estate space in the club's home country as well as overseas to provide goods and services and operate supply chains.

19   The economic multiplier effects of a successful Olympic bid are substantial; for example, research by Avison Young (2003) suggests that the 2012 Vancouver Winter Olympics will create demand for up to 600 000 ft^2 of offices, as 3 000 new jobs will be created. Similarly, in Sydney, Australia (NSW, Department of State and Regional Development 2001), the 2000 Olympics attracted some 64 companies to the city between 1996 and 2001, creating more than 200 jobs and increasing demand for office, retail, call centre and distribution space.

20   Mitchell (2003) also suggests that ICT can reinvent residential neighbourhoods in three main ways: firstly by envisioning buildings and cities retaining their current structures, but with goods and services consumption facilitated by ICT; secondly, that ICT will drive an anti-urban agenda through homeworking, teleworking and so on; or thirdly by using ICT to reinvent small-scale neighbourhoods for the twenty-first century.

21   In the UK, ODPM (2003) have drafted new proposed Building Regulations (Requirement Q) that are designed to ensure electronic communications can be installed at any time in domestic property with the minimum of disruption. This is part of the drive to widen broadband participation in the UK. Lobbying from the house-building industry may also lead to developers of new housing having the option of installing either wired or wireless connections in new homes.

22   See also Box 3.2.

23   This combines elements of a telework centre with a business incubator (Johnson 2003).

24   See the Craig Business School website which showcases the e-village at the Digital Economy Center homepage (www.deconline.csufresno.edu).

8

Real Estate Service Providers and ICT

Introduction

In a collection of papers exploring the future of the built environment professions, Curry and Howard (2003) suggest a future scenario in which the landscape is dominated by a small number of large service-delivery companies driven by shareholders and shareholder value, with new financial models built around 'whole service management' (or the lifetime value of buildings). This requires not only deal-making skills to design the financial vehicles needed to underwrite and fund developments, but also service innovation skills to identify new income streams for the developer and owner. The growth of a service-based economy and digitally networked companies has driven this pattern together with the growing emphasis on sustainability in the public and private sectors, underpinned by a preference for leasing rather than owning and the relative weakness of capital markets as a source for funding (which leads to innovative financing). As Curry and Howard (2003) point out, the traditional value chain model is being supplanted by an exploded business model (Figure 8.1), where outsourcing of various activities, which were considered essential, has occurred. These tasks previously took up management time, resources and attention but can be outsourced to third parties or stand-alone units within the company. Networks have also promoted faster response times and allow businesses to focus and specialise on factors that are essential to business success.

Therefore just as ICT is impacting on business and its organisational structure so ICT is impacting on real estate services. This is leading to two principal models for successful real estate service provision:

- Model A. Core competencies are based around deal making and financial packaging with the brokerage role fulfilled by the gap left by

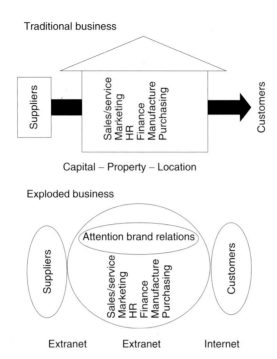

Figure 8.1   Traditional and exploded business model (adapted from DTI/Foresight 2000).

financial markets. Here the emphasis is on deals rather than building relationships.

- Model B. In this model the emphasis is on long-term relationships and servicing the needs of building occupiers over time.

How the future landscape of real estate services pans out is open to debate, but in terms of sheer size, the real estate service sector[1] is substantial, and ICT has played a major role in driving change in the form and shape of services offered. In 2000 the real estate sector in the EU comprised about 755 000 companies, and has been increasing over time, with some 1.7 million persons employed in the same sector in the EU in 2000 (European Commission 2003). In the UK the sector has some 68 000 enterprises employing 371 000 people with a turnover in excess of 47 bn euros (European Commission 2003).

We explore below how these changes are beginning to manifest themselves in the real estate sector. This chapter explores the transformation brought about in this sector from both the demand and supply sides by ICT, acting in conjunction with other forces for change. The chapter therefore covers:

- the changing nature of real estate investment;
- owners and owners' managers;
- occupiers and occupiers' managers;
- appraisers; and
- brokers.

We have not developed a separate section for developers. The commercial real estate development sector consists of a wide spectrum of diverse commercial organisations, and many of the largest developers (e.g. British Land, Land Securities Trillium, Slough Estates, Brixton) are also in essence long-term investors.

The changing context of real estate investment

The last decade has seen important changes in the way that both investors and occupiers finance the procurement of real estate, real estate services and business support services, the legal arrangements for occupation and the ways that real estate is configured and used by occupiers. Although sometimes caricatured as 'lethargic', over the last decade the real estate sector has witnessed the emergence of new types of occupational, financing and investment products. The section first outlines some of the main areas where innovation has occurred.

New developments in corporate finance

In the area of corporate finance, the 1990s saw acceleration in the application of innovative financial techniques to the real estate market. The real estate industry has increasingly adapted products and techniques from the capital markets. In addition to the emergence of the corporate outsourcing sector, Lizieri *et al.* (2001) identify a range of innovations including:

- increased use of asset- and mortgage-backed securitisation;
- the development of real estate derivative products;
- new forms of sale and leaseback and off-balance sheet structures; and
- growth of limited partnerships and special purpose (offshore) vehicles.

Lizieri *et al.* (2001: 53) conclude that:

> ... a breed of finance-led real estate professionals have emerged in the UK, less influenced by the 'all-risk yield' than a concern for total returns and cash-flow-generated performance.

Interestingly, they identified appraisers as stifling innovation, arguing that the use of traditional appraisal methods is problematic for the pricing of differing cash-flow patterns. Whilst these transactions often involve large single assets and portfolios of properties, at the same time, there is a growing recognition that individual real estate assets can be 'unbundled' (or deconstructed) to create a value-added product.

Deconstructing the asset

There is an increasing appreciation amongst investors of the complexity of commercial real estate as an asset class, the flexibility inherent in commercial real estate investments and the potential to exploit these characteristics to improve returns. The single real estate asset consists of a package of diverse financial interests each of which has different risk–return characteristics. Importantly, each can also be traded separately from the ownership of the real estate asset. Innovative investors such as Rotch Property Group are reported to have 'stripped out' the different elements of the income stream. Investors have achieved arbitrage gains by securitising the fixed income components of properties let on long leases. They can then either retain or sell the rights to the residual value and/or future increases in rent at rent reviews. In turn, innovative insurance products have also emerged in the commercial lending sector which enable borrowers to insure against tenant default and low residual values.

It is interesting to note that this market change has had implications for appraisal. Motivated by the 'deconstruction' of the real estate asset, innovative approaches to the appraisal of commercial real estate assets pioneered by one actuarial firm (William M. Mercer Ltd) in particular have been used by Rotch Property Group to appraise their assets. However, the so-called 'actuarial' approach is still at an embryonic stage and is still not fully in the public domain. However, it is interesting that the approaches are based upon option pricing methods.

Changing lease structures

Closely linked to the issue of ICT-driven change in business processes is the increasing demand for flexibility from real estate assets. As we have seen, driven and facilitated by the interrelated forces of globalisation, technological innovation and increased competition, a proportion of businesses needed to be more agile in their production of goods and services. Lease contracts are not trivial matters for business that need to respond quickly to rapidly changing business conditions. Prior to 1990, in the UK the landlord had typically managed to shift many of the risks associated with ownership of real estate to the tenant. The normal long lease (20 years) with upward-only rent reviews every five years and full repairing and insuring terms meant that tenants bore the risks of:

- space becoming surplus to operational requirements;
- space requiring major expenditure on repair and maintenance; and
- rental value falling.

The recessionary conditions of the early 1990s saw a clear change in leasing practices for institutional grade property. Such a market environment empowered tenants, seeking greater flexibility and reduced risk, to secure shorter leases and/or an option to break at least once during the term of the lease. Figure 8.2 illustrates how for all sectors of the market, the 1990s saw a fall in lease lengths.

It is methodologically difficult to disentangle the effects of market conditions, government intervention, technological innovation and accounting regulation in explaining the changes to lease lengths in the UK. However, it is clear that real estate owners in the UK are becoming increasingly comfortable with flexible leasing patterns, as they have become established. Figure 8.3 illustrates how there is now a diversity of lease structures.

In the real estate literature, Gibson and Lizieri (1999) have drawn an analogy between the concepts of core and peripheral labour forces and

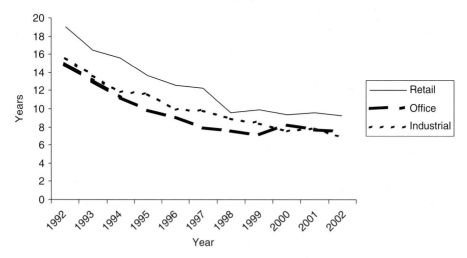

Figure 8.2   Average lease length in the UK (adapted from DETR 2000; ODPM 2004).

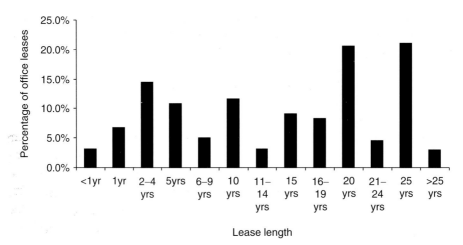

Figure 8.3   Distribution of UK office lease lengths (ERV weighted) (adapted from ODPM 2004).

real estate assets. They argue that the same drivers leading businesses to require more flexibility in their labour force are also producing demand for flexibility in their real estate portfolios. Whilst initially forced by market pressures to introduce flexi-leases, it is clear that some real estate owners have now identified the opportunity provided by the demand for flexibility and have attempted to develop real estate products to fulfil this demand. The outcome of this market and structural shift is a much more diverse pattern of lease lengths within the UK. The main change has been a decrease in effective length of lease in all sectors and the disappearance of a standard market lease. Further, in the corporate sector, some large companies are in the process of disposing of their real estate assets completely and occupying through service contracts rather than leases.

The emergence of corporate real estate outsourcing

A key development in the real estate sector in the 1990s has been intermediation as organisations have emerged which have 're-engineered' the landlord and tenant relationship. In response to corporate and public sector demand to outsource the provision of real estate and associated services and to release the value of their assets, companies such as Mapeley, MWB and Trillium provide accommodation and FM services to corporate and public sector occupiers. Typically, in return for a capital payment, the organisation gives up ownership of their portfolio and enters into a long-term contract to occupy space and to receive a range of services. There is unitary charging for the space and services. Whilst this PFI type of agreement has been restricted to large organisations (see, for example, Dixon *et al.* 2003) another service that experienced rapid expansion in the 1990s has been serviced offices. In this sector the market has been small and medium-sized enterprises and short-term corporate project teams and, arguably, the emphasis has been more on the services than the offices (see Chapters 7 and 9).

It is clear from the discussion above that the procurement and supply of real estate has fundamentally changed in the last decade. The growing interest in landlords providing additional services represents continuing evolution in the sector. Below, the main drivers and facilitators of this shift are assessed.

Linkages to ICT innovation

We have seen above that Internet-centred technology, in particular, has expanded the range of options that businesses have to structure their production, procurement, distribution, marketing and retailing functions. The DTI (2001) argues that the key consequences of these factors are likely to be:

- an increase in the importance of brands and relationships as 'signals' of quality, with a consequent ability to leverage brand presence and reputation from one market to another at reduced entry cost;
- a reduced role for some intermediaries and the creation of new intermediaries such as 'best buy' sites, quality guarantors and information brokers;
- more amorphous market and company structures with a continuation of the trend away from vertically integrated companies towards networks.

It will become apparent that these three outcomes are central to market shifts that are beginning to emerge in the real estate sector and have the potential to transform the role of real estate owners and their managers.

A major impact of technological innovation is that it has enabled businesses to re-structure the supply chain in order to improve productivity. This re-structuring provides opportunities for real estate owners to enhance their contribution to the supply chain and Internet-centred technology has facilitated the market entry of real estate owners. Essentially, the technology provides real estate owners with a relatively low-cost means of extending their relationship with their tenants. Although it could be reasonably argued that costs of communication with clients have not been a major barrier in the past, it is interesting to note that the most advanced providers of additional services offer a largely web-based method of procurement.

Outsourcing

Probably the most significant change in the organisation of production of goods and services over the last decade has been the expansion of outsourcing. The 'ideology' of core competency focus has led businesses to critically examine their production organisation in order to concentrate on sectors where they can be pre-eminent and to outsource functions in which they do not have competitive advantage. The key advantages of outsourcing are regarded as being reduced capital investment and operating costs, access to 'best in class' providers, shared risks and ability to focus on core functions (see Moore 2000; Kistler 1999). Internet-centred technology has reduced the transaction costs associated with outsourcing such as costs of search, contracting and monitoring. A direct consequence has been rapid expansion in the demand for a whole range of business support services such as IT support, facilities management and back-office functions.

Outsourcing not only provides opportunities for real estate owners at the business level; it is clear that potential business opportunities are emerging at the level of the individual. Affluent office workers may wish to 'outsource' a number of their domestic tasks in order to be able to devote more time to professional activities. A consequence is that real estate owners *inter alia* have identified concierge services as a potential source of revenue in buildings occupied by 'money rich, time poor' employees.

Bundling services

A paradox of business evolution in the 1990s was the growth of bundling alongside the spread of outsourcing. Bundling refers to 'the practice of marketing two or more products and/or services in a single "package" for a special price' (Guiltinan 1987: 74). It is found practically everywhere in the consumer sector and is increasingly common in the commercial sector. For instance, it has been observed that companies such as Lucent, GE and General Motors have become increasingly involved in providing finance to such an extent that manufacturing may be becoming a loss-leader in the profit chain. For clients the main benefits of bundling are reduced search costs and lower transaction costs, whilst providers gain additional income streams and also gain from lower transaction costs.

For bundling to occur in the commercial real estate sector, an obvious prerequisite is that real estate owners have a range of products and services to bundle. This has rarely been the case, as owners have tended to offer a uniform commodity – a standard unit of space let on standard terms at a single price. The most obvious example where it does occur is in the serviced office sector where occupiers are typically offered a 'package' which includes flexibility of occupation, utilities, some business support services and equipment for a single price whilst having the option to source other services (catering, IT support, etc.). If we regard the 20-year FRI lease and the serviced office sector as two extremes, we can observe that some real estate investors are attempting to develop products that blend the two. A good example is Arlington's Total Workspace Solution which offers terms of occupation from three to five years fully inclusive of (some) utilities with the option to access FM and a range of other services. Consistent with their acquisition of Trillium, Land Securities are exploring the potential of introducing unitary charging for a 'bundle' of real estate and additional services.

New products

The DTI research discussed above highlighted the potential of the Internet to allow intermediaries to occur, offering existing products and services through new channels. The emergence of new technology is proving disruptive to established, often inherently passive, models of real estate management. As well as facilitating the development of new relationships between real estate owners and occupiers, the rapid development of Internet-related technology has forced some real estate owners to respond to demand for connectivity. For instance, the growing broadband sector provides an example of how real estate owners have been forced to consider their traditional relationship with their tenants. The growth of Internet-centred technology has enabled the provision of a whole range of web-based services, leading a number of real estate companies to develop specialist software products. There is a general consensus that landlords who wish to keep their buildings competitive should consider growing business demand for services and flexibility.

Towards a service industry?

There is a view that the real estate industry is the last major business sector to embrace the importance of customer relations and quality of service. The long-term, and essentially asymmetrical, nature of traditional lease contracts has provided little incentive for owners to be concerned about quality. However, the shift towards more flexible leases, the growth of corporate real estate outsourcing and serviced offices create a context in which quality of service and customer satisfaction are increasingly relevant to investment performance. In the context of markets where tenants were increasingly wishing to outsource many services, there is a recognition that landlords who are able to offer an attractive package of services (as well as space) can obtain a competitive advantage and be in a position to retain existing and attract new tenants. This, in turn, should lead to fewer voids and improved income return and security.

In summary, it is clear that the supply of services by landlords is being facilitated by the emergence of web-based technologies and driven by increased pressures on landlords to be innovative and customer focused. The demand is being created by the trend for businesses to outsource non-core functions. As a result, landlords are beginning to 'bundle' space and services provision to tenants.

We now focus on four categories of real estate professionals: managers (owners and occupiers), appraisers and brokers, and assess the implications of these changes for their professional activities.

The owner's manager

Unlike 'paper' securities such as bonds and equities, real estate assets also include real options. Ownership of real estate assets provides opportunities to raise additional revenues from the asset and the tenant base. The increased interest of real estate owners in the potential to add value to their portfolios by providing services is one of a number of market innovations in the real estate sector in the 1990s. A unique feature of real estate as an investment class is that it requires a relatively substantial (if variable) management input by the owner or a manager acting on the owner's behalf. Indeed, a key decision for the owner is whether to retain the management functions, outsource them to real estate management service providers or some combination of these two options.

In addition to the standard investment management tactical and strategic allocation decisions common to all investment portfolios, real estate investors have the opportunity to improve investment returns by entrepreneurial and efficient management and strong negotiation and marketing skills. Conversely, unimaginative and inefficient management and lack of negotiation and marketing expertise can produce relative underperformance. In this section we examine how innovations in ICT have affected how real estate is managed.

Clearly, ICT innovation has transformed the traditional functions of the real estate manager in the same way that the use of email, mobile telephony, the Internet and specialist software has affected all professional activities. However, we focus in this section on the additional opportunities generated by ICT innovation. These changes in the roles and functions of the real estate manager are currently embryonic. Nevertheless, it will be argued that they are irreversible.

Defining the real estate manager

First, we must understand what a real estate manager is and does and, therefore, address a number of questions:

- What is management and, in particular, in the real estate context what is the distinction between an active and passive approach to management?
- What functions does the real estate manager perform?
- What skills and knowledge does the real estate manager need?
- How is the role of the real estate manager changing and what growth areas are emerging?

It is important to bear in mind that attitudes concerning many real estate management issues will vary with perspective and position. Who is the 'client'? Landlord, tenant, public, other? Large company/small company? What is the objective? Return maximisation? Optimise contribution to business? Public good? What is being managed? Regional shopping centre or single tenant high street shop? Serviced office or single tenant unit? Short leases or long leases? What is the level of manager? It is possible to identify a broad hierarchy as follows:

- 'Real estate manager' is concerned with day-to-day functions, problem solving, tenant liaison, etc. This role may not even be necessary in a single tenant asset let on a long FRI lease.
- 'Asset manager' is concerned with issues such as letting, rent reviews, assignments, improvements, etc. Works closely with real estate manager.
- 'Portfolio manager' takes a more strategic role focused on investment performance, disposal decisions, major expenditures, lease re-structuring.

So the impact of ICT on the analysis of real estate management and ICT issues needs to consider explicitly:

- the characteristics of the asset managed;
- the objectives of the manager; and,
- the category (hierarchy) of management.

The focal point?

The real estate manager can also be viewed as a key intermediary between a range of professionals involved in the ownership, occupation and management of the real estate portfolio. Some potential relationships are set out below in Figure 8.4.

Active vs passive management
During the same period that ICT began to be assimilated into business processes, the attitude of some of the major real estate investors towards their asset began to change. In essence, there has been a growing realisation that real estate is a 'management play' and that entrepreneurial management is possible. A distinction has been drawn between two styles of, or approaches to, real estate management – active and passive. The dissimilarity between active and passive management is often presented in Manichean terms. In reality, different styles will be appropriate for different assets. For instance, where a single office has been let on a 20-year lease to a tenant with a strong credit risk who is responsible for all repairs and maintenance, the management may be minimal and simply

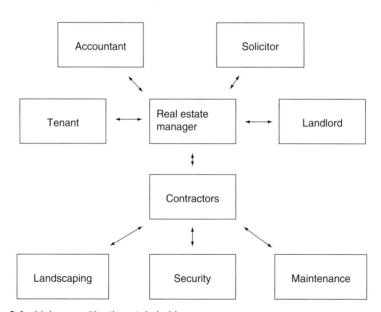

Figure 8.4   Linkages with other stakeholders.

consist of collecting the rent, periodic inspections and responses to tenant enquiries. At the other extreme, a serviced office provider is involved in all aspects related to attracting occupiers (skills: marketing and negotiating), administering a business (skills: finance, HRM), providing services (skills: purchasing and procurement) and managing a real estate (skills: all of the above). Their management style can only be active.

The culture and philosophy of the organisation will also be an important determinant of the general attitude to asset management. How is manager/asset performance monitored? How are staff incentivised and rewarded? What is the attitude to risk? What aspects of risk are important? With the caveat that we are often dealing in caricatures, the essential characteristics and differences between the two styles of real estate management are set out below in Table 8.1.

Commercial landlords have been criticised for their desire to shift the risk of real estate occupancy to users. In 2000, Howard Bibby (MD of Arlington) summed up some of their faults as:

- over-reliance on legal rights and monopoly power;
- still treating tenants as 'revolting peasants';
- resistant and vulnerable to change;
- no attempt to understand let alone satisfy occupier needs;
- single win/lose transaction focus; and,
- zero 'service'.

It is likely that this caricature of the traditional landlord–tenant relationship struck a few chords. However, it is also becoming increasingly out of date.

The traditional responsibilities of and key areas in which the real estate manager will be involved therefore include such activities as: practice management; tenant liaison; inspection and monitoring; environmental

Table 8.1 Styles of real estate management.

Active	Passive
Entrepreneurial	Risk averse
Proactive	Reactive
Positive	Cautious
Maximising	Satisficing
Hands on	Hands off
Accessible	Remote

management; lease management; service charges; rent collection; health and safety; procurement management; record and information systems; facilities management and maintenance; and fund management. We discuss below some of the new options available to owners and how they may be exploited.

Generating additional revenue streams

Although the traditional functions of the real estate manager will always be required, there are a number of potential areas where real estate owners may be able to develop new business opportunities. Currently, a relatively small number of real estate investors are pioneering the introduction of the services and products discussed below. Consequently, many of the models are embryonic and still evolving. However, it seems clear that opportunities exist in both the retail and commercial sectors and that the new revenue streams are in both landlord-to-business (L2B) services and landlord-to-consumer (L2C) services. Moreover, whilst ICT innovation is not a *sine qua non* of the exploitation of many of the opportunities, it is also the case that web-based delivery and administration of the business processes involved is often at the core of the new models.

Facilities management

Given that owners typically have a 'head start' in terms of detailed knowledge concerning their buildings and the associated mechical and electrical (M&E) services, there has been an obvious potential opportunity to market maintenance services to occupiers. Owners have the potential to offer a range of real estate services which occupiers otherwise have to procure elsewhere. It should also be borne in mind that many real estate owners already provide varying levels of FM services in shopping centres and other multi-let buildings. The main areas are:

- landscaping;
- security;
- external fabric maintenance and cleaning;
- internal fabric maintenance and cleaning;
- waste management; and
- mechanical and electrical maintenance.

Currently, very few mainstream commercial landlords offer comprehensive FM services. Where real estate owners provide FM services, it may be structured as a separate 'spin-off' company. For instance, British Land provide FM services in the City through Broadgate Estates Plc. This was originally set up to provide FM services to tenants of British Land at Broadgate. However, the company has subsequently won FM tenders for other buildings close to Broadgate and expanded accordingly. However, it is also clear that landlords regard FM as a low margin business with substantial cost pressures. Whilst it is recognised that they may need the capability to offer the service, there is limited enthusiasm about its potential to generate significant revenue streams.

Relocation and fitting out

The one-off event of moving into the premises and rendering them suitable for operational purposes involves substantial outlay by the tenant. Real estate owners are well placed to exploit the business opportunities concerning any relocation and occupation due to their existing relationship with the tenant, the associated information of their plans and their knowledge of the building itself. In order to illustrate the potential of this sector, the range of services offered by Arlington as part of their workspace support are outlined in Table 8.2.

Procurement

Procurement services provide another opportunity for real estate owners with scale often cited as the critical variable. Many SMEs and relatively autonomous business units of corporations are unlikely to possess either the resources and/or skills to optimise the procurement process or the market power to obtain bulk discounts. Aggregation is the key to volume discounts. Although any landlord can attempt to aggregate the buying power of their tenants, large landlords, in particular, have the potential to use their purchasing power to achieve discounts and then to exploit potential arbitrage opportunities in procurement. Using preferred provider models or bulk purchase, they can obtain a range of business goods and services at discounted prices for their tenants whilst obtaining a margin on the revenue generated.

eProcurement, in particular, has been identified by real estate owners as a potential growth area. The main benefits have been identified as:

Table 8.2   Relocation and fitting out services.

● Inventory and layout	● Fit-out, cabling, telecoms and services installation
● Project management of move	● Finance, lease purchase options
● Space audit	● Approvals and consents
● Services integration and compliance	● Competitive tendering
● Interior design and space planning	● Fit-out management
● Building appraisal	● Commissioning and testing
● Service and system design	● After care
● Furniture selection	● Relocation and moving
● Insurance approvals and liaison	● Risk assessment

- reduced costs of processing transactions, particularly due to the elimin-ation/reduction of paper documentation;
- reduced costs of items due above, bulk purchasing and elimination of intermediaries such as wholesalers and distributors; and
- improved organisational control of procurement process and reduced costs of data collection and monitoring.

A number of landlords and real estate consultancies in the UK have been pioneering the introduction of online procurement facilities through intra-nets. Driven initially by an attempt to create 'virtual communities' in business parks, sites are being upgraded to allow for a wider range of services to be offered. These fall into two main areas:

- landlord-to-consumer – information, online shopping, retail services (e.g. dry cleaning); and,
- landlord-to-business – procurement of goods and services.

Intermediation can produce a win–win outcome for both landlord and tenant. It is not difficult to envisage the list of services where this may be possible – business travel, recruitment, professional services, database management, graphic design, equipment hire, financing, etc. The potential opportunity seems to lie in generic business support services rather than in sector-specific goods and services. Outside utilities, a likely model is a joint venture or partnership with a specialist procurement company or a specialist provider in single area (e.g. IT).

However, there is some scepticism among a number of landlords concern-ing the revenue-generating potential of intermediation and eProcurement. A number of questions can be posed. Given the convenience of the Inter-net as a procurement tool, it can be questioned whether landlords were likely to have a competitive advantage over established intermediaries. Is it reasonable to expect that established intermediaries will permit market entrants to capture a proportion of their margin without a reaction? To be successful, landlords would need to be able to offer tenants a high-quality service at lowest cost. It is likely that this would only be achievable in sectors where existing intermediaries were earning supernormal profits or business costs of search were high. Even where these conditions held, the product or service offered by the landlord would have to be amongst 'best in class'.

Back-office functions

Competitive pressures to consolidate costs and focus on the core business have facilitated the emergence of a relatively new business sector special-ising in outsourcing back-office functions. Major corporations have been able to create 'spin-off' companies who both provide back-office functions to both their 'parent' firm and other organisations. However, a key point is that typically the model has been for firms with established expertise and other infrastructure in a given sector to separate out the back-office functions and create new businesses. There seem to have been relatively few 'from scratch' start-ups. This is particularly advanced in the banking and fund management sectors. In the US, a number of landlords have been attempting to exploit this market by offering back-office functions to tenants. It is likely that landlords will only be able to enter the market for outsourcing generic back-office functions such as human resource administration, accounts, credit control, data processing and IT services – and only then with a suitable partner. In addition there is potential to use the access to the tenant to market new business support products. A good example is the joint venture between Deloitte and Touche, Flint House Limited and Land Securities which has developed specialist software for managing tax reporting requirements. Again for landlords the main market for such services and products seems to be with SMEs. In terms of a reality check, it is difficult to envisage a large expansion of this area. It is revealing that there are no reported examples of landlords providing back-office functions in the UK.

Retail: an example

The prime retail sector is largely divided between free-standing retail units and shopping centres. It is the latter which is the focus of this discussion since shopping centres, in particular, provide useful insights into the potentially changing roles of real estate managers and appraisers. Besides being forced to provide a relatively full FM service, owners of shopping centres have always generated additional non-rental income streams linked to their asset. These include revenues from:

- car parks;
- market stalls;
- advertising sites;
- ATMs;
- mobile telephony infrastructure; and
- other concessions.

However, the emergence of Internet-centred technology has also created opportunities for owners to develop their relationships with both visitors and tenants in shopping centres.

A topic generating particular interest is the sheer size of the consumer base that uses shopping centres. For instance, the Annual Report of Land Securities states that:

> ... There are in excess of 150 million visits each year to our various centres and we are currently pursuing a number of initiatives to generate additional income from companies keen to access the high levels of consumer visits.
>
> (Land Securities 2004, p. 19)

Real estate companies are considering a number of ways to exploit the brand and consumer loyalty associated with regional and sub-regional shopping centres. These include:

- virtual malls;
- improved advertising (video walls, plasma screens);
- loyalty cards;
- CCTV;
- endorsements;
- data acquisition; and
- in-centre mobile phone marketing schemes and price searching facilities.

The tenant base also presents retail-specific opportunities to generate additional revenues. A particular area was logistics management. It has been argued that the inventory control by a large number of UK retailers was relatively undeveloped and that landlords could improve the supply chain. For instance, British Land noted that in Meadowhall a number of the retailers had acquired storage facilities in the vicinity for logistics purposes. Consequently, they have developed a managed warehouse, providing storage but also with potential to provide pre-retailing services and pick-up and drop-off services to consumers on behalf of retailers. The development of replenishment centres could enable retailers to improve their customer/sale conversion rates, reduce storage space and increase sales space (Box 8.1).

Further potential opportunities provided by broadband technology have been identified including:

- rapid credit authorisation for credit card purchases;
- webcam facilities;
- training and recruitment;
- video-conferencing;
- EPoS;

Box 8.1   Shared local distribution draws on eCommerce technology

Retailers with outlets at Sheffield's Meadowhall out-of-town shopping centre are co-operating in a pioneering scheme to pool local storage capacity and use a shared delivery system to shuttle goods into their stores. They include Miss Selfridge, Top Shop, Top Man, Allsports and Adams. Others are understood to be considering joining the scheme. The system is heavily reliant on information technology from MetaPack, the start-up, eFulfilment company. Whilst not strictly an eLogistics application in itself, it harnesses similar concepts. In the Meadowhall trial, a handful of retailers have transferred stock that would normally be held in stores to a refurbished warehouse building on the periphery of the site. This has been refitted and re-racked by logistics group Exel, which is managing the operation. From here product is shuttled into the stores on a shared van (a 7.5-tonner will be used eventually).

MetaPack's software intelligently allocates goods to storage positions, and manages picking, cross-docking and local despatch in response to individual retailers' specific requirements. According to MetaPack's Matthew Hardcastle, early research indicated that retailers could reclaim over 7% of space for shopfloor use by holding local stocks externally. 'Some have moved out slower-moving products, some faster-moving items.' The scheme is sponsored by British Land, which controls the Meadowhall site, but MetaPack says the concept would apply equally to high street locations, 'providing some organisation is prepared to take overall responsibility for it'. Whilst in principle MetaPack remains an eFulfilment company, it is now putting increasing emphasis on its technology side. By mutual agreement it has handed operational responsibility for its big fulfilment contract with Wellbeing.com over to Boots, one of the two companies behind the venture. Now it concentrates on running the IT side of the business, although it continues to liaise directly with carriers (one of its specialities). MetaPack is also targeting what sales and marketing director Nigel Rzemieniecki calls 'the retail mainstream' alongside eCommerce activities. And in a further expansion step, it is focusing on direct despatch and supply management: fulfilment for companies such as supermarket giants who want to market product not actually held in stores.

Extracted from http://www.elogmag.com/magazine/22/distribution.shtml

---

- Active server page services; and
- customer relationship management.

Although it is emphasised that for the majority of examples highlighted the value currently lies in the option to provide rather than the actual provision of services, it is clear that additional non-rental revenues have been obtained from shopping centre developments for decades.

A reality check

The discussion above argued that the changing business and technological environment has provided opportunities for new intermediaries, quality guarantors and risk sharers. It is these types of roles that owners have been developing. However, it is also apparent that there is a wide range of potential revenue opportunities with diverse risk–return characteristics. Landlords also have a number of decisions regarding the structure of the service operation. The model selected will affect the income profile generated and the linkage with the real estate asset. This section discusses the types of options open to landlords and identifies some barriers that deter landlords from developing this market.

Vertical integration?

While many real estate analysts are focused on the opportunities and potential of the real estate sector, it is clear that many of the problems raised or implied are neither new nor restricted to the real estate sector. The micro-economics and business management literature devoted to the theory of the firm contains an enormous quantity of empirical and theoretical analysis related to optimisation of product range. The concepts and framework within these disciplines are extremely relevant to this topic and many of the points raised have parallels in the business economics literature.

The ability of real estate owners to develop new products can be analysed as a form of forward and backward vertical integration.[2] Vertical integration typically involves the production of a range of distinct goods and services within the single firm. The outsourcing discussion above highlights the fact that vertical integration has been somewhat out of fashion with clear trends towards vertical *disintegration* in many business sectors. Ironically, disintegration in some sectors is providing opportunities for integration in the real estate sector. Currently the trend in the real estate sector seems to be towards what Michael Porter (1980) labels 'quasi-integration'. This refers to the range of alternatives that firms have between integration and disintegration to enter, for example, into partnerships and alliances.

The potential benefits of the product range diversification often associated with vertical integration are echoed in the literature on bundling and procurement strategies. The debate concerning the merits of vertical integration overlaps in many instances with the whole topic of outsourcing and focus on core competencies. Customers benefit from the logistical efficiencies of 'one-stop shopping' whilst the supplier benefits from customer retention, control over the quality of the product and potential new customers (see Kline 2001). Echoing concerns about real estate owners entering new markets, vertical integration is criticised in terms of draining away resources, diluting management focus and misallocating capital (see Roever 1992). Indeed, the additional services should be assessed in terms of whether they are *complementary* products and services,[3] i.e. complementary to the business of real estate investment.

Figures 8.5 and 8.6 illustrates how the pattern of services procurement by occupiers may evolve. Currently, the majority of landlords are not involved in the provision of real estate-related and business support services to their tenant base. These functions are typically provided 'in-house' or outsourced to a range of independent providers. As Figure 8.5 indicates, the real estate owner has usually no relationship with these service providers. The owner has the opportunity to become both an intermediary and a provider. The service may be provided either directly by the owner, by a provider appointed by the owner, by a subsidiary of the owner's business or by a joint venture with a service provider.

In common with the impact of ICT on business processes, it is important to note that the adoption of these changes will vary between both real estate owners and real estate occupiers. It seems clear from this analysis that the interactions of changing business structures and new technology are creating demand for, and facilitating, the provision of a range of business support services. In addition to the advantage of scale, existing relationships and knowledge of the building and tenants provide landlords

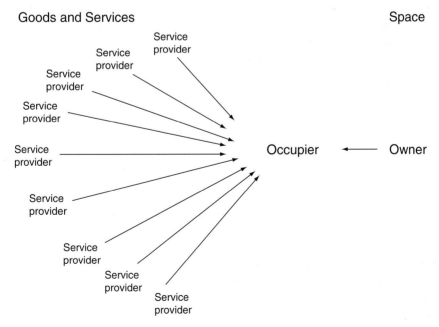

Figure 8.5   Current model of occupier services procurement.

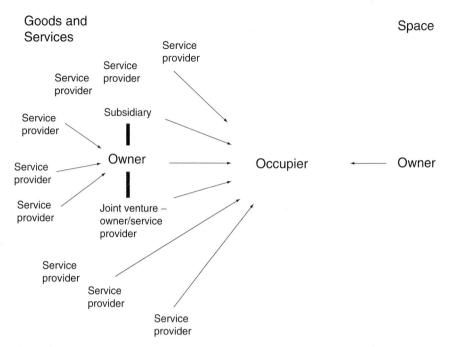

Figure 8.6   Potential model of occupier services procurement.

with an obvious head start in the development and exploitation of the
business opportunities. However, the extent of the opportunity is limited
to where landlords are the optimal provider. Real estate owners by definition are the optimal providers of space but it is not always obvious that
they are the optimal provider for real estate-related services and, indeed,
other services.

A limited market?

Given the pervasive role of procurement in the value chain, one of the
obvious objectives of any commercial organisation will be to optimise this
function. Of course, optimisation cannot be judged solely according to cost
minimisation with impact on product quality and risk of non-production
being other critical variables. The nature of the procurement itself will be
crucial whether it is a one-off, straight re-buy or modified re-buy since
each has different cost–benefit implications. It seems relatively certain
that landlord intermediation offers potential for SMEs to access the benefits of the economies of scale achieved by larger organisations. Such organisations are likely to welcome intermediaries who can share risk and
profit, guarantee minimum prices and supply. Moreover, in terms of the
attraction of eProcurement, SMEs are unlikely to have the resources and

technology skills to develop their own strategy. On the other hand, larger corporations should have well-established supplier networks and partnering arrangements. A key factor for large corporations is likely to be organisational structure with the balance between centralisation and decentralisation being fundamental. The arguments for the economies of scale produced by corporate centralisation against the increased responsiveness and flexibility associated with decentralisation have been well rehearsed. Hence, for the individual business unit of a large corporation the degree of autonomy in procurement will be a significant variable.

It is difficult to assess how the market will evolve. The speed of evolution and adoption will vary according to the characteristics of the building, the occupier and the owner. It is apparent from the discussion above that different types of tenants are likely to have different levels of demand for services. There is also an important distinction between a multi-let building and a single tenancy premises. The former tends to require more management involvement than the latter and is also more likely to contain the critical mass of SMEs. The size and location of the building will also influence the viability of offering services with the additional complication that different services will have different viability thresholds. Given variations in incentives and business culture, it is also relatively apparent that different types of real estate owner will exploit the opportunities at different speeds and to different extents (see Table 8.3).

The occupier's manager

From the perspective of the occupier, real estate is a corporate asset to be managed. Recognition that corporate real estate (CRE) has a shared experience across organisational boundaries has led to growth in the theoretical and organisational underpinning of the area through organisations such as CoreNet Global. Research commissioned by occupier.org (Haynes *et al.* 2002) defines the CRE territory in terms of a schematic model (Figure 8.7).

Their definition of the CRE territory places technology at its heart:

> Occupier organisations procure property, which, with other services and resources, creates a workplace. That workplace supports an occupier organisation in the delivery of goods, services or knowledge to its customers; no suggestion of permanence is intended...As property ages technology changes and so does the fit between an organisation's needs and its workplace. Property life cycles and obsolescence affect the occupier organisation, particularly in a world where the

Table 8.3 The adoption of services provision – market scenarios.

Scenario 1 – Full engagement	Effects on pattern of occupation	Effects on asset	Implications for appraisal
• Real estate owners proactively develop the opportunity to service the tenant base • Real estate owners commonly provide FM services to occupiers • Real estate owners (or coalitions of owners) combine with major utilities providers to provide a range of utilities to the majority of occupiers • Real estate owners offer a range of web-based services to the majority of their tenants • Real estate owners offer broadband services in majority of premises • Real estate owners develop joint ventures and strategic alliances with business support services providers to offer a range of procurement and consultancy services and products	• Bundling of space–services packages commonly occurs • Diversity of space–service–flexibility packages increases dramatically • Real estate management functions are transformed	• Heterogeneity of real estate lease structures increases dramatically • Market transparency decreases • Non-rental revenues account for a substantial proportion of income return • Complexity of income flows increases dramatically	• Comparable approach less reliable • Cash flow approaches typically used

Scenario 2 – Low hanging fruit only	Effects on pattern of occupation	Effects on asset	Implications for appraisal
• Real estate owners opportunistically service the tenant base in high-quality, multi-let, large-scale schemes • Real estate owners provide FM services to occupiers in high-quality, multi-let, large-scale schemes • Real estate owners (or coalitions of owners) combine with major utilities providers to provide utilities in high-quality, multi-let, large-scale schemes	• Bundling of space–services packages occurs in high-quality, multi-let, large scale schemes • Diversity of space–service–flexibility packages concentrated in high-quality, multi-let, large–scale schemes • Increased diversity of real estate management functions • Tiered market for properties requiring intensive and limited management	• Heterogeneity of real estate increases for certain categories of real estate only • Market transparency decreases for certain categories of real estate only • For the majority of buildings non-rental revenues account for a small proportion of income return	• Comparable approach less reliable for certain categories of real estate only • Cash flow approaches increasingly required for certain categories of real estate only

	Effects on pattern of occupation	Effects on asset	Implications for appraisal
• Real estate owners offer a range of web-based services to tenants in high-quality, multi-let, large-scale schemes • Real estate owners offer broadband services in high-quality, multi-let, large-scale schemes • Real estate owners develop a limited number of joint ventures and strategic alliances with business support services providers to a limited number of new products and services		• Complexity of income flows increases for certain categories of real estate only	

Scenario 3 – Proceed with caution

	Effects on pattern of occupation	Effects on asset	Implications for appraisal
• Real estate owners 'defensively' service the tenant base • Real estate owners provide FM services to occupiers only where the real estate and tenants demand it • Real estate owners leave provision of utilities to occupier • Real estate owners fail to offer a range of web-based services to tenants in high-quality, multi-let, large-scale schemes • Real estate owners offer broadband services only where and when competitive pressures force them • Real estate owners largely ignore the business support services sector	• Bundling of space–services packages rarely occurs • Diversity of space–service–flexibility packages is rare • Real estate management functions fail to change • Specialist market for properties requiring intensive and limited management	• Limited change within real estate sector • Market transparency remains stable • Non-rental revenues rarely account for a significant proportion of income return • Complexity of income flows remains stable	• The reliability of comparable approach is largely unchanged • Cash flow approaches rarely used

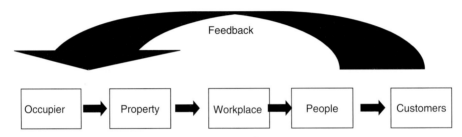

Figure 8.7   The scope of corporate real estate (adapted from Haynes *et al.* 2002).

physical ageing of property remains relatively slow but an organisation's needs change fast. Innovation in technology, the changing nature of business and environmental pressures are encouraging new ways of working.

The traditional role of CRE was to find facilities based on specifications set by corporate operations, negotiate the best price, manage the space, then dispose of it when no longer required. This typifies a transaction-based corporate real estate function, with the strategic decision making handled outside CRE (Veale 1989). Using this model the corporate real estate manager is not involved in the company's strategic planning process. Real estate decisions are made on a property-by-property basis with no overall guiding plan for real estate assets.

Research by Joroff *et al.* (1993) identified five evolutionary stages of corporate real estate unit development:

- taskmaster;
- controller;
- dealmaker;
- 'intrapreneur' (i.e. entrepreneur within a large firm); and
- business strategist.

This sequence identifies the move from the transaction-based focus of the traditional model to a modern strategic asset management role.

Increasing awareness of the importance of corporate property assets dates back to 1983 to when Zeckhauser & Silverman (1983) first observed that a major portion of all corporate assets (approximately 25% to 41%) were invested in real property, and Veale (1989) noted that occupancy costs of corporate space represented some 10% to 20% of operating expenses, or 41% to 50% of corporate net operating income. Over the ensuing 20 years, researchers (Veale 1989; Nourse 1990; Nourse & Roulac 1993; Rodriguez

& Sirmans 1996) have discussed the relative neglect of corporate real estate assets. Since 1992, the CRE management literature has begun to address issues in the context of wider business drivers (Joroff 1992; Nourse 1992; Duckworth 1993; Joroff *et al.* 1993; Becker & Joroff 1995; Lambert *et al.* 1995; Manning *et al.* 1999). Structural CRE issues such as outsourcing (Kimbler & Rutherford 1993; Bergsman 1994; Manning *et al.* 1997; Carn *et al.* 1999) and the contribution of CRE to shareholder wealth (Manning & Roulac 2001) have also been addressed.

The work of Franklin Becker particularly during this period has introduced some important concepts. The 'Total Workplace' (Becker & Steele 1995) is a flexible framework according to which employees are able to consider the entire office as their workplace. In other words, their work is not merely confined to their workstations, but rather wherever they work and are able to increase their productivity in the office premises, be it the cafeteria, boardroom, corridors or even restrooms. This directly relates to the idea of organisational ecology within which the total workplace exists. Organisational ecology here is the broader picture or business setting, which allows for this flexibility to arise and work towards the fundamental business goals of that organisation. Becker (1990) also identified a trend towards the centralisation and standardisation of facilities in corporations. The role of technology as a facilitator runs through the majority of this research.

The concept of the intelligent building attempts to define a framework in which the CRE manager operates. According to the Intelligent Building Institute (IBI) (reported in So *et al.* 1999), an Intelligent Building is one which provides a productive and cost-effective environment through optimisation of its structure, systems, services and management and the relationships between them (Figure 8.8).

Intelligent buildings help building owners, property managers, and occupants realise their goals in the areas of cost, comfort, convenience, safety, long-term flexibility and marketability. There is no intelligence threshold above which a building 'passes' or 'fails'. Optimal building intelligence is the matching of solutions to occupant needs. Furthermore, the IBI stated that 'there is no fixed set of characteristics that defines an Intelligent Building'. In fact, the only characteristic which they share is a structure designed to accommodate changes in a convenient, cost-effective manner.

CRE therefore encompasses all the aspects of real estate from the occupier's perspective, in particular:

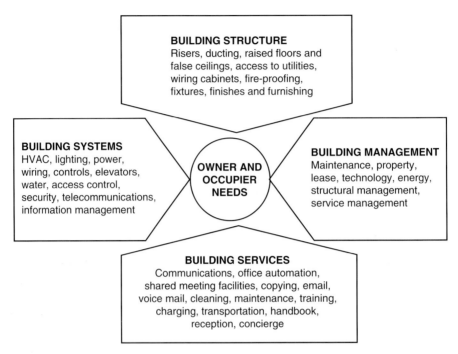

Figure 8.8   Intelligent buildings and occupier needs (adapted from So *et al.* 1999).

- **Occupied asset management** – in respect of tenure, location and suitability of the asset, together with its impact upon other aspects of the business.
- **Lease management** – with respect to operation and accounting.
- **Operational facilities management** – focused upon the efficient operation of the asset.

At one level this overlaps with the structure of the building owner and owner's manager; indeed the functionality is often identical since the occupier usually needs to know the same information. However, CRE is charged with the strategic management of the asset as economic capacity and consequently has a far wider remit. ICT has had an impact upon all these areas at both operational and structural levels.

Occupied asset management

The role of the occupier's asset manager is to deliver competitive advantage through the efficient use of capital to provide capacity for the business. Consequently this remit covers the strategic aspects of the asset, its location, operational efficiency and role in the business. It covers the following aspects:

- location/relocation;
- efficiency;
- lease management; and,
- contingency planning.

Location

The influence of ICT on location is evident in the provision of telecommunications infrastructure to specific sites and buildings. The provision of infrastructure to support voice telecommunications has been universal throughout developed economies for the last three decades. The growth of bespoke networking solutions has also facilitated a broadband infrastructure particularly in urban areas. However, the growth in demand for networking as business processes have become Internet enabled over the last decade has placed a considerable strain upon its provision in certain locations. ICT has also had an impact upon the ability to research and compare locations independent of third parties. The optimisation of location may be pulled by business development or pushed by cost or efficiency pressures. In all cases, the factors taken into account vary according to the broad nature of the accommodation required.

Table 8.4 shows some of the ICT influences applicable to different generic types of building. Each of these tools is available using geographic information systems (GIS) technology overlaid with spatially referenced information on, for example, labour availability and skills.

In some industries (for example, retailing) the location of premises is a crucial determinant in profitability and acquisition or relocation is an ongoing task, positioning the property to best serve the income stream. In others, consideration of location may be very rare, the optimum location being a function of proximity to a particular market or pool of labour specialism. The inertia of existing locations remains a powerful force, but through ICT it faces the threat of further erosion (see Box 8.2).

Table 8.4 Tools for locational analysis by use type.

Generic building type	ICT influence
Office	Labour catchment modelling
Manufacturing facility	Spatial modelling of distribution
Warehouse	Spatial modelling of supply chain
Shop	Demographic modelling

Box 8.2   Crossroads

Crossroads is a spatial interaction model developed by the RETRI Group that evaluates any given site (or set of co-ordinates) as a location for warehousing. The underlying assumption is that the optimum warehouse location for any supply chain is a function of the reach of the site in terms of consumption and the distance from importation or production. The model uses a GIS together with data on the location of production, the location and volume of imports and the location and numbers of population at settlement level. The objective of Crossroads was to create a variable that encapsulates demand for national or pan-national distribution facilities at a particular spatial reference point. For each chosen location the model produces a distribution quotient (DQ) using:

- the reach of the site – how many consumers can be reached within a 4.5 hour isochrone;
- the position of the site relative to the main ports for import/ export; and
- the position of the site relative to the main airports for import/export.

The distribution quotient is a weighted measure of the distribution suitability of the site from a demand perspective. A low DQ does not necessarily render a location bad for distribution. Other factors may counterbalance the score, including:

- particular distribution patterns in terms of volume;
- the value of the product being distributed; or
- distribution to a particular network of locations.

The primary use of Crossroads is at the site appraisal stage of an acquisition when it can be used to compare the site with benchmarks developed for pan-European, national, regional and local distribution. It has also been used to evaluate existing portfolios to show the potential for distribution uses.

Operational efficiency

Workplace efficiency is a function of the interaction between process and space. An efficient workplace is one in which the facilities provided exactly match the requirements of the process. As a result, this covers the accommodation of alternative working practices, workplace planning, and the monitoring of the performance of the workplace itself.

Figure 8.9 shows the potential stakeholder groups and working practices that need to be supported by workplace planning. Each of these groups has the potential to place demands upon operational space. In purely practical terms these demands may include:

- extension of the working day – the ability to have full access to workplace facilities at any time;

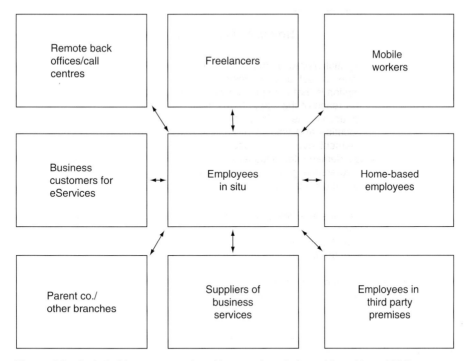

Figure 8.9 Stakeholder groups and working practices (adapted from Huws 2001).

- mobility inside and outside the premises – the ability to work anywhere, inside or outside the workplace; and
- reduced or eliminated territorial space within the building – changing the balance between dedicated and shared facilities.

Workplace planning strategies to meet these kinds of demand are predicated upon a strong ICT infrastructure. A secure, robust network with facilities for remote and mobile working is a prerequisite for planning a workplace of any size. However, these methods of working also place demands upon other aspects of asset management including:

- asset identification and control – mobility of work implies mobility of corporate assets such as computers, mobile phones and PDAs;
- health and safety compliance – may need to be extended to remote locations, employees' homes for example; and
- support and maintenance – mobility also offers up a higher probability that computers will be damaged and that breakdowns will happen in remote locations.

Asset location and control is a feature of computer assisted facilities management (CAFM) systems. Typically CAFM systems are designed to identify and keep track of people, places and things.

In a survey for CoreNet and CB Richard Ellis (NOP 2003), 85% of the companies responding indicated that they had implemented alternative working practices within the last two years. Home working (52%) and hot-desking/hotelling (52%) were the main practices adopted together with flexible working hours (41%). In order to manage space efficiency effectively this must be measurable. Research by NOP for Ernst & Young (2002) showed that 23% of respondents used no formal measurement of what is likely to be one of the most important areas of cost (Figure 8.10). For the 77% that are measuring the efficiency of space within the organisation, however, this research demonstrates the importance of information to CRE.

Contingency planning
The provision of capacity to the business is doubly important in the event of threats to physical plant or locations. Research by Witty and Scott (2001) showed that two out of five enterprises that experience a disaster – such as the World Trade Center attack – go out of business within five years. ICT is not just critical to the protection of corporate records, but also in the ability to switch to an alternative workplace in the event of disaster, and this has also been recognised as a strong driver by the Lyons review (2004)

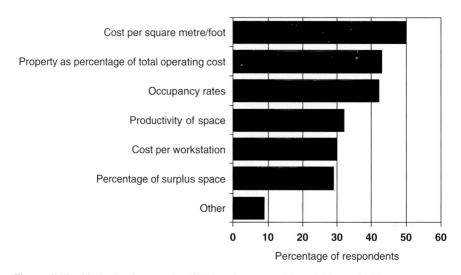

Figure 8.10   Methods of measuring CRE performance (Ernst & Young 2002).

in its analysis of UK government department relocation from London and the South East. Elliot *et al.* (2002) also describe business continuity management (BCM) as a new and evolving discipline, the roots of which lie in information systems (IS) protection. They go on to identify that technological advances, specifically in the areas of information technology, were key to the development of BCM.

Lease management

Lease management covers the complete spectrum of financial and management accounting but at its core has developed from rent and service charge accounting programmes developed for landlords. The main impact of ICT upon value has been to facilitate the maintenance of a detailed record. Operationally, CRE asset management systems cover areas such as location, valuation, depreciation and document management. Increasingly applications such as lifecycle management and asset utilisation tools are also being provided.

Operational facilities management

In its broadest interpretation, facility management (FM) co-ordinates the physical resources of an organisation. Becker (1990) describes it thus:

> Facility management is responsible for coordinating all efforts related to planning, designing, and managing buildings and their systems, equipment, and furniture to enhance the organisation's ability to compete successfully in a rapidly changing world.

However, in the context of this chapter, this definition describes the totality of the occupier's role rather than the operational nature of FM described here. Given the breadth of this interpretation it is clear that FM runs laterally through the hierarchy of an organisation, servicing and interacting with all functions and levels.

In some respects FM is a project management discipline, particularly with respect to the implementation of change. In most cases, however, it is characterised primarily by a service ethic providing an optimum working environment. FM can be subdivided into services concerned with the physical fabric of a building, access or environmental control, for example, and services concerned with its occupation such as catering, cleaning, security, postroom and concierge. From an ICT perspective the latter are concerned with monitoring and control, while the former may have application considerations.

Detailed considerations of hardware for monitoring and control are outside the scope of this book. However, hardware sensors and actuators have long been a feature of building control systems covering areas such as access control, security and environmental management. The majority of these devices are either used in complex specialist systems, fire control for example, or in small closed loop situations, proximity switches controlling lighting in lavatories perhaps. Although effective in isolation, these systems suffer from a number of problems:

- Monitoring and evaluation is either done retrospectively on the basis of data captured by the system or visually, requiring regular on-site inspections.
- Typically the systems are stand-alone and cannot be easily balanced at a building level.
- Cabling systems are complex and independent.

The growth of Computer Aided Facilities Management (CAFM), together with changes in sensor technology, is are improving the efficiency and resilience of these systems. Finch (2003) reports that in 1997, the US President's advisors on science and technology asserted that the development of wireless sensors could improve production efficiency in the manufacturing sector by 10% and reduce emissions by more than 25%.

In essence a smart sensor can be thought of as a 'network-enabled sensor'. It involves the integration of a sensor with signal processing and network communications. Added to this are the capabilities of modern battery technology and radio telemetry.

In essence, a smart sensor can be thought of as a 'network-enabled processor' that:

- makes logical decisions at the source of the information, either acting on that information or passing on a rich message rather than raw data;
- can receive and send data;
- is able to perform self-testing and adaptive calibration; and,
- offers a simple set-up process.

The combination of CAFM with smart sensors and broadband allows the creation of a system that monitors and balances the environment in a building, interfaces with fire control and security systems, manages access control and facilitates maintenance, thereby improving asset life. Using broadband means that cabling systems for data, control, video and audio systems can be routed via a common carrier cabling infrastructure, eliminating the problems of complex stand-alone wiring loops. Additionally the control and monitoring of these systems can be undertaken remotely giving the opportunity for buildings to be managed from different time zones to cover 24-hour working.

Appraisers

Real estate change and the valuation profession

Like many other professional functions, valuation has been transformed by the development and application of specialist software.[4] This considerably improved the productivity of valuation professionals and either reduced the cost of and/or improved the quality of valuations. However, the changes discussed above in terms of increased heterogeneity in lease practices and occupational forms have also impacted upon the nature of the task being performed. In essence, the cash flows generated are becoming both more complicated and diverse. Complex cash flows are not difficult to price when there are numerous similar assets being traded. Their prices can be observed and the information applied appropriately. Problems emerge when there is complexity without reliable market pricing signals. This has posed new problems.

Purposes of valuations

Property owners and investors may require valuations of their property assets for a number of purposes:

- Sale/acquisition process.
- Performance measurement.
- Public accounts.
- Lending.
- Insurance.

Valuation is essentially an attempt to estimate market price. Formally, market value is defined as:

> The estimated amount for which a property should exchange on the date of the valuation between a willing buyer and a willing seller in an arm's-length transaction after property marketing wherein the parties have each acted knowledgeably, prudently and without compulsion.

This has become the internationally accepted definition of market value.

The valuation profession in the UK is also increasingly being asked to provide calculations of 'investment value' (or 'worth'). The RICS has adopted the international definition of investment value, which is:

> The value of the property to a particular investor, or class of investors, for identified investment objectives.

This subjective concept relates specific property to a specific investor, group of investors or entity with identifiable investment objectives and/ or criteria. It covers both the individual and the group.

In the UK, the majority of mainstream commercial property assets are valued (market value is estimated) by the income approach. This involves the application of a capitalisation rate (the all-risks yield) to the income stream. In essence, it is a comparison approach. The capitalisation rate is generally derived from the analysis of market transactions involving comparable properties. Given the effects of the heterogeneity of the property market, thin trading and lengthy transaction times, valuers are required to adjust market-derived capitalisation rates to reflect variations between comparables and the subject property. The main task of the valuer is to obtain data on market transactions and perceptions and apply this information to the subject property.

Consequently, the efficiency and reliability of this method are dependent upon the availability of transaction evidence. Where income profiles are similar, for instance where a single lease structure dominates the market, capitalisation rates derived from transactions involving comparable assets with similar income streams will provide a good indication of market value. Relative homogeneity in income profile is therefore an important variable. It seems reasonable to propose that the more heterogeneous income profiles become, the less efficient will be comparison methodologies.

Flexi-leases and serviced offices

Driven partially by the need for corporate flexibility and agility, we have already seen earlier in this chapter that there is now more diversity of lease lengths creating, in turn, more diversity in expected cash flows from property assets. The result is that valuation practice is having to adapt. There are a wide variety of factors affecting the financial implications of short leases and break clauses. Valuers are faced with the task of reflecting the rental and capital value implications of this diversity within their appraisals. It is well documented that when faced with relatively novel lease structures, valuers tend to adopt conservative practices. Indeed there are rational grounds for such an approach. Consistent with other appraisal approaches to 'anomalies', the initial research on this topic found that valuers tend to use rather *ad hoc* adjustments to reflect the effects of break clauses (Herd & Lizieri 1994). Although it may be argued that any application of generalised risk adjustments by market participants to account for uncertainty should also be used by valuers in assessing market values, previous research has shown that established rules-of-thumb in valuation practice are often at odds with activities in the market or that there is diversity of application within the market (O'Roarty *et al.* 1997). Further, given the combination of asset heterogeneity, confidentiality and 'thin' trading, the usefulness of direct comparison methods of valuation will be limited.

The growth of the serviced office market has also raised a number of questions for appraisers. Critically their appraisal has blurred the boundaries between market value and investment value. There is much debate in the serviced office sector about whether there is a mismatch between price and worth. There are numerous reasons why the 'rental' differences between the serviced office sector and traditional office accommodation appear to be so large. First, we are not comparing like with like. In a traditional office the tenant, or their outsourced supplier, is responsible for providing the FM services, the office infrastructure and the office management services. These total to a significant expense, but one which occupiers are often unable to quantify. Assessing whether the overall charge for a serviced office is reasonable is, therefore, difficult.

Additionally, serviced offices offer a level of flexibility not found in the traditional office market both in terms of speed of access and length of stay. Both of these have considerable value to an occupier for certain types of activities or business situations. It could be argued that this value should be passed to the serviced office operator for the extra risk they are carrying. Therefore, estimating the worth of serviced offices becomes more problematic. It is necessary not only to understand the property income and costs but also the service-related income and costs. Furthermore, the 'appropriate' level of profitability needs to be estimated, reflecting both the risk and entrepreneurial skill.

Valuing the more unusual contractual arrangements with profit-related elements has often posed problems for appraisers. Rather than using traditional approaches, more transparent appraisal techniques using cash flows and an explicit assessment of risk tend to be required. Considering what a serviced office operator could pay for a particular property requires a real understanding of both the business potential of a unit and the total cost of fitting out, servicing and managing that space. As with undertaking any appraisal to assess the residual income, it is also necessary to include a profit element for the serviced office operator. An assessment of worth is, therefore, only really possible through a full cash flow analysis with each of the figures estimated, and the sources of risk identified through sensitivity analysis. This cash flow analysis will be an integral part of any appraisal, not least because it gives the required information base for an appraisal report.

Revenue from services

The appraisal of revenue raised from the provision of services to tenants raises some similar issues to serviced offices. A critical question concerning the effect of non-rental revenues is whether income goes with the property or to landlord. Two key questions emerge:

- Is it reasonable to expect that the income stream will remain with the property upon disposal?
- Does the generation of revenues from the provision of services affect the revenues from rent?

Although it has already been noted that there is an emerging recognition that the different elements of the income stream in a property investment can be stripped out and sold separately, it is also clear that investors do feel that some of the revenues from services provision are inextricably linked to ownership. In the case of broadband, existing owners feel that it is very unlikely that they would retain broadband revenues from an asset subsequent to disposal of the freehold. In essence, the rationale was that prospective purchasers would regard it as an encumbrance to their management of the asset. Thus, liquidity, investment demand and values may be adversely affected. Where contracts exist, the solution has been to allow for them to be assigned upon disposal.

With regard to the second question, the bundling of space and service provision, especially where there is a unitary charge, has the potential to create problems of market transparency for valuers. Valuers have always experienced problems in making price and valuation adjustments to reflect non-standard lease terms. For instance, differences in liability for repair and maintenance have tended to be accounted for by crude measures. It is possible to identify a number of potential effects:

- **Blurring** – where unitary charging occurs it may be difficult to disentangle the charge for the rent and other services. A good example is serviced offices where the tenant pays a single charge for rent, flexibility of entry and exit, office infrastructure, running costs and support services.
- **Substitution** – particularly where some of the services are high margin, landlords may opt to accept a lower rent to obtain contracts to provide these services. This is analogous the activities of companies such as CE Capital and Rolls Royce who sell capital equipment at a loss where they can secure the contracts to maintain, service and finance the purchasing of the equipment. Alternatively, the landlord can opt to provide services at cost (or even below cost) in the expectation of achieving higher rents instead of additional revenue streams.
- **Enhancement** – where the services are better than average, tenants may pay a higher rent to access them (as long as superior provision of services exists). This is likely to place increased importance on factors such as branding, reputation, quality of business model, etc. In many cases, rental 'premiums' paid for access to superior services will not be sustainable as other property owners react and mimic. However, owners able to establish a strong reputation and brand may be able to maintain higher rents in the medium to long term. Further, it is implicit in the defensive motivation of a number of major property owners that the objective is to maintain rental income rather than generate additional revenues. One motivation of investors in providing services has been to make tenants 'stickier' in order to reduce the costs associated with tenant vacation.

It is evident from this discussion that, in addition to generating additional income, the provision of services is capable of having compound effects on the rental income stream from a property asset. It is possible to envisage circumstances where the valuer will need to be able to allocate the rental income (separate from income generated by payment for services) that is being paid for:

- the occupation of the property;
- the provision of services where no explicit charging takes place;
- access to the ability to source high-quality services and, if appropriate;
- the provision of these services by an organisation with an established reputation, successful track record and brand.

Further, the valuer may have to assess the extent to which a 'premium' rent is attached to the property. As we have noted above, typically it will dissipate after either a sale of the building to a new owner or the setting of a new rent.

A number of salient points for valuers came out of the discussions of flexi-leases, serviced offices and revenues from services:

- There may be a 'skills gap' since not all valuers are comfortable with business valuation techniques. It is no coincidence that where these skills have been required in the past, it has been accountants or specialists who have taken a share of the business.
- Understanding the risk–return characteristics of non-rental income streams in terms of transferability, growth, sustainability and risk will become increasingly important as the relative size of these income streams grows.
- Understanding the interdependencies between rental income and the level and quality of the provision of additional services will be a key issue in the long term.

More obviously, professional guidance will need to reflect the changing nature of the valuation process implied by this analysis.

Brokers

Disintermediation

The real estate market has historically been characterised by a lack of transparency. Real estate is a non-standardised product, where buyers and sellers have often lacked information. Yet, real estate is an information-intensive and information-driven business, heavily transaction based with high value and asset specificity (Crowston & Wigand 1999; Crowston *et al.* 2001). This is also true of real estate brokers or agents. Agents act as the connection between buyers and sellers in what Buxmann and Gebauer (1998) refer to as a 'centralised market'. Brokers (or agents)[5] therefore act as intermediaries between sellers and buyers in both residential and commercial markets, not only to help match demand and supply, but also to improve market co-ordination and help the market reach equilibrium point (see Box 2.2, page 56). Intermediaries in the real estate business also exhibit some of the 'critical mass' effects achieved by other types of network: therefore the more buyers an intermediary serves, the higher the value for sellers wanting to use the intermediary as a distribution channel, and the same effect holds true for the buyer. In a market with n sellers and m buyers therefore, an intermediary reduces the number of contacts from

n^*m to $n + m$ (Baligh & Richartz 1967), and as long as the information costs are the same within the network, the available intermediaries will provide overall value provided these costs are zero. This is represented by Figure 8.11 which shows the reduction in links between a centralised and fragmented market.

The Internet provides the potential to create an even more centralised market by transforming the role of the intermediary, and the process of removing the middleman from a transaction has commonly been referred to as 'disintermediation' (see also Box 2.2 and Chapter 5). As Tapscott (1995: 56) put it:

> Middleman functions between producers and consumers are being eliminated through digital networks. Middle businesses, functions, and people need to move up the food chain to create new value, or they face being disintermediated.

At that time, during the mid-1990s, the conventional wisdom that emerged from much of the management and eCommerce literature was that the Internet would mean the death of the middleman (see, for example, Baatz 1996). In the case of real estate brokers, buyers and sellers would be brought together by real estate information provided on the web. In fact, as Evans and Wurster (2000) point out, disintermediation is not new: bankers used the term in the 1970s to describe how securities markets could displace corporate banking and how money market funds captured a large portion of deposits from retail banks. Moreover, they suggest that disintermediation has two meanings:

- Instances where the ultimate supplier of a good or service sells directly to customers by short-circuiting the intermediary.[6]

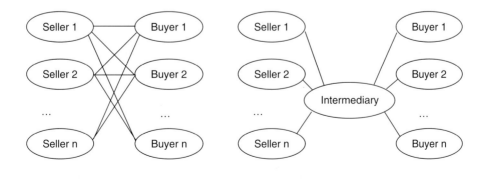

Figure 8.11   Basic market forms (Buxmann & Gebauer 1998).

- The emergence of a new intermediary who employs a lower cost way of distributing the good, or service, in place of the existing intermediary.

However, others (see Garven 2002, for example) have used the term 're-intermediation' (Table 8.5) to encapsulate new forms of intermediation. Moreover, the term 'transintermediation' has been used to conceptualise the situation where offline middlemen are replaced by online specialists (Birch *et al.* 2000).

The situation is therefore a complex one, with transintermediation and reintermediation becoming commonplace in real estate markets. The Internet does, however, offer a number of advantages to the agency/broker-age industry because the real estate value chain is founded on the exchange of commodity goods and services. These include (Dixon & Marston 2001):

- reduced transaction costs through reduced property search costs; a reduction in co-ordination costs; and faster and more efficient negotiating; and
- closer customer contact through improved customer service and customer loyalty as well as new customer relationships.

The real estate agency industry therefore offers a large potential for eCommerce because of its nature (i.e. people intensive; paper intensive; time intensive; information intensive; work intensive and fragmented). Essentially by listing properties on the Internet, a broker is transferring the cost of the property search to the buyer (Gwin 2004), although a broker can risk disintermediation if too much information is provided, which is why almost no real estate websites provide full address details. Before the Internet, the business model for agency was very much a 'gateway'

Table 8.5 Intermediaries (adapted from Birch *et al.* 2000).

Disintermediation	Transintermediation	Reintermediation
Middlemen disappear . . .	*Middlemen migrate to the Internet . . .*	*New types of middlemen set up on the Internet . . .*
Digital products	Brokerage business	Virtual markets
• Software • Information • Music • Travel	• Discount brokers • Employment agencies • Dating agencies • Real estate agents/brokers	• Industry specific (autos) • Auctions • Internet services • Search engines • Marketing • Payment services

(Tuccillo 1999) with the real estate professional guiding the buyer through the real estate purchase process. Key to this process were people, organisational and networking skills. Multiple listing in the USA was part of this process and roughly 80% of homes bought and sold in the USA were through an agent. The Internet's arrival was set to change all of that, but how much difference has it really made?

In practice, Gwin (2004) found that, internationally, brokers tend to provide more information on their websites if their prospective buyers have high search costs, and that brokers do tend to take disintermediation into account when deciding how much information to provide on their websites. Green and Vandell (2001) suggest that lower level product innovations (Table 8.6) such as information gathering and analysis are being provided first and most completely by the Internet, but they also believe there is scope for greater consolidation in the sector. Buxmann and Gebauer (1998), on the other hand, see the Internet as offering new opportunities for agents and brokers: global markets become a reality and so the numbers of potential buyers and sellers entering the marketplace may increase. Competition is therefore potentially increased, and may lead to further specialisation with unbundling of services and more outsourcing of functions (perhaps mimicking the horizontal and vertical division of work, or 'flexible specialization', among flexible companies, highlighted in the work of Pralahad and Hamel 1990).

In the commercial brokerage market Gyourko and Nakahara (2001) estimate the industry in the USA is worth some $11.8 bn in commissions. They also suggest that ICT is likely to bring about three broad changes in the commercial brokerage industry in the USA:

- Development of new, specialist firms which perform only part of the brokerage process such as the research or listings function. This has been directly promoted by the web and the lowering of inter-firm transaction costs has allowed greater global reach (for example, the CoStar Group in the USA). There is therefore likely to be competition for such business between a stand-alone, for-profit firm, versus a co-operative, multiple-listing type arrangement that is anchored in the brokerage community. Ultimately it is likely that research and listings/marketing will be outsourced to specialist firms, however.
- Outsourcing promoted from traditional brokerage with a growing emphasis on project-based fees (fees per hour) rather than commission-based fees. Research, for example, may be increasingly outsourced as a discrete function (see also Arthur Andersen 2000). Also, increased transparency through the web will drive clients' demands for a fee

Table 8.6 Opportunities to apply Internet technology to the real estate market (adapted from Green & Vandell 2001).

Information
- Property listing services (sales, leasing)
- Property sales and rental information
- Property performance information
- Assessment/real estate tax data
- Legal conditions
- Market data – current and historical
- Available financing terms
- Secondary market/pool data
- Zoning and planning information
- Mapping data
- Architectural drawings/specifications and plan data
- Personnel data

Analysis
- Market and feasibility analysis (including acquisition, disposition, redevelopment)
- Appraisal/assessment
- Portfolio diversification
- Deal structuring
- Tax analysis
- Accounting
- Property management
- Asset management
- Institutional structuring/office management
- Default, interest rate, prepayment risk evaluation
- Pricing of loans and pools
- Due diligence
- Employment decisions and performance evaluation

Transaction facilitation online
- Sales and leasing
- Loan application and approval
- B2B procurement (e-commerce)
- Joint product offerings (e-commerce services for tenants)
- Tax payment
- Purchase of syndication units
- Secondary market/pool purchases and sales
- Contracting for maintenance services and repair
- Insurance purchasing (property, liability, mortgage)
- Bill paying (on-line banking)
- Employee acquisition retention/disposition(?)

Transformation of the transaction function online
- Shop.bots (search engines for related/competing services)
- Property auctions for sales or leasing
- Central auction market for security interests (REITs, REOCs, MBS, CMBS)
- Central auctions market for B2B procurement
- Central auctions for maintenance services and repairs
- Central auctions for insurance (property, liability, mortgage)
- Central auctions for temporary workers

structure akin to other service professions (for example, lawyers and accountants).

- Discount brokerage models, with a growing emphasis on smaller, relatively low-margin transactions. Here the business model mirrors the high-volume low-cost approach of discount stock firms such as Charles Schwab, which gave rise to pure Internet-based companies such as E*Trade. This is already being seen with the growth of tenant representative services online (search, negotiation and execution through Tenantwise.com in the USA, for example).

Theoretical approaches to transformation

ICT is frequently described as a transformational technology because of its perceived power to transform entire industries. Size and complexity issues, however, often rule out anything more than superficial studies (Dess & Beard 1984; Crowston *et al.* 2001).

Indeed much research at this level has been limited to examining simple relationships between use of ICT (for example, measured by investment) and industry-level outcomes (for example, firm size, or profitabilty). Crowston *et al.* (2001) therefore argue that deeper studies are needed to understand ICT transformation and this is especially the case with the real estate brokerage industry. In these terms, they view ICT use as being enacted by individuals who through their actions adapt their work in response to ICT. This is also associated (Figure 8.12) with changes in (Crowston *et al.* 2001):

- organisational process, or the way in which tasks are undertaken and performed;
- organisational structure, which reflects how individuals are organised for management and reporting;
- industry structures, which reflect the division of work among companies (i.e. boundaries between firms); and,
- value chains, which are processes extending across a number of firms.

These changes must also be seen in the context of strong organisation and industry forces influencing work patterns (Abbott 1995), which also affect how individuals do their work. In the case of real estate, despite the impact of multiple listings services, agents/brokers still continue to have privileged physical access to listed properties, which is independent of the ICT system itself.

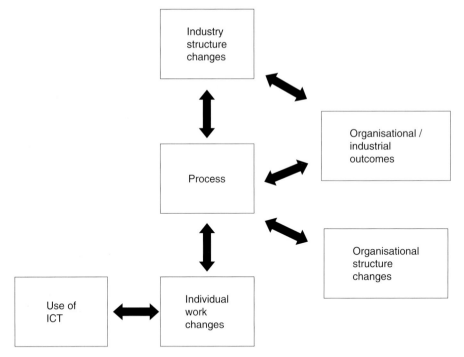

Figure 8.12 Conceptual framework for ICT transformation (adapted from Crowston *et al.* 2001).

At an industry level, the logic of this framework is that (in conceptual terms) to understand ICT transformation in the real estate agency industry, we must understand individual, organisational, and industrial levels simultaneously. Crowston *et al.* (2001) therefore adopt a 'structuration theory' approach based on the work of Orlikowski (1992), which is founded on the idea that human actors or agents are at once both enabled and constrained by structures, which themselves are the result of previous actions by agents. The resultant social system consists of rules and resources used in the everyday interaction of agents. Crowston *et al.* (2001) use this framework to examine the residential real estate industry in the USA. They found that from a market/economic perspective ICT growth is creating the mechanism for disintermediation. However, in practice real estate agents were helping to restructure their roles, by refocusing their business on service with the provision of resources from their social network such as information on mortgage providers, house inspectors and skilled workers. In this way they provided a value-added service to potential buyers. Also agents were guiding both buyers and sellers through a series of steps to complete the transaction. This suggests that real estate agents were fulfilling three distinct roles as a result of ICT impact:

- information intermediaries between buyers and sellers;
- drawing on large social networks to provide value-added services; and,
- acting as process or transaction consultants.

Although ICT is impacting on the first component, agents are still using their knowledge to create new roles for themselves (see also Dermisi 2002). This suggests that ICT is both the product and shaper of human action. For example, increased use of web-based systems can both help and harm agents' current roles: help by extending the agent's ability to market listings and harm by reducing the agent's control over information, thus allowing other intermediaries to participate.

Evidence of transformation

Property or real estate is a unique product, and so the informational content of a transaction is high, which means that any principal or intermediary has to supply the relevant information that allows parties to reach agreement on price. However, this leads to a high degree of fragmentation, with many smaller players (Dixon & Marston 2001). The trend in the UK has been towards a one-stop shop service, which mirrors the evolution in the USA. The number of consumers and real estate providers using the Internet has increased dramatically. According to NAR (1999) the number of buyers using the Internet to search for homes increased from 2% in 1995 to more than 55% in 2001. Muhanna (2000) suggested that in the USA, buyers' searching was most impacted by the Internet, followed by property listing and property evaluating. Negotiating and executing were seen as more risky, however, and this point was also highlighted by Chin and Liu (2004).[7] Examples of sites providing residential listings in the UK include:

- Asserta.com, which lists some 200 000 properties with one-third of UK estate agents online;
- Rightmove, the website of Countrywide Assured; and
- Fish4homes, with some 300 000 properties, including other services, such as legal advice and mortgage information.

As regards commercial property listings in the UK, we have certainly come a long way since the mid-1980s when online property services such as Focus, Pride and Applied Property Research began life. These were dial-up subscription services with no agreed standards and were relatively expensive. Perhaps in those days the property industry was more 'technophobic' than it is today and the added value of using data as a resource was not generally recognised. Moreover, strategic alliances in the property industry were not the norm, and UK practices tended to compete rather than collaborate. But as Mantle (2001) points out, various factors changed all this. The late 1990s property boom gave added impetus to growth in the property service industry and many European property advisers founded strategic alliances with their US counterparts who had already implemented sophisticated IT systems. Commercially based pressures were also impacting at this time (Dixon & Marston 2001):

- Barriers to entry fell because property services became easier and less costly to supply over the web, and this was overlaid by a move to outsourcing generally across the service sector.
- Firm differentiation became easier.
- Data were no longer proprietary in nature.
- Critical mass became an issue, as size of firm is dependent on the demand for particular services. Firms had to decide whether to stay small or expand and merge.
- Capital resources became a critical issue as property service providers became listed companies, and had to battle to maintain market share in a world with reduced margins and competition for capital.

In general, therefore, increased fee pressures, reduced margins and lower profits have reinforced the impact of eCommerce and the web and the way data and information are rapidly migrating from the virtual world. A key development in the commercial property world was the launch of Estates Gazette Interactive in 1997, which offered industry news, a large database of articles and market information as well as add-on services. Similarly Property Link became the UK's first commercial property listing service. Other services are included in Box 8.3.

Box 8.3   Commercial property listings in the UK

This is a rapidly evolving marketplace but at the time of writing, key examples from the UK include:

- PropexProfessional – a subscriber investment marketplace (www. primepitch. com).
- Primepitch – subscriber investment service (www.primepitch.com).[8]
- First Property Online – property investment exchange (www.fprop.com).
- EGPropertyLink – open access property service (www.egipropertylink. com).
- Pridenet – database of commercial property with over 17 000 available properties (www.2pride.com).

Summary

This chapter has shown how ICT, in conjunction with other related forces for change, has transformed key areas of real estate service provision, including those services provided by:

- owners and owners' managers;
- occupiers and occupiers' managers;
- appraisers; and
- brokers.

This has come at a time when important changes have occurred in the procurement of real estate, including new developments in corporate finance; deconstructed real estate asset provision; flexible leases; corporate outsourcing; and bundled service provision. Part 3 of the book draws together key themes from previous sections and poses some searching questions for the future. The first part of Chapter 9 begins with a summary of the main themes emerging from this transformation of real estate products and services.

Notes

1   e-BusinessW@tch (2002) categorises the 'real estate sector' according to the NACE rev 1 classification which combines letting, broking and managing real estate. Real estate activities are very much part of the service sector and are distinct from construction activities, which also includes architects and real estate banks and funds.
2   For instance, entry to the market for FM and fit-out services can be viewed as forward vertical integration whilst for relocation services it can be seen as a form of backward integration.
3   Activities are defined as complementary when the cost of producing one reduces the cost of doing the other.
4   For an historical perspective see Dixon *et al.* (1991).
5   The terms 'real estate broker' and 'estate agent' are used interchangeably in this chapter. The former is generally used in the USA and the latter in the UK. The term 'agent' in the latter should be distinguished from the use of the term 'agent' in the actor network theory and related theories.
6   Monks (2004) highlights Office of Fair Trading evidence in the UK to suggest that 10% people now sell houses privately in the UK. HouseWeb.com has seen a dramatic increase in private business sales since 1996, with some 3500 properties online. Other evidence of house sales on eBay also exists.

7 In the USA, the Electronic Signatures in Global and National Commerce Act, or E-Sign legislation, was passed in 2000, and this reduced many of the barriers to paperless transactions. In the UK, the equivalent legislation is the Electronic Communications Act 2000 and the Land Registration Act 2002.

8 Propex own both the PropexProfessional service and Prime Pitch service.

Part 3

THE FUTURE

9

New Directions and Policy Implications: The Future of Real Estate in the New Economy

Introduction

In Part 1 of this book we examined the ways in which ICT has, in alliance with a range of social, economic and political factors, led to a transformation in the ways that businesses, governments and citizens interact economically, socially and culturally. We argued that ICT cannot be treated in isolation: to do so is to be guilty of technological determinism. We also examined the concept of a new economy (as part of the information society) and highlighted an increasing body of evidence to support the view that such an economy is not only strongly technology driven, but that productivity, organisational structures and consumer demand patterns are also interacting and creating a potent mix of forces for change. We also suggested that any form of technology can only be understood in the context of forces which shape and are shaped by it. Our perspective therefore led us to formulate a 'socio-technical framework', which we believe is the first time that such an approach has been adopted at a real estate level[1] in explaining ICT transformation.

In Part 2 of this book we looked in more detail at how ICT was transforming real estate products/assets and services. We examined how concepts of space were changing, as ICT transformed real estate markets. We also saw how the concepts of traditional real estate use were becoming blurred through a combination of technology-led change with other social and economic factors. This was creating flux and change in location; layout and intensity of use; leasing arrangements; value and market patterns; and support services. In the same way, ICT was transforming real estate services such as trading, valuation and management operations, and therefore altering the very nature of the relationships between real estate clients and their advisors.

In the final part of this book (Part 3), which comprises the current chapter, we seek to draw together the key themes of the book, and to look not only to the future evolution of real estate in the new economy and the related research agenda, but also to the policy implications of the transformations we have highlighted in this book. To do this, we pose some key questions:

- How successful is the socio-technical framework at explaining real estate transformation?
- What new forms of real estate have emerged as a result of technological change in the new economy?
- How can existing property cope with technological change, and what are the implications in terms of depreciation and obsolescence?
- What are the policy implications of ICT transformation for real estate?
- What are the future visions of real estate?
- Is there still a future for real estate in the new economy?

To address these questions, the chapter is divided into the following sections:

- A review of the socio-technical framework.
- New forms of real estate.
- Implications for existing buildings.
- Policy implications.
- Future visions.

The socio-technical framework

The framework that we have adopted in this book has always sought to place ICT in context. We have contended throughout the book that ICT must be seen in the context of stakeholder interaction, set within a framework that reflects social economic and political factors. In many ways, we believe that the role of ICT has frequently been either underplayed or overplayed by those examining and analysing its transformative effect on real estate.

'Sceptics' have frequently argued that the case for technological change is either not proven, or is modified by institutional or market barriers in what are inherently conservative or change-resistant domains. In other words, the lack of impact is due to the fact that many managers have insufficient power or authority to influence corporate strategy, or that institutional lease structures work against change (see, for example, Lizieri 2003). Spinks (2002) has also highlighted the importance of cultural and human resource management (HRM) issues in a Japanese context, and how HRM legacy can affect the adoption of new work practices.

However, recent research (see, for example, Dixon & Marston 2002; Marston & Dixon 2003; Worzala *et al.* 2002; Dixon *et al.* 2002a, 2003) has found a growing impact of ICT in both the retail and office sectors. Also, in our view the issue is not one of lack of impact of ICT; rather, part of the problem with much of the research in this field is that it is often cross-sectional in nature, preferring to take snapshots in time rather than tracking trends longitudinally in the same organisations. This suggests we may therefore be missing changes caused by ICT, because in organisational management and business process, the changes are much harder to map. Often, the majority of studies do not explicitly compare current working practices with historic work practices; it is inherently more difficult to identify 'step changes' in process if you have only recently become part of the 'revolution' in technology, and part of the issue may also be connected with who is surveyed in these studies, what their role is in the organisation, and how they see technological change as altering their business models. Focusing too narrowly on the institutional barriers to ICT could therefore compound the problems we must resolve in order to measure and identify the precise nature and impact of technological change.

In contrast, many at the opposite end of the spectrum (i.e. those that have overplayed the ICT impact) have heralded and hyped the role of ICT in creating huge transformations and upheavals in real estate markets, leading to reductions in floor-space demand (retail and offices are prime cases). Such views fall into the trap of technological determinism, which is predicated on the belief that ICT acts in a linear fashion, and frequently eschews any form of social or economic context to the transformation (see, for example, Borsuk 1999).

In our view, both perspectives may be contested, and both oversimplify and miss the point. This is on the basis of a number of counts, which are now summarised.

Barriers and research focus

Some survey evidence has often suggested that new work practices promoted by ICT may in some instances lie outside corporate culture (see, for example, Gerald Eve 2001). Although cultural and institutional barriers are important, however, there is growing evidence of productivity change from ICT feeding through into the economy, into businesses and into new working practices, all of which is a result of organisational change and related economic and social factors acting in unison.

But the research focus of studies does have a strong bearing on what is taken from the evidence, as we saw earlier in this section. For example, we may also be seeing the effect of SME response in some surveys: where these companies form a large proportion of the sample, they may also be more resistant to ICT implementation because of their size. This point has been the subject of much concern at a national policy level in the UK, and research by Dixon *et al.* (2002a) (and Dixon *et al.* 2003) found substantial evidence of a digital divide in the City of London in terms of size and access to ICT with smaller companies less likely to have evidence of ICT transformation.[2] Also, those studies that simply focus on large, best practice exemplars can be accused of skewed analysis, because their sample does not represent the real-world size distribution of companies. Finally, the trend towards younger managers who are more ICT literate than their forebears is also bound to reduce corporate conservatism in ICT implementation.

Real estate assets and service provision

New kinds of real estate have emerged (for example, call centres, data centres and serviced offices) and real estate service provision has been transformed through the provision of online listing services, bundled service provision and shorter leases, again driven by technology acting with other forces. This has had implications for the way in which real estate managers manage buildings and client relations and the way in which appraisers, FM specialists, and brokers all offer services. Arthur Andersen (2000), for example, suggest eight possible future business models to unlock the value chain for real estate service provision:

- **Advertising**: advertising through owned channel on behalf of product or service suppliers.
- **Direct commerce**: supply of product directly to customers, bypassing other channel intermediaries.

- **Transaction facilitation**: facilitates the matching of buyers or sellers in any market.
- **Service provision**: provision of a general or specialist service to the customer, often on an *ad hoc* basis.
- **Utility provision**: provision of product/service which can be paid for as it is used.
- **Online community**: provision of community of common interest.
- **Information trading**: provision of information about markets, products, services and/or market traders.
- **Market aggregation**: aggregation of demand or supply through a digital marketplace providing products and services.

Productivity impacts

Despite the evidence for productivity change, those hyping ICT transformation have frequently oversimplified the debate. In fact there is an element of 'fallacy'[3] in productivity arguments (Bean 2003; Bootle 2003) and the way in which they are often posited in terms of real estate impact. Technological advance does not automatically reduce jobs. Although technology may lead to job losses in some firms and some sectors by enabling the same output with less labour, this may not necessarily be the case, because the lower cost of production may allow a firm to lower prices and so boost demand for its product. It is simplistic to argue that improved productivity created by ICT automatically leads to job loss and reduced space demand. For example, although teleworking is widespread it does not necessarily reduce the demand for office space and may increase the demand for residential office space (Greater London Authority 2002). Also, research (Gerald Eve 2001) has shown that net densities have increased over time and that new working practices increase densities (see Table 7.2, page 241), other factors such as firm size and length of occupation are also 'important' factors to consider.

Clustering and dispersion

As we saw in Chapter 6, changing concepts of personal, public and work space can aid our understanding of ICT transformation in connection with real estate, although some of the views of space and their impact on clustering and dispersion are not new. At the height of the dot.com boom there were those who argued that the revolution brought about by the new economy would lead to the 'death of geography', and remove the need for people to be physically located together.[4] Some used these arguments to suggest the imminent demise of real estate. Telecommuting, for example, would reduce demand and would create dispersion.

As long ago as the nineteenth century, Marshall (1890) suggested that three forces act to pull economic activity to the centre (the 'Marshallian Triad') whilst three act to pull activity to the margin, stemming from transportation or congestion costs (Table 9.1).

The Forum for the Future (Digital Europe 2001) also suggests that there are key stages in the eBusiness process which may significantly alter the traditional dynamic between agglomeration and dispersion forces. As Table 9.2 shows, search and matching costs of finding a new partner are potentially reduced by the Internet, email and mobile telecommunications. This means that demand and cost linkages are weakened and so dispersion is increased. However, there is still also a need to be located close to customers and buyers for the conclusion of search and matching transactions.

In terms of direct shipping cost it can be argued that the cost of time in transit means that production is more likely to be located close to suppliers and Klier (1999) found that 70–80% of US automobile suppliers are located within a day's drive of the assembly plant, and that this concentration has increased with the arrival of just-in-time methods. However, when services (such as accounting, insurance, advertising) are examined, the situation is not straightforward: on the one hand, demand and cost linkages are weakened, but on the other hand the need for face-to-face contact remains. Similarly, as we saw earlier in Chapter 1, research by Dixon *et al.* (2002a)[5] on City of London-based office occupiers identified four key centrifugal factors:

- ICT.
- Transport problems.
- Sustainable development.
- Human resources (demands and needs of employees and home working).

Table 9.1 Marshall's centripetal and centrifugal forces (adapted from Marshall 1890; Digital Europe 2001).

Centripetal	Centrifugal
Market size effect: local concentration leading to demand linkages and cost linkages	Immobile factors: land, labour and capital slow down agglomeration
Thick labour markets: local concentration of employees and employers	Land rents: high cost of land in centre
Pure external economies: information spill-overs	Pure external diseconomies: increased traffic, congestion, pollution and crime

Table 9.2 The effect of eBusiness on dispersion and agglomeration forces (adapted from Digital Europe 2001).

Costs affected by the development of eBusiness	Dispersion/ agglomeration forces	Explanation
Reduction in search and matching costs	Increase dispersion	Reduction in the cost of searching and finding trading partners
Reduction in direct shipping costs	Increase dispersion	No need to locate close to producers or other ICT firms as transport costs fall
	Increase concentration	No need to follow dispersed customers
Costs of personal interaction: relative roles of codifiable and tacit knowledge	Increase dispersion	Codifiable knowledge: less dependent on geographic proximity
	Increase concentration	Tacit or non-codifiable knowledge: requires geographic proximity
Reduction in control and management costs	Decrease or do not affect dispersion	ICT alone is not sufficient. Face-to-face contact is also required
Increase in the costs of time in transit	Increase concentration	As the marginal value of time increases, the desire to be closer to the market increases
Reduction in the costs of commuting	Increase dispersion (at the urban level)	One of the major limits to urban growth in industrial cities is weakened
Reduction in the costs of relocation	Increase dispersion (at the national and regional level)	Fast information and communication facilitates relocation at lower costs, which may be emphasised by national/regional policy.

In practice, ICT may also partly act as a centripetal force if technology maps itself onto existing economic activity and continues to promote 'clustering'. If home working and other ICT-based activities grow then ICT will clearly promote 'dispersion'. Similarly there is an argument for saying sustainable development (see later in this chapter) would be promoted by encouraging living and working in the City. The aftermath of the 11 September 2001 terrorist threat was also a major concern for many, reinforcing dispersion trends. Acting in the opposite direction, and pulling businesses towards the City, were centripetal forces such as:

- face-to-face contact;
- clustering benefits;
- locational advantage; and
- clients' demands.

In some cases, other forces encourage dispersion. For example, outsourcing and foreign direct investment has resulted in firm fragmentation and production, which is split into separate geographic and organisational units (for example, call centres). However, research by Venables (2001) has shown that ICT can increase the value of further time reduction, and actually increase the need to concentrate, if the market itself is also concentrated.

The type of knowledge embedded in the good or service is also important: codified knowledge, or knowledge that can be reduced to digital information, is less dependent on geographic proximity than tacit (or non-codifiable) information, or knowledge embedded in practical experience and social practice through customers, clients, suppliers and so on. If codified knowledge increases in extent, then dispersion would be likely to increase. Initiatives such as teleworking and home shopping might also be expected to reduce costs and therefore lead to greater dispersion. Also, firms may decide to relocate because the 'sunk costs' of doing so are reduced by ICT. These issues have important ramifications for policy-makers and spatial development patterns internationally, nationally, regionally and at the urban and real estate levels (see later in this chapter).

In short, perhaps the best summary of the clustering/dispersion debate comes from Gillespie *et al.* (2001) who conclude:

> Communications technologies should not be seen as simply pulling the balance of centrifugal and centripetal forces in one direction at the expense of the other, but rather as simultaneously strengthening both.

Summary

We argue therefore that previous real estate studies have often oversimplified the key issues. In our view, using our framework enables us to identify changes more easily and to better understand their context and the role played by businesses, consumers and governement. As evidence of how ICT has transformed real estate in alliance with other factors, we examined a number of real estate sectors in Chapter 7. Table 9.3 summarises this in detail, by identifying key drivers; real estate transformations (in terms of location, layout/intensity, leasing arrangements, values/markets and support services); and overall future impacts. Also in Chapter 8 we examined real estate service provision and the transformations brought about by ICT which are highlighted in summary form in Table 9.4 for the four types of service provision we identified.

Table 9.3 Real estate transformations and overall impact (by sector).

Sector	Real estate transformations to date						Overall future impact	
	Key drivers (with ICT)	Location	Layout/intensity of use	Leasing	Value/market	Support services	Short–medium term (up to 5 years)	Long term (5–10 years and beyond)
Sales	Demographic factors Wealth Economic factors	Multichannel shopping Changes to supply chain	'Shoppertainment' promoted in urban areas Blurring between distribution and stores	Shorter and more flexible leases Wired leases	Some impact in marginal areas	Bundling of services	Impact in marginal locations and in travel/books/CDs goods	Continuing impact depending on nature of goods/services
Processing	Organisational change Demographic factors Transport and supply chains	Continued clustering Some outsourcing and separation of functions and hence dispersion of key activities	Evidence of reducing floor-space requirements and technology-driven density changes New types of workspace and office design evolving	Shorter and more flexible leases	Further outsourcing and off-shoring reducing floorspace demand Growth of teleworking and homeworking Two-tier market between ICT-enabled and other types of buildings	Bundling of services Serviced office arrangements	Evidence of some reduced demand and dispersion, but with continued clustering Variation dependent on type of knowledge (tacit or codifiable)	Likely to be more substantial, as ICT and other factors impact on demand and use of space Other issues: transport and sustainable development
Manufacturing	Demographic factors Wealth Transport Supply chains	Continued clustering Some 'footloose' industries	Trend towards smaller units	Shorter and more flexible leases	Build to order offers greater flexibility	Bundling of services	Falling inventory: sales ratios Increased demand for more flexible space	Greater space efficiencies in future as customisation increases

continues

Table 9.3 (continued)

	Real estate transformations to date					Overall future impact	
Storage	Demographic factors Wealth Transport Supply chains	Focus on transport hubs	Larger units	Shorter and more flexible leases	Shortening supply chains	Bundling of services	Falling inventory: sales ratios Increased demand for more flexible space	May be further reduction in demand but new types of space required for faster distribution
Leisure	Demographic factors Economic factors Work–life balance Transport	City centres still important: some dispersion Clustering of production	Wider market scope and reach Social interaction maintains and increases space demand	Shorter and more flexible leases in relevant sectors	Revenue streams increasing through Internet marketing	Bundling of services Serviced office arrangements in leased premises	Continued clustering	May be some reduction in demand, as home entertainment increases in popularity
Living	Demographic factors Work–life balance Economic factors Transport	Development of wired communities Some dispersion Homeworking/teleworking	Smart home concept only available to higher income groups although broadband availability increasing Changes in home design from teleworking/homeworking	Not applicable	Not applicable	Not applicable	Low penetration of smart home concept Space impacts on homeworking	Growth of wired communities concept Interaction with sustainable development agenda

Table 9.4 Summary of real estate services transformation.

Service function	Forces for change (with ICT)	Transformation by ICT
Owners/owners' managers	Corporate finance Unbundled assets Outsourcing Lease structures	Additional revenue streams Flexi-leases New products
Occupiers/occupiers' managers	Corporate finance Unbundled assets Outsourcing Lease structures	Growth of FM services Intelligent buildings Lease management Asset management
Appraisers	Corporate finance Unbundled assets Outsourcing Lease structures	Changing skills Flexi-leases New products
Brokers	Increased transparency Competition	Disintermediation and reintermediation

However, we also believe there needs to be more research to address the transformations to real estate brought about by ICT impacts. For instance, the research we have identified and highlighted needs to be extended to address, for example, the issue of rental and capital value impact in more detail. Previous research (College of Estate Management 2001) has examined and analysed rental value impact in retail property caused by eCommerce. Using an analysis based on migration of sales from stores and mail order, the study suggested that rental growth in the UK would be reduced by between 0.2% and 0.5% per annum over the period 2000–2005. Retail provides an example of how ICT can create a new distribution model, which affects turnover and rents. In the case of offices the transformation brought about by ICT is rather different: here there is likely to be a premium between ICT-enabled space and non-ICT-enabled space, and the work of Thompson and Hills (1999) and Tien Foo (2002) and Tien Foo *et al.* (2004) remain the best-known studies here. Developing a new research agenda to address such issues is dealt with in more detail later in this chapter.

Similarly, continued innovation in real estate service provision requires continuing monitoring and benchmarking to learn from best practice as landlords and tenants come to terms with a landscape of service provision that has been transformed by ICT.

In summary, whilst the continued transformation of real estate by ICT requires a new research agenda, we believe that our framework provides a foundation not only to enable us to examine current ICT transformation, but also to consider new types of real estate which have emerged directly as a result of ICT and other related factors.

As an example of how technology can potentially transform access patterns, consider the recent French moves to upgrade existing copper wire phonelines to ASDL and pipe TV channels into French homes (Guardian 2004). This service is already available in Paris and will be rolled out in French cities during 2004. This comes at a time when Internet telephony is making great inroads into conventional telephone calls, especially in Japan. In this sort of scenario would telephone exchanges become defunct, and if so, what would telecoms companies do with the redundant property? Given the moves towards sustainable inner city communities, the possibilities are intriguing.

New types of real estate

In Chapters 1 and 5 we highlighted how the concept of an 'eProperty' could aid our understanding of how ICT is transforming real estate. The new types of real estate that have emerged represent shifts in technology infrastructure, logistics and process re-engineering within organisations. Examples include co-location centres; distribution centres and collection/delivery points; call centres and serviced offices, which are now summarised.

Co-location centres

Co-location centres (also known as data centres, server farms or web hotels) are, put simply, very large banks of computers used to store web information.[6] The growth of these has partly been driven by the global network of Internet backbones that carry long-distance Internet traffic across the world. However, initial growth in the sector was also driven by the need to meet the disaster recovery requirements on investment banks, in relation to terrorist activity (Property Advisory Group 2002).

Traffic flows are exchanged at 'peering points' or 'Internet exchanges', which act as magnets for other traffic generators (DTZ Research 2000a) and may include Internet service providers, content providers and other enterprises. The co-location provider market is diverse, offering a range of facilities and services. Primetrica (2003) divide 'colos' into three groups (see Table 9.5):

- bandwidth providers offering co-location (or 'colo') within their point of presence;
- real estate and investment companies providing basic space within their carrier hotels; and
- colo specialists focusing heavily on co-location and hosting services.

Table 9.5 Co-location provider typology (adapted from Primetrica 2003).

	Carrier hotel property managers	Colo specialists	Bandwidth provider
Average unit size	560 369 sq ft	49 486 sq ft	29 401 sq ft
Typical basic colo services	Shell and core	Racks Locked cabinets Cages	Racks Locked cabinets
Typical managed services	Equipment installation	Equipment installation Remote hands Data management	Equipment installation IP bandwidth
Examples	Insignia/ESG Tishman GVA Williams	Global switch Telecity TELEHOUSE	Level 3 COLT

In basic terms colo centres offer customers housing for equipment but may also offer power, air-conditioning and security systems. Various forms of outsourcing may also operate in the colo market. DTZ Research (2000b) highlight three examples of outsourcing (of which colo is one) which carry benefits of cost savings, speed to market and access to IT skills:

- Leasing space but installing dedicated equipment (customer looks after equipment and the colo landlord looks after the facility, bandwidth and other services).
- Outsourcing facilities management where the server is maintained by colo management and the customer is responsible for application programs (this is called web hosting).
- Renting applications programs from an application service provider associated with systems integration and other customised software.

Colo space is usually rented out in a variety of configurations (racks, cabinets, cages, suites, vaults and shell and core space). The price paid by a tenant is usually on the basis of racking (where the equipment supplied is from the colo supplier or the customer) or in terms of floor area (where a self-contained area is rented). Bundling of services (such as private storage, first- and second-line maintenance, meeting rooms or even office space) is common so headline rent figures can be misleading.

Although colo space in both the USA and UK experienced consolidation, and some reduction in overall area, during the late 1990s, reuse of such buildings is generally feasible; in the USA, for example, cases of colo space being reclaimed for warehouse or even retail space are not uncommon. In terms of space provision early colo space was often core office space in city centres. However, sophisticated clients required greater security and customisation, so that today new build (and refurbished space, which often still is warehousing or industrial space) for colo facilities is driven by (DTZ Research 2000b):

- minimum floor to ceiling heights of 4 m;
- structural floor loading of 10–15 kilonewtons per m^2;
- efficient column-free space; and
- large goods lifts and riser capacity if the building is multi-storey.

The extent of colo space in a city is also a measure of its importance globally. Telehouses need to be located near fibre-optic cables, have adequate power supplies and access to skilled IT staff and also require proximity to customers for support services (Property Advisory Group 2002).

Colo space and ICT infrastructure are driven by supply and demand forces at a city and regional level, and there is strong linkage between global cities and infrastructure provision. The important role of technology-led infrastructure in 'world winning' cities has also been recognised in research by Jones Lang LaSalle (2003) who highlight the importance of technology-rich cities such as Helsinki, Austin, and Raleigh Durham in a global economy. Research by Hackler (2002) has also highlighted that cities with greater telecommunications capacity are more likely to have positive growth in their hi-tech industry sector. This follows Gorman's (2002) work in the USA which found that eBusiness location is highly skewed towards ICT agglomerations such as New York and San Francisco. Also, Dixon *et al.* (2002a) point out that London is the leading eBusiness centre in Europe because it has more capacity in use in terms of Internet infrastructure than any other world city.[7] It is a hub for three of the five largest Internet city-to-city connections, including the top two, and is in the top four European cities in terms of average and total space for Internet data centre co-location centres. When web hosting is included, London is the largest centre in Europe (Local Futures Group 2001), and London to New York (77.7 Gbps) is one of the world's key Internet backbone trunks. This provides further evidence of ICT clustering around ICT infrastructure.

Distribution centres and collection/delivery points

The increasing importance of eCommerce and online sales activity has also altered existing distribution networks (DTZ Research 2000a). Simple linear models of distribution have become outmoded (Figure 9.1). Traditionally networks comprised a fairly discrete set of intermediaries with a series of satellite warehouses around a high bay distribution hub. However, with the advent of online shopping, supply chains no longer end at retailers' ware-

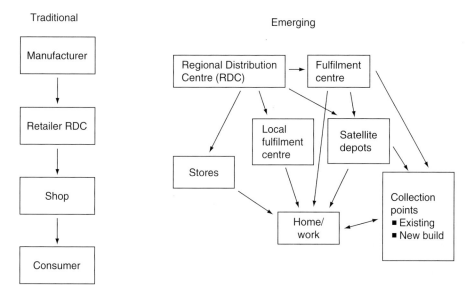

Figure 9.1 Traditional and emerging supply chains (adapted from DTZ Research 2000a; DTZ Pieda 2000).

houses, but instead link directly to people's homes. Suarez-Villa (2003) sees these changes as being driven by a phenomenon known as 'technocapitalism' (or the evolution of market capitalism rooted in rapid technological innovation and its supporting intangibles) and relates changing transport infrastructures to three separate eras as outlined in Table 9.6.

As a result of the change in transport from point-to-point to e-networks, and the growth of ICT infrastructure, three alternative models of distribution have evolved (DTZ Research 2000a; DTZ Pieda 2000), although there are other variations (see DTI/Foresight 2000a).[8]

Table 9.6 Organisational eras and transportation (adapted from Suarez-Villa 2003).

Era	Firm type	Transportation				
		Distribution patterns	Logistics	Modal characteristics	Pricing criteria
Middle industrial capitalism (1910s–1960s)	Fordist	Point-to-point	Shipping firms	Send-and-warehouse	Weight, bulk (regulated)
Late industrial capitalism (1960s–1990s)	Post-Fordist	Network-based	Third party Providers	Just-in-time	Timing, weight (deregulated)
Techocapitalism (1990s–?)	Experimental	e-network based	e-3PLs and infomediaries	Fast-in-time	Value, speed

Maintaining the status quo

For some online goods such as CDs and books, consumer demand can still be fulfilled from existing distribution networks. The point here is that e-tailers still require property. Generally, e-tailers tend to lease office and distribution space rather than own it. For example, Amazon does not own any real estate – it leases all its portfolio, including the headquarters in Seattle. Box 9.1 gives a breakdown of Amazon's portfolio and sales data.[9]

Home delivery

Here online sales provide an additional channel to add to existing mail order services, and create a more complex system of product flows, requiring additional warehouse facilities such as dedicated fulfilment centres, as well as retailer and cross-dock facilities. The overall impact on the warehousing market depends very much on the type of strategy adopted by the retailers. In the UK grocery industry the choice seems to be between

---

Box 9.1   Amazon's real estate model. *Source: SEC filings and CEM 2001.*

Amazon is undoubtedly one of the most successful pure online retailers worldwide which has quickly expanded from its base in the book and music sectors. It built on pre-existing electronic book distribution systems that were being used by the wider bookselling industry by using its own warehouse space in each of the countries in which it operates. Based on this and Amazon's marketing strategy, DTI/Foresight (2000b) described the company as a 'traditional tangible retailer' – it experiences the same difficulties of supply and demand that conventional retailers face. However, it is the consumer side of its business that is different for Amazon with a vast network of affiliates and partners that link through or trade through Amazon's z-shops and second-hand. Amazon also needs substantial amounts of real estate space in which to operate.

	Floor-space (ft^2)	
US office space	730 000	
European office space (UK & Germany)	121 000	
Total office space		851 000
US distribution space	3 800 000	
European distribution space	690 000	
Marston Gate distribution centre (UK)	500 000	
Total distribution space		4 990 000
TOTAL SPACE		5 841 000
Net sales ($000s)	$1 639 839 (£1 015 175)	
Net sales per ft^2		$281 (£74)
Net sales per ft^2 office space		$1927 (£1193)

US$ 1 = £ 0.61907

dedicated picking centres of J Sainsbury and the expanding superstore model of Tesco. Alternatively smaller retailers have also outsourced ordering and customer management functions to intermediaries, whose core function is to pass stock, order and delivery information between the customer and the retailer (Murphy 2003).

Collection points
The idea of delivery to convenient local points is not new: French mail order company La Redoute has for some years delivered goods for collection at launderettes. This model envisages a network of existing facilities and new-build collection points designed to provide a halfway house between supplier and final customer. Collection points, which put the onus on the customer for collection, either make use of existing real estate facilities or emerge from new-build dedicated facilities. Existing facilities include food superstores, petrol stations, post offices, shopping centres, retail parks and public transport nodes. Alternatively, new, dedicated facilities may therefore include future models based around (DTZ Pieda 2000; DTI/Foresight 2000a, 2000b):

- national hubs with large distribution centres of 30 000 m^2 designed to serve national markets;
- fulfilment centres with regional space of 10 000–30 000 m^2;
- satellite depots, comprising units of 3000–5000 m^2 serving smaller sub-regional markets and used as transhipment points;
- local fulfilment centres with units of 2000–3000 m^2 located in major urban areas; and,
- collection points of between 500–2000 m^2 close to centres of urban population.

Call centres, serviced offices and peripheral space

These were examined in some detail in Chapter 7 as part of the processing section, and it is clear that their evolution has been driven by ICT in combination with other factors. Ironically, ICT and lower labour costs are beginning to threaten the future of call centres based in the UK and USA, as 'offshoring' to India and the Far East grows in popularity. The serviced office sector has primarily been driven by organisational change, as companies seek flexible space, but ICT has also driven change in the sector through its ability to decentralise certain functions, particularly back-office space. There are now some 985 serviced offices in the UK,[10] with Regus, MWB and HQ Executive Offices the top three providers. London and Manchester lead in terms of the highest number of facilities, and demand from government departments has increased over the last few years. Tenants are attracted by fast and short-term occupation, flexibility, no up-front capital expenditure and no long-term commitments.

Prudential UK's new Flexible Working Environment (FWE) is a good example of the way in which office environments are being redesigned to suit different ways of working (Thomas 2004; Mackaness 2004). The FWE concept was introduced in Prudential's London Paddington office in 2002 (Box 9.2), and is based on occupancy and mobility within the office, recognising that employees may be out of the office or working away from their desks. In fact, research by Prudential revealed that average utilisation of an assigned desk was only 43%. In the Paddington office all designated offices and assigned desks are removed, with each department having a neighbourhood of desks plus a range of space for more general use (i.e. meeting rooms, 'touch-down' desks, short-term project areas and informal areas which all represent the growth in collaborative working).

Other companies are pursuing similar policies; examples include Sun Microsystems iWork programme and Nokia's workplace technology. The former is claimed to have led to global savings of 7400 desks and real estate costs of £37.2 million (Thomas 2004).

Box 9.2   Space and cost efficiencies from FWE at Paddington (adapted from Mackaness 2004)

The Prudential's Paddington office is 3.623 m^2 on three floors and the default desk: employee ratio is 7:10. Cost savings are shown below.

	Traditional office	FWE
Staff	325	465
Desk count	325	318
Net internal area	39 000 ft^2 (3623 m^2)	39 000 ft^2 (3623 m^2)
Desks:employees ratio	1:1	7:10
Floor 7	**Conventional**	**FWE**
Floor-space	13 471 ft^2 (1252 m^2)	13 471 ft^2 (1252 m^2)
No. of work settings (excl. meeting rooms)	112	145 (incl. fixed desks, shared desks, touch-down desks)
Area / employee	120 ft^2	87 ft^2
Employees accommodated	112	c.155
Cost/employee @ rent of $78/ft^2	$9432	$6814
Savings/100 employees @ rent of $78/ft^2		$404 000 pa

Implications of ICT transformation for existing real estate

Sceptics may argue that the 'new' types of real estate outlined in the previous section represent a small part of the real estate sector. But what about existing, 'conventional' space? How has ICT transformed this space, and what are the implications for investment value, for example?

Commercial real estate investment provides an asset class which involves a trade-off between risk and return. Risks may include structural risk associated with high repair and maintenance costs, refurbishment and rebuilding due to obsolescence (Bottom *et al.* 1999). Previous studies on the depreciation of commercial real estate in the UK (see, for example, CALUS 1986; Baum 1991; Dixon *et al.* 1997, 1999) have all highlighted the importance of physical deterioration and obsolescence in causing the loss in real existing-use value of buildings. In this sense, Baum (1991) defined obsolescence as a decline in utility not directly related to physical usage or the passage of time. Khalid (1992) extended the taxonomy of obsolescence to include 'functional' and 'technological' obsolescence. For example, functional obsolescence can occur as a product of technological change, leading either to changes in occupiers' requirements or the introduction of new building products. Examples might include a defective layout or an inability to accommodate new ICT. This term is used for the whole building, whereas technological obsolescence refers to components in a building, which can become technologically inefficient. Functional obsolescence is therefore incurable, whereas technological obsolescence is often curable.

Building quality is also an important issue in depreciation studies. In the debates over depreciation methodologies, age has often been used as a proxy for building quality, which is the product of the individual attributes of a building (see Dixon *et al.* 1997). These attributes can change over time; for example, changing services technology originally caused certain office building designs to produce inefficiency of operation due to demand for increased floor to ceiling height. During the 1990s, however, further advances in cordless technology reduced the need for height, therefore bringing previously obsolescent buildings back into service.

Nonetheless, given the 'legacy' stock (built pre-1980) of commercial real estate in the UK, which in 2000 represented some 50% of insurance and pension fund commercial real estate investment (Investment Property Databank 2001), investors, occupiers and their advisors all need to plan strategically for refurbishment to enable the building to be wired and avoid technological obsolescence. In a US-based study, Slaughter (2001) showed that building design frequently has inbuilt obsolescence because of changes which can occur in the building and its functions. Essentially three types of change can occur:

- Functional change, arising from upgrades, incorporating new functions or modifying functions.[11]
- Capacity changes arising from load or volume changes in the building.
- Flow changes, resulting from changes in environment or changes in the flows of people or things.

Slaughter (2001) therefore argues for greater flexibility in design so that the functional life of a building can be increased, and accommodation and services can be changed quickly over the life of the building as the need arises (Figure 9.2). Simply improving design strategies (for example, creating specific areas or zones for particular activities, or enhancing system access proximity) can lead to the recoupment of any increased construction costs (which across the 26 buildings in the study was only a 2% increase on average) and also to improved design flexibility.

Despite these considerations, however, older buildings are not necessarily inefficient in terms of floor-space density or backward in their implementation of ICT. Firstly, although currently relatively expensive, wireless technology has reduced the need for cabling, making ICT infrastructure

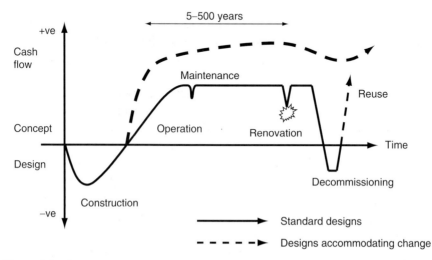

Figure 9.2 Expected life cycle of facilities and potential impact of design to accommodate change (adapted from Slaughter 2001).

much easier to install. Secondly, evidence suggests that older buildings are not always necessarily inefficient in space terms. Findings from the Gerald Eve (2001) study, for example, found that older, converted buildings had higher densities than purpose-built buildings.[12] Moreover, pre-1945 office buildings in the survey had a density of $15.3\,m^2$ per employee, which matched that of modern, post-1980 buildings. This may be due to the fact that although older buildings generally provided less efficient cellular space with large amounts of support space, newer premises during the 1990s tended to have more creative and informal space, thereby leading to convergence in the two age categories. Storage space in offices has reduced, however, due to ICT: this was 12% of space in pre-1945 buildings, but only 7–8% in post-1960 buildings.

Nonetheless, to remain competitive and avoid obsolescence with its ramifications for real estate value, owners and occupiers will seek out the best space offering the latest ICT infrastructure. Research by Colwell and Ramsland (2001) has shown that in retail property, the early years of a building's life are characterised by obsolescence that may not be able to be offset by reinvestment, and can be as high as 1.7% pa in the early years. Increasingly therefore, alongside the development of state-of-the-art new space, we are seeing older, commercial office space refurbished to a high standard, with wired and wireless infrastructure and flexible leasing packages (Box 9.3).

Policy issues

In the view of Gillespie and Rutherford (2004), planners, developers and local authorities frequently fail to recognise the importance of ICT in driving change in the built environment. There is also a danger that ICT is viewed as a 'fix' for current problems and may reinforce and extend the socio-spatial disparities in cities, and if digital divide issues are to be resolved, further public sector intervention to integrate ICT within new real estate developments will be needed.

Previous research by Dixon and Marston (2002) has also highlighted the important implications that ICT will have for real estate and urban form. Policymakers, for example, will need to consider the following issues:

- **Planning** – eCommerce and eBusiness renew the need for policy changes which have already become apparent, particularly to resolve the tensions between conservation and development, to plan for technology-led growth and new patterns of living and working. This is

---

Box 9.3   Empress State, London

Empress State, a 1960s office block, is a landmark building and, as London's fourteenth tallest, has dominated the west London skyline for nearly 40 years. A major £102 million refurbishment of the building was completed by Land Securities in 2003 and the completed building comprises 40 000 m^2 of office space on 30 floors with a conference bar, 200 seat restaurant and coffee bar, fitness club, child-care facilities and a top-floor revolving bar. The building has a central IT room with server racks and is pre-wired with Cat 6 cabling, making IT installations quick and easy. Land Securities is also considering including a wireless network (Tinworth 2003a). The units in the building are offered under Land Securities flexible lease structure (Land-flex), which is an integrated accommodation package that allows a company to match their business accommodation requirements to their business plan and minimise their total accommodation costs. This is achieved by providing a choice of lease lengths for a range of different sized units priced in terms of 'occupational cost' rather than rent. This was developed against the backdrop of the Code of Practice for commercial leases which suggested that landlords should offer priced alternatives to their tenants on a number of aspects of their lease including length, rent review process and break clauses. Land Securities has ambitions to expand Landflex to some 1.5 million ft^2 across Central London (www.landflex.com).

---

particularly true of the development plan system to make it more flexible with regular updating. Also, the Lyons (2004) review high-lighted the importance of resolving tensions between continued growth in the South East of the UK at the expense of the rest of the country and the review also stressed the important role that ICT could have in driving government department relocation.

- **Regeneration** – urban areas at the margin and locations within those areas are likely to become more marginalised. Opportunities to use ICT-led developments for regeneration exist, but trends towards online retailing will have an impact on the suburbs and smaller town centres. Travel agents and estate agents supplanted by online services will produce vacancies in prime areas which will be filled with new office types or relocated secondary businesses moving up. Secondary locations may deteriorate further as businesses move out to relocate or them-selves are impacted by eCommerce.

- **Sustainable development** – the impact on sustainable development is complex. On the one hand, the ability of the economy to grow more rapidly without inflationary constraints is likely to result in a higher trend rate of economic growth, but on the other hand this growth may be less resource intensive and more sustainable than before. Transport patterns will also be affected, with teleworking and online retailing potentially reducing and changing some types of traffic flow.

Concerns over the issue of home deliveries and its impact on transport and the environment have also led to research being commissioned by the DTI (Browne *et al.* 2001) on home deliveries in the UK. This research was part of the continuing work commissioned by the DTI into eCommerce and home shopping, reflected by previous reports (Retail Logistics Taskforce 2000a, 2000b).[13] Their research showed that the home delivery sales of grocery products, small packages and large items made up approximately 11% of total UK retail sales. Given current growth trends, online grocery sales were expected to increase from £350 million in 2000 to £4.6 bn by 2005, which would increase the number of grocery home delivery trips dramatically from 6.6 million in 2000 to 62.5 million by 2005. As we saw earlier there are varying approaches to fulfilment in groceries: using existing stores; using dedicated centres; or operating a hybrid approach. However, if the growth forecast becomes a reality, then achieving customers' preferred delivery time windows may become increasingly difficult and costly, and overall transport and environmental effects become important to consider. A dramatic increase in home delivery traffic may replace some trips, leading to changes in the choice of transport mode. However, this is a complex area and so far little research has been carried out to examine it in more detail, although Hop Associates (2002) have explored the links between transport, technology and land use in policy-related research for the Office of the Deputy Prime Minister.

As another example of growing awareness of the spatial impacts that eCommerce and eBusiness are having on the built environment, the Office of the Deputy Prime Minster's (ODPM) Planning Advisory Group (Property Advisory Group 2002) has also undertaken work on studies of eCommerce in the UK in four discrete areas where ICT transformation trends are already discernible:

- Geographical and spatial impacts.
- Infrastructure impacts.
- Impact on urban areas.
- Building use issues.

The Group was careful to examine only the drivers for change and not the likely government response to that change. In general, the Group sees the impact of eCommerce leading to further clustering but also marginalisation. As far as retail is concerned, cities' spatial mix may be shaped in the following ways:

- City core – increased sales, pressure for accommodation, offset by dis-intermediation of some retailers. Some retreat to prime areas, contraction of secondary areas.
- Inner city – more abandonment on Central Business District (CBD) borders as secondary retail retreats to prime areas.
- Suburbs and urban fringe – the effects of disintermediation might ease some of the pressures for growth.

The Group also looked at the impact in different types of area. Again in relation to retail:

- Central London – special location, hit less than most retail centres.
- Outer London and South East – attractive and larger towns do better than more ordinary towns. Generally more penetrated than northern towns, given greater affluence (to purchase hardware) and more white-collar families.
- Metropolitan areas (excluding South East) – larger choice of goods, therefore less badly affected than small towns.
- Towns (excluding South East) – unless these towns have other attractions, such as a pleasant environment, could lose trade to larger towns.
- Country towns – could find eCommerce particularly attractive. However, probably already have more of a (less affected) convenience role.

Similarly for office functions, with increasing 'disintermediation' in some service sectors, there may be less demand for inner city locations with more suburban growth as office locations follow a decentralisation trend. However, demand in central business districts is likely to be maintained as high bandwidth users agglomerate around ICT infrastructures. Space requirements are also likely to change as more communal space is in demand and wireless technology will mean less need for raised floors (Property Advisory Group 2002).

There has also been an increasing realisation among policymakers that the twin agendas of the 'new economy' and 'sustainable development' are interlinked. As we have seen, the new economy requires us to rethink the nature of goods and services and the transformations in networks and real estate structures that can ensue, and in parallel with this, the sustainable development agenda requires a similar shift in thinking.

The Brundtland Commission (1987) defines sustainable development as 'development which meets the needs of the present without compromising the ability of future generations to meet their own needs'. This is usually taken to mean that the 'triple bottom line' (Elkington 1997) of sustainable development must be linked through interconnecting economic, environmental and social pillars. Therefore, as well as setting goals for economic performance, businesses and economies should also set social and environmental performance goals. The drive towards sustainability is also a very real one in the corporate world, and shareholder pressure, legislation and green ethics have all played their part in promoting a corporate social responsibility (CSR) theme for businesses that encompasses a sustainable development goal (Mansley 2000). There is a growing body of work therefore (see, for example, EITO 2002; Park & Roome 2002; Alakeson *et al.* 2003) that has focused on how the growing use of ICT can offer environmental and sustainable development benefits, and this has also been identified in several European-wide policy initiatives (see, for example, the Lisbon European Council 2000).[14]

Forum for the Future (Digital Europe 2001), for example, offers a useful framework for conceptualising the impacts of ICT on the environment in environmental, economic and social terms (Table 9.7). For example, in terms of primary impacts, the evidence suggests that production of ICT equipment does not use up as many natural resources or pollute as much as other industries, although data centres create substantial demands on the electricity grid, and other negative impacts do occur, especially on

Table 9.7 Categorisation of the environmental effects of the Internet and its applications (adapted from Fichter 2001; EITO 2002).

Effect	Caused by	Examples	Aspects
Primary effects (physical existence of ICT and processes)	Infrastructure	Terminal equipment such as the PC, mobile phones Net infrastructure Servers and routers	Energy consumption Material consumption Toxicity of end-of-life equipment
Secondary effects (ongoing use and application of ICT)	Application	B2B – supply chain management – product development – logistics B2C B2G	Energy consumption Material consumption Traffic Land use
Tertiary effects (aggregated effects of widespread use of ICT)	Changes in consumption pattern, new habits, rebound effects	Increase in consumption Substitution effects Side effects	Energy consumption Material consumption Traffic Land use

disposal.[15] Transmission masts, dishes and earth stations will also have environmental implications (see Property Advisory Group 2002).

In terms of second-order impacts, ICT can create efficiencies through 'dematerialisation' or 'weightlessness' in a product, through a reduction in the quantity of raw materials required to support human activity. It should be stressed that there is a strong relationship between telecommunications and its ability to affect urban form through the medium of travel behaviour. The spread of ICT into the workplace, combined with the energy crises of the 1970s, emphasised the role that telecommuting and teleconferencing could play in reducing travel and energy consumption (Mokhtarian 2000; Hop Associates 2002). But despite a growing awareness of the issues, the ICT revolution has not so far been accompanied by an overall decrease in travel. Complex forces are at play; communication can occur at three levels: face to face, through transfer of an information object or through telecommunications. Moreover, several different relationships can co-exist and occur simultaneously in these alternative modes: substitution (elimination or replacement); generation (stimulation or complementarity); modification; and neutrality. Forecasting the impacts of ICT on travel can be very difficult therefore and it should be recognised that cost of travel is only one of many influences, including the quality of a location-based experience compared with a virtual alternative, and the ability to carry out multiple activities at the real location (i.e. business, social and recreational).

There is therefore conflicting evidence on the impact of ICT on travel; for example, Figure 9.3 shows that although eCommerce and telework reduce the need for travel, and telematics (or intelligent traffic guidance systems) can make car transport more efficient, the number of deliveries may increase and longer supply chains may be created. At an international level, Arnfalk (2003), for instance, shows how new technology such as videoconferencing and related ICT use can drastically reduce business travel. However, there is also a potential 'rebound' effect for more local travel, because it is unclear what people may do with the increased time they save in making a car journey to the shops if they are shopping online instead. It is still also unclear as to whether home delivery is more sustainable than supermarket shopping, and research by Galea and Walton (2003) found that Webvan's US distribution model may be unsustainable: moving warehouse operations away from the city core to service deliveries can accelerate sprawl, for example.

However, other research has shown that ICT can also decrease the amount of material product in some sectors of the economy. Research under the

Decrease?   **Increase?**

- eCommerce reduces need to travel
- Teleworking reduces need to travel to work
- Telematics reduces congestion and journeys

- More deliveries
- Geographically longer supply chains
- Rebound effects

Environmental impact?

Figure 9.3 Sustainable development, eCommerce and transport (adapted from EITO 2002).

Digital Europe (2002) programme,[16] for example, shows that the materials intensity needed for a conventional payment through a bank is 2.87 kg, and for an online transaction it is 0.26 kg, which reflects savings in energy, consumables and other materials. Similarly Romm *et al.* (1999) suggested that as much as 25% of the reduced US energy consumption during 1996 to 1999 was due to structural changes brought about by eCommerce such as the switch from retail to distribution stores in the USA as online shopping grew in popularity during this period: for instance, a square metre of warehouse holds far more merchandise than a square metre of shop but uses 16 times less energy.

Finally, at a macro level, third-order effects (or the aggregated effect of widespread use of ICT) also need to be examined, although EITO (2002) points out that this may be difficult to unravel because of the synergy between ICT and other social and economic forces. Economic theory perhaps helps provide the explanation for the spatial patterns of economic activity we see at different scales of resolution (Digital Europe 2001). This may be characterised as a balance between centripetal and centrifugal forces referred to earlier.

Future visions

The penultimate section of this chapter seeks to shed light on how real estate might evolve in the future, as a result of ICT and other factors. In order to focus on how real estate sectors may develop, we firstly examine some examples based on previous futures studies. Then, in the final section of the chapter, we examine whether there is a future for real estate, and how future research should also evolve to address the key issues that require further work.

Future studies of the transformation of real estate have often adopted a 'scenario planning' approach, and there has been a flourishing production of 'futures research', using these techniques. Proponents of scenario planning[17] argue that it provides a way of identifying timelines to possible outcomes without being tied to forecasts or predictions, although the empirical underpinning of some of these badges is open to question. Many generalist, 'utopian' studies of the future therefore concur that of the trends in science and technology, ICT factors will have the greatest impact (Cabinet Office 2001). Processing power is likely to continue and 'quantum' processing is likely to revolutionise processing speed and by 2020 computers may be 4000 times more powerful than today (Labour Party 2003). Storage capacity and network connectivity will grow at even faster rates and PC functionality is likely to be embedded in a range of devices from smart mobile phones to consumer appliances. Within 5–10 years, most domestic consumers could have 'always on' Internet with speeds 10–20 times faster than today. Other developments may include (Labour Party 2003):

- artificial intelligence and virtual reality technologies allowing organisations to solve problems well in advance of today's capabilities;
- by 2011, 75% of the UK population with Internet access, and wireless technologies outstripping voice data by 2006;
- workers using ICT as their agents, performing increasingly complex tasks.

However, work by the Socio-economic Trends Assessment for the Digital Revolution (STAR) research project team (STAR 2003) highlighted four main paths for the future of the information society (Table 9.8), one of which is a negative, information-less scenario.

Some specific examples of the scenario approach, firstly from the commercial real estate sector and secondly from retail, are now identified.

Table 9.8 Scenarios for an information society (adapted from STAR 2003).

Scenario	Characteristics
Connected lives	A society governed by interpersonal media allowing emotional relationships and preserving communities. Mobile technologies dominate and enable interlinking of range of media. ICT has a limited impact on the economy and productivity
The Internet galaxy	ICT plays a minor role in society, industry and government. Products and services offer ambient intelligence as objects are able to communicate. ICT has a much greater role in productivity impacts
Web impact or effective relations	This combines interpersonal media and relationships, creating new organisations. Individually led projects are key and people communicate and do business in different ways enabling them to compete with other organisations. There is strong decentralisation
The information-less society	This is a negative scenario and technology does not progress at the pace expected. There is low impact on productivity and a strong ambivalence towards the positive features of ICT (in terms of sustainable development, health and environment). Society is weakly impacted by ICT

Commercial real estate futures: examples

Scenario studies in office real estate have generally been less common than in retail.[18] However, as a specific example of ICT transformation, wireless technology has been heralded by many as an enabler of change in both the office and the home (Ross & Davies 2003). Personal area networks (PANs) are likely to form the focus for this, providing 'office bubbles' within which everything is connected. This could lead to innovations such as:

- proximity features for automatic logon when individuals walk into a room;
- furniture embedded with connectivity technology to provide gateways between users, their equipment and corporate networks;
- real estate with smart identification functions to recognise people occupying or passing through the space. Global system for mobile communication (GSM) has already begun to enable owners to send text messages to phone users entering particular spaces. Bluetooth technology offers a richer way of incorporating base station information to provide information and obtain information from mobile technology users.

Wireless is also likely to impact on home use, through smart home technology, leisure use, through gaming and dating services, and retail use as

Local Infotainment Points may become more common. These are already being installed in advertising hoardings and billboards to allow interactive communication with potential or existing customers.

The development of bubble spaces is also likely to increase the drive towards 'nomadic' workers, who use touch-down space and hot-desking facilities. A good example of how wired technology is becoming mainstream[19] is shown in Box 9.4.

More concrete uses of scenario planning and visions of the future can be found in retail (CEM 2001). For example, the DTI/BRC/Foresight (1999) study produced three scenarios:

- The 'sustainable development' scenario, where town centres are revitalised through urban regeneration, but where environmental legislation leads to higher prices and congestion from home delivery.
- The 'internationalisation of UK and domestic markets' scenario, where lower prices are suggested but the UK is dominated by international retailers.
- The 'small and smart' scenario, where small retailers using smart technology outperform large retailers with IT and virtual presence, resulting in a backlash against big business.

This was extended with a follow-up report (DTI/Foresight 2000a), which took four scenarios: 'Explosive', 'Dynamic', 'Active' and 'Sluggish'.

Sparks and Findlay (2000) built on this and work by Scase (2000) to suggest that the two key drivers for change are the role and impact of technology and the danger of inequality. In turn they suggest three different scenarios:

Box 9.4   Spinningfields, Manchester, UK

This is a development of offices (220 000 m^2) and shopping/entertainment (37 250 m^2) designed to be a major part of Manchester's regeneration strategy. Residential space is also planned. The Spinningfields project is a joint venture between Manchester City Council and Allied London, and the IT infrastructure is provided by MiSpace. At the heart of the development is an open access wireless network, which provides a flexible way for occupiers to connect to Internet services and dedicated broadband (Tinworth 2003b) with bilateral connections to buildings, the ability to upgrade quickly and 24/7 support facilities.

- 'Wired wonderland', where the e-tail future is fully embraced and socio-economic tensions are resolved.
- 'Social security', a 'middle path' scenario, where balance is achieved between social and economic futures, and where technology is important, but not dominant.
- 'Compound calamity', in which tensions in society and economy have forced massive divisions between the 'haves' and 'have nots'.

Were any scenario or combination of scenarios to become a reality, Sparks and Findlay argue that the future of shopping and retailing may be impacted in a variety of ways:

- Retailers will be bigger companies with targeted formats (and may be based overseas).
- Local retailers will be important as will the service and leisure component of shops.
- E-tailing will lead to some replacement of existing retailing at the mundane (or 'convenience') end of the spectrum.
- Environments will be enhanced and rebuilt regularly.
- The needs of the older consumer will be important.

Jones Lang LaSalle (2000) drew on a database of one million interviews with consumers across Europe to produce three scenarios. Overlaid on their scenarios are four preconceptions (or drivers) which are likely to remain important for the next 10–15 years:

- The continuing growth of globalisation and new technology.
- The continuing integration of the EU.
- Changing consumer lifestyles, particularly the power of the 'grey pound' as the population ages.
- The way people shop: the typology of shopping will continue in its present shape (i.e. 'household/personal management', 'morale boosting', 'top-up and leisure').

Three scenarios were then constructed:

- The 'fresh air and free markets' scenario, where the current brand of post-Thatcherite capitalism spreads to Europe.
- The 'stakeholder' scenario, where the current continental, social-democratic model spreads to the UK.
- The 'new lifestyle, new rules' scenario, where a new-age blend of 1960s values and Californian social fluency becomes the vogue.

As with other 'future studies' the study is characterised by a 'top-down' approach but is somewhat more incisive about the potential and specific impact on property. Nonetheless, it hedges its bets by stressing that the extent to which each is realised is 'scenario dependent' and it can be argued that the badges may oversimplify the subtleties of future change. Nonetheless, Jones Lang LaSalle (2000) suggest that certain retail sectors will be 'winners' and others 'losers' (Table 9.9).

Deconstructing myths: the case of retail

The danger with future studies of the type presented in the previous section is that 'hype' overshadows 'reality' in many instances. To attempt to present a balanced view of the retail sector, therefore, further work by CEM (2001) (see also Dixon & Marston 2002; Marston & Dixon 2003) identified a number of 'myths' relating to the demise of traditional retail real estate, which three UK-based surveys of retailers and investors/ developers over the period 2000–2003 sought to deconstruct. The myths that were highlighted in the 2000 study (CEM 2001) comprised the following:

- **'eCommerce will mean the death of the high street...'**. This was found to be false. Although parts of the high street were found to be under threat (particularly financial services and travel), those stores that integrated eCommerce and had a strong brand would continue to be successful. What is difficult in any research of this kind is to tease out the impact eCommerce will have alongside all the other concerns there are over retailing, including price deflation, falling margins and rents outstripping sales. Certainly there will still be concerns for retailers operating on low margins, despite the future impact B2B may have on their costs. Technology changes rapidly, however, and so the research stressed that it is vital to monitor and benchmark progress as we move towards a future where fast Internet access will widen in scope.

Table 9.9 Sectors with opportunities and threats (adapted from Jones Lang LaSalle 2000).

Sectors with opportunities	Sectors under threat
Large own-brand fashion stores	Middle market, low impact, fashion format
Express supermarkets – town centre formats	Formal menswear
Themed bars, restaurants, Internet cafés, coffee/juice bars	Department stores
High street health and beauty-related stores	Large mixed use and variety store sector
Fitness centres	Banks and building societies
Financial services centres	Travel agents and estate agents

- **'Retail property values will be hit...'.** This was found to be only partly true. There was mounting evidence to suggest that this had already happened during the early 'noughties', and not just because of eCommerce. Retail yields moved out during 2000 because of more pessimistic investor sentiment over such factors as the weak retail market and oversupply of accommodation. But the research suggested that eCommerce would be likely to increase the polarisation between prime and secondary property and between towns. Also as eCommerce slowed rental growth then we would see yields moving further to accommodate this fall, if they had not done so already.
- **'The future lies with dot.coms...'.** This was found to be false. Evidence suggested that the future was seen as being multichannel with 'bricks and clicks' dominating (i.e. a physical presence combined with an online sales channel). 'Shoppertainment', combining shopping with entertainment, was also found to be a key feature of the most successful retail schemes.
- **'Retail property will be deadweight...'.** This was found to be false. Even e-tailers need property to operate. Retailers want more flexible leases and are looking in some instances to move property off their balance sheets because of accounting changes and other drivers. 'Reverse convergence' may become more common as e-tailers move into physical property and retailers move into virtual space.

This survey and the follow-up CEM surveys (Dixon & Marston 2002; Marston & Dixon 2003) also suggested that retailers were more sanguine than developers/investors and their advisers about the impact that eCommerce would have on rental and capital values, yields and returns. Overall, respondents thought rental values, yields, capital values and returns were mainly at low to medium risk.[20] [21]

The benchmark surveys of 2000–2003 research also enables follow up users to track changes in sentiment over this period in the UK. The key issues raised were as follows:

- **Barriers to eCommerce**. Security, although still regarded as an important barrier, showed the greatest decrease in importance since 2000. Generally, all the barriers presented to respondents have shown a fall in the mean score over the three years of the research.
- **Perceived impact of eCommerce**. In terms of perceived impact, the survey work suggested that in 2000 there was a reasonably strong view that eCommerce could have an impact on the property market in the short term. However, by the time of the 2001 survey, that attitude had shifted in favour of the longer. That attitude follows

through into the results from the 2003 survey and is consistent with the view that eCommerce is not seen as the great threat to the retail sector that was once feared.

- **At-risk property**. Over the three surveys, relative to one another, the same property types have been viewed to be at the greatest risk (Figure 9.4). However, the magnitude of that risk fell in most cases. Banks and travel agents have consistently been perceived to be at greatest risk from eCommerce (see Chapter 7). This was because both services convert well to the online environment, offering goods and services which, at the point of sale, are intangible. A holiday, for instance, only becomes tangible at the moment it is experienced. Until that point it is merely a description in a brochure, and in that sense makes it perfect for transition onto the Internet. Overall, properties located in the best parts of major centres were perceived to be the least at risk from eCommerce-related change. This included major regional shopping centres (e.g. Meadowhall, Bluewater), and the large city centre shopping centres and the prime retail units in their vicinity. Secondary retail areas occupy the middle ground on this risk spectrum. The level of risk faced by properties in these areas is likely to vary depending on local circumstances and urban regeneration policies that are in place to enhance the vitality of these areas. After banks and travel agents, retail warehouses are seen to be the most at risk of the other retail property types.
- **At-risk centres**. These findings associated with retail property types also transfer over to the wider responses connected to retail centres and goods

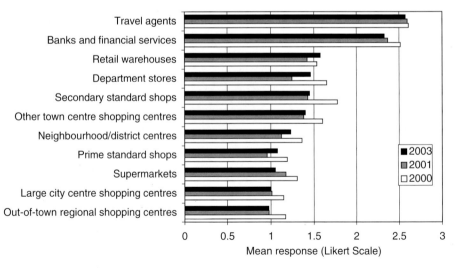

Figure 9.4   Perceived level of risk for different retail property types (adapted from Marston & Dixon 2003).

type. Respondents were presented with a matrix comprising four types of retail centre (big city, medium-sized town, small metropolitan town and small rural town) and three product categories (convenience, comparison and niche). They were asked to identify which combination of centre and product would be most at risk from eCommerce. The results from the three surveys are shown in Figure 9.5 sorted by the 2003 responses. A clear pattern has emerged here in terms of product types. Convenience retailing is seen to be the least at risk, particular in large city locations. Niche product retailing attracts a similar level of responses to convenience, and again the larger city locations have the lowest scores. Comparison goods retailing is regarded as the most at risk with a similar distribution for the centre types – large cities receiving a more favourable score than smaller centres.

These results therefore reinforce the message that:

- changes in other factors acting in alliance with ICT can transform real estate; and
- there is still a future for retail real estate.

In relation to the first factor, Richard Scase (2000) makes the point that our understanding of ICT impact on society must be interpreted within a broader social, economic and business context. This is a more realistic

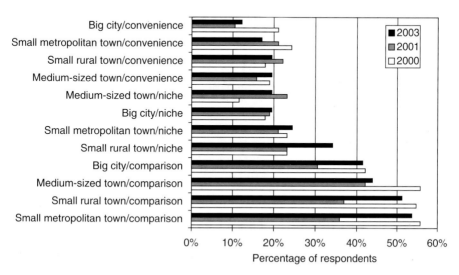

Figure 9.5 Centres and products at most risk from eCommerce (adapted from Marston & Dixon 2003).

approach than that adopted by those who may be described as 'utopian technologists', he suggests. As he states (Scase 2000: 112):

> Although ICTs possess the capabilities of changing work and employment patterns, it is organisational cultures and practices that will determine whether such capabilities are realised...although ICTs may support a huge growth in electronic shopping, this is unlikely to take off while retail shopping is central to personal lifestyles. For those who retire early, shopping will remain a central sphere for personal decision-making...as well as for social interaction. Conversely there are single professional people...who will grasp at the opportunity to shop through the Internet.

The importance of the 'digital divide' at economy, business and citizen levels cannot be overestimated in this respect, and this is a point recognised in the future development of housing by Gillespie and Rutherford (2004), who also highlight the 'splintering' nature of ICT, spaces and interests in contemporary urban environments (see Graham & Marvin 2001).

ICT, in alliance with other factors at more marginal locations and in more marginal urban areas, may therefore lead to transformations in space and usage patterns, but varying consumer demand patterns will be important to consider. We are also seeing differences in ICT usage and impact internationally, with Nordic and Northern European countries (plus the USA) leading Southern Europe in Internet access and online shopping. This reflects key differences in the size and extent of retail networks as well as cultural differences (see Dixon & Marston 2002; Scase 2000). However, real estate managers and owners should not be complacent (Marston & Dixon 2003).[22]

Is there still a future for real estate in the new economy?

It is clear from what we have written previously in this book that rumours of the death of real estate are grossly exaggerated. All the evidence points to a continued future for real estate, but as an asset it is not immune to changes and fluctuations in demand brought about by ICT and other factors. There is growing evidence to suggest that in terms of shape, layout and intensity of use, real estate is shifting in emphasis. Pea (1985) wrote that we can think of technology in two ways: as a set of tools that amplify or extend what we do (make it better, faster or stronger), or as something with the potential to change radically what we do and how we do it. The impact of ICT upon business processes and business tools over the past 30 years has been radical, irrespective of the framework in which it has been implemented, and this has caused radical changes in all sectors of real estate. Data from CBECS (1999) in the USA show, for example, that in 1992 there were 463 computers per million ft^2 of commercial office space; by 1999 the equivalent figure was 859.

Indeed, because its impact has been so pervasive, the day-to-day implications of ICT-enabled change tend to be forgotten as the processes that they facilitate become the norm. The ubiquitous word processor is a classic example of this phenomenon. Thirty years ago the electronic typewriter held sway in the office as the main engine for document production; now it is consigned almost entirely to the museum. This, alongside the concomitant ability to share and distribute the creation of documents, has changed the physical organisation of office space.

As we have seen, the decreasing size and increasing power of microprocessors has allowed them to be embedded within tools and processes to an ever greater extent, making the tools and processes smarter or safer and extending their capabilities. As this 'transparent' ICT becomes more prevalent – within the physical infrastructure of buildings, for example – they redefine the parameters against which changes are measured.

Also, as we have seen, new types of real estate are emerging, there is a blurring of emphasis between the traditional sectors, and more marginal and secondary locations and property types are at risk. Real estate service functions are also changing in emphasis, to reflect modified customer and service provider relationships brought about by ICT and other factors. As Gillespie and Rutherford (2004) point out, technological infrastructure is just one element of the built environment and does not in itself make a home, neighbourhood, or city more 'liveable' in its own right. Rather, individual lifestyle choices determine how people use technology.

The work of Green and Vandell (2001) and Winograd *et al.* (2000) help place this view in an economic context. Green and Vandell (2001) suggest that although real estate's share of total wealth has declined in the US economy, its absolute value in real terms has increased over the period 1950–1997. They point to the fact that in the long run the supply of productive assets would increase to the point at which their marginal productivity (or the productivity of one more unit of production) is the same across all sectors. Because assets other than real estate (for example, financial services) have become more productive, they have grown more and increased in value more. But real wealth increase has created higher values and demands for all asset classes. If the overall value of assets is increasing, for real estate to experience a real decline in value and absolute decline in demand for the product would entail both:

- an absolute decline in marginal productivity of real estate assets; and
- a substantial substitution effect as IT replaced real estate in production functions.

This is very unlikely, and Winograd *et al.* (2000) support this view with analysis over the period 1899–1997 in the US economy. Comparing ICT to other technologies throughout US history, they argue that advances in technology increase productivity and wealth and therefore both the demand and value of real estate.

Of course, this is not to deny that ICT will have an impact in particular sectors, but rather to suggest that ICT will continue to create shifts and transformations in subtle ways, and that it will change the needs and preferences of owners, occupiers and their customers. This being the case, it will be vital to maintain an active research agenda in the field to monitor and benchmark changes and for professionals to recognise the role of ICT in transforming real estate. We believe that at a 'meta' level it will be important to continue carrying out benchmarking and monitoring research and address questions such as:

- How is ICT impacting at a real estate sector level?
- How is ICT impacting on productivity?
- How are businesses responding in terms of real estate space demands?
- What are the key drivers and barriers to ICT implementation in real estate sectors?
- What are the real estate value and market impacts of ICT?
- How best can ICT transformation be unravelled from other forces for change?

We hope that this book has gone some way towards addressing these questions, but in our view, more work still remains to be done, as ICT continues to transform real estate products and services in the new economy.

Notes

1   The important previous work on understanding technological change at an economy level and urban and regional level should not be underestimated. We acknowledge the important contribution that this work has made to our ideas in Chapter 1, not only in advancing our understanding and helping to highlight key themes and issues, but also in helping anchor our own framework and ideas on a robust base.

2 See also Dixon *et al.* (2002b) for a literature review of ICT in the SME sector generally.

3 See Chapter 5 for a full discussion.

4 The extreme consequence of this is a 'dystopic' view of a technological future found in the fictional work of E.M. Forster (*The Machine Stops*) and George Orwell (*1984*).

5 See also Dixon *et al.* (2003) and Dixon and Marston (2004).

6 The term 'co-location centre' is distinguished here from the term 'teleport'. The latter are larger in size, usually involve a satellite ground station, and can include a sizeable amount of infrastructure, including adjoining business park space. Examples of teleports exist at Fareham and Sunderland in the UK and Staten Island, USA. For further information on teleports see World Teleport Association (2001).

7 Note, however, the importance of measuring bandwidth per capita (see Thompson 2002). On this measure London would trail other cities such as Geneva.

8 The DTI/Foresight (2000a) study identified two basic models for grocery retailers: store-based picking and eFulfilment centres. However, three other variants were identified: eFulfilment centres at the same location as existing stores; eFulfilment centres at the same location as existing regional distribution centres; and a centralised eFulfilment centre with the picked orders being distributed to existing stores for onward distribution to the consumer (see also Reynolds 2000; DTI/Foresight 2000b).

9 Unfortunately it is not possible to specify UK sales.

10 This and other data on serviced offices in this section was kindly supplied to us by Robert Hamilton of Instant Offices.

11 A function is defined by Slaughter (2001) as a set of activities or components to achieve a specific objective. Functions can relate to the facility itself (e.g. shelter) or to human activities (e.g. transportation).

12 Research by Swanke Hayden Connell (cited in Freemans 2000) found that density also varies by sector. Management consultants' space occupancy ratios were 1:110 (net internal area (in ft^2) per person), compared with industrial oil and petrochemicals at 1:256.

13 See also the DTI-funded Oxford Templeton website at http://mww.temp.ox.ac.uk/marketspace/about.htm

14 Heads of state agreed to make Europe 'the most competitive and dynamic knowledge-based economy in the world, capable of sustainable economic growth with more and better jobs and greater social cohesion' (EITO 2002).

15 Co-location centres (also known as server farms, data centres or web hotels) are very large banks of computers used to store web information. They concentrate energy use in one place and although this leads to economies of scale, a single server farm can consume as much energy as a small airport or four large hospitals. Server farms can therefore drain local electricity supplies in their locations (for example, Silicon Valley or London) (EITO 2002). To combat this, iXGuardian, a UK computer services firm, has built a server farm with a dedicated 24 MW gas-fired power station to supply all its energy requirements

on the outskirts of London. Beck (2001) suggests that energy efficient design could also make considerable energy consumption savings in the US market.

16   See http://www.digital-eu.org

17   Scenario planning is a form of strategic planning, often used by corporates to aid decision making. The process involves developing 'stories' about potential futures. Porter (1985) defines a scenario as:

> An internally consistent view of what the future might turn out to be – not a forecast, but one possible future outcome.

Scenarios were first created in 1960s America by Herman Kahn at the RAND Corporation. He pioneered 'future-now' thinking – the art of writing reports as if they had been written at some point in the future. He went on to co-author *The Year 2000* (Kahn & Weiner 1967) which exposed his ideas to greater attention. The technique was used during the 1970s and 1980s at major international corporates such as General Motors and Shell. Shell successfully used scenarios to foresee the oil crisis and the end of the Soviet Union. During the 1970s most of the 1000 top US companies were using scenarios of some kind. There was a revival in use for strategic planning during the 1990s by information age companies (for example, ICL: see Ringland 1998). This is mainly due to the increased uncertainties in the modern world, and the possibility that the world may be on the brink of major changes.

18   Although see Green and Shackleton (2000) for alternative work scenarios that have ramifications for real estate. They highlight three options: economic competitiveness; environmental sustainability; and social inclusion, each with differing impacts.

19   RealComm (www.realcomm.com) showcase a number of international, wireless offices and wireless communities at their website.

20   Retailers were more likely than the property industry to consider these factors to be at no risk, and a greater number of retailers also considered all factors except rentals to be at high risk. This suggests a greater polarisation of views in the retailer group.

21   The 2001 survey (Dixon & Marston 2002) also compared results with a US survey and found the overall results to be broadly comparable in terms of impact in both the UK and USA (see also Worzala *et al.* 2002).

22   Floor-space statistics derived from Goad in this research provided an overview of how much floor-space was 'at risk' in certain comparison and service sectors. On a crude basis, this was about 17% of floor-space in Britain in 2001. Service sector space has increased in the high street over the last ten years and can be expected to continue in financial services and travel. Within categories the balance has shifted, however. Floor-space falls (in proportional terms) occurred in estate agents, building societies, and video/music. Gains were made in banks/financial, travel agents and books. Clearly eCommerce is one of a number of forces impacting on retail space and in fact, the overall 'at-risk' floor-space fell from a total of 18.2% to 17.5% over the period 1991–2001, with only the latter three years of this period coinciding with eCommerce growth. Finally, over the same period, nationally, the proportion of restaurants,

cafés, fast food outlets and takeaways increased from 6.19% in 1991 to 7.81% in 2001. Such an admittedly simple analysis does, however, reveal that many centres need to monitor the health and vitality of their retail environments, as eCommerce continues to grow.

References

Preface

Kelly, K. (1998) *New Rules for the New Economy*, Viking Penguin, New York.

1 Introduction

Aibar, E. & Bijker, W.E. (1997) 'Constructing a city: the Cerda plan for the extension of Barcelona', *Science, Technology and Human Values*, vol. 22, no. 1, pp. 3–30.

Audirac, I. (2002a) 'Information technology and urban form', *Journal of Planning Literature*, vol. 17, no. 2, pp. 212–226.

Audirac, I. (2002b) 'Information technology and urban form: challenges to smart growth', available at: http://www.smartgrowth.umd.edu/events/pdf/IT-UrbanForm&SmartGrowth.pdf

Audirac, I. & Fitzgerald, J. (2003) 'Information technology (IT) and urban form: an annotated bibliography of the urban deconcentration and economic restructuring literatures', *Journal of Planning Literature*, vol. 17, no. 4, pp. 481–511.

Becker, F. (1990) *The Total Workplace: Facilities Management and the Elastic Organisation*, van Nostrand Reinhold, New York.

Becker, F. (1998) 'Beyond alternative offices: infrastructure on demand', *Journal of Corporate Real Estate*, vol. 1, pp. 154–168.

Becker, F. & Joroff, M. (1995) *Reinventing the Workplace*, Corporate Real Estate 2000 Project. IDRC, Norcross, GA.

Becker, G. (1996) *Accounting for Tastes*, Harvard University Press, Cambridge, MA.

Beniger, J.R. (1986) *The Control Revolution: Technological and Economic Origins of the Information Society*, Harvard University Press, Cambridge, MA.

Berry, B. (1973) *The Human Consequences of Urbanization*, Macmillan, London.

Bijker, W.E. (1995) 'Sociohistorical technology studies', in S. Jasanoff *et al.* (eds) *Handbook of Science and Technology Studies*, MIT press, Cambridge, MA.

Bijker, W.E., Hughes, T.P. & Pinch, T.J. (eds) (1987) *The Social Construction of Technological Systems: New Directions in the Sociology and History of Technology*, MIT Press, Cambridge, MA.

Borsuk, S. (1999) *Nowhere Yet Everywhere*, The Space Place Paper, available at: www.thespaceplace.net

Brock, J.K.U. (2000) 'Information and communication technology in the small firm', in S. Carter & D. Jones-Evans (eds) *Enterprise and Small Business: Principles, Practice and Policy*, Financial Times-Prentice Hall, Harlow, Essex.

Brooks, H. (1971) 'Technology and the Ecological Crisis', paper presented at Lecture given at Amherst, May 9.

Bruland, K. (2001) *Technological Revolutions, Innovation Systems and Convergence From a Historical Perspective*, University of Oslo.

Bruun, H. & Hukkinen, J. (2003) 'Crossing boundaries: an integrative framework for studying technological change', *Social Studies of Science*, vol. 33, no. 1, pp. 95–116.

Brynjolfsson, E. & Hitt, L.M. (1998) 'Beyond the productivity paradox: computers are the catalyst for bigger changes', *Communications of the ACM*, vol. 41, no. 8, pp. 49–55.

Buchanan, D.A. & Boddy, D. (1983) *Organisations in the Computer Age*, Gower, Aldershot.

Buchanan, D.A. & Huczynski, A.A. (1985) *Organisational Behaviour*, Prentice Hall, London.

Capital Economics Ltd (2002) *Property in Business – A Waste of Space?* RICS, London.

Carn, N., Black, R. & Rabianski, J. (1999) 'Operational and organization issues facing corporate real estate executives and managers', *Journal of Real Estate Research*, vol. 17, pp. 281–299.

Cash, J.I. & Konsynski, B.R. (1985) 'IS redraws competitive boundaries', *Harvard Business Review*, pp. 134–142.

Castells, M. (2000) *The Information Age: Economy, Society and Culture: Volume 1 – The Rise of the Network Society*, 2nd edn, Blackwell, Oxford.

Christie, I. & Hepworth, M. (2001) 'Towards the sustainable e-region', in J. Wilsdon (ed.) *Digital Futures: Living in a dot.com World*, Earthscan, London.

Clark, W.A.V. & Kuijpers-Linde, M. (1994) 'Commuting in restructuring urban regions', *Urban Studies*, vol. 31, no. 3, pp. 465–483.

Coyle, D. & Quah, D. (2002) *Getting the Measure of the New Economy*, The Work Foundation, London.

Dempsey, J., Dvorak, R.E., Holen, E., Mark, D. & Meehan, W.F. (1998) 'A hard and soft look at IT investment', *McKinsey Quarterly*, vol. 1, pp. 126–137.

Dixon, T. & Marston, A. (2001) *e-Property=e-Business+e-Commerce*, CPD Study Pack Series, College of Estate Management, Reading.

Dixon, T.J. & Marston, A.D. (2002a) 'eProperty = eBusiness + eCommerce: The new digital economy and UK commercial property', paper presented at the European Real Estate Society Conference, Glasgow, June.

Dixon, T. & Marston, A. (2002b) *eRPUK 2001: eCommerce and Retail Property in the UK: Annual Survey and International Comparison*, College of Estate Management, Reading.

Dixon, T., Pottinger, G., Marston, A. & Beard, M. (2000) *Occupational Futures? Real Estate Refinancing and Restructuring*, College of Estate Management, Reading.

Dixon, T.J, Marston, A.D., Elder, B. & Thompson, B. (2003) 'eBusiness and City of London offices', *Journal of Property Finance and Investment*, vol. 21, no. 4, pp. 348–365.

Dosi, G. (1982) 'Technological paradigms and technological trajectories', *Research Policy*, vol. 11, pp. 147–162.

Drucker, P. (1977) *Management: Tasks, Responsibilities, Practices*, Pan Books, London.

DTI/Spectrum (1996) *Development of the Information Society: An International Analysis*, HMSO, London.

Earl, M.J. (1991) *Management Strategies for Information Technology*, Prentice Hall, New York.

Fink, D. (1998) 'Guidelines for the successful adoption of information technology in small and medium enterprises', *International Journal of Information Management*, vol. 18, no. 4, pp. 243–253.

Fishman, R. (1990) 'America's new city: Megalopolis unbound', *Wilson Quarterly*, vol. 14, no. 1, pp. 24–45.

Florida, R. (2000) *Competing in the Age of Talent: Environment, Amenities and the New Economy*, R.K. Mellon Foundation, Pittsburgh, PA.

Freeman, C. & Louca, F. (2001) *As Time Goes By – From the Industrial Revolutions to the Information Revolution*, Oxford University Press, Oxford.

Frey, W. (1993) 'The new urban revival in the United States', *Urban Studies*, vol. 30, no. 4/5, pp. 741–774.

Friedman, J.P., Harris, J.C. & Lindeman, J.B. (1993) *Dictionary of Real Estate Terms*, 3rd edn, Barron's, New York.

Garreau, J. (1991) *Edge City: Life on the New Frontier*, Doubleday, New York.

Garrison, W. (1990) 'Impacts of technological systems on cities', *Built Environment*, vol. 6, no. 2, pp. 120–130.

Gepts, E. (2001) *The Relation Between ICT and Space*, Vienna University of Technology, Vienna.

Gerald Eve (2001) *Overcrowded, Under-Utilised or Just Right? Report of a Study of Occupational Densities*, Gerald Eve in association with RICS, London.

Gibler, K., Black, R. & Moon, K. (2002) 'Time, place, technology and corporate real estate strategy', *Journal of Real Estate Research*, vol. 24, pp. 235–262.

Gibson, V. & Lizieri, C. (1999) 'New business practices and the corporate property portfolio', *Journal of Property Research*, vol. 16, pp. 201–218.

Gibson, V. & Lizieri, C. (2001) 'Friction and inertia: corporate change, real estate portfolios and the UK office market', *Journal of Real Estate Research*, vol. 21, pp. 59–79.

Gillespie, A., Richardson, R. & Cornford, J. (2001) 'Regional development and the new economy', *European Investment Bank, Cahiers Papers*, vol. 6, no. 1, pp. 109–131.

Gordon, R.J. (2000) 'Does the new economy measure up to the great inventions of the past?', *Journal of Economic Perspectives*, vol. 14, no. 4, pp. 49–74.

Gottman, J. (1991) 'Megalopolis and antipolis: the telephone and the structure of the city', in I. de Sola Pol (ed.) *The Social History of the Telephone*, MIT Press, Cambridge, MA.

Graham, S. (1998) 'The end of geography or the explosion of place? Conceptualizing space, place and information technology', *Progress in Human Geography*, vol. 22, no. 2, pp. 165–185.

Graham, S. & Marvin, S. (1996) *Telecommunications and the City: Electronic Spaces, Urban Places*, Routledge, London.

Graham, S. & Marvin, S. (2001) *Splintering Urbanism: Networked Infrastructures, Technological Mobilities and the Urban Condition*, Routledge, London.

Green, R.K. & Vandell, K.D. (2001) 'The Impact of Technology and the Internet on Real Estate', paper presented at International Real Estate Conference, July 27, Girdwood, Alaska.

Grubler, A. (1998) *Technology and Global Change*, Cambridge University Press, Cambridge.

Guy, S. & Shove, E. (2000) *A Sociology of Energy, Buildings and the Environment*, Routledge, London.

Hall, P. (1997) 'Modelling the post-industrial city', *Futures*, vol. 29, no. 4/5, pp. 311–322.

Hanseth, O. & Monteiro, E. (1998) *Understanding Information Infrastructure*, available at: http://heim.ifi.uio.no/~oleha/Publications/bok.html

Hawley, A.H. (1986) *Human Ecology: A Theoretical Essay*, University of Chicago Press, Chicago.

Kanter, R.M. (1989) *When Giants Learn to Dance: Mastering the Challenges of Strategy, Management and Careers in the 1990s*, Routledge, London.

Kellerman, A. (2002) *The Internet on Earth: A Geography of Information*, John Wiley & Sons Ltd, Chichester.

Kling, R. (2000) 'Learning about information technologies and social change: the contribution of social informatics', *The Information Society*, vol. 16, pp. 217–232.

Kling, R., Olin, S. & Poster, M.E. (1995) *Postsuburban California: the Transformation of Oregon County Since World War II*, University of California Press, Berkeley, California.

Kuznets, S. (1971) *Population, Capital and Growth, Selected Essays*, W.W. Norton, New York.

Latour, B. (1987) *Science in Action*, Harvard University Press, Milton Keynes.

Latour, B. (1993a) *Aramis, or the Love of Technology*, Harvard University Press, London.

Latour, B. (1993b) *We Have Never Been Modern*, Harvester Wheatsheaf, London.

Lemola, T. (2000) *Perspectives on Technology*, Gaudeamus, Helsinki.

Lichtenberg, F.R. (1995) 'The output contributions of computer equipment and personnel: a firm-level analysis', *Economics of Innovation and New Technology*, vol. 3, May, pp. 201–217.

Lizieri, C. (2003) 'Occupier requirements in commercial real estate markets', *Urban Studies*, vol. 40, no. 5-6, pp. 1151–1169.

Manning, C. & Roulac, S. (2001) 'Lessons from the past and future directions for corporate real estate research', *Journal of Real Estate Research*, vol. 22, pp. 7–58.

Marshall, A. (1890) *Principles of Economics*, Macmillan, London.

McFarlan, F.W. (1984) 'Information technology changes the way you compete', *Harvard Business Review*, pp. 98–103.

McGrath, K. (2003) *Organisational Culture and Information Systems Implementation: A Critical Perspective*, PhD thesis, London School of Economics.

Medda, F., Nijkamp, P. & Rietveld, P. (1999) 'Urban industrial relocation: the theory of edge cities', *Environment and Planning B: Planning and Design*, vol. 26, no. 5, pp. 751–761.

Mintel (2004) *British Lifestyles (2004)*, Mintel, London.

Mitchell, W.J. (2000) *E-Topia*, MIT Press, Cambridge, MA.

Mokhtarian, P.L. (1998) 'A synthetic approach to estimating the impacts of tele-commuting on travel', *Urban Studies*, vol. 35, no. 2, pp. 215–241.

Mol, A.P.J. & Spaargaren, G. (2003) 'Towards a Sociology of Environmental Flows: A New Agenda for 21st Century Environmental Sociology', paper presented at International Conference on Governing Environmental Flows, June 13–14, Wageningen, Netherlands.

OECD (2000) *OECD Information Technology Outlook: ICTs, E-Commerce and the Information Economy*, Information Society, OECD, Paris.

OECD (2003) *ICT and Economic Growth: Evidence From OECD Countries, Industries and Firms*, Information and Communication Technologies, OECD, Paris.

O'Mara, M. (1999) *Strategy and Place: Managing Corporate Real Estate and Facilities for Competitive Advantage*, Free Press, New York.

Perez, C. (2002) *Technological Revolutions and Financial Capital: The Dynamics of Bubbles and Golden Ages*, Edward Elgar, Cheltenham.

Peters, T. (1987) *Thriving on Chaos: Handbook for a Management Revolution*, Pan, London.

Pettigrew, A.M. (1973) *The Politics of Organisational Decision-Making*, Tavistock, London.

Pinch, T.J. & Bijker, W.E. (1997) 'The social construction of facts and artifacts: or how the sociology of science and the sociology of technology might benefit each other', in W.E. Bijker, T.P. Hughes & T.J. Pinch (eds) *The Social Construction of Technological Systems: New Directions in the Sociology and History of Technology*, MIT Press, Cambridge, MA.

Porter, M. (1998) 'Clusters and the new economics of competition', *Harvard Business Review*, pp. 77–90.

Porter, M.E. & Millar, V.E. (1985) 'How information gives you competitive advantage', *Harvard Business Review*, July–August, pp. 149–160.

Progressive Policy Institute (1998) *New Economy Index*, Progressive Policy Institute, Washington DC.

Rodriguez, M. & Sirmans, C. (1994) 'Managing corporate real estate: evidence from the capital markets', *Journal of Real Estate Literature*, vol. 4, pp. 13–33.

Rogers, E.M. (1995) *Diffusion of Innovations*, 4th edn, Free Press, New York.

Rowlatt, A., Clayton, T. & Vaze, P. (2002) 'Where, and how, to look for the New Economy', *Economic Trends*, vol. 580, March, pp. 29–35.

Ryder, M. (2003) *The Global Digital Divide: Technical Responses and Social Implications*, available at: http://carbon.cudenver.edu/~mryder

Sassen, S. (1991) *The Global City: New York, London, Tokyo*, Princeton University Press, Princeton, NJ.

Sassen, S. (1994) *Cities in a World Economy*, Pine Forge Press, Thousand Oaks, CA.

Scarbrough, H. & Martin Corbett, J. (1992) *Technology and Organization*, Routledge, London.

Schumpeter, J. (1939) *Business Cycles: a Theoretical, Historical and Statistical Analysis of the Capitalist Process*, McGraw Hill, New York.

Smith, M.R. & Marx, L. (1994) *Does Technology Drive History? The Dilemma of Technological Determinism*, MIT Press, Cambridge, MA.

Soros, G. (1994) 'The Theory of Reflexivity', paper presented at MIT Department of Economics World Economy Laboratory, April 26, Washington DC.

Storper, M. (1997) *The Regional World: Territorial Development in a Global Economy*, Guilford Press, New York.

Suarez-Villa, L. (2003) 'The E-economy and the rise of technocapitalism: networks, firms and transportation', *Growth and Change*, vol. 34, no. 4, pp. 390–414.

Thong, J.Y.L. & Yap, C.S. (1995) 'CEO characteristics, organisational characteristics and information technology adoption in small businesses', *Omega-International Journal of Management Science*, vol. 23, no. 4, pp. 429–442.

Veblen, T. (1934) *The Theory of the Leisure Class*, Modern Library, New York.

Veblen, T. (1964) *The Engineers and the Price System*, Augustus M. Kelley, New York.

Winner, L. (1996) 'Who will we be in cyberspace?', *Information Society*, vol. 12, pp. 63–72.

Zaltman, G., Duncan, R., & Holbek, J. (1973) *Innovations and Organisations*, Wiley & Sons, New York.

Zmud, R.W. & Apple, L.E. (1992) 'Measuring technology incorporation/infusion', *Journal of Product Innovation Management*, vol. 9, no. 2, pp. 148–155.

2   The Social, Economic and Political Context of ICT Transformation

ABN-AMRO (1999) *E-Commerce: From Here to Eternity*, ABN-AMRO, New York.

Abrams, P. (1982) *Historical Sociology*, Open Books, Shepton Mallet.

Allen, J. (2000) 'Power/economic knowledge: symbolic and spatial formations', in J. Bryson (ed.) *Knowledge–Space–Economy*, Routledge, London.

Alvarez, I. & Kilbourn, B. (2001) 'Mapping the information society literature: topics, perspectives and root metaphors', *First Monday*.

Analytical (1998) *Our Competitive Future: Building the Knowledge Driven Economy (Technical Report)*, DTI, London.

Auray, N., Beauvallet, G., Charbit, C. & Fernandez, V. (2003) *WiFi: An Emerging Information Society Infrastructure*, Rep. No. Issue Report 40 (Draft), STAR, Paris.

Bangemann, M. (1994) *Europe and the Global Information Society*, European Commission, Brussels, available at: http://europa.eu.int/ISPO/infosoc/backg/bangeman.html

Barkham, R. (2003) 'Demographic change and real estate', *IPF Newsletter Forum View*, pp. 6–7.

Baudrillard, J. (1983) *Simulations*, Semiotext(e), New York.

Begg, I. (ed.) (2002) *Urban Competitiveness: Policies for Dynamic Cities*, Policy Press, Bristol.

Bell, D. (1973) *The Coming of Post-Industrial Society: A Venture in Social Forecasting*, Penguin, London.

Beniger, J.R. (1986) *The Control Revolution: Technological and Economic Origins of the Information Society*, Harvard University Press, Cambridge, MA.

Berger, D. (1999) 'Letters: the great disruption', *Atlantic Monthly*, vol. 3, pp. 10–14.

Beyers, W.B. (2002) 'Services and the New Economy: elements of a research agenda', *Journal of Economic Geography*, vol. 2, pp. 1–29.

Booz Allen Hamilton/INSEAD (2002) *The World's Most Effective Policies for the e-Economy*, Booz Allen Hamilton/INSEAD, London.

BT (2002) *Do Modern Communications Technologies Make Life Better or Worse?*, BT, London.

Cabinet Office (1999) *Modernising Government*, Cabinet Office, London.

Cabinet Office (2000) *E-Government: A Strategic Framework for Public Services in the Information Age*, Cabinet Office, London.

Castells, M. (2000) *The Information Age: Economy, Society and Culture: Volume 1 – The Rise of the Network Society*, 2nd edn, Blackwell, Oxford.

Christie, I. & Hepworth, M. (2001) 'Towards the sustainable e-region', in J. Wilsdon (ed.) *Digital Futures: Living in a dot.com World*, Earthscan, London.

Cohen, S.S., DeLong, J.B. & Zysman, J. (2000) *Tools for Thought: What Is New and Important About the E-Conomy*, BRIE Working Paper 138, University of Berkeley, California.

College of Estate Management (CEM) (2001) *Future Shock or E-Hype? The Impact of Online Shopping on UK Retail Property*, British Council of Shopping Centres, London.

Competition Commission (2003) *Safeway Plc and Asda Group Limited (Owned by Wal-Mart Stores Inc); Wm Morrison Supermarkets PLC; J Sainsbury Plc; and Tesco Plc: A Report on the Mergers in Contemplation*, Rep. No. Cm 5950, Competition Commission, London.

Coyle, D. (1997) *The Weightless World*, Capstone and MIT, London and MA.

Coyle, D. & Quah, D. (2002) *Getting the Measure of the New Economy*, The Work Foundation, London.

Crabtree, J. & Roberts, S. (2003) *Fat Pipes, Connected People: Rethinking Broadband Britain*, The Work Foundation, London.

Crabtree, J., Nathan, M. & Reeves, R. (2002) *Reality IT: Technology and Everyday Life*, ISociety, The Work Foundation, London.

CSTB (Computer Science and Technology Board) (2001) *Broadband: Bringing Home the Bits*, National Academies Press, Washington DC, available at: http://www7. nationalacademies.org/cstb/pub_broadband.html

Dahlman, C. & Andersson, T. (2000) *The Korean Knowledge Economy*, IBRD, World Bank, OECD, Paris.

Daniels, P. (2003) *Old Economy, New Economy and Services*. University of Birmingham, School of Geography, Earth and Environmental Sciences, Birmingham.

Digital Europe (2003) *Inclusion in the Information Society*, European Commission, Brussels.

DTI (1998) *Our Competitive Future: Building the Knowledge Driven Economy*, Department of Trade and Industry, London.

DTI/Spectrum (1996) *Development of the Information Society: An International Analysis*, HMSO, London.

DTI/Spectrum (1998) *Moving into the Information Age: International Benchmarking Study*, DTI, London.

Ducatel, K., Webster, J. & Hermann, W. (2000) 'Information infrastructures or societies?', in K. Ducatel, J. Webster & W. Hermann (eds) *The Information Society in Europe: Work and Life in an Age of Globalisation*, Rowman & Littlefield Publishers, Lanham, ML.

Dutta, S., Lanvin, B. & Paua E (2003) *The Global Information Technology Report: Readiness for the Networked World*, Oxford University Press, New York.

Dutton, W., Gillett, S., McKnight, L. & Peltu, M. (2003) *Broadband Internet: The Power to Reconfigure Access*, Forum Discussion Paper, Oxford Internet Institute, Oxford, available at: http://www.oii.ox.ac.uk/resources/publications/OIIFD_Broadband_0803.pdf

Dyson, E., Gilder, G., Keyworth, G. & Toffler, A. (1996) 'Cyberspace and the American dream', *Information Society*, vol. 12, pp. 295–308.

Economist Intelligence Unit (EIU) (2003) *The 2003 E-Readiness Rankings*, available at: www.ebusinessforum.com.

Edmonds, T. (2000) *Regional Competitiveness and the Role of the Knowledge Economy*, Rep. No. 00/73, House of Commons Research Library, House of Commons, London.

ERICarts (2001) *Making Information Society Work for Culture*, Council of Europe NIT Project, Bonn.

Eurescom (2001) *Telework and Quality of Life*, European Institute for Research and Strategic Studies in Telecommunications, Heidelberg.

European Commission (2000) *Statistical Indicators for the New Economy (SINE)*, Information Society Technologies.

FLEXCOT (2000) *Flexible Work Practices and Communication Technology*, European Commission, Brussels.

Foley, P. (2000) *Whose Net? Characteristics of Internet Users in the UK: Report Submitted to the Department of Trade and Industry*, De Montfort University, Leicester.

Forstater, M., Raynard, P. & Zadek, S. (2003) *BT and the Digital Divide*, BT, London.

Freeman, C. & Perez, C. (1988) 'Structural crises of adjustment business cycles and investment behaviour', in Dosi, G. *et al.* (eds) *Technical Change and Economic Theory*, Pinter, London.

Gareis, K. & Mentrup, A. (2001) *On the E-Work Frontier: Developments Towards an Internet-Based Labour Market in a Forerunner Industry*, STAR Issue Report No. 8, Empirica, Bonn.

Giddens A. (2000) *The Third Way and Its Critics*, Polity, London.

Greenspan, A. (1999) 'Testimony of Chairman Alan Greenspan Before the Committee on Banking and Financial Services', July 22, US House of Representatives.

Heller, F.A. (1987) 'The technological imperative and the quality of employment', *New Technology, Work and Employment*, vol. 2, pp. 19–26.

Henneberry, J. (1987) *British Science Parks and High Technology Developments – Progress and Change: 1983–86*, Sheffield City Polytechnic (now Sheffield Hallam).

Hepworth, M. & Spencer, G. (2002) *A Regional Perspective on the Knowledge Economy in Great Britain: Report for DTI*, Local Futures Group, London.

IBM (1997) *The Net Result – Report of the National Working Party for Social Inclusion*, IBM Community Development Foundation, New York.

Indergaard, M. (2003) 'The webs they weave: Malaysia's multimedia super-corridor and New York City's Silicon Alley', *Urban Studies*, vol. 40, no. 2, pp. 379–401.

Indergaard, M. (2004) *'Silicon Alley: The Rise and Fall of a New Media District'*, Routledge, London.

Ismail, S. & Wu, I. (2003) *Broadband Internet Access in OECD Countries: A Comparative Analysis*, Staff Report of the Office of Strategic Planning and Policy Analysis and International Bureau, OECD, Paris, available at: http://yamachan.hept. himeji-tech.ac.jp/DOC-239660A2.pdf

ITU (International Telecommunications Union) (2003) *Birth of Broadband*, ITU, Geneva.

Jessop, B. (2000) *The State and the Contradictions of the Knowledge-Driven Economy*, Department of Sociology, University of Lancaster, Lancaster.

Johnson, J.H. & Sinder J.H. (2003) *Breaking the Chains: Unlicensed Spectrum As a Last-Mile Broadband Solution*, Rep. No. Issue Brief 11, New America Foundation, Washington DC.

Jones Lang LaSalle (2003) *Shopping for New Markets: Retailers' Expansion Across Europe's Borders*, Jones Lang LaSalle, London.

Katz, J.E. & Aakhus.M. (eds) (2002) *Perpetual Contact: Mobile Communication, Private Talk, Public Performance*, Cambridge University Press, Cambridge.

Kearns, I. (2002) *Code Red: Progressive Politics in the Digital Age*, Institute of Public Policy Research, London.

Kuhn, T. (1962) *The Structure of Scientific Revolutions*, Chicago University Press, Chicago.

Leadbeater, C. (1999) *Living on Thin Air: The New Economy*, Viking, London.

Lengrand and Associates (2002) *Innovation Tomorrow*, EU-Directorate General for Enterprise, Brussels.

Lessig L. (2001) *The Future of Ideas: The Fate of the Commons in a Connected World*, Random House, New York.

Lever, W. (2002) 'The knowledge base and the competitive city', in I. Begg (ed.) *Urban Competitveness: Policies for Dynamic Cities*, Policy Press, Bristol.

Liikanen, E. (2000) *eEurope: An Information Society for All*, European Commission, Brussels.

Livingstone, S. (2002) *Young People and New Media*, Sage Publications Ltd, London.

Livingstone, S. & Bovill, M. (1999) *Young People New Media: Summary*, London School of Economics, London.

Local Futures Group (2001) *The Geography of the Knowledge Economy in Britain*, Local Futures Group, London.

Machlup, F. (1962) *The Production and Distribution of Knowledge in the United States*, Princeton University Press, Princeton, NJ.

Malecki, E. (1997) *Technology and Economic Development: The Dynamics of Local, Regional and National Competitiveness*, Addison-Wesley Harman, Harlow.

Mansell, R. (1998) 'The Scarcity-Abundance Dialectic: The Dynamics of Communication and Access', paper presented at Amsterdam School of Communication Research, Amsterdam University.

Mansell, R. (ed.) (2002) *Inside the Communication Revolution: Evolving Patterns of Social and Technical Interaction*, Oxford University Press, Oxford.

Mansell, R. (2003) *The Nature of the Information Society: an Industrialised World Perspective*, Visions of the Information Society, International Telecommunications Unit, Geneva.

Mansell, R. & Nikolychuk L (2002) *The Economic Importance of Electronic Networks: Assessing the Micro-Level Evidence Base*, Report prepared for the Prime Minister's Strategy Unit, Media@LSE, London.

Martin, R. (2003) 'Putting the Economy in its Place: on Economics and Geography', paper presented at Cambridge Journal of Economics Conference, 17–19 September, Cambridge.

Masuda, Y. (1990) *Managing in the Information Society: Releasing Synergy Japanese Style*, Blackwell, Oxford.

Meyer, C. (1999) 'What's the matter?' *Business*, 2.0, April.

Miles, I. (2000) 'Rethinking Organisation in the Information Society', paper presented at SOWING Conference, Karlsruhe.

Millar, J.E. (2002) *The Globalisation of Information Processing Services? The Implications of Outsourcing for Employment and Skills in Europe*, STAR Issue Report No 26, STAR/SPRU, Paris.

Mumford, L. (1964) *The Myth of the Machine: The Pentagon of Power*, Harcourt Brace Jovanovich Inc, New York.

Murdock, G. (2002) 'Tackling the Digital Divide: Evidence and Intervention', paper presented at the Digital Divide Day Seminar, 19 February, British Educational Communications and Technology Agency, Coventry.

Myers, M.B. & Rosenbloom R.S. (1996) 'Rethinking the role of industrial research', in R.S. Rosenbloom & W.J. Spencer (eds) *Engines in Innovation: US Industrial Research at the End of an Era*, Harvard Business School Press, Harvard, MA.

Nafus, D. & Tracey, K. (2002) 'Mobile phone consumption and concepts of parenthood', in J. Katz & M. Aakhus (eds) *Perpetual Contact: Mobile Communications, Private Talk, Public Performance*, Cambridge University Press, Cambridge.

Neice, D. (2002) 'Cyberspace and social distinctions: two metaphors and a theory', in R. Mansell (ed.) *Inside the Communication Revolution: Evolving patterns of Social and Technical Interaction*, Oxford University Press, Oxford.

Norton, R.D. (2000) *The Geography of the New Economy – The Web Book of Regional Science*, available at: www.rriwvu.edu.

OECD (1995) *Industry and Technology: Scoreboard of Indicators*, OECD, Paris.

OECD (2001) *Understanding the Digital Divide*, OECD, Paris.

OECD (2002) *Measuring the Information Economy*, OECD, Paris.

Paltridge, S. (2003) *The Social Divide: The Deployment and Adoption of Broadband Within Nations and Across Nations and Regions*, Oxford Internet Institute, Oxford.

Pepper, S. (1942) *World Hypotheses: A Study in Evidence*, University of California, Berkeley, CA.

Performance Innovation Unit (PIU) (1999) *Ecommerce@Its.Best.Uk*, Performance Innovation Unit, London.

Peters, M. (2001) 'National education policy constructions of the "knowledge economy": towards a critique', *Journal of Educational Enquiry*, vol. 2, no. 1, pp. 1–22.

Porat, M. (1997) *The Information Economy: Definition and Measurement*, US Department of Commerce, Washington DC.

Robins, K. & Webster, F. (1999) *Times of Technoculture*, Routledge, London.

Roszak, T. (1986) *The Cult of Information*, Lutterworth, Cambridge.

Sawyer, S., Crowston, K., Wigand, R. & Allbritton, M. (2003) 'The social embeddedness of transactions: evidence from the residential real estate industry', *The Information Society*, vol. 19, pp. 135–154.

Schiller, R. (2001) *The Dynamics of Property Location*, Spon, London and New York.

Selhofer, H. & Husing, T. (2002) *The Digital Divide Index – A Measure of Social Inequalities in The Adoption of ICT*, Empirica, Bonn.

Selwyn, N. (2003) *Defining the Digital Divide: Developing a Theoretical Understanding of Inequalities in the Information Age*, Rep. No. Occasional Paper 49, Report for the Adults Learning @ Home Project (ESRC), Cardiff University.

Sheerin, C. (2002) 'UK material flow accounting', *Economic Trends*, June, 53–61.

Siegfried, C. (2001) *E-Government and E-Commerce: German Experience in the Construction of Virtual Townhalls and Marketplaces*, Centre of Excellence for Electronic Government, Universisitat St Gallen, Switzerland.

Slevin, J. (2000) *The Internet and Society*, Polity Press, Cambridge.

STAR (2003) *Images of Tomorrow*, Annual Report, STAR, Paris.

Steinmueller, E. (2003) *Taking Stock of Socio-Economic Research on IST*, STAR Report No. 22, STAR, Paris.

Strategy Unit (2002) *Electronic Networks: Challenges for the Next Decade*, Stationery Office, London.

Tapscott, D. (1996) *The Digital Economy: Promise and Peril in the Age of Networked Intelligence*, McGraw Hill, New York.

Tauber, E.M. (1972) 'Why do people shop?', *Journal of Marketing*, vol. 36, no. 4, pp. 46–49.

Toffler, A. (1980) *The Third Wave*, Collins, London.

Tuomi, I. (2001) *From Periphery to Center: Emerging Research Topics on The Knowledge Society*, Technology Review 116/2001, TEKES, Finland.

UKSPA (2003) *United Kingdom Science Park Association Annual Statistics*, Cambridge.

UNCTAD (2003a) *Information Society Measurements: the Case of EBusiness*, UNCTAD Trade and Development Board, New York.

UNCTAD (2003b) *E-Commerce and Development Report*, Internet edition, New York and Geneva (www.unctad.org).

United Nations (2001) *Benchmarking E-Government: A Global Perspective-Assessing the Progress of the UN Member States*, Report for Public Economics and Public Administration and the American Society for Public Administration, United Nations, Geneva.

Urry, J. (2000) *Sociology Beyond Societies: Mobilities for the Twenty-First Century*, Routledge, London.

US Department of Commerce (1995) *Falling through the Net*, US Department of Commerce, Washington DC.

Verdict (2000) *Verdict Forecasts Retailing 2005*, Verdict, London.

Warf, B. (2001) 'Segueways into cyberspace: multiple geographies of the digital divide', *Environment and Planning B: Planning and Design*, vol. 28, no. 1, pp. 3–19.

Webster, F. (2002) *Theories of the Information Society*, Routledge, London.

Webster, F. (ed.) (2004) *The Information Society Reader*, Routledge, London.

Westhead, P. & Batstone, S. (1998) 'Independent technology-based firms: the perceived benefits of a science park location', *Urban Studies*, vol. 35, no. 12, pp. 2197–2219.

Westhead, P. & Batstone, S. (1999) 'Perceived benefits of a managed science park location', *Entrepreneurship and Regional Development*, vol. 11, pp. 129–154.

Wilsdon, J. & Stedman Jones, D. (2002) *The Politics of Broadband: Network Innovation and Regulation In Braodband Britain*, DEMOS, London.

Winner, L. (1996) 'Who will we be in cyberspace?', *Information Society*, vol. 12, pp. 63–72.

Woolgar, S. (ed.) (2002) *Virtual Society? Technology, Cyberpole, Reality*, Oxford University Press, Oxford.

World Bank (1998) *World Development Report 1998/99: Knowledge and Information for Development*, Oxford University Press/World Bank, New York.

World Economic Forum/INSEAD (2003) *Global Information Technology Report*, available at: http://www.weforum.org/site/homepublic.nsf/Content/Global+Programme%5CGlobal+Information+Technology+Report

Wresch, W. (1996) *Disconnected: Haves and Have Nots in the Information Age*, Rutgers University Press, New Brunswick, NJ.

3 Technological Change: Diffusion and Adoption of ICT by Consumers, Businesses and Government

Aldrich, F. (2003) 'Smart homes: past, present and future', in R. Harper (ed.) *Inside the Smart Home*, Springer-Verlag, London.

Arthur, B. (1989) 'Competing technologies, increasing returns, and lock-in by historical events', *The Economic Journal*, vol. 99, pp. 116–131.

Barlow, J. & Gann, D. (1998) 'A Changing sense of Place: Are Integrated IT Systems Reshaping the Home?', paper presented at Technological Futures, Urban Futures, 23–24 April, Durham.

Bassanini, A. & Scarpetta, S. (2003) 'Growth, technological change and ICT diffusion: recent evidence from OECD Countries', *Oxford Review of Economic Policy*, vol. 18, no. 3, pp. 324–344.

Bastow, S., Dunleavy, P. & Margetts, H. (2003) *Progress in Implementing E-Government at Central and Local Levels in England: 1998–2003*, Government on the Web, London School of Economics and University College London.

Becker, F. & Steele, F. (1995) *Workplace by Design: Mapping the High Performance Workscape*, Jossey Bass, New York.

Betcherman, G. & McMullen, K. (1998) *Impact of Information and Communication Technologies on Work and Employment in Canada*, Canadian Policy Research Network, Ottawa.

Bijker, W. & Law, J. (1992) *Shaping Technology/Building Society: Studies in Sociotechnical Change*, MIT Press, Cambridge, MA.

Booz Allen Hamilton (2003) *Business in the Information Age – International Benchmarking Study*, Department of Trade and Industry, London.

Booz Allen Hamilton/INSEAD (2002) *The World's Most Effective Policies for the E-Economy*, Booz Allen Hamilton/INSEAD, London.

Bowden, S. & Offer, A. (1994) 'Household appliances and the use of time: the United States and Britain since the 1920s', *Economic History Review*, vol. XLVLL, no. 4, pp. 725–748.

Bresnahan, T.F., Brynjolfsson, E. & Hitt, L. (2002) 'Information technology, workplace organization, and the demand for skilled labor: firm-level evidence', *Quarterly Journal of Economics*, vol. 117, February, pp. 339–376.

Brynjolfsson, E. & Hitt, L. (2002) *Digital Organisation, Preliminary Results From an MIT Study of Internet Organisation, Culture and Productivity*, MIT and University of Pennsylvania, Philadelphia.

Carr, N. (2003) 'IT Doesn't Matter', *Harvard Business Review*, May, pp. 41–49.

Charles, D. & Lever, W. (1996) 'Information technology and production systems', *The Global Economy in Transition*, Longmans, London.

City University Business School (2002) *Total Office Cost Survey*, Actium Consult, London.

College of Estate Management (2001) *Future Shock or E-Hype? The Impact of Online Shopping on UK Retail Property*, British Council of Shopping Centres, London.

Coyle, D. & Quah, D. (2002) *Getting the Measure of the New Economy*, The Work Foundation, London.

Crabtree, J., Nathan, M. & Reeves, R. (2002) *Reality IT: Technology and Everyday Life*, ISociety, The Work Foundation, London.

CURDS (Centre for Urban and Regional Development Studies) (2004) *Public Sector Relocation From London and the South East*, Report for English Regional Development Agencies, CURDS, University of Newcastle upon Tyne.

Curthoys, N. & Crabtree, J. (2003) *SmartGov: Renewing Electronic Government for Improved Service Delivery*, ISociety, The Work Foundation, London.

David, P. (1985) 'Clio and the economics of QWERTY', *AEA Papers and Proceedings*, vol. 75, no. 2, pp. 332–337.

Davidow, W.H. & Malone, M.S. (1992) *The Virtual Corporation*, Harper Business, London.

De Kare-Silver, M. (2000) *E-Shock 2000: The New Rules – E-Strategies for Retailers and Manufacturers*, Palgrave, Basingstoke.

Deloitte Research (2003) *The Cusp of a Revolution: How Offshoring Will Transform the Financial Services Industry*, Deloitte, New York.

Dixon, T. & Marston, A. (2002) *eRPUK 2001: ECommerce and Retail Property in the UK: Annual Survey and International Comparison*, College of Estate Management, Reading.

Dixon, T., Thompson, R. & McAllister, P. (2002) *The Value of ICT for SMEs in the UK: A Critical Literature Review and Scoping Study for Further Research*, College of Estate Management, Reading.

Douglas, M. & Isherwood, B. (1979) *The World of Goods*, Routledge, London.

DTI (2001) *Business in the Information Age: International Benchmarking Study*, DTI, London.

DTI (2002) *Business in the Information Age: International Benchmarking Study, 2002*, DTI, London.

DTI/MORI (2001) *Informing Consumers About E-Commerce*, DTI, London.

Duffy, F. (1997) *The New Office*, Conran Octopus, London.

e-BusinessW@tch (2003) *The European E-Business Report: 2003 Edition*, European Commission, Luxembourg.

ECATT (2000) *Benchmarking Telework and E-Commerce in Europe: Final Report*, ECATT, Bonn.

e-Envoy (2003) *Annual Report*, Office of the e-Envoy, London.

EITO (2002) *European Information Technology Observatory (EITO): 2002*, EITO, Frankfurt.

European Commission (2000) *Telework Pilot Project in the European Commission: External Evaluation Panel Report*, European Commission, Brussels.

European Commission (2003) *European Competitiveness Report: Competitiveness and Benchmarking*, European Commission, Brussels.

Felstead, A., Gallie, D. & Green, F. (2002) *Work Skills in Britain*, Centre for Labour Market Studies, University of Leicester, Leicester.

FLEXCOT (2000) *Flexible Work Practices and Communication Technology*, European Commission, Brussels.

Fulton, C., Halpin, E. & Walker, S. (2001) 'Privacy meets home-based eWork', paper presented at eWork 2001: Working Together on the Net, 12–14 September, Helsinki.

Hamill, L. (2003) 'Time as a rare commodity in home life', in R. Harper (ed.) *Inside the Smart Home*, Springer-Verlag, London.

Hardman (1973) *The Dispersal of Government Work from London*, Cmnd 5322, June, Stationery Office, London.

Harkin, J. (2003) *Mobilisation: The Growing Public Interest in Mobile Technology*, DEMOS, London.

Harper, R. (2003) 'Inside the smart home: ideas, possibilities and methods', in R. Harper (ed.) *Inside the Smart Home*, Springer-Verlag, London.

Hotopp, U. (2002) 'Teleworking in the UK', *Labour Market Trends*, June, pp. 311–318.

Huws, U. (2001) *Where the Butterfly Alights: the Global Location of EWork*, Rep. No 378, Institute for Employment Studies, Brighton.

Huws, U. & O'Regan, S. (2001) *EWork in Europe: Results From the EMERGENCE 18-Country Survey*, Report No 380, Institute for Employment Studies, Brighton.

Huws, U., Korte, W.B. & Robinson, S. (1990) *Telework: Towards the Elusive Office*, Wiley, New York.

Kellerman, A. (2002) *The Internet on Earth: A Geography of Information*, John Wiley & Sons Ltd, Chichester.

Kinsmann, F. (1987) *The Telecommuters*, Wiley, New York.

Kling, R. & Tilquist, J. (2000) *Conceiving IT-Enabled Organisational Change*, CSI Working Paper No. 98–02, Indiana University, Bloomington, IN.

Leamer, E. & Storper, M. (2001) 'The economic geography of the Internet age', *Journal of International Business Studies*, vol. 32, no. 4, pp. 641–665.

Levin, M.R. (1998) *Teleworking and Urban Development Patterns*, University Press of America, New York.

London Economics (2003) *ICT Investment and Productivity in the UK: a Regional Assessment*, Economic Brief, London.

London Economics/CISCO (2003) *ICT and GDP Growth in the United Kingdom: A Sectoral Analysis:* CISCO, New York and London.

Lyons, M. (2003) *Independent Review of Public Sector Relocation: Interim Report*, UK Treasury, London.

Lyons, M. (2004) *Well Placed to Deliver? Shaping the Pattern of Government Service*, HM Treasury, London.

Malecki, E.J. (2002) 'The Internet: a preliminary analysis of its evolving economic geography', *Economic Geography*, vol. 78, pp. 399–424.

Mansell, R. (2003) *The Nature of the Information Society: an Industrialised World Perspective*, Visions of the Information Society, International Telecommunications Unit, Geneva.

Mansell, R. & Nikolychuk L (2002) *The Economic Importance of Electronic Networks: Assessing the Micro-Level Evidence Base*, Report prepared for the Prime Minister's Strategy Unit, Media@LSE, London.

Mansell, R. & Steinmueller, W.E. (2000) *Mobilizing the Information Society*, Oxford University Press, Oxford.

Margetts, H. & Dunleavy, P. (2002) *Better Public Services Through E-Government: Academic Article in Support of Better Public Services Through E-Government*, Report by the Comptroller and Auditor General HC 704-III – Session 2001–2002, National Audit Office, London.

McCarthy, H. & Miller, P. (2003) *London Calling: How Mobile Technologies Will Transform Our Capital City*, DEMOS, London.

Mesenbourg, T. (2001) 'Measuring the Digital Economy Available', paper presented at Netcentric Economy Symposium, March 30, University of Maryland.

Mitel (2000) *Teleworking Britain*, Mitel, London.

Murphy, M. (2002) *Organisational Change and Firm Performance*, STI Working Paper 2002/14, OECD, Paris.

Nathan, M., Carpenter, G. & Roberts, S. (2003) *Getting By, Not Getting on: Technology in UK Workplaces*, ISociety, The Work Foundation, London.

National Audit Office (NAO) (2002) *Better Public Services Through E-Government*, Report by the Comptroller and Auditor General: HC 704–1 Session 2001–2002, NAO, London.

National Statistics (2003a) *Family Spending: A Report on the 2001–2002 Expenditure and Food Survey*, National Statistics, London.

National Statistics (2003b) *Internet Access: Individuals and Households*, National Statistics, London.

National Statistics (2003c) *2002 E-Commerce Survey of Business:Value of E-Trading*, National Statistics, London.

National Statistics (2004) *Social Trends: 34*, Stationery Office, London.

Nilles, J.M., Carlson, F.R., Gray, P. & Hanneman, G.J. (1976) *The Telecommunications Transportation Trade-Off*, Wiley, New York.

OECD (1999) *The Economic and Social Impact of Electronic Commerce*, OECD, Paris.

OECD (2002) *Measuring the Information Economy*, OECD, Paris.

OECD (2003) *ICT and Economic Growth: Evidence From OECD Countries, Industries and Firms*, Information and Communication Technologies, OECD, Paris.

Oulton, N. (2002) 'ICT and productivity growth in the United Kingdom', *Oxford Review of Economic Policy*, vol. 18, no. 3, pp. 363–379.

Oxford Internet Institute (2004) *Oxford Internet Survey 2003 – How Much Is Enough of the Internet?*, Oxford Internet Institute, Oxford.

Percival-Straunik, L. (2001) *E-Commerce*, The Economist Books, London.

Perez, C. (2001) 'Technological change and opportunities for development as a moving target', *Cepal Review*, vol. 75, December, pp. 109–130.

Perez, C. (2002) *Technological Revolutions and Financial Capital: The Dynamics of Bubbles and Golden Ages*, Edward Elgar, Cheltenham.

Performance Innovation Unit (1999) *Ecommerce@Its.Best.Uk*, Performance Innovation Unit, London.

Performance Innovation Unit (2000) *E.Gov: Electronic Government Services for the 21st Century*, Performance Innovation Unit/Cabinet Office, London.

Pragnell, M., Spence, L. & Moore, R. (2000) *The Potential Market for Smart Homes*, Joseph Rowntree Foundation, York.

Rogers, E.M. (1995) *Diffusion of Innovations*, 4th edn, Free Press, New York.

Shapiro, A.L. (1999) *The Control Revolution: How the Internet Is Putting Individuals in Charge and Changing the World*, Public Affairs, New York.

Shapiro, C. & Varian, H. (1999) *Information Rules*, Harvard University Press, Boston, MA.

SIBIS (2003) *Benchmarking e-commerce in the Information Society Europe and the US, Statistical Indicators: Benchmarking the Information Society* (SIBIS), available at: http://www.empirica.biz/sibis/files/download/reports2.htm

Sorenson, K.H. (1998) *Learning Technology, Constructing Culture: Socio-Technical Change As Social Learning*, Centre for Technology and Society, Norwegian University of Science and Technology.

Stoneman, P. (1983) *The Economic Analysis of Technological Change*, Oxford University Press, Oxford.

Thompson, M., Ellis, R. & Wildavsky, A. (1990) *Cultural Theory*, Westview Press, Colorado.

Toffler, A. (1980) *The Third Wave*, Collins, London.

US Department of Commerce (2003) *E-Commerce Statistics*, US Department of Commerce, available at: http://www.census.gov/mrts/www/current.html

Verdict (2002) *Verdict on Electronic Shopping*, Verdict, London.

Zuboff, S. (1988) *In the Age of the Smart Machine: The Future of Work and Power*, Basic Books, New York.

4   Business Process and Organisational Change

Bashein, B.J., Lynne Markus, M. & Riley, P. (2001) *Business Process Reengineering: Preconditions for Success and How to Prevent Failures*, Information Systems Management, Boca Raton, FL.

Benchmark Research (2002) *Commerce One Global Procurement Report*, Benchmark Research, Kent.

Beniger, J.R. (1986) *The Control Revolution: Technological and Economic Origins of the Information Society*, Harvard University Press, Cambridge, MA.

Burton, R.M. & Obel, B. (1984) *Designing Efficient Organizations: Modeling and Experimentation*, North Holland, New York.

Cairncross, F. (2001) *The Death of Distance 2.0: How the Communications Revolution Will Change Our Lives*, Texere, London and New York.

Davenport, T.H. (1993) *Process Innovation*, Harvard University Press, Harvard, MA.

Davenport, T.H. & Short, J.E. (1990) 'The new industrial engineering: information technology and business process redesign', *Sloan Management Review*, Summer, pp. 11–27.

Dixon, T., Marston, A., Thompson, B. & Elder, B. (2002) *The Impact of eBusiness on the City of London Office Market*, College of Estate Management, Reading.

Dixon, T., Marston, A., Thompson, B. & Elder, B. (2003) 'eBusiness and the City of London office market', *Journal of Property Investment and Finance*, vol. 21, no. 4, pp. 348–365.

Duffy, F. (1997) *The New Office*, Conran Octopus, London.

Evans, P. & Wurster, T.S. (2000) *Blown to Bits: How the New Economics of Information Transforms Strategy*, Harvard Business School Press, Boston, MA.

Gerald Eve (2001) *Overcrowded, Under-Utilised or Just Right? Report of a Study of Occupational Densities*, Gerald Eve in association with RICS, London.

Groth, L. (1999) *Future Organizational Design: The Scope for the IT-based Enterprise*, Wiley, Chichester.

Jacka, J.M. and Keller, P.J. (2001) *Business Process Mapping*, Wiley, New York.

Kling, R. & Lamb, R. (2001) 'IT and organizational change in digital economies: a sociotechnical approach', in B. Kahin (ed.) *Understanding the Digital Economy*, MIT Press, Boston, MA.

Malone, T.W. & Smith, S.A. (1988) 'Modeling the performance of organizational structures', *Operations Research*, vol. 36, no. 3, pp. 421–436.

Mintzberg, H. (1979) *The Structuring of Organizations*, Prentice Hall, New York.

Moore, G.E. (1965) 'Cramming more components onto integrated circuits', *Electronics*, vol. 38, no. 8, pp. 1–4.

Negroponte, N. (2002) 'Wearable Wallets, Vacant Malls', keynote address presented at Internet Commerce Expo, April, Tokyo.

Pfeffer, J. & Leblebici, H. (1977) 'Information technology and organization structure', *Pacific Sociological Review*, vol. 20, pp. 241–261.

RETRI Group (2003) *Office Futures*, RETRI, UK.

Robey, D. (1995) 'Theories that Explain Contradiction: Accounting for the Contradictory Organizational Consequences of Information Technology', paper presented at Proceedings of the 16th International Conference on Information Systems, Atlanta, GA.

Taylor, F.W. (1911) *The Principles of Scientific Management*, Harper Brothers, New York.

University of California (2003) *How Much Information 2003?*, Berkeley School of Information Management, available at: http://www.sims.berkeley.edu/research/projects/how-much-info-2003/printable_report.pdf

UNECE (2003) *World Robotics*, United Nations Economic Commission for Europe (UNECE), Geneva.

Wang, S. (2000) 'Managing the organizational aspects of electronic commerce', *Human Systems Management*, vol. 19, no. 1, pp. 49–59.

Weiser, M. (1991) 'The computer for the 21st century', *Scientific American*, vol. 265, pp. 94–104.

Whisler, T.L. (1970) *Information Technology and Organizational Charge*, Wadsworth, London.

Womack, J.P., Jones, D.T. & Roos, D. (1991) *The Machine That Changed the World*, Harper Collins, New York.

Zuboff, S. (1988) *In the Age of the Smart Machine: The Future of Work and Power*, Basic Books, New York.

5 The New Economy and Real Estate

Arthur Andersen (2000a) *eReal Estate Companies: the Impact of eBusiness and the Internet in the New Economy*, Arthur Andersen/Rosen Consulting Group, New York.

Arthur Andersen (2000b) *eReal Estate: A Virtual Certainty*, Arthur Andersen/Rosen Consulting Group, New York.

Baldwin, J.R. & Sabourin, D. (2002) *Impact of the Adoption of Advanced Information and Communications Technologies on Firm Performance in the Canadian Manufacturing Sector*, STI Working Paper 2002/1, OECD, Paris.

Bartelsman, E.J. & Hinloopen, J. (2004) 'Unleashing animal spirits: investment in ICT and economic growth', in Soete, L. and ter Weel, B. (eds) *The Economics of the Digital Economy*, Edward Elgar, Cheltenham.

Bean, C. (2003) *Economists and the Real World*, Lecture at the London School of Economics, 29 January.

Black, S.E. & Lynch, L.M. (2001) 'How to compete: the impact of workplace practices and information technology on productivity', *The Review of Economics and Statistics*, vol. 83, no. 3, pp. 434–445.

Bootle, R. (2003) *Money for Nothing: Real Wealth, Financial Fantasies and The Economy of the Future*, Nicholas Brealey Publishing, London and Maine.

Boulton, R., Libert, B. & Samek, S. (2000) *Cracking the Value Code: How Successful Businesses Are Creating Wealth in the New Economy*, Harper Business, New York.

Bresnahan, T.F. & Greenstein, S. (1996) *Technical Progress and Co-Invention in Computing and the Use of Computers*, Brookings Papers on Economic Activity: Microeconomics, Brookings Institution, Washington DC.

Brynjolfsson, E. & Hitt, L.M. (1998) 'Beyond the productivity paradox: computers are the catalyst for bigger changes', *Communications of the ACM*, vol. 41, no. 8, pp. 49–55.

Business Week (2000) 'Americans see the new economy all around them', *Business Week*, 19 May, available at: www.businessweek.com

Cairncross, F. (2001) *The Death of Distance 2.0: How the Communications Revolution Will Change Our Lives*, Texere, London and New York.

Cannon, T., Nathan, M. & Westwood, A. (2003) *Welcome to the Ideopolis*, The Work Foundation, London.

Capital Economics Ltd (2002) *Property in Business – A Waste of Space?*, RICS, London.

Caroli, E. & Van Reenen, J. (2003) *Organisation, Skills and Technology: Evidence From a Panel of British and French Establishments*, IFS Working Paper Series W99/23, Institute of Fiscal Studies, London.

Clayton, T. & Waldron, K. (2003) 'e-Commerce adoption and business impact: a progress report', *Economic Trends*, vol. 591, February, pp. 33–40.

Colecchia, A. & Schreyer, P. (2001) *The Impact of Information Communications Technology on Output Growth*, STI Working paper, 2001/7, OECD, Paris.

College of Estate Management (CEM) (2001) *Future Shock or E-Hype? The Impact of Online Shopping on UK Retail Property*, British Council of Shopping Centres, London.

Coyle, D. (1997) *The Weightless World*, Capstone and MIT, London and MA.

Coyle, D. (2002) 'Still Seeking the New Paradigm', paper presented at IAOS Conference, 27–29 August, London.

Coyle, D. & Quah, D. (2002) *Getting the Measure of the New Economy*, The Work Foundation, London.

Crafts, N. (2001) *The Solow Productivity Paradox in Historical Perspective*, London School of Economics, London.

Daniels, P. (2003) *Old Economy, New Economy and Services*, Working Papers in Services, Space, Society, University of Birmingham, School of Geography, Earth and Environmental Sciences, Birmingham.

Daveri, F. (2002) *The New Economy in Europe, 1992–2001*, Discussion Paper No. 2002/70, UNU World Institute for Development Economic Research, Helsinki.

De Kare-Silver, M. (2000) *E-Shock 2000: The New Rules – E-Strategies for Retailers and Manufacturers*, Palgrave, Basingstoke.

Deloitte Research (2003) *The Cusp of a Revolution: How Offshoring Will Transform the Financial Services Industry*, Deloitte, New York.

Deng, Y. & Gyourko, J. (1999) *Real Estate Ownership by Non-Real Estate Firms: the Impact of Firm Returns*, Lurie Real Estate Center at Wharton University of Pennsylvania.

Dixon, T.J. & Marston, A.D. (2002) 'eProperty = eBusiness + eCommerce: The New Digital Economy and UK Commercial Property', paper presented at European Real Estate Society Conference, June, Glasgow.

Dixon, T., Pottinger, G., Marston, A. & Beard, M. (2000) *Occupational Futures? Real Estate Refinancing and Restructuring*, College of Estate Management, Reading.

Donaldsons (2003) *Research Proves that Leasing Property helps Boost Company Performance*, Donaldsons, London.

Florida, R. (2002) *The Rise of the Creative Class*, Basic Books, New York.

Gerald Eve (2001) *Overcrowded, Under-Utilised or Just Right? Report of a Study of Occupational Densities*, Gerald Eve in association with RICS, London.

Gibson, V. & Louargand, M. (2001) 'The workplace portfolio as contractual arrangements', in Gartner (ed.) *The Agile Workplace: A Research Partnership Between Gartner, MIT and 22 Industry Sponsors*, Gartner and MIT, Massachusetts.

Gordon, R.J. (2000) 'Does the new economy measure up to the great inventions of the past?', *Journal of Economic Perspectives*, vol. 14, no. 4, pp. 49–74.

Greenspan, A. (1999) 'Testimony of Chairman Alan Greenspan Before the Committee on Banking and Financial Services', July 22, US House of Representatives.

Gust, C. & Marquez, J. (2002) *International Productivity Growth: The Role of Information Technology and Regulatory Practices*, Finance Discussion Papers, No. 727, Federal Reserve Board, Washington DC.

Harberger, A. (1998) 'A vision of the growth process', *American Economic Review*, vol. 88, no. 1, pp. 1–32.

Harrison, A. (2002) 'Accommodating the new economy: the SANE space environment model', *Journal of Corporate Real Estate*, vol. 4, no. 3, pp. 248–265.

Jacobs, J. (1961) *The Death and Life of Great American Cities*, Random House, New York.

Johnson, B.C. (2002) 'Retail: the Wal-Mart effect', *The McKinsey Quarterly*, available at: www.mckinseyquarterly.com

Kelly, K. (1998) *New Rules for the New Economy*, Viking Penguin, New York.

Kirschbraun, T.C. (2000) 'News of real estate's death is greatly exaggerated: real estate in the new economy', *Journal of Corporate Real Estate*, vol. 2, no. 4, pp. 343–350.

Kolko, J. (2002) 'Silicon mountains, silicon molehills: geographic concentration and convergence of internet industries in the US', *Information Economics and Policy*, vol. 14, no. 2, pp. 211–232.

Kotkin, J. (2001) *The New Geography: How the Digital Revolution Is Reshaping the American Landscape*, Random House, New York.

Landmann, O. (2002) *Employment, Productivity and Output Growth*, World Employment Report – Background Paper, University of Freiberg, Freiberg.

Leamer, E. & Storper, M. (2001) 'The economic geography of the Internet age', *Journal of International Business Studies*, vol. 32, no. 4, pp. 641–665.

Lohr, S. (1999) 'At last, economists see a high-tech payoff', *International Herald Tribune*, 15 April.

Marshall, A. (1890) *Principles of Economics*, Macmillan, London.

McGuckin, R. & van Ark, B. (2001) *Making the Most of the Information Age: Productivity and Structural Reform in the New Economy*, Rep. No. 13012-01-RR, Perspectives on Global Economy.

McGuckin, R.H., Strietweiser, M. & Doms, M. (1998) 'The effect of technology use on productivity growth', *Economics of Innovation and New Technology*, vol. 7, pp. 1–26.

Meyer, C. (1999) 'What's the matter?', *Business 2.0*.

Momentum Research Group (2003) *Net Impact: Driving Networked Business Productivity*, Momentum Research Group, Austin, TX.

Moore, G.E. (1965) 'Cramming more components onto integrated circuits', *Electronics*, vol. 38, no. 8, pp. 1–4.

Motohashi, K. (2001) *Economic Analysis of Information Network Use: Organisational and Producitvity Impacts on Japanese Firms*, METI, Research and Statistics Department, Tokyo.

National Statistics (2003) *UK 2003: The Official Yearbook of the United Kingdom of Great Britain and Northern Ireland*, National Statistics, London.

OECD (2001) *The New Economy: Beyond the Hype – Final Report on the OECD Growth Project – Executive Summary*, OECD, Paris.

OECD (2003) *ICT and Economic Growth: Evidence From OECD Countries, Industries and Firms*, Information and Communication Technologies, OECD, Paris.

O'Mara, M.A. (1999) 'Strategic drivers of location decisions for information-age companies', *Journal of Real Estate Research*, vol. 17, no. 3, pp. 365–386.

O'Sullivan, F. (2002) *Dot Com Clusters and Local Economic Development: A Case Study of New Media Development in London's City Fringe*, Centre for Enterprise and Economic Development Research, Middlesex University.

Perez, C. (2002) *Technological Revolutions and Financial Capital: The Dynamics of Bubbles and Golden Ages*, Edward Elgar, Cheltenham.

Pilat, D. (2003) *Sources of Productivity Growth in the 21st Century – Findings From the OECD Growth Project*, OECD, Paris.

Pohjola M. (2002) 'The new economy: facts, impacts and policies', *Information Economics and Policy*, vol. 14, no. 2, pp. 133–144.

Porter, M. (1998) 'Clusters and the new economics of competition', *Harvard Business Review*, pp. 77–90.

PriceWaterhouseCoopers (2000) *Physical Assets – Virtual World: How Do They Reconcile?*, New York

Progressive Policy Institute (1998) *New Economy Index*, Progressive Policy Institute.

Property Council of Australia & Andersen (2001) *Digital Property*, Property Council of Australia, Sydney, NSW.

Putnam, R. (2000) *Bowling Alone: The Collapse and Revival of the American Community*, Touchstone, Simon and Schuster, New York.

Rifkin, J. (1994) *The End of Work – The Decline of the Global Labor Force and the Dawn of the Post-Market Era*, Tarcher/Putnam, New York.

Rowlatt, A., Clayton, T. & Vaze, P. (2002) 'Where, and how, to look for the New Economy', *Economic Trends*, vol. 580, March, pp. 29–35.

Sheerin, C. (2002) 'UK material flow accounting', *Economic Trends*, vol. 583, June, pp. 53–61.

Solow, R. (1987) 'We'd better watch out', *New York Times Book Review*, July 12, p. 36.

Storper, M. & Venables, A.J. (2002) 'Buzz: The Economic Force of the City', paper presented at DRUID Summer Conference: 'Industrial Dynamics of the New and Old Economy: who is embracing whom?', 6–8 June, Copenhagen/Elsinor.

Strassmann, P.A. (1997) *The Squandered Computer: Evaluating the Business Alignment of Information Technologies*, The Information Economics Press, New Cannan, CT.

Tapscott, D. (1996) *The Digital Economy: Promise and Peril in the Age of Networked Intelligence*, McGraw Hill, New York.

Tayyaran, M. & Khan, A. (2003) 'The effects of telecommuting and intelligent transportation systems on urban development', *Journal of Urban Technology*, vol. 10, no. 2, pp. 87–100.

Triplett, J.E. & Bosworth, B.B. (2002) *Baumol's Disease Has Been Cured: IT and Multifactor Productivity in US Services Industries*, Brookings Institution, Washington DC.

van Ark, B., Inklaar, R., and McGuckin, R. (2002) *Changing Gear–Productivity, ICT and Service Industries: Europe and the United States*, Research Memorandum GD-60, Groningen Growth and Development Centre, Groningen.

van Ark, B., Inklaar, R. & McGuckin, R. (2003) 'ICT and Productivity in Europe and the United States', paper presented at SOM PhD Conference, 29 January 2003, De Nieuwe Academie, Groningen.

Varian, H., Litan, R.E., Elder, A. & Shutter, J. (2002) *The Net Impact Study: The Projected Economic Benefits of the Internet in the United States, United Kingdom, France and Germany*, Momentum Research Group, Austin, TX.

Visco, I. (2000) 'The new economy: fact or fiction?' *OECD Observer*, June 27 available at: www.oecdobserver.org, 1–4.

Westwood, A. & Nathan, M. (2003) *Manchester: Ideopolis*, The Work Foundation, London.

6   Real Estate Spaces

Allen, J., Massey, D. & Pryke, M.E. (1999) *Unsettling Cities*, Routledge, London.

Amin, A. & Graham, S. (1998) 'The ordinary city', *Transactions of the Institute of British Geographers*, vol. 22, pp. 411–429.

Batty, M., Chapman, D., Evans, S., Haklay, M., Kueppers, S., Shiode, N., Smith, A. & Torrens, P. (2000) *Visualising the City*, Centre for Advanced Spatial Analysis, University College, London.

Berne, E. (1972) *What Do You Do After You Say Hello?*, Transworld Publishers Ltd, London.

Borsuk, S. (1999) *Nowhere Yet Everywhere*, The Space Place Paper, available at: www.thespaceplace.net

Bourdakis, V. (1997) 'The Future of VRML on Large Urban Models', paper presented at Proceedings of VR -SIG '97, Brunel University, pp. 55–61.

Boyer, C. (1996) *The City of Collective Memory*, MIT Press, Cambridge, MA.

Britton, F. (1994) *Rethinking Work: an Exploratory Investigation of New Concepts of Work in a Knowledge Society*, Ecoplan International, Paris.

Cairncross, F. (2001) *The Death of Distance 2.0: How the Communications Revolution Will Change Our Lives*, Texere, London and New York.

Carr, S., Francis, M., Rivlin, L. & Stone, A. (1992) *Public Space*, Cambridge University Press, Cambridge.

Castells, M. (2000) *The Information Age: Economy, Society and Culture: Volume 1 – The Rise of the Network Society*, 2nd edn, Blackwell, Oxford.

DEGW (1992) *The Intelligent Building in Europe: Study Report*, DEGW, London.

Dixon, T. (2003) 'Real Estate, Technology and the New Economy: The Paradox of Location (Plenary Paper)', paper presented at ERES, June, Helsinki.

Farenc, N., Raupp, M.S., Schweiss, E., Kallmann, M., Aune, O., Boulic, R. & Thalmann, D. (1998) *One Step Towards Virtual Human Management for Urban Environment Simulation*, Swiss Federal Institute of Technology, Lausanne.

Gepts, E. (2001) *The Relation Between ICT and Space*, Vienna University of Technology, Vienna.

GL Hearn (2003) 'Workspace audits: a matter of fact, not opinion', *Viewpoint*, vol. 7, pp. 1–6.

Gordon, G.E. (1988) 'The dilemma of telework: technology vs tradition', in W. Korte, S. Robinson & W. Steinle (eds) *Telework: Present Situation and Future Development of a New Form of Work Organisation*, Elsevier, London; New York.

Graham, S. & Marvin, S. (1996) *Telecommunications and the City: Electronic Spaces, Urban Places*, Routledge, London.

Graham, S. & Marvin, S. (2001) *Splintering Urbanism: Networked Infrastructures, Technological Mobilities and the Urban Condition*, Routledge, London.

Hall, E.T. (1966) *The Hidden Dimension*, Doubleday, New York.

Hiltz, S.R. (1984) *Online Communities: A Case Study of the Future*, Ablex Publishing Corporation, Norwood, NJ.

Holti, R. & Stern, E. (1986) *Distance Working: Origins, Diffusion, Prospects*, Futuribles, Paris.

Jepson, W., Liggett, R. & Friedman, S. (1995) 'An environment for real-time urban simulation', in ACM (ed.) *ACM Symposium on Interactive 3D Graphics*, ACM, New York.

Khalili, A., Mathur, V. & Bodenhorn, D. (1974) 'Location and the theory of production: a generalisation', *Journal of Economic Theory*, vol. 9, pp. 467–475.

Levy, P. (1998) *Becoming Virtual*, Plenum, New York.

Levy, R.M. (1995) 'Visualization of urban alternatives', *Environment and Planning B*, vol. 22, pp. 343–358.

Makimoto, T. & Manners, D. (1997) *Digital Nomad*, John Wiley, New York.

Marshall, A. (1890) *Principles of Economics*, Macmillan, London.

McCalman, J. & Anderson, C. (2002) 'Design oases for corporate nomads', in P. Jackson & R. Suomi (eds) *eBusiness and Workplace Design*, Routledge, London.

McCann, P. (1998) *The Economics of Industrial Location*, Springer-Verlag, London.

McKinsey Global Institute (2004) *Offshoring: Is It a Win-Win Game?* McKinsey World Economic Forum, New York.

Moorcroft, S. & Bennet, V. (1995) *European Guide to Teleworking: A Framework for Action*, Office for Official Publications of the European Community, Brussels.

Moses, L. (1958) 'Location and the theory of production', *Quarterly Journal of Economics*, vol. 72, pp. 259–272.

Pawley, M. (1997) *Terminal Architecture*, Reaktion Books, London.

Porter, M. (1990) *The Competitive Advantage of Nations*, Macmillan, London.

Predoehl, A. (1928) 'The theory of location in its relation to general economics', *Journal of Political Economy*, vol. 36, pp. 371–390.

Probert, B. & Wajcman, J. (1988) 'Technological change and the future of work', *Journal of Industrial Relations*, vol. 30, pp. 432–448.

Solomon, C.M. (1995) 'Global teams: the ultimate collaboration', *Personnel Journal*, 74(9), pp. 49–58.

Stanworth, J. & Stanworth, C. (1991) *Telework: the Human Resource Implications*, Institute of Personnel Management, London.

Van der Linden, M. (2002) 'Transition! The transformation of the design and use of corporate architecture' in P. Jackson & R. Suomi (eds) *eBusiness and Workplace Redesign*, Routledge, London.

Weber, A. (1909) *Theory and Location of Industries*, University of Chicago Press, Chicago.

Wexelblat, A. (1999) *Footprints: Interaction History for Digital Objects*, PhD Program in Media Arts and Sciences, MIT.

7   Real Estate Use and ICT

Ahrentzen, S. (2001), 'Housing home businesses in urban neighbourhoods: implications for the city of Milwaukee', *University of Wisconsin (Milwaukee) Research and Opinion*, vol. 14, no. 1, pp. 1–11.

Almond, N. (2001) 'Broadband Communications: The Implications for the UK Office Market', paper presented at RICS Foundation Cutting Edge Conference, 5–7 September, Oxford.

Arthur Andersen (2000) *eReal Estate: A Virtual Certainty*, Arthur Andersen/Rosen Consulting Group, New York.

Avison Young (2003) *Olympics and Beyond: Implications for Greater Vancouver's Office Market*, Avison Young, Vancouver.

Baen, J.S. (2000) 'Effects of technology on retail sales, commercial property values and percentage rents', *Journal of Shopping Center Research*, vol. 7, no. 1, pp. 85–101.

Barlow, J. (2000) *The Future of Housing*, 20:20 Visions of the Future, RICS Foundation, London.

Barlow, J. & Venables, T. (2003) 'Smart home, dumb suppliers? The future of smart homes markets', in R. Harper (ed.) *Inside the Smart Home*, Springer-Verlag, London.

Barratt, M. (2001) 'E-business – catalyst for next generation supply chain management', *Supply Chain Practice*, vol. 3, no. 1, pp. 20–29.

Barrett, C. (2003) 'Overseas call', *Property Week*, 18 July.

Beniger, J.R. (1986) *The Control Revolution: Technological and Economic Origins of the Information Society*, Harvard University Press, Cambridge, MA.

BPI (2004) *Legal Downloads Begin to Make Their Mark*, British Phonographic Industry Ltd, London.

BRE (2003) *Client Report: Trends in Smart Home Systems, Connectivity and Services*, Report for Department of Trade and Industry's Nextwave Programme, BRE, available at: http://nextwave.org.uk/downloads/

British Phonographic Industry (2003) *Music Downloading: Consumer Research*, Rep. No. 202, Market Information, BPI, London.

BT (1992) *A Study of Homeworking Environments*, British Telecommunications, London.

Byrne, P., Lizieri, C. & Worzala, E. (2002) 'The Location of Executive Suites and Business centers in the United States: An Exploratory Analysis', paper presented at American Real Estate Society Annual Meeting, April, Naples, FL.

Cabinet Office (2001) *Short Survey of Published Material on Key UK Trends: 2001– 2011*, Cabinet Office/Performance Innovation Unit, London.

Cap Gemini Ernst & Young (2002) *Third Party Logistics (3PL) Study – Results and Findings of Seventh Annual Survey*, Cap Gemini Ernst & Young, London.

Capital Economics Ltd (2002) *Property in Business – A Waste of Space?*, RICS, London.

Celner, A., Gentle, C., Lowes, P. & Nikolic, P. (2003) 'The offshoring imperative', *Waters Magazine*, pp. 1–8.

Chatterton, P. & Hollands, R. (2002) 'Theorising urban playscapes: producing, regulating and consuming youthful nightlife city spaces', *Urban Studies*, vol. 39, no. 1, pp. 95–116.

Chatterton, P. & Hollands, R. (2003) *Urban Nightscapes: Youth Culture, Pleasure Spaces and Corporate Power*, Routledge, London and New York.

Church, R. (2001) *Sport on the Internet*, Screen Digest, London.

College of Estate Management (2001) *Future Shock or E-Hype? The Impact of Online Shopping on UK Retail Property*, British Council of Shopping Centres, London.

Comedia (2003) *Releasing the Cultural Potential of Our Core Cities*, Report for Core Cities Group, Comedia, London, available at: www.comedia.org.uk

Cortright, J. (2001) 'Transportation, Industrial Location and the New Economy: How will the Knowledge Economy Affect Industrial Location and the Demand for Transportation?', paper presented at Transportation Research Board Conference on Transportation and Economic Development, September, Portland, Oregon, USA.

David, P. (1990) 'The dynamo and the computer: An historical perspective on the modern productivity paradox' *American Economic Review*, vol. 80, no. 2, pp. 355–361.

Davis, S.M. (1987) *Future Perfect*, Addison Wesley, Boston.

De Moragas Spa, M. (2001) 'Internet and Olympic Movement', paper presented at 11th International Association for Sports Information World Congress, May, Lausanne.

De Moragas Spa, M., Kennett, C. & Sedo, R. (2003) 'The Impact of the Internet on the Sports Industry', paper presented at SportCongress, 15–16 May, Barcelona.

Department of Labor (2000) *Telework and the New Workplace of the 21st Century*, Department of Labor, Washington DC.

DETR (2000) *Using ICT to Help Regeneration Objectives*, Department of Environment, Transport and Regions, London.

Din, R. (2000) *New Retail*, Conran Octopus, London.

Dixon, T. & Marston, A. (2002) *eRPUK 2001: eCommerce and Retail Property in the UK: Annual Survey and International Comparison*, College of Estate Management, Reading.

Dixon, T., Marston, A., Thompson, B. & Elder, B. (2002) *The Impact of eBusiness on the City of London Office Market*, College of Estate Management, Reading.

Dixon, T., Marston, A., Thompson, B. & Elder, B. (2003) 'eBusiness and the City of London office market', *Journal of Property Investment and Finance*, vol. 21, no. 4, pp. 348–365.

DTI (1998) *Working Anywhere: Exploring Telework for Individuals and Organisations*, Information Society Initiative, Department of Trade and Industry (DTI), London.

Duffy, F. (1997) *The New Office*, Conran Octopus, London.

Duffy, R. & Fearne, A. (2004) 'Partnerships and alliances in UK supermarket supply networks', in M.A. Bourlakis & P.W.H. Weightman (eds) *Food Supply Chain Management*, Blackwell, Oxford, pp. 137–152.

Economist (2003) 'The Internet in a cup', *The Economist*, vol. 369, no. 8355, pp. 88–90.

ECOTEC (2000) *Call Centres in Leicestershire: A Report to Leicestershire Development Agency and TEC*, ECOTEC, Birmingham.

e-HQ (2003) *Leeds: The E-Location for 2003*, e-HQ and Leeds Development Agency, Leeds.

Eppli, M.J., Hendershott, P.H., Mejia, L.C. & Shilling, J.D. (2000) 'Lease Overage Rent Clauses: Motivation and Use', paper presented at American Real Estate Society Conference, April, Santa Barbara, CA.

ESA (2000) *Office Business Center Industry Survey*, Executive Suites Association and Industry Insights, Columbus, OH.

Evans, A.W. (1985) *Urban Economics: An Introduction*, Blackwells, Oxford.

Field, C. (1999) *The Future of the Store: Competing Successfully in the New Millennium*, Financial Times, London.

Forrester (2000) *eCommerce Integrators Exposed*, Forrester Research, Cambridge, MA.

Gaming Board of Great Britain (2002) *Internet Gambling: Report to the Home Secretary*, Gaming Board of Great Britain, London, available at: http://www.gbgb.org.uk/intgambling.html

Gerald Eve (2001) *Overcrowded, Under-Utilised or Just Right? Report of a Study of Occupational Densities*, Gerald Eve in association with RICS, London.

Gibson, V. & Lizieri, C. (2000) 'Space or service? The role of executive suites in corporate real estate portfolios', *Journal of Real Estate Finance*, Spring, pp. 21–29.

Gore, T. (2001) *Accommodating E-Business Growth: The Leeds E-HQ Initiative, Yorkshire and Humberside: A UK Case Study for the NWDMA INTERREG SPECTRE Report*, Centre for Regional Economic and Social Research (School of Environment and Development), Sheffield Hallam University, Sheffield.

Gorman, S.P. (2002) 'Where are the web factories: the urban bias of E-business Location', *Tijdschrift Voor Economische En Sociale Geografie*, vol. 93, no. 5, pp. 522–536.

Graham, S. & Marvin, S. (2001) *Splintering Urbanism: Networked Infrastructures, Technological Mobilities and the Urban Condition*, Routledge, London.

Green, H., Strange, A. & Trache, H. (2000) 'The homeworking revolution: considering the property dimension', *Regional Studies*, vol. 34, no. 3, pp. 303–307.

Greenfield, S. (2003) *Tomorrow's People: How 21st Century Technology Is Changing the Way We Think and Feel*, Penguin/Allen Lane, London.

Hallberg, G. (1995) *All Consumers Are Not Created Equal: The Differential Marketing Strategies for Brand Loyalty and Profits*, John Wiley, New York.

Hampton, K. & Wellman, B. (2003) 'Neighbouring in Netville: how the Internet supports community and social capital in a wired suburb', *City and Community*, vol. 2, no. 4, pp. 277–311.

Hargrave, S. (2004) 'Terminal decline', *Guardian*, Media Guardian, p. 44.

Hendershott, P., Hendershott, R. & Hendershott, T.J. (2000) 'Will the Internet reduce the demand for mall space?', *Real Estate Finance*, vol. 17, no. 1, pp. 41–47.

Hendershott, P., Hendershott, R. & Hendershott, T.J. (2001) 'The future of virtual malls', *Real Estate Finance*, vol. 18, no. 1, pp. 25–32.

Henderson, R. (1995) 'European retail banking: innovation strategies', *International Journal of Business Studies*, vol. 3, no. 1, pp. 11–30.

HM Treasury (2003) *The Location of Financial Activity and the Euro*, HM Treasury, London.

Hodson, N. (2003) *Property and Telework*, available at: http://www.noelhodson.com/index_files/property_telework.htm

Hounshell, D.A. (1984) *From the American System to Mass Production, 1800–1932: Development of Manufacturing Technology in the United States (Studies in Industry and Technology)*, Johns Hopkins University Press, Baltimore.

Hubbard, P. (2003) 'A good night out? Multiplex cinemas as sites of embodied leisure', *Leisure Studies*, vol. 22, July, pp. 255–272.

Intelligent Community Forum (2000) *Smart Communities Profile: Ennis*, Intelligent Communities Forum, New York, available at: http://www.intelligentcommunity.org/art/pdf/EnnisIreland.pdf

Intelligent Community Forum (2001) *The Top Seven Intelligent Communities of 2001*, Intelligent Community Forum, available at: http://www.intelligent community.org/art/pdf/TopSevenIC2001.PDF

Intille, S. (2002) 'Designing a home of the future', *Pervasive Computing*, April–June, pp. 76–82.

Jenkins, C. (2001) *E-London – An Outline of London's Opportunities and Challenges*, Greater London Authority, London.

Johnson, L. (2003) *The Co-Workplace: Teleworking in the Neighbourhood*, University of British Columbia Press, Vancouver.

Jones Lang LaSalle (2001) *London: The New Economy and the Dot Com – Time for Perspective*, Jones Lang LaSalle, London.

Jones Lang LaSalle (2002) *The Gambling Review and Casino Culture in the UK*, European Retail and Leisure Research, Jones Lang LaSalle, London.

Katz, M.L. & Shapiro, C. (1994) 'Systems competition and network effects', *American Economic Review*, vol. 75, no. 3, pp. 424–440.

Kirkup, M.H. & Rafiq, M. (1999) 'Marketing shopping centres: challenges in the UK context', *Journal of Marketing Practice: Applied Marketing Science*, Vol. 5, no. 5, 119–133.

Knight Frank (1996) *Retail Review: Winter 1996/7*, Knight Frank, London.

Knight Frank (2003) *UK Hotel Review (Autumn)*, Knight Frank, London.

Kolko, J. (2002) 'Silicon mountains, silicon molehills: geographic concentration and convergence of internet industries in the US', *Information Economics and Policy*, vol. 14, no. 2, pp. 211–232.

Koski, H., Rouvinen, P. & Yla-Anttila (2001) *ICT Clusters in Europe: The Great Central Banana and Small Nordic Potato*, Rep. No. 2001/6, UNU/WIDER, Helsinki.

Kotha, S. (1995) 'Mass customization: implementing the emerging paradigm for competitive advantage', *Strategic Management Journal*, vol. 16, Summer, pp. 21–42.

Kotler, P. (1989) 'Public Relations vs Marketing: Dividing the Conceptual Domain an Operational Turf', Position paper prepared for the Public Relations Colloquium, San Diego, January 24, unpublished.

Kotzab, H. (1999) 'Improving supply chain performance by efficient consumer response? A critical comparison of exisiting ECR approaches', *Journal of Business and Industrial Marketing*, vol. 14, no. 5/6, pp. 364–377.

KPMG (2001) *Loyalty Cards: A Research Report on Loyalty Cards in European Retailing*, KPMG, London.

Labour Party (2003) *Forethought: Britain in 2010*, Labour Party, London, available at: http://www.labour.org.uk/britainin2020/

Leadbeater, C. & Oakley, K. (2001) *Surfing the Long Wave: Knowledge Entrepreneurship in Britain*, Demos, London, available at: www.demos.co.uk/surfingthelongwave_pdf_media_public.aspx

Levin, S., Meisel, J. & Sullivan, T. (2003) *The Impact of the Internet on the Law and Economics of the United States Motion Picture Industry*, Department of Economics and Finance, Southern Illinois University, Edwardsville, IL.

Local Futures Group (1999) *The Role of the City in London's Knowledge-Driven Information Economy*, Corporation of London, London.

Local Futures Group (2001) *E-London and the London Plan: A Report to the GLA From the Local Futures Group*, Local Futures Group, London.

Lorente, S. (1997) 'The global house', *Trends in Communication*, vol. 3, pp. 117–141.

Malecki, E.J. (2002) 'The Internet: a preliminary analysis of its evolving economic geography', *Economic Geography*, vol. 78, pp. 399–424.

Marcussen, C.H. (2003) *Trends in European Internet Distribution of Travel and Tourism Services*, Center for Regional Tourism Research, Bornholm, Denmark.

Marston, A. & Dixon, T. (2003) *eRPUK 2003: eCommerce and Retail Property in the UK: Third Annual Benchmarking Survey*, College of Estate Management, Reading.

McAllister, P. (1996) 'Turnover rents: comparative valuation issues', *Journal of Property Valuation & Investment*, vol. 14, no. 2, pp. 6–23.

McConnell, T. (2004) 'Call centres: the wake-up call', *Property Week*, 9 January, pp. 53–57.

McMichael, H., Mackay, D. & Altmann, G. (2000) 'Quick response in Australian TCF industry: a case study of supplier response', *International Journal of Physical Distribution and Logistics Management*, vol. 30, no. 7/8, pp. 611–626.

Miller, N.G. (2000) 'Retail leasing in a web enabled world', *Journal of Real Estate Portfolio Management*, vol. 6, no. 2, pp. 167–184.

Mintel (2002) *The UK Cinema Market*, Leisure Intelligence Reports, London.

Minton, A. (2002) *Building Balanced Communities: The UK and US Compared*, RICS, London.

Mitchell, W.J. (1995) *City of Bits*, MIT Press, MA.

Mitchell, W.J. (2003) 'Emerging digital neighbourhoods', in P. Neal, (ed.) *Urban Villages and the Making of Communities*, Spon, London and New York.

Morrell, S. (2003) *UK Contact Centres in 2003*, ContactBabel, UK.

Mulani, N.P. & Lee, H.L. (2002) 'New business models for supply chain excellence' in N. Mulani (ed.) *Achieving Supply Chain Excellence Through Technology (Vol. 4)*, Montgomery Research Inc., USA.

Murray, C.J. (2003) 'Privacy concerns mount over retail use of RFID technology', *Electronic Engineering Times*, 1 December, pp. 4–28.

Myerson, J. & Ross, P. (2003) *The 21st Century Office*, Laurence King Publishing, London.

National Statistics (2003) *UK 2003: The Official Yearbook of the United Kingdom of Great Britain and Northern Ireland*, National Statistics, London.

New South Wales, Department of State and Regional Development (2001) *Business and Economic Benefits of the Sydney 2000 Olympics: A Collation of Evidence*, New South Wales, Department of State and Regional Development, Sydney.

Nortel (2003) *Nortel Networks Teams to Create High-Performance Internet Village in California*, Nortel, available at: www.nortelworks.com

ODPM (2003) *Electronic Communications Services (Draft Approved Document – Q)*, Office of Deputy Prime Minister, London.

ODPM (2004) *Commercial and Industrial Floorspace Statistics 2003*, Office of Deputy Prime Minister, London.

Ohno, T. & Rosen, C.B. (1988) *Toyota Production System: Beyond Large Scale Production*, Productivity Press, New York.

O'Roarty, B. (2000) *Converging Re-Tail and E-Tail Windows – Opportunity or Threat?*, Jones Lang LaSalle, London.

Passingham, J. (1998) 'Grocery retailing and the loyalty card', *Journal of the Market Research Society*, vol. 40 (1), pp. 55–63.

Perry, M. & Sohal, A.S. (2000) 'Quick response practices and technologies in developing supply chains: a case study', *International Journal of Physical Distribution and Logistics Management*, vol. 30, no. 7/8, pp. 627–639.

Pine, J.B. (1993) *Mass Customisation – The New Frontier in Business Competition*, Harvard Business School Press, Boston, MA.

Piore, M.J. & Sabel, C.F. (1985) *Das Ende Der Massenproduction*, Wagenbach, Berlin.

Policy Action Team (PAT) 13 (2000) *Improving Shopping Access for People Living in Deprived Neighbourhoods*, Department of Health, London.

Policy Action Team (PAT) 15 (2000) *Closing the Digital Divide*, Department of Trade and Industry, London.

Pragnell, M., Spence, L. & Moore, R. (2000) *The Potential Market for Smart Homes*, Joseph Rowntree Foundation, York.

Priemus, H. (2003) *Changing Urban Housing Markets in Advanced Economies*, OTB Research Institute, Delft University of Technology, Delft.

Quinn, J.P. (2004) 'Retailers face the question: is the future in RFID?', *Supply Chain Management Review*, vol. 8, no. 1, pp. 1–4.

RETRI Group (2003) *Industrial Futures*, RETRI, UK.

Ross, P. & Davies, W. (2003) *Bytesized Guide to Bluetooth: Technology, Impacts and Futures*, Unwired, London.

Sauvé, P. & Dihel, N. (2002) 'Services Liberalisation and Evolving Regulation: Trends and Outcomes in OECD Countries', paper presented at Symposium on Assessment of Trade in Services, March, Geneva.

Schiller, R. (2001) *The Dynamics of Property Location*, Spon, London and New York.

Schwarz, L.B. (2004) 'The state of practice in supply-chain management: a research perspective', in E. Akçali *et al.* (eds) *Applications of Supply Chain Management and E-Commerce Research in Industry*, Kluwer, Dordrecht, The Netherlands, pp. 1–37.

Screen Digest (2002) *Screen Digest Report on the Implications of Digital Technology for the Film Industry*, Department for Culture, Media and Sport, London.

Shapiro, A.L. (1999) *The Control Revolution: How the Internet Is Putting Individuals in Charge and Changing the World*, Public Affairs, New York.

Sparks, L. (1994) 'Delivering quality: the role of logistics in the post-war transformation of British food retailing', in G. Jones & N.J. Morgan (eds) *Adding Value: Brands and Marketing in Food and Drink*, Routledge, London, pp. 310–335.

Sparks, L. & Wagner, B.A. (2003) 'Retail exchanges: a research agenda', *Supply Chain Management: An International Journal*, vol. 8, no. 3, pp. 201–208.

Spurge, V. (2002) 'Broadband technology in the office: an appraisal of the perception and needs of office occupiers and the potential impact on the office market', *Pacific Rim Property Research Journal*, vol. 8, no. 3, pp. 183–202.

Stec Group (2000) *The Impact of E-Business on the Netherlands Real Estate Market*, Stec Group/IVBN, Netherlands.

SUSTEL (2003) *Is Teleworking Sustainable? An Analysis of Its Economic, Environmental and Social Impacts*, SUSTEL (Sustainable Teleworking), UK Centre for Economic and Environmental Development, Peterborough, UK, available at: http://www.sustel.org/

Taylor, T., Beaverstock, J., Cook, G. & Pandit, N. (2003) *Financial Services Clustering and Its Significance for London*, Corporation of London, London.

Telegeography (2001) *Packet Geography 2002*, Telegeography, Washington DC.

Thompson, R. (2002) 'A New Urban Hierarchy: Connected Cities?', paper presented at European Real Estate Society (ERES), June, Glasgow.

Thompson, R. (2003) 'Wake up and smell the coffee', *Estates Gazette*, 18 October.

Thompson, R. & Hills, M. (1999) 'Wired up for extra value', *Journal of Real Estate Research*, vol. 17, no. 1/2, pp. 245–255.

Tien Foo, S. (2002) 'Impact of Information and Communication Technology on Office Space Demand', paper presented at ERES Conference, June, Glasgow.

Tien Foo, S., Kin Pang, L. & Ah Long, W. (2004) *Network Effects and Broadband Connectivity in Office Buildings*, Pacific Rim Conference, forthcoming.

Toffler, A. (1970) *Future Shock*, Cologny.

Toffler, A. (1980) *The Third Wave*, Collins, London.

Trends Business Research (2001) *Business Clusters in the UK*, Department of Trade and Industry, London.

Tseng, M. & Jiao, R. (2001) Mass customization, in *Handbook of Industrial Engineering*, Wiley Europe, Chichester.

United States General Accounting Office (2002) *Internet Gambling: An Overview of the Issues*, United States General Accounting Office, Washington DC.

University of West of England Facilities Innovation Centre (2003) *The UK Flexible Working Survey*, University of West of England, Bristol.

Wilson, P. (2004) 'E-mail campaign clicks with Vancouver's Olympic bid', *Vancouver Sun*, February 10.

Womack, J.P., Jones, D.T. & Roos, D. (1991) *The Machine That Changed the World*, Harper Collins, New York.

Wrigley, N. (1998a) 'Understanding store development programmes in post-property-crisis UK food retailing', *Environment and Planning A*, vol. 30, pp. 15–35.

Wrigley, N. (1998b) 'How British retailers have shaped food choice', in A. Murcott (ed.) *The Nation's Diet: The Social Science of Food Choice*, Longman, London, pp. 112–128.

Zipkin, P. (2001) 'The limits of mass customization', *Sloan Management Review*, vol. 42, Spring, pp. 81–87.

8   Real Estate Service Providers and ICT

Abbott, A. (1995) 'Sequence analysis: new methods for old ideas', *Annual Review of Sociology*, vol. 21, pp. 91–113.

Arthur Andersen (2000) *EReal Companies: The Impact of eBusiness and the Internet in the New Economy*, Arthur Andersen, New York.

Baatz, E.B. (1996) 'Will the web eat your job?', *Webmaster Magazine*, 1.

Baligh, H. & Richartz, L. (1967) *Vertical Market Structures*, Allyn and Bacon, Boston, MA.

Becker, F. (1990) *The Total Workplace: Facilities Management and the Elastic Organisation*, van Nostrand Reinhold, New York.

Becker, F. & Joroff, M. (1995) *Reinventing the Workplace*, Corporate Real Estate 2000 Project, IDRC, Norcross, GA.

Becker, F. & Steele, F. (1995) Understanding organizational ecology, in *Workplace by Design: Mapping the High Performance Workscape*, Jossey-Bass, San Francisco.

Bergsman, S. (1994) 'The bloom is off: why real estate outsourcing isn't always the low-cost solution it's been hyped to be', *Corporate Finance*, vol. 4, pp. 26–29.

Birch, A., Gerbert, P. & Schneider, D. (2000) *The Age of E-Tail*, Capstone Publishing, Oxford.

Buxmann, P. & Gebauer, J. (1998) 'Internet-based Intermediaries – The Case of the Real Estate Market', paper presented at Proceedings of the 6th European Conference on Information Systems (ECIS'98), June, Aix-en-Provence, France.

Carn, N., Black, R. & Rabianski, J. (1999) 'Operational and organization issues facing corporate real estate executives and managers', *Journal of Real Estate Research*, vol. 17, pp. 281–299.

Chin, L. & Liu, J. (2004) 'Risk management in real estate electronic transactions', *Journal of Real Estate Literature*, vol. 12, no. 1, pp. 53–66.

Crowston, K. & Wigand, R. (1999) 'Real-estate war in cyberspace: an emerging electronic market', *Electronic Markets*, vol. 9, no. 1/2, pp. 1–8.

Crowston, K., Sawyer, S. & Wigand, R. (2001) 'Investigating the interplay between structure and information and communications technology in the real estate industry', *Information Technology and People*, vol. 14, no. 2, pp. 163–183.

Curry, A. & Howard, L. (2003) 'Economic scenario', in S. Foxell (ed.) *The Professionals' Choice: The Future of the Built Environment Professions*, Building Futures (CABE/RIBA), London.

Dermisi, S.V. (2002) 'Impact of the Internet on international office markets', *Journal of Real Estate Portfolio Management*, vol. 8, no. 4, pp. 140–148.

Dess, G.G. & Beard, D.W. (1984) 'Dimensions of organisational task environments', *Administrative Science Quarterly*, vol. 29, pp. 52–73.

DETR (2000) *Monitoring the Code of Practice for Commercial Leases*, Department of the Environment, Transport and the Regions, London.

Dixon, T. & Marston, A. (2001) *e-Property = e-Business + e-Commerce*, CPD Study Pack Series, College of Estate Management, Reading.

Dixon, T.J., Hargitay, S.E. & Bevan, O.A. (1991) *Microcomputers in Property: A Surveyor's Guide to Lotus 1–2–3 and dBASE IV*, Spon, London.

Dixon, T., Jordan, A, Marston, A., Pinder, J. & Pottinger, G. (2003) *Lessons From UK PFI and Real Estate Partnerships: Drivers, Barriers and Critical Success Factors*, Foundation for Built Environment, Watford.

DTI (2001) *Converging Technologies: Consequences of the New Knowledge-Driven Economy*, Department of Trade and Industry (DTI), available at: http://www.innovation.gov.uk/projects/converging_techn/summary.html

DTI/Foresight (2000) *Clicks and Mortar: The New Store Front*, Department of Trade and Industry (DTI), London.

Duckworth, S.L. (1993) 'Realizing the strategic dimension of corporate real property through improved planning and control systems', *Journal of Real Estate Research*, vol. 4, pp. 495–509.

e-BusinessW@atch (2002) *ICT & E-Business in the Real Estate Sector*, European Commission, Brussels.

Elliott, D., Swartz, E. & Herbane, B. (2002) *Business Continuity Management: A Crisis Management Approach*, Routledge, London.

Ernst & Young (2002) *Views of Corporate Real Estate from the Boardrooms of Europe*, Ernst & Young, London.

European Commission (2003) *European Business: Facts and Figures (1991–2001)*, European Commission, Luxembourg.

Evans, P. & Wurster, T.S. (2000) *Blown to Bits: How the New Economics of Information Transforms Strategy*, Harvard Business School Press, Boston, MA.

Finch, E. (2003) 'The untethered facilities manager', *Facilities*, vol. 21, no. 5/6, pp. 126–133.

Garven, J. (2002) 'On the implications of the Internet for insurance markets and institutions', *Risk Management and Insurance Review*, vol. 5, no. 2, pp. 105–116.

Gibson, G. & Lizieri, C. (1999) 'New business practices and the corporate property portfolio: how responsive is the UK property market?', *Journal of Property Research*, vol. 16, no. 3, pp. 210–219.

Green, R.K. & Vandell, K.D. (2001) 'The Impact of Technology and the Internet on Real Estate', paper presented at International Real Estate Conference, July 27, Girdwood, Alaska.

Guiltinan, J. (1987) 'The price bundling of services: a normative framework', *Journal of Marketing*, vol. 51, April, pp. 74–85.

Gwin, C. (2004) 'International comparisons of real estate e-nformation on the Internet', *Journal of Real Estate Research*, vol. 26, no. 1, pp. 1–23.

Gyourko, J. & Nakahara, A. (2001) *The Impact of New Information Technologies on the Commercial Brokerage Industry: What Does New Information Technology Make Possible and Under What Conditions Will Changes Occur?*, Working Paper No. 378, The Wharton School, University of Pennsylvania.

Haynes, B., Matzdorf, F., Nunnington, N., Ogunmakin, C., Pinder, J. & Price, I. (2002) *Does Property Benefit Occupiers? An Evaluation of the Literature*, Occupier.org, Sheffield.

Herd, G. & Lizieri, C. (1994) 'Valuing and appraising new lease forms: the case of break clauses in office markets', *Government Procurement*, vol. 7, no. 6, pp. 74–77.

Huws, U. (2001) *Where the Butterfly Alights: the Global Location of EWork*, Rep. No. 378, Institute for Employment Studies, Brighton.

Joroff, M. (1992) *Corporate Real Estate 2000, Management Strategies for the Next Decade*, Industrial Development Research Foundation White Paper, Norcross, GA.

Joroff, M., Louargand, M., Lambert, S. & Becker, F. (1993) *Strategic Management of the Fifth Resource: Corporate Real Estate*, Industrial Development Research Foundation, Atlanta, GA.

Kimbler, L. & Rutherford, R.C. (1993) 'Corporate real estate outsourcing: a survey of the issues', *Journal of Real Estate Research*, vol. 4, pp. 525–541.

Kistler, R. (1999) 'Outsourcing frees agencies to focus on core competencies', *Product Finishing*, vol. 54, no. 4, pp. 65–69.

Kline, S. (2001) 'Growth and diversification through vertical integration', *PF Online* (www.pfonline.com).

Lambert, S., Poteete, J. & Waltch, A (1995) *Generating High-Performance Corporate Real Estate Service*, Industrial Development Research Foundation, Atlanta, GA.

Land Securities (2004) *Report and Financial Statements*, Land Securities, London.

Lizieri, C., Ward, C. & Lee, S. (2001) 'No free lunch? An examination of innovation in UK commercial property markets', *Journal of Property Investment and Finance*, vol. 19, no. 4, pp. 361–374.

Lyons, M. (2004) *Well Placed to Deliver? Shaping the Pattern of Government Service*, HM Treasury, London.

Manning, C.A., Rodriguez, M. & Roulac, S.E. (1997) 'How much corporate real estate management ahould be outsourced?', *Journal of Real Estate Research*, vol. 14, no. 3, pp. 259–274.

Manning, C.A., Rodriguez, R.M. & Ghosh, C. (1999) 'Devising a corporate facility location strategy to maximize shareholder wealth', *Journal of Real Estate Research*, vol. 17, no. 3, pp. 321–340.

Manning, C. & Roulac, S. (2001) 'Lessons from the past and future directions for corporate real estate research', *Journal of Real Estate Research*, vol. 22, pp. 7–58.

Mantle, P. (2001) 'Like your e-thinking', *Urban Land Europe*, pp. 21–25.

Monks, H. (2004) 'Keen to cut out the estate agent?', *Observer (Cash)*, April 11.

Moore, P. (2000) 'Core competency companies', *McKinsey Quarterly*, vol. 1, pp. 48–71.

Muhanna, W.A. (2000) 'e-Commerce in the real estate brokerage industry', *Journal of Real Estate Portfolio Management*, vol. 3, no. 1, pp. 1–16.

National Association of Realtors (NAR) (1999) *The Impact of Online Technologies on the Real Estate Industry*, NAR, New York.

NOP (2003) *Property in Turbulent Times*, CBRE/CoreNet, London.

Nourse, H.O. (1990) *Managerial Real Estate, Corporate Real Estate Asset Management*, Prentice Hall, New York.

Nourse, H.O. (1992) 'Real estate flexibility must complement business strategy', *International Real Estate Review*, vol. 4, pp. 25–29.

Nourse, H.O. & Roulac, S.E. (1993) 'Linking real estate decisions to corporate strategy', *Journal of Real Estate Research*, vol. 3, pp. 475–494.

ODPM (2004) *Monitoring the 2002 Code of Practice for Commercial Leases: Interim Report*, Office of Deputy Prime Minister (ODPM), London.

Orlikowski, W. (1992) 'The duality of technology: rethinking the concept of technology in organizations', *Organization Science*, vol. 3, no. 3, pp. 398–427.

O'Roarty, B., McGreal, S. & Adair, A. (1997) *The Impact of Retailers' Store Selection Criteria on the Estimation of Retail Rents*, RICS, London.

Porter, M.E. (1980) 'Competitive strategy', *McKinsey Quarterly*, vol. 2, pp. 97–105.

Pralahad, D. & Hamel, G. (1990) 'The core competence of the corporation', *Harvard Business Review*, May–June, pp. 79–91.

Rodriguez, M. & Sirmans, C.F. (1996) 'Managing corporate real estate: evidence from the capital markets', *Journal of Real Estate Literature*, January, pp. 13–33.

Roever, M. (1992) 'Cursing the Disease of Overcomplexity', paper presented at RICS Cutting Edge Conference, June, London.

So, A.T.P., Wong, A.C.W. & Wong, K.C. (1999) 'A new definition of intelligent buildings for Asia', *Facilities*, vol. 17, no. 12/13, pp. 485–491.

Tapscott, D. (1995) *The Digital Economy: Promise and Peril in the Age of Networked Intelligence*, McGraw Hill, New York.

Tuccillo, J. (1999) *The Eight New Rules of Real Estate*, Dearbourn Financial Publishing, USA.

Veale, P.R. (1989) 'Managing corporate real estate assets: current executive attitudes and prospects for an emergent discipline', *Journal of Real Estate Research*, vol. 4, pp. 1–22.

Witty, R. & Scott, D. (2001) *Disaster Recovery Plans and Systems Are Essential*, Gartner First Take, New York.

Zeckhauser, S. & Silverman, R. (1983) 'Rediscovering your company's real estate', *Harvard Business Review*, vol. 61, no. 1, pp. 111–117.

9   New Directions and Policy Implications: the Future of Real Estate in the New Economy

Alakeson, V., Aldrich, T., Goodman, J. & Jorgensen, B. (2003) *Making the Net Work: Sustainable Development in a Digital Society*, Xeris, Teddington.

Arnfalk, P. (2003) 'Information and communications technologies and business travle: environmental possibilities, problems and implications', in J. Park & N. Roome (eds) *The Ecology of the New Economy: Sustainable Transformation of Global Information, Communications and Electronics Industries*, Greenleaf Publishing, Sheffield.

Arthur Andersen (2000) *eReal Companies: The Impact of eBusiness and the Internet in the New Economy*, Arthur Andersen, New York.

Baum, A. (1991) *Property Investment Depreciation and Obsolescence*, Routledge, London.

Bean, C. (2003) *Economists and the Real World*, Lecture at the London School of Economics, 29 January.

Beck, F. (2001) *Energy Smart Data Centers: Applying Energy Efficient Design and Technology to the Digital Information Sector*, Rep. No. 14, Renewable Energy Policy Project, Washington DC.

Bootle, R. (2003) *Money for Nothing: Real Wealth, Financial Fantasies and The Economy of the Future*, Nicholas Brealey Publishing, London and Maine.

Borsuk, S. (1999) *Nowhere Yet Everywhere*, The Space Place Paper, available at: www.thespaceplace.net

Bottom, C.W., McGreal, W.S. & Heaney, G. (1999) 'Appraising the functional performance characteristics of office buildings', *Journal of Property Research*, vol. 16, no. 4, pp. 339–358.

Browne, M., Allen, J., Anderson, S. & Jackson, M. (2001) *Home Delivery in the UK*, Transport Studies Group, University of Westminster, London, available at: available at: http://www.wmin.ac.uk/transport/projects/homedel.htm

Brundtland Commission (1987) *Our Common Future*, European Commission, Brussels.

Cabinet Office (2001) *Short Survey of Published Material on Key UK Trends: 2001–2011*, Cabinet Office/Performance Innovation Unit, London.

CALUS (1986) *Depreciation of Commercial Property*, CALUS/College of Estate Management, Reading.

CBECS (1999) *Energy Information Administration Commercial Buildings Energy Consumption Survey (CBECS)*, Energy Information Administration (CBECS), Washington DC.

College of Estate Management (CEM) (2001) *Future Shock or E-Hype? The Impact of Online Shopping on UK Retail Property*, British Council of Shopping Centres, London.

Colwell, P.F. & Ramsland, M. (2001) *The Pace of Technological Change: the Case of Retail*, Rep. No. 2001–02, Department of Land Economy, University of Aberdeen, Aberdeen.

Digital Europe (2001) *Digital Europe: EBusiness and Sustainable Development*, Forum for the Future/Digital Europe, Brussels, available at: http://www.digital-eu.org/

Digital Europe (2002) 'eBusiness and Sustainable Development', paper presented at CBI Conference, London.

Dixon, T. & Marston, A. (2002) *eRPUK 2001: ECommerce and Retail Property in the UK: Annual Survey and International Comparison*, College of Estate Management, Reading.

Dixon, T. & Marston, A. (2004) *The Impact of EBusiness on the City of London Office Market: 2004 Survey*, College of Estate Management, Reading.

Dixon, T., Law, V. & Cooper, J. (1997) *The Dynamics and Measurement of Depreciation in Commercial Property*, College of Estate Management, Reading.

Dixon, T.J., Crosby, N. & Law, V. (1999) 'A critical review of methodologies for measuring rental depreciation applied to UK commercial real estate', *Journal of Property Research*, vol. 16, no. 2, pp. 153–180.

Dixon, T., Marston, A., Thompson, B. & Elder, B. (2002a) *The Impact of EBusiness on the City of London Office Market*, College of Estate Management, Reading.

Dixon, T., Thompson, R. & McAllister, P. (2002b) *The Value of ICT for SMEs in the UK: A Critical Literature Review and Scoping Study for Further Research*, College of Estate Management, Reading.

Dixon, T., Marston, A., Thompson, B. & Elder, B. (2003) 'eBusiness and the City of London office market', *Journal of Property Investment and Finance*, vol. 21, no. 4, pp. 348–365.

DTI/Foresight (2000a) *Clicks and Mortar: The New Store Front*, Department of Trade and Industry (DTI), London.

DTI/Foresight (2000b) *Smoke on the Water. A Fire in the Sky. Electronic Task Force Report for Consultation*, Department of Trade and Industry (DTI), London.

DTI/BRC/Foresight (1999) *Take a Look at the Future of Retailing: 2003*, Department of Trade and Industry (DTI), London.

DTZ Pieda (2000) *E-Commerce and the Physical Transportation of Goods*, DTZ Pieda, London.

DTZ Research (2000a) *A Research Study into Potential Collection Points*, DTZ Research, London.

DTZ Research (2000b) *The Co-Location Market in Europe*, DTZ Research, London.

EITO (2002) *European Information Technology Observatory (EITO): 2002*, EITO, Frankfurt.

Elkington, J. (1997) *Cannibals With Forks: The Triple Bottom Line of 21st Century Businesses*, Capstone, Oxford.

Fichter, K. (2001) 'Sustainable business strategies in the Internet economy', in H. Loreny & P. Gilgen (eds) *Sustainability in the Information Society*, Metropolis Marburg, Marburg.

Freemans (2000) *Property Guide*, Freemans, London.

Galea, C. & Walton, S. (2003) 'Is e-commerce sustainable? Lessons from Webvan', in J. Park & N. Roome (eds) *The Ecology of the New Economy: Sustainable Transformation of Global Information, Communications and Electronics Industries*, Greenleaf Publishing, Sheffield.

Gerald Eve (2001) *Overcrowded, Under-Utilised or Just Right? Report of a Study of Occupational Densities*, Gerald Eve in association with RICS, London.

Gillespie, A. & Rutherford, J. (2004) *The Brave New World of the 21st Century Home*, Commission for Architecture and the Built Environment (CABE), London.

Gillespie, A., Richardson, R. & Cornford, J. (2001) 'Regional development and the new economy', *European Investment Bank, Cahiers Papers*, vol. 6, no. 1, pp. 109–131.

Gorman, S.P. (2002) 'Where are the web factories: the urban bias of E-business location', *Tijdschrift Voor Economische En Sociale Geografie*, vol. 93, no. 5, pp. 522–536.

Graham, S. & Marvin, S. (2001) *Splintering Urbanism: Networked Infrastructures, Technological Mobilities and the Urban Condition*, Routledge, London.

Greater London Authority (2002) *Demand and Supply of Business Space in London*, SDS Technical Report 21, Greater London Authority, London.

Green, A. & Shackleton, A. (2000) *The Future of Work*, 20:20 Visions of the Future, RICS Foundation, London.

Green, R.K. & Vandell, K.D. (2001) 'The Impact of Technology and the Internet on Real Estate', paper presented at International Real Estate Conference, July 27, Girdwood, Alaska.

Guardian (2004) 'Broadband: revolutions in waiting', *The Guardian*, March 27.

Hackler, D. (2003) 'Invisible infrastructure and the city', *American Behavioral Scientist*, vol. 46, no. 8, pp. 1034–1055.

Hop Associates (2002) *The Impact of ICTs on Travel and Freight Distribution Patterns*, Department of Transport, Local Government and the Regions, London.

Investment Property Databank (2001) *Property Investors' Digest*, Investment Property Databank, London.

Jones Lang LaSalle (2000) *Retail Futures*, Jones Lang LaSalle Research, London.

Jones Lang LaSalle (2003) *Rising Urban Stars: Uncovering Future Winners*, Jones Lang LaSalle, London.

Kahn, H. & Weiner, A.J. (1967) *The Year 2000: A Framework for Speculation on the Next 30 Years*, Macmillan, London.

Khalid, A.G. (1992) *Hedonic Price Estimation of the Financial Impact of Obsolescence on Commercial Office Buildings*, unpublished PhD thesis, University of Reading (Construction Management).

Klier, T.H. (1999) 'Agglomeration in the US auto supply industry', *Economic Perspectives, Federal Reserve Bank of Chicago*, vol. 1, pp. 18–34.

Labour Party (2003) *Forethought: Britain in 2010*, Labour Party, London, available at: http://www.labour.org.uk/britainin2020/

Lisbon European Council (2000) *eEurope – An Information Society For All – Progress Report For the Special European Council on Employment, Economic Reforms and Social Cohesion*, European Commission, Brussels, available at: http://europa.eu.int/scadplus/leg/en/cha/c10241.htm

Lizieri, C. (2003) 'Occupier requirements in commercial real estate markets', *Urban Studies*, vol. 40, no. 5–6, pp. 1151–1169.

Local Futures Group (2001) *The Geography of the Knowledge Economy in Britain*, Local Futures Group, London.

Lyons, M. (2004) *Well Placed to Deliver? Shaping the Pattern of Government Service*, HM Treasury, London.

Mackaness, E. (2004) 'Transforming workplace productivity: Prudential UK's flexible working environment', *Corporate Real Estate Leader*, pp. 11–13.

Mansley, M. (2000) *Socially Responsible Investment: A Guide for Pension Funds and Institutional Investors*, Monitor Press, Sudbury, Suffolk.

Marshall, A. (1890) *Principles of Economics*, Macmillan, London.

Marston, A. & Dixon, T. (2003) *eRPUK 2003: ECommerce and Retail Property in the UK: Annual Survey and International Comparison*, College of Estate Management, Reading.

Mokhtarian, P. (2000) *Telecommunications and Travel*, Committee on Telecommunications and Travel Behavior, Travel Research Board, Washington DC.

Murphy, A. (2003) *The Web, The Grocer and The City: On the (In)Visibility of Grounded Virtual Retail Capital*, Working Papers in Services, Space, Society, University of Birmingham, School of Geography, Earth and Environmental Sciences.

Park, J. & Roome, N. (eds) (2002) *The Ecology of the New Economy: Sustainable Transformation of Global Information, Communications and Electronics Industries*, Greenleaf Publishing, Sheffield.

Pea, R.D. (1985) 'Beyond amplification: using the computer to reorganize mental functioning', *Educational Pychologist*, vol. 20, no. 4, pp. 167–182.

Porter, M. (1985) *Competitive Advantage*, Free Press, New York.

Primetrica Inc. (2003) *Colocation 2004*, Primetrica Inc, New York.

Property Advisory Group (2002) *Annual Report 2001*, Department of Transport, Local Government and the Regions, London.

Retail Logistics Taskforce (2000a) *@ Your Service*, Department of Trade and Industry, London.

Retail Logistics Taskforce (2000b) *Bricks and Clicks*, Department of Trade and Industry, London.

Reynolds, J. (2000) 'eCommerce: a critical review', *International Journal of Retail and Distribution Management*, vol. 28, no. 10, pp. 415–444.

Ringland, G. (1998) *Scenario Planning: Managing for the Future*, John Wiley, Chichester.

Romm, J., Rosenfeld, J.A. & Herrmann, S. (1999) *The Internet and Global Warming: A Scenario of the Impact of E-Commerce on Energy and the Environment*, Centre for Energy and Climate Solutions, Arlington VA.

Ross, P. & Davies, W. (2003) *Bytesized Guide to Bluetooth: Technology, Impacts and Futures*, Unwired, London.

Scase, R. (2000) *Britain in 2010: The New Business Landscape*, Capstone Publishing, Oxford.

Slaughter, E.S. (2001) 'Design strategies to increase building flexibility', *Building Research and Information*, vol. 29, no. 3, pp. 208–217.

Sparks, L. & Findlay, A. (2000) *The Future of Shopping*, 20:20 Visions of the Future, RICS, London.

Spinks, W. (2002) 'Structural legacies and flexible work: Japanese challenges', in P. Jackson & R. Suomi (eds) *eBusiness and Workplace Design*, Routledge, London.

STAR (2003) *Scenarios for the Information Society*, Socio-Economic Trends Assessment for the Digital Revolution, STAR, Paris.

Suarez-Villa, L. (2003) 'The E-economy and the rise of technocapitalism: networks, firms and transportation', *Growth and Change*, vol. 34, no. 4, pp. 390–414.

Thomas, H. (2004) 'Flexible friends', *Property Week Supplement: International Corporate Real Estate*, pp. 27–28.

Thompson, R. (2002) 'A New Urban Hierarchy: Connected Cities?', paper presented at European Real Estate Society (ERES), June, Glasgow.

Thompson, R. & Hills, M. (1999) 'Wired up for extra value', *Journal of Real Estate Research*, vol. 17, no. 1/2, pp. 245–255.

Tien Foo, S. (2002) 'Impact of Information and Communication Technology on Office Space Demand', paper presented at ERES Conference, June, Glasgow.

Tien Foo, S., Kin Pang, L. & Ah Long, W. (2004) *Network Effects and Broadband Connectivity in Office Buildings*, forthcoming.

Tinworth, A. (2003a) 'In the event horizon', *Estates Gazette*, 26 July.

Tinworth, A. (2003b) 'Wave power rules', *Estates Gazette*, 18 October.

Venables, A.J. (2001) 'Geography and International Inequalities: the Impact of New Technologies', paper presented at World Bank Annual Conference on Development Economics, May, Washington DC.

Winograd, B., Conner, P., Liang, Y. & Whitaker, W. (2000) 'Conjectures on the impact of technology on real estate', *Real Estate Finance*, vol. 17, no. 2, pp. 11–20.

World Teleport Association (2001) *Intelligent Communities*, World Teleport Association, New York.

Worzala, E.M., Dixon, T.J., McCarthy, A. & Marston, A. (2002) 'Ecommerce and retail in the UK and USA', *Journal of Property Investment and Finance*, vol. 20, no. 2, pp. 142–157.

Index

Page numbers in *italics* refer to figures, those in **bold** to tables and boxes.

24 hour cities, 266–67

accounting, 146, **149**
active management, 290–91
actor network theory (ANT), 14–15, **15**, 25–6, 35, 324–25, 327–28
advertising, 269–70
agents, *see* brokers
agglomeration, **121**, 245, **337**
airlines, *see* travel and retail
Amazon, 153, 191, **211**, 227, **346**
appraisal, 281–88, 313–18
Arcadia, 48
Arlington, 249–50
Asda, 49
asset deconstruction, 282
asset management, 306–11
asset manager, 289
asset returns, 188–90
ATMs, 228–30, *229*
automobiles, see motor industry
avatars, **207**, 210

B2B, **62**, 64,115, 269, **355**
B2C, **62**, 109, **355**
back offices, 227, 238–39, 294–95
balance sheet, 188–90, 281
banking, 170, 202, 228–30, *229*, 248–49, 319–20, 357
Barclays, **157**
Beniger, James, **6**, 12, 250–51
Bluetooth, 273
Bluewater, 364
BMW, 255–57, **256**
Boots, **297**
Britart, 268
British Land, 292–93, 296
British Telecommunications, 181
broadband, 23, 28 44, **68**, *72*, 72–6, *75*, 90–91, 239–40, 244, *246*
Broadgate Estates, 292–93
brokers (or agents), 194, 318–26, 327–28, 334
brokerage, 321–26
  commercial, 321–23

theories, 323–25, *324*
transformation, 325–26
  UK property listings, 325–26, **326**
Brundtland Commission, 354–55
BT Openzone, **222**
building quality, 349–51
Building Regulations, 278
bundling, 286–88
BUPA, **145**
business models, 277–78
business process, 128–59
  defined, 135–36
  outsourcing, 239
  re-engineering, 17, 129, 148
  generic, 135–39, *137*, *138*
  real estate, *186*, 186–95

computer assisted design (CAD), 204–205
call centres, 101, 124, **149**, 157, **157**, 204, 238–39, 248–50, 277, 347–48
Castells, Manuell, 4, **6**, 23–4, **24**, 39, 52–3, 82–3, **103**, 201
  informational cities, 20, 22
  informational economy, 201–02
  space of flows 24
  space of places 24
CCTV, 223–24, 272, 296
central banana, 245
centralised market, 318–19, *319*
centrifugal, 20, 36, *36*, 201–02, **336**
centripetal, 20, 36, *36*, 201, **336**
change, technological, 5–6, *18*
Charles Schwab, **130**
Chivers, **156**
cinemas, 47, 265–67, 269–70
City of London offices, *see* offices
clickstream, 211
clusters, 38, 93, 196, 203, 245–46, 276
  financial services, 245
clustering, 36, 80, **121**, 124, 182, 183, 335, 337
commercial mortgage-backed securities (CMBS), 28
co-invention, 176

collection points, 347
co-location centres, 122, 342–44, **343**, 369
commercial brokerage, *see* brokerage
commercial real estate, 158
comparison shopping, 364–65, *365*
computer assisted facilities
    management (CAFM), 310, 312
computer integrated manufacturing
    (CIM), *see* manufacturing
connectivity, 263–64, 358
conspicuous consumption, 48
constructivism, 14
consumers, 88–93
contingency planning, *310*, 310–11
control revolution, 12, 250–51
convenience shopping, 364–65, *365*
convergence, 58–9, *59*
core cities, 267, 277
core space, 194, 239, 244–46
corporate finance, 281–82
corporate real estate, 30, 184–85,
    301–05, *304*
corporate social responsibility, 355
CoStar, **144**
Covisint, **142**
Countdown, **222**
creative human capital theory, 182
cross docking, **297**, 346, *see also*
    distribution
Crossroads, **308**
customer relationship management,
    111, 145–46, **149**

data centres, 355
data protection, 212
death of distance, 80, 152, 181–82, 187
death of geography, 335
death of real estate, *see* real estate
Debenhams, 270
deconcentration, *see* perspectives
DEGW SANE, 184
Dell, **154**
demographics, 35, 45, 46–7, 66–7, 270–71
densities, 369
depreciation, 349–51
determinism, 8, 14, 17, 19, 26, 29, 33,
    34, 99, 116, 148, 199, 331
diffusion, 84–7, *86*, 178
digital divide, 44, 69–71, *70*, 334, 366
digital property, 196

diseconomies, 336
disintegration, 298–99
disintermediation, **56**, 319–20, **320**, 354
dispersion, 121, 335, **337**, 338
disruptive technology, 190
distributed workplace, 183–84
dynamic flexibility, **100**
distribution, 155–56, **156**, 256–58,
    260–65, 356, 357
    centres, 344
    changing focus, *258*
    clear span, 263
    drivers, 260–65
    eaves height, 257, 263
    security, 263
    superflat floors, 263
    supply chains, 257–58, **258**
    warehouses, 155–56
domestic appliances, 88–9, **88**, *89*, *90*
dot.coms, 51, 244–46, 363
Duffy, Frank, 133–34, 236–37
dystopia, 369

e-adoption ladder, 62, 99, *100*, **100**, 103,
    125
eBusiness, **36**, 39, 53, 66, *100*, 107–12,
    111, 184–85, 245, 336–38, **337**
    defined, 107–08
eCommerce, *29*, 39, *53*, 60, 64, **65**, *100*,
    144, 112–15, **297**, 319
    defined, 108–09
    distribution costs, **113**
    hype, 227–28
    productivity, 177
    retail, 35–36, **297**
    systems, 144
economics, evolutionary, 7, 13–14, 86
edge cities, 20–21
Electronic Data Interchange (EDI),
    115–16, 140–41, 177, 233
eFulfilment, 369
eGovernment, 58–66, **63**, 64, 99–102,
    102, **103**
electronic cottage, 117, 271
electronic shopping, 109–10, 114–16
electronic space, 201
e-maturity, 68–69
Empress State (London), **352**
enhancement, 25, 202, *202*
Ennis (Ireland), **274**

entertainment, 88
environment, *357*
eOutsourcing, **123**,124
EPoS, 233, 276, 296
eProcurement, **111**, **139**, 294
eProperty, 39, 161, 186–87, 342
e-readiness, 83
e-shopping, *see* electronic shopping
E-sign legislation, 328
e-tailing, 109–10, 360–63
e-village, 274, **274**
eWork, 116–20, **123**, 214
  defined, 108, 117–18
exabyte, 150, **151**
executive suites, 246–48

facilities lifecycle, *350*, 350–51
facilities management, 30, 284, 295, 315,
    334, 343, 292–93, **302–03**, 311–13,
    334
Fifth Revolution, **11**, 12
financial management, 147–48, **149**
financial services, 130
fitting out, 293, **293**
Fleet Street, 267
flexible leases, *see* leases
flexible work, 45, 267, 348, **348**
food retailing, 232, 239
Fordism, 22, 31, **252**
Fordist, **345**
future studies, 358–68, **359**, **362**

gambling, 277
gated communities, 275
general-purpose technology (GPT), 82,
    87, 98,163–65, 178
generation, 25, 202, *202*
geographic information systems (GIS),
    207, 307, **308**
global cities, 20, 122, 239, 344
global positioning system (GPS), 212
globalisation, 30, 36, 44, *45*, 49–50, 282
Gordon, Robert, **6**, 12–13, 162–63,
    167–68
Greenspan, Alan, 38, 51
grocery retailers, 239, 353, 369
groupware, 116

hardware, 55
hi-tech estates, 79–80

high street, 362–63
home delivery, 346–47, 353
home shopping, 338
homeworking, 22, 240–41, 337
hot-desking, 180, 240
hotelling, 180, 240
hotels, 268–69
household expenditure, 266–67, *266*
Hoxton (London), 267–68
human resource management, 333

IBM, **217**, 239
implementation research, 15
Information and Communications
    Technology (ICT), *see* technology
ideopolis, 182
industrial real estate, 154–55
Industrial Revolution, 12–13, 168
information society, 3, 44, *45*, *53*, 54,
    66–9
  defined, 4–5, 50
  differences to new economy, 51
  drivers, **60**
  emergence, 43
  literature, 53
  measurement, 66–9, **68**
  models, 53
  origins, 50
  policy development, 58–66
  scenarios, 358–59, **359**
  theories, 54–5
information character, 121–22, **121**
informationalisation, 203
infrastructure obsolescence, 257
innovation, *18*, 58, 76, 341, 285–86
  commons, 75–6
  defined, 85
  systems, 7
intangible goods, 160–61
intelligent buildings, 225, 305, *306*
Intelligent Virtual Environments,
    205–06, **207**
intermediation, 175, 287
internet cafes, 270, 362
Internet Quarter (Leeds), 246–47, **247**
Internet, 28, 52, 63, **65**, 66–7, 89–90, *90*,
    111, 122, 130–31, *130*, 168, 183–85
    343–44
  access, 92–93
  business access, 93–5, *95*, *96*

environmental impact, **355**, 355–56
exchanges, 342
productivity, 175
purchases, *92*
real estate market, 321–23, **32**
use, *139*
iPod, 229

just-in-time, **252**, 259

knowledge economy, *see* knowledge
knowledge, *18*, 44, 55, 56–8, 78, 161, 338
divide, 76–80
economy, 19, 43, 44, 51, 57–8, 245,
250, *see also* new economy
definition, 77–8
society, 56–7
workers, 32
Kuznets, Simon, 10

La Redoute, 347
Labour government, 57–58
Land Registration Act, **106**, 328
Land Registry, 105–06, **106**
Land Securities, 287, 295–96, **352**
Land Securities Trillium, 181, 284, 287
landlord-to-business, 292, 294
landlord-to-consumer, 292, 294
Lastminute.com, 227
lean production, **252**
leases, 283–84, *284*, 290–91, 311
flexible, 30, 283–84, 314–16, **341**,
352
lengths, 283–84, *283*, *284*, 290–91
management, 311
structures, 282–84, *283*
wired, 235
Leeds (UK), 246–47, **247, 249**
leisure, 19, 47, **47**, 205, 265–75, *266*
consumption, 268–69
production, 267–68
spending, 266–67
linear model, 1, 17–19, *18*, 99, 333
location, 148–49, 200, 243, 259, 307–08
analysis, **307**
choice, 182–83, **183**
paradox, 200–204
logistics, 175, **256**, 258–59, 261–62, **262**
cross-docking, 262–63
loyalty cards, 296

lump of labour fallacy, 178, 335
Lyons Review, 106–07, **108**, 352

Madera County (California), **274**
manufacturing resource planning
(MRF), 147
manufacturing, 28, 165–66, *167*, 250–57
build to order, 253–57, **256**
build to stock, 251–53
computer integrated manufacturing
(CIM), 254
ICT, 171
real estate, 250–57
resource planning, 147
Mapeley, 284
market forms, *319*, 319–20
marketing, 143–44
Marks & Spencer, **262**
Marshall, Alfred, 24, 201, 336, **336**
mass customisation, 253–55
Meadowhall (Sheffield, UK), 296, 231,
297, 364
mediation, 55–6
megalopolis, 20–21
Metcalfe's law, 196
microprocessor, *see* processing power
Mintzberg, Henry, 132–34
mobile office, **217**
mobile phones (3G), 64, **72**, 123, 212,
224, 358
Moore's Law, 134, 158–59, 162–63, *163*
motor industry, **11**,135, 200–01, 254–57,
256, 336
multifactor productivity, 170–72,
175–76, *see also* productivity
multiple listing, 321–22, **326**
music industry, 211, 277–78
MWB, 284

NASDAQ, 162
neighbourhood shops, 36
neo–liberalism, 76, 77, 82–3
Nestle, **147**
network society, *see* networks
networked enterprise, 185–86
networks, 61–63, 101–02
brokers, 319
computer-mediated, 162
connectivity, *63*
electronic, 61, *62*, **62**

networks (*cont'd*)
  productivity, 175
  real estate, **56**
  society, 44
  wireless, 61
new economy, 2, 43, *53*, 160–77, 354
  defined, 4, 77–8, 161–65
  emergence, 160–61
  employment, 166–68, *167*
  evidence, 165–78
  evolution, 51
  measurement, 165–69
  old economy, **166**
  USA, 160
  weightlessness, 52
new urbanism, 20, 23, 32
new working practices, 240–41, **241**
Nordic potato, 245

obsolescence, 349–51
occupier's manager, 301–13
offices, 149–150, 235–50, 367
  broadband, 244
  City of London, 36–7, 36, **36**, 138–39,
    139, 239–44, 334, 336
  communications, 152–53
  defined, 235–36
  densities, 180–81, 240–41, **241**, 276,
    351, 335
  floor-space changes, *242*
  future changes, *242*
  global cities, 239–44
  information processing, 151, **151**
  information storage, 150–51, *150*
  leases, 247–48, *284*
  narrative, 237
  neighbourly, 235
  nodal, 237
  nomadic, 237
  non-territorial, 216–17
  rents, 341
  serviced, *see* serviced offices
  types, 236–38
offshoring, 192–93, 203–04, 249, 347
Olympics, 269–70, 278
online auctions, 141
online communities, 273
online orders, 115, *115*
online retailing, 29–30, 144, 190–92
open market value, 313–14

operational efficiency, 308–309
operational management, 142–43
options, 288
Oracle (Reading), 231
organisational design, 131–35, **132**
organisational informatics, 129–30
outsourcing, 30–31, 39, 106–107, **123**,
    123–24, 160, 260–61, 284–85, 286,
    298
owner's manager, 288–301

passive management, 290–91
PDA, 212, **222**, 277, 309
peer-to-peer models, 63
Perez, Carlota, 4, **6**, 7–13, 86–7, 162
  constellation, 9–10
  technological revolution, 9, **9**, **11**
  trajectory, 86–7
peripheral space, 347–48
Personal Area Networks (PANs), 359
perspectives, 5–32
  deconcentration school, 20–26
  non-spatial, 6–19
  non-spatial, firm-level, 14–19
  restructuring school, 22
  spatial, 19–38
  spatial, real estate level, 26–32
  spatial, urban and regional, 19–29
  technology, **6**
political factors, 43, 56–80
Porter, Michael, 15–16, 200–01, 203,
    298–99
portfolio manager, 289
post-industrial, 54
PPG6, 267
primary impacts, 355
printing industry, 202
Private Finance Initiative (PFI), 31,
    284–85
processing power, 163–64, *164*,
    195–96
procurement, 139–42, *140*, **149**, 187,
    285, 293–94, *299*, *300*
production function, 27–8
productivity, 98–9, 101, 148, 161,
    165–78, 253, 335, 368
  drivers, 176–78
  fallacy, 178, 335
  paradox, 167–68, 174
  real estate, 178–81

proxemics, 206–08
Prudential, 348, **348**

QVC, **220**

real estate, 1–5, 26–38, 121–35,
    148–58,160–94,199–224, 226–76,
    279–327, 331–68
  business, 97
  death, 181–86, 195
  defined, 5
  distribution sector, 257–65
  future, 366–68
  investment, 47, 281–88
  leisure and living sector, 265–75
  management, 289–90, *290*, **291**
  manufacturing sector, 250–57
  market (US), 235–36
  new and old economies, *185*
  new forms, 342–48
  processing sector ('offices'), 235–50
  role, 366–68
  sales ('retail') sector, 153–54, 226–35
  service industry, 287–88
  services, 111–12, **112**, 278, 298–99
  technology/policies, 351–56
  transformations, 121–25, 148–58,
    339–40, **341**, 349–51
rebound effects, 356
recruitment, 146
regeneration, 273, 352, **360**
Regional Development Agencies
    (RDAs), 107, 246–47, 249
regional divide (UK), 79
Regus, 247
reintermediation, **56, 320**, 320–21
REITS, 27–8
relocation, 106–07, 293, **293**
research reflexivity, 22–3, 38
restructuring, 20–26
retail, *29*, 32, 47–50, **111**, 153–54,
    295–97, 357, 370–71
  at-risk property, 364–65, *364, 365*
  cannibalisation, 235
  consolidation, 35, 48
  demographics, 35, 47
  eCommerce, 64–6, **65**,153–54,
    227–28, 363
  EU, 49–50
  exchanges, 232–33, **233**

future studies, 359–66
globalisation, *see* globalisation
Internet, 191–92
leisure, 35
loyalty schemes, 234
music, 227, 229–30
networks, 366
online sales, 203
price deflation, 49
productivity 169–70, 173
property values, 363
real estate, 153–54
rents, eCommerce, 341
sales densities, 35, 48–49
sales online, 114–15
sectors, **362**
superstores, 48
supply chain, 231–34, 344–46, *345*,
    345
travel, 230–231
revenue streams, 292, 316–18
RFID, 147, 224, 234, 263–64, **264**
robots, 154–56, *155*
Rotch, 282

sale and leaseback, 193
scenario planning, 358, 370
Schumpeter, Joseph, **6**, 7–8, 13
science parks, **79**, **80**, 79–80
second order impacts, 356
service industries, 166–67, 173
service provision, 301–03, **302–03**,
    334–35
serviced offices, 246–48, 285, 314–16,
    347–48
shareholder value, 191–92
shopping centres, 233–35, 266–67, 276,
    292, 364–65, *364*
Silicon Alley (New York), 77
Silicon Valley (California), 10, 202, 245
silver surfers, 114, 361
Singapore (office market), 243–44
smart homes, 28, **94**, 270–75, **272**
  defined, 271
SMEs, 60, **80**, 94–5, *95*, **112**, 188, 241,
    243, 293, 295, 300–01, 334
social capital theory, 182
social construction of technology
    (SCOT), 13–14, **14**, 35
social inclusion, 69, 275

social informatics, 33
socio–technical framework, 2, 26, 32–3,
    33, **34**, 34–5, 35–7, 43–4, *99*,
    199–200, 332–38
software, 55
Solow, Robert, 167–68, 174
space, 23–5, 148–57,199–225, 299–300
    categories, 208–09, *210*
    electronic, 25
    living, 218–21, **220**
    office, 236–37, *236*
    peripheral, 246–48
    personal, 209–12
    private, 213–24
    public, 221–24, **222**
    socio-fugal, 213–14
    space of flows, 23–5, *24*, 201, *202*
    space of places, *see* space of flows
spatial metaphors, 25
spillover, 172, 174, 182
spinoff companies, 294–95
Spinningfields (Manchester), **360**
sport, 278
start-up companies, 162, 267–68
stock management, 146
Strassmann, Paul, 168–69
substitution, 25, 201–02, *202*, 317
Suntec City (Singapore), 244
supply chains, *345*
Surrey County Council, **216**
sustainable communities, 32
sustainable development, *36*, 336,
    352–53, 354–57, **355**, *357*, 360
synergy, 25, 201–02, *202*

Taylorism, 236
techno-capitalism, 10, 345
techno-economic, 12
technology (including ICT), *see also*
    productivity
    adoption, 75
    defined, 3, 6, 26–7, 29
    diffusion, 9, 66, 84–7, *86*
    GDP growth, 171–72, *172*
    government, 99–107
    home, 88–89
    impact on real estate, 148–57
    institutional barriers, 29–30
    mobile, 90–91, **91**
    myths, 104–06, *105*

offices, 32, 36–7, 243–44, *243*
productivity, economy level, 169–73,
    171, **172**
productivity, firm level, 173–78
pull, 45
push, 45, 71
real estate impacts, 121–25
regeneration, 273
revolution, 4, **11**, 8–12, 45, 167–68,
    202–03
strategy, 15–17, **16**
work, 96–8, *97*
telecommuting, *see* teleworking
teleport, 369
telework centres, 215
teleworking, 22, 45–6, 117, **118**,
    123,123–24, 273–75, 338, 356
    defined, 214–15
    home-based, 215–16, **216**
    taxonomy, *214*
terabyte, 150–51, *150*, **151**
Tesco, 48, **141**
third order effects, 29, 357
Third Way, 43, 82
Tibbett & Britten, **262**
time budgets, 88–9
TMT, 244–46
Toshiba, 273
total quality management (TQM), 129,
    252
total workplace, 305
Toyota, **252, 253**
transactions, 206–09
transintermediation, 319–21, **320**
transport, 46, **46**, 336, **345**, 353–54, 356,
    357
travel, 22, 227–28, 362
Trillium, *see* Land Securities
Trocadero (London), 267
turnover (or percentage) lease, 235
TV, 61, *62*, 87–90, 88, **89**, 219–20, 238,
    342

Urban Tapestries, 267, 277
Utopia, 366

valuation, 313–14
value dynamics, 189–90
vertical integration, 298–99, 327
video-conferencing, 239–40, 356

virtual business, 248–49
virtual London, **207**, 267
virtual malls, 234–35, 296
virtual reality 204–06, 358
virtual teams, 218
virtual workgroups, 116

Wal-Mart, 49, 169–70, 234, 264
warehouse, 259–60, **260**
web firms, 245–46, *246*
web-hosting, 246
Webvan, 356
weightlessness, 52, 54, 160, 167, 195, 356
West Quay (Southampton), 231
Whitetooth, 273

whole service management, 279
Wide Area Networks (WANs), **112**
WiFi, 61, **72**, 73–4, **73**, *74*, 76, **91**, 270, 350, 359–60
wired buildings, 244
wired communities, **274**
wired leases, *see* leases
wireless, *see* WiFi
work delocalisation, 118–19, **119**
work paradigm, 120, **120**
working practices, *309*
work-life balance, 179
workplace strategies, 192–94, *193*
workspace, 213–15

Zara, 49, **153**, 232, 276